Council Fires
on the Upper Ohio

Council Fires

on the Upper Ohio

A Narrative of Indian Affairs
in the Upper Ohio Valley until 1795

Randolph C. Downes

With Headpiece Illustrations by Alex Ross

University of Pittsburgh Press

THIS BOOK is one of a series relating Western Pennsylvania history, written under the direction of Western Pennsylvania Historical Survey sponsored jointly by The Buhl Foundation, the Historical Society of Western Pennsylvania and the University of Pittsburgh.

Library of Congress Catalog Card Number 40-34394
ISBN 0-8229-5201-7
Copyright 1940, University of Pittsburgh Press
Copyright © 1968, Randolph C. Downes
Paperback reissue, 1969
Second paperback printing, 1977
Feffer and Simons, Inc., London
Manufactured in the United States of America

Contents

Council Fires
on the Upper Ohio

Preface

THIS BOOK is a narrative of the coming of the Indians to the upper Ohio Valley and of their struggle with the white men from 1755 to 1795 for the control of that region. The sequence of events involved is both a postlude to the history of eastern Pennsylvania when that section was the keystone of colonial and revolutionary America and a prelude to the history of the whole commonwealth when it became the Keystone State of modern times. From the early 1720's, when the first Delawares and Shawnee appeared in the Allegheny Valley, to 1792, when Major General Anthony Wayne made his headquarters at Legionville to organize his army for the conquest of the Ohio country, western Pennsylvania played a dominant part in the great drama that took place. During a large part of this period the region was the rendezvous for armies and the assembling point for supplies. And finally it became the resting place for the body of Wayne, whose death in 1796 at Presque Isle marked the passing from the Pennsylvania scene of a primary interest in the Indian problem.

The story of the conquest of the upper Ohio Valley has been told many times from the white man's point of view without a real consideration of the point of view of the Indian. Both are essential to a true interpretation of the problem. The historian has here the opportunity to portray a spectacle that is unusual in the history of any civilization, the spectacle of that civilization in conflict with another and in the process of eliminating it. It must be left to the ethnologist to analyze the problems inherent in the origins and development of the different techniques and standards of these two civilizations and to answer the mooted questions of their superiority or inferiority. Although this work confines itself to the facts of the conflict, the reader should be able to gain, from the presentation of the two conflicting sets of values involved, a better basis from which to judge their relative merits. The author has assumed the attitude that the Indian civilization was neither better nor worse than that of the white man, but that it was a distinctive civilization and that the Indians believed it worth defending.

Words cannot convey the full measure of gratitude the author feels toward those who have helped to make this work possible. There is The Buhl Foundation of Pittsburgh, whose beneficence in creating the Western Pennsylvania Historical Survey has provided the funds both for research and publication. There is Dr. Solon J. Buck, former director of the Survey, under whose direction the work was begun and whose searching reading of parts of the manuscript was productive of the most helpful criticisms. There are Franklin F. Holbrook, acting director of the Survey, and Dr. Leland D. Baldwin, assistant director of the Survey, both of whom rendered equally effective aid. The author feels especially grateful to Elisabeth M. Sellers, assistant editor of the *Western Pennsylvania Historical Magazine,* for her critical reading and editorial revision of the entire manuscript. To all who have helped, in whatever capacity, the author extends his heartfelt thanks.

1

The Indian
Point of View

An american indian arose from the circle around
a council fire to address his fellow tribesmen and his brothers,
the white men. It matters not who, or when, or where. It was
a treaty council at the close of a brief but bloody racial war,
the inevitable outcome of which had been a crushing defeat
for the Indians. The terms, of course, were settled; to his white
listeners, therefore, the Indian spoke to no purpose save that
of repentance. His talk was the description of a dream, by
which he meant to symbolize his message, which was the narrative of the history of his tribe. In this dream he had seen his
people as the original people of the world living on an island.
They lived by the hunt and never lacked for food and clothing
and shelter, which were provided by the game and vegetable

growth that abounded in the forests, salt licks, and river bottoms of their island home. One morning a ship appeared on the horizon and, ushered in by the sun, revealed to their wondering eyes a great number of fair-skinned visitors. "Behold," said the Indians, "the gods have come to visit us."

The Indians received these gods with reverence and provided them with food and water. In return the gods gave them strange, roaring, fire-belching weapons, which, though they frightened the game, could kill at a much greater distance than bows and arrows. The gods told them not to be dismayed if these weapons frightened the game away so that it did not come back, but to go farther into the forests and bring back furs and skins from regions where the Indians had never hunted before. They did so, but found other Indians, who resisted their coming and told them to go home and hunt in their own forests. The gods, however, were angry, and told the Indians that the forests belonged to the Great Spirit. "Go," they commanded, "and hunt in those distant forests. If bad men impede your progress, tell them that you are sent by the Great Spirit. And if they still resist, tell them that the Great Spirit has commanded that they die. Do not fear. We will buy all your furs and skins, and will provide you with new guns when the old ones wear out, and you will never want for bullets and powder."

Evil days thus fell upon the island; man had been set against man, and the forest was stained with the blood of the Indians. The anger of the Great Spirit stirred, and he sent other gods to befriend the enemies of the Indians. And all the time the game became less and less plentiful and war more and more frequent. When the game disappeared, the Indians had no need for the lands, and the white gods bought them for their children to build homes upon. But the children of the gods were undutiful and forgot the precepts of their parents. They were unkind to the Indians and treated them with contempt. And so the red men had fought against the children of the gods, who were more powerful and had defeated the Indians.

The Indian Point of View

The Indian speaker paused before the council fire, as the interpreter translated his words to the American general and his advisers. He saw the proud and dignified bearing of these conquerors, resplendent in their military uniforms, as his dream was conveyed to them. He became conscious that his words were falling on the ears of men who did not understand dreams. He was a fool in the eyes of these soldiers, who thought that his words ill befitted a man and a warrior who had just come from the battlefield. The Indian was abashed and humiliated. His fellow warriors in the council circle who had heard him speak cast their countenances and eyes upon the ground. Then, in the shadow of the great fortress near which all treaties with the white men must be held, he turned to the American general with words of apology, and said, "This is the finishing of the dream. I am but a foolish man that you see here standing."

This is, of course, an allegory. Yet something very similar actually took place many times in those years in which the American Indians were expelled from their native hunting grounds. It took place in the forests of the upper Ohio Valley, where from time to time the tribes assembled to settle the problems involved in the great racial struggle between the red men of that part of the world and their white antagonists. And in these assemblies and their proceedings is illustrated a phase of Indian-American diplomacy that tempts the philosopher and disturbs the patriot.

The story here narrated is one of a conflict between two civilizations, that of the Indians and that of the white men; or, more definitively, between two methods of living, one based on hunting and fishing, the other on farming and commerce. This conflict, grim and unceasing, was born of the utter incompatibility of two different sets of folkways, and it was nourished by the profound conviction of each race that its ways were superior to those of the other. In the white man this conviction was aggressive and militant and justified the displacement or extermination of the Indian. In the Indian it was defensive and heroic and gave strength, in the face of despair and overwhelming force, for resistance against the hated conqueror.

It is easy to understand why the whites considered themselves superior to the Indians. The civilization of the white men has today triumphantly displaced that of the red men, and judgment on the relative merits of the two civilizations is rendered accordingly. Likewise, in other days, the onward march of the white race produced the same sense of superiority. To the whites of the generation living in 1774 the Indians were savages—untamed and wild—mere children of nature. In their roving life they were thriftless and improvident, wasteful of a land that was intended by God to be parceled out into farms for a more thickly settled population. The Indians were not versed in the finer arts; above all, they were illiterate—a manifest sign of inferiority. Nor were they much more fortunate in the material arts. They knew little of the efficient cultivation of the soil. Their home life was primitive and crude. In their natural state they hunted with the bow and arrow. In the use of the gun and rifle they were quite dependent upon the whites. Moreover, they were heathen, whose Mannitto was not God and whose pagan rites and beliefs must be changed by the Christian missionary.

With this attitude toward the red men as a racial heritage, it is naturally quite difficult for white men today to understand how the Indians could possibly have considered themselves a superior race. Yet in all sincerity they believed themselves to be a chosen people in the sight of God. This belief was justified, in their opinion, by the fact that the whites were a race of mongrels, while they themselves were thoroughbreds. The uniformity of their physical characteristics revealed them as aristocrats among the races of men. According to the Moravian missionary, John Heckewelder, the Delawares said of the white men, "The hair of their heads, their features, the various colours of their eyes, evince that they are not ... *Lenni Lenape,* an ORIGINAL PEOPLE, a race of men that

4

has existed unchanged from the beginning of time." Their neighbors, the Wyandot, also relied, with a simple and intense faith, upon the belief that, in their homes on the shores of Lakes Erie and Huron, their nation "was the first . . . that the Great Spirit Placed upon this Ground."

Moreover, in this world in which they dwelt as an original and favored people, the Indians believed that they lived a life superior to that of their pale-faced brothers. The Delawares declared that the great Mannitto had ordained that the whites should "till the ground and raise by cultivation the fruits of the earth" but that he had assigned to the Indians "the nobler employment of hunting, and the supreme dominion over all the rest of the animal creation." The Indians believed themselves highly favored by the Great Mannitto "not only in having been created different in shape and in mental and bodily powers from other animals, but in being enabled to controul and master them all, even those of an enormous size and of the most ferocious kinds."[1]

The Indians believed they were an original, a superior, race, and the student of American Indian affairs should master this concept if he is to hope to understand his subject. Before the white man came to disillusion the Indians there was no world other than theirs; they were the only existing race. They were the supreme earthly creatures, the chosen of God, and the only other forms of animal life were the beasts of forest and field, the fish of the river and sea, the birds of the air. These constituted the other "races," over which it was given them to rule. Implicit in this conviction that they were God's favorites was the belief that "if the Great Mannitto could reside on earth he would associate with them and be their great chief." Thus it was natural for these forest folk, when Henry Hudson sailed into their vision in 1609, to believe that the gods had come to visit them.[2] Mannitto, the Great Spirit, had come to his chosen people. Little did they dream of the

[1] Heckewelder, *History . . . of the Indian Nations,* 100, 187; Draper MSS, 23U116.
[2] Heckewelder, *History . . . of the Indian Nations,* 72, 100.

5

doom that this visit foretold, or that these men were not gods, but the representatives of a great and conquering race to whose mastery the Indians, once masters of all "races" known to them, were destined in their turn to be subjected.

A glimpse at certain techniques and characteristics contributive to this concept of Indian mastery will lead to a more intelligent appreciation of it. The Indians were quite conscious that they were more skilled in certain arts than the white men. These were the arts of hunting, trapping, and fishing, all of which required a versatility and a craftsmanship of a type superior to that of the farmer, the trader, and the mechanic. In contrast with wild game, the plants and tools and domestic animals of the white men were tame and easily controlled.

The young Indian's object in life was to acquire a mastery of these arts. The ambition of every Indian boy was "by following the advice of the most admired and extolled hunter, trapper or warrior," to attain a degree of fame equal to that possessed by his superior. This was an Indian's education. It was part of the normal process of living unaccompanied by such artificial devices as schools, elections, and written law codes. This living produced, without friction, a body of skilled hunters and warriors, from whose ranks were selected the rulers, or, as they were called, the "wise men." "Thus," writes Heckewelder, "has been maintained for ages, without convulsions and without civil discords, this traditional government . . . a government in which there are no positive laws, but only long established habits and customs, no code of jurisprudence, but the experience of former times, no magistrates, but advisers, to whom the people, nevertheless, pay a willing and implicit obedience, in which age confers rank, wisdom gives power, and moral goodness secures a title to universal respect." Nor did the Indians' sense of superiority suffer when measured by the tests of character frequently made the standards of merit and virtue by white men. For genuine integrity, bravery, mercy, and hospitality, the Indian was not to be despised, and he was conscious of his own high standing. The

Delawares believed that the Great Spirit, knowing the wickedness of the white men's disposition, had given them "a great Book" and taught them to read it, but that the Indians "had sufficient discernment given to them to distinguish good from evil, and by following that guide, they are sure not to err."

Having found a sense of rest and of social equilibrium in the great forces of nature, the Indians seem to have attained a state of peace and contentment in which the pressure of population on subsistence did not produce a concept of private property with its attendant evils, artificial privacies, and defense institutions. Hospitality, good will, and a general spirit of sharing in common permeated their relations with one another. They believed that the Great Spirit "made the earth and all that it contains for the common good of mankind . . . Every thing was given in common to the sons of men. Whatever liveth on the land, whatsoever groweth out of the earth, and all that is in the rivers and waters flowing through the same, was given jointly to all, and every one is entitled to his share."[3]

Nature constituted reality and therefore defined the Indians' virtues for them, and comparisons with white standards did not lessen their self-esteem. Their lives stood the daily test of direct comparisons with nature and natural forces. The sincerity with which they lived according to their beliefs is evidenced in their spoken language, in which there were no abstractions, but in which natural objects and forces were used to create ideologies and definitions. Their leaders were "wise and beloved men"; other tribes were brothers, nephews, cousins, or grandfathers; the whites might be elder brothers or great fathers. The United States were the thirteen fires; time was expressed in terms of sun and moon. To make friends was to "take by the hand"; to confer was to smoke together; to pray was to entrust the spoken word to the rising smoke. To trade was to keep the road open, and when trade was interrupted, trees and branches had fallen across the road.

[3] Heckewelder, *History . . . of the Indian Nations,* 101, 114, 117, 187.

7

When there was friendship between nations, the council fire burned brightly; when trouble was brewing, it was obscured. In times of peace the tomahawk was buried, but in war it was taken up, brightened, and made sharp. Treaties or conferences were invariably begun by the ceremony of wiping tears from the eyes and dust from the faces, opening the ears, cleansing the hearts, and covering the bones of those killed in conflict. Treaties were symbolized by wampum (belts of many strings of beads woven together in different designs), which was passed around from tribe to tribe. White wampum signified peace and property; black was used to indicate war, sorrow, and mourning. Soldiers were warriors, and the Virginians were the "Long Knives." Wisdom was to these naïve savages a synonym for right.

The Indians most directly concerned in the narrative that follows were the Iroquois or Six Nations, the Shawnee, the Delawares, and the Mingo. The Iroquois were really a confederacy consisting of the Seneca, Onondaga, Oneida, Tuscarora, Mohawk, and Cayuga. Their domain in which their towns were located and in which they did most of their hunting extended from the upper Allegheny in Pennsylvania to the Adirondack Mountains in eastern New York. In the course of Dutch- and British-inspired imperialism during the seventeenth and eighteenth centuries, the Iroquois made enemies of many tribes, among which were the Shawnee and the Delawares, the two largest tribes that were to make their homes in western Pennsylvania. There was a certain amount of intertribal conflict even before the coming of the white man; and gradually the practice of the Indian theory that "every one is entitled to his share" had come to be limited to Indians within their own tribes. The dissent between tribes was furthered by the whites for their own ends. Thus by the end of the seventeenth century the Iroquois, spurred on by Dutch and British fur traders, with whom they had established friendly relations, had extended their authority, in some cases by direct warfare and in others by more subtle methods, over

The Indian Point of View

a territory from the Ottawa River in Canada to the Tennessee River and from the Kennebec in the district of Maine to the Illinois River and Lake Michigan.

The Shawnee nation during most of the seventeenth century existed in two widely separated groups, one in the lower Cumberland River Valley and the neighboring Illinois country, and the other on the South Carolina frontier. Their own traditions were that the island of Cuba was their native habitat, whence they were expelled by the Spaniards,[4] although ethnologists have been able to trace them definitely only as far south as the Cumberland River.[5] About 1690 the Indians of the southern section were at war with their neighbors, the Catawba, and those of the Cumberland group were uneasy as a result of their unsatisfactory relations with the tribes of the Illinois. Hence by 1690 both sections of the tribe were ready to migrate into Pennsylvania. Circumstances had thus made this nation a migratory one—a fact that put them in a most dependent situation, as their moving from place to place worked repeatedly to their disadvantage.

The Delawares, or Lenni Lenape, were a tribe inhabiting the Delaware River Valley both in New Jersey and in Pennsylvania and whose towns and hunting grounds extended as far west as the Susquehanna River. They were nominally dependents of the Iroquois, but actual dependence did not exist until somewhat later. The Mingo did not exist as a tribe in 1690 but became a separate group in the years after 1754 when Iroquois who had moved into the upper Ohio Valley since 1690 returned to New York and left behind some of their brethren. The Indians that remained became known as the Mingo.

These Indian nations felt that their actual relations with the whites need not necessarily be belligerent; they believed that the two races could maintain separate existence side by side. The history of Indian trade relations with the whites,

[4] Draper MSS, 3U613.
[5] Hodge, *Handbook of American Indians,* 2:531.

9

however, shows that no tribe was able to preserve its territorial integrity, because the white man desired land more than trade. Moreover, the white man chose to ignore the deeply rooted beliefs and concepts of the Indians. The whites learned the forms of Indian address and procedure at treaties and followed them in order to placate the tribes, but it is doubtful if many of them ever rightly understood the true meanings of Indian symbolism or attempted to abide by the Indian code. Faced with repeated evidences of aggression and often of bad faith, the naïve belief of the tribes in the possibility of harmonious living with the whites began to fade, until, in bewilderment and indignation, the Indians finally came to consider the white men as dangerous and powerful enemies. The frontier then became to them a place of drunkenness, debauchery, and disease, where the old beliefs were vitiated by contact with Christianity and where the tribes gradually were forced to surrender to an agricultural mode of living with the despised tameness of domestic animals and plant life. It came to mean contact with and forced adoption of the white man's great weapon of "divide and conquer," which set tribe against tribe, man against man, friend against friend; it became the scene of humiliation, of scuffles and fights and murders resulting from the contempt in which a proud people were held by frontier riffraff; and it became the scene of the destruction of a natural way of life and of the substitution of an unnatural code represented by such things as money, parcels of land, fences, and branded stock. In short, the triumph of the white man on the frontier came to be synonymous to the Indian with the triumph of chicanery and of false values.

Out of the disparity between the two civilizations grew long decades of conflict on the North American continent. This disparity may be illustrated by the respective attitudes of the whites and the Indians in regard to the hunting grounds of the Shawnee, which were transferred by the Iroquois to the English at the treaty of Fort Stanwix in 1768. The causes and the results of this cession of land will be dealt with in another chapter; the situation arising from it was one of the immediate sources of Indian discontent that culminated, in 1774, in the first episode, known as Dunmore's War, of the long contest between the Indians and the whites. It is sufficient to point out here that when the Indian title to the land south of the Ohio River, especially the Kentucky country, was ceded to the English, the rights of the Shawnee, who hunted in the region, were ignored. As the white hunters began to appear in these hunting grounds, the Shawnee, in defense of what they considered their rights, made resistance.

One of the first of these white hunters was Daniel Boone. It has been customary for historians to laud the skill and self-reliance of this rugged frontiersman and to point with pride to his service in blazing a trail for civilization into Kentucky. As a matter of fact, Boone's hunting and exploring was more destructive and hateful to the Indians than the buccaneering of Drake and other Elizabethan sea dogs was to the Spaniards of another generation. For Boone and his "long hunters" threatened to wipe out the game of the forest—the very essence of the domain over which the Indians considered themselves rulers.

On Boone's very first trip to Kentucky—the famous one of 1769—this menace was clearly perceived and emphatically dealt with by the Shawnee, the dominant hunters of this ground. Boone's partner in this expedition was John Findlay, a fellow Pennsylvanian and Indian trader, whom the Shawnee had guided in 1752 to the salt licks of Kentucky. There Findlay had beheld the thousands of buffalo and deer that now, seventeen years later, enticed Boone across the Cumberland Gap. Visions of the profits from the sale of the skins of these animals lured Boone and Findlay to these haunts on a mission fraught with peril to the Indians. After seven months of slaughtering and curing and packing at various camps in the valley of the Kentucky River, the party was suddenly surprised by a band of Shawnee returning from a fall hunt on Green River, led by the chief, Captain Will. The

Indians immediately noticed the telltale evidence of wasteful hunting and "sternly demanded" that the traders "show their camps." Although Boone, made prisoner, sought to give his camp guards warnings of the approach of the Shawnee, the camps were surprised, one by one, and the pelts, guns, ammunition, horses, and all other appurtenances of this forbidden business were either destroyed or confiscated.

Having thus rendered Boone's expedition fruitless, the Shawnee, with true Indian generosity and consideration, "dismissed their captives, presenting each with two pairs of moccasins, a doe-skin for patch-leather, a little trading gun, and a few loads of powder and shot, so that they might supply themselves with meat on their way back to the settlements." Most significant of all, they gave Boone this parting advice, which shows in clear and simple terms the Indian view of this invasion of their rights: "Now, brothers, go home and stay there. Don't come here any more, for this is the Indians' hunting ground, and all the animals, skins and furs are ours; and if you are so foolish as to venture here again, you may be sure the wasps and yellow-jackets will sting you severely."[6] Thus is illustrated the truth of the statement made by a well-known historian of border warfare: "An Indian sees no difference . . . between the right of property, acquired by the actual cultivation of the earth, and that which arises from its appropriation to other uses."[7]

From the Indian standpoint the encounter had been handled with the utmost restraint and generosity. A destructive party had invaded the hunting grounds that had belonged to the Indians since the beginning of time and had begun a policy of butchering the game that eventually would have completely exterminated it and rendered the country useless to hunters. Indeed, this slaughtering of game in such a way that the meat was thrown away and the herds threatened with irreparable destruction must have excited in the Indian

---

[6] Draper MSS, 2B169.
[7] Withers, *Border Warfare*, 140.

breast an attitude toward wastefulness akin to that of the whites, who considered the Indian wasteful and improvident of land. Moreover, the expulsion of the intruders was accomplished without bloodshed—without the hum and sting of the wasps and yellow jackets. He who remembers only the tales of Indian cruelties, of scalpings and torturings, might well ponder the significance of this treatment of these intruders into Kentucky, when the whites were sent back home well provided for by the red men.

The whites, however, considered their treatment by the Indians an outrage—a wanton destruction of the fruits of seven months' hunting. Boone immediately, but unsuccessfully, sought to recover his horses so that his hunt might still be fruitful with the aid of rifles and ammunition that could be brought back from the East. Repetition and retaliation were the only thoughts of the whites, who believed that they had as much right to hunt as had the Indians. The rights of property and labor were at stake. Lyman C. Draper comments that Boone and his party had worked hard and suffered much hardship, that "the deer they had killed belonged no more to the Indians than to themselves, and as for the horses, guns and other articles, the Indians had not the shadow of a claim to them."[8]

Encouraged by Boone's discoveries in the hunting field, new parties of long hunters crossed the mountains into Kentucky to continue the slaughter. Boone himself returned early in 1770 for a winter hunt and again in 1771, when he was again plundered. A party under Casper Mansker, including Abraham and Isaac Bledsoe, was organized on New River in June, 1769, and, although robbed by Cherokee, who likewise hunted in the Kentucky wilderness, obtained enough ammunition to return and complete the hunt. In 1772 a party under Benjamin Cleveland set out from the Yadkin River in North Carolina and was plundered by Cherokee. Late in 1771 Joseph Drake and Henry Skaggs conducted a large party to

[8] Draper MSS, 2B170.

the region, some of whose members were plundered by the Shawnee at one of their camps, where the returning Skaggs, upon discovering the disaster, engraved upon a tree, "Fifteen hundred skins gone to ruination." This setback, however, did not prevent the return of the party to the East "well laden with peltries."[9]

So the toll went on. Plunder and destruction of the hunters' camps by the Indians did not improve matters, because the determined hunters could too easily obtain the necessary munitions to make their labor productive. There is evidence to indicate that the kind of white hunter typified by Boone had characteristics that lost him not only the respect of the Indians, but also that of some of the whites. Sir William Johnson, British superintendent of Indian affairs in the northern department, wrote in 1774 that "for more than ten years past the most dissolute fellows united with debtors, and persons of a wandering disposition" had been migrating from Pennsylvania and Virginia into Indian territory. He spoke of them as idle persons who occupied themselves with hunting, "in which they interfere much more with the Indians than if they pursued agriculture alone, and the Indian hunters . . . already begin to feel the scarcity this has occasioned, which greatly encreases their resentment."[10]

Not only does this Kentucky example serve to illustrate the difference between the Indian and the white civilizations, but it also indicates the disadvantages under which the Indians labored. In the general conflict between the two races, the Indians were at similar disadvantages throughout. They might win the day as in the massacres that took place in 1755-57, 1763, and 1777-82 and in such conflicts as those that ended in William Crawford's defeat, in the battle of the Blue Licks, and in the defeats of Generals Harmar and St. Clair. But such victories always had a sequel of disaster for the Indians. After 1757 came Forbes, after 1763 came Bouquet and Bradstreet,

[9] Draper MSS, 3B179ff., 223, 227, 229, 238, 245-247.
[10] *New York Colonial Documents*, 8:460.

after 1782 came the American invasion of the Northwest, and after Harmar and St. Clair came Wayne. The reasons for the inevitable defeat of the Indians are not hard to find. Knowing only the simpler arts needed to sustain a small population in a state of nature, they were no match for those whose arts were capable of harnessing nature to more effective uses in sustaining large units of population. Even though in the days of conflict the Indians were not greatly outnumbered by the actual frontier invaders, there were always the legions of white people to the east who could be hired to crush the red men. Unable to make a gun or to repair it and supply it with powder and bullet, lacking horses and wagons needed to move them quickly to battle and facilities to sustain a siege, they were forced to rely on foreign allies and on bush fighting. Unfortunately they chose the wrong allies for their purposes: first the French and then the English. And as for their methods of fighting, a knowledge of these was easily acquired by the American frontiersman, who, with superior force of arms and ammunition, soon learned not only ways in which to defend himself, but also ways by which the Indians could be deprived of their main source of sustenance, their hunting grounds.

2
The Indians
of Allegania,
1720-1745

THERE was peace in the hills and forests of western Pennsylvania in 1700. The waters of the Allegheny and the Monongahela flowed untroubled to their union, where no trader's fort, nor even an Indian's wigwam, marred the prospect. No man had learned to call this land a homeland. Tombs and graves there were, of a people called the Mound Builders, whose bones were now piled high to remind those who should come after that here man once had lived and died. But these were vain mockeries, like the pedestal of Ozymandias; for these folk were utterly forgotten—those in the grass-covered mounds were no more remembered than were the more recent but extinct Erie who slept in unmarked graves. But unlike the pillar of Ozymandias, these tombs were not placed in a trackless desert. Fish and game abounded all the year round in forest, field, and stream and were generously treated by a temperate sun and gentle rains.

But the peace was but an interlude. It seems a little strange indeed that country so abundantly stocked with game, especially with beaver, should not in 1700 be inhabited by man. The most recent inhabitants had been the Erie, who in 1656 had been dispersed from their native hunting grounds by the imperial Iroquois. Since then no Indian tribe had reoccupied the deserted lands. The Shawnee were the most eligible candidates for such a reoccupation, but the history of their wanderings shows that they did not improve their opportunity. Members of a section of their tribe that had been living and hunting in the lower Cumberland Valley and probably in the Illinois country began in 1692 a migration to the Delaware and Susquehanna valleys, where in the course of the next two decades many of their western colleagues and all of their South Carolina fellow tribesmen joined them. But they did not venture into the western country.[1]

The reasons for the failure of the Shawnee to select the upper Ohio Valley for their new home are difficult to discover. Probably they were afraid of the Iroquois, whose chastisement of the Erie could not have been unknown to them and whose war with the Illinois, Foxes, and other western tribes in the 1680's involved the Shawnee directly.[2] Perhaps they understood that it was unwise to establish homes in a region that was not really close enough to either of the contending imperial powers, the French and the English, to enable the Indians to depend on the protection of either power against the other. And since they had reason to know that British trading goods were cheaper than French, it may be that the Shawnee believed that the Delaware and Susquehanna valleys combined satisfactorily the factor of good trading with that of

---

[1] Hodge, *Handbook of American Indians*, 2:530-536; Hanna, *Wilderness Trail*, 1:126-160.

[2] Kellogg, *French Régime*, 215, 235; Hanna, *Wilderness Trail*, 1:124.

immunity from French attacks. Moreover, they had probably heard of the benevolent Indian policy of "Onas," Indian name for the proprietor of the new colony of Pennsylvania. This policy of "kindness and good neighborhood," by which the Indians and the English were to "live in love as long as the sun and moon give light," to use Penn's own words, may have been as much of a factor in the willingness of the Delaware and the Susquehanna Indians to share the land as it was a factor in the migration there of the Shawnee.[3] Another reason for the friendliness of the Indians inhabiting the Susquehanna region was that they shared with the Shawnee a hatred of the Catawba, who had assisted in the expulsion of the Shawnee from South Carolina. When Governor John Evans of Pennsylvania visited the Susquehanna Shawnee at Pequea, in the southwestern part of the present Lancaster County, in June, 1707, their leader, Opessa, told him that his people were "happy to live in a country at peace, and not as in those parts where we formerly lived, for then, upon our return from hunting, we found our town surprised, and our women and children taken prisoners by our enemies."[4] A factor inducing the English to acquiesce in the advent of the Shawnee in the Susquehanna region included the desire to rob France of as many Indian allies as possible in the Anglo-French war (King William's War) then raging. Thus in their migration the Shawnee passed by the forests of the upper Ohio, and for almost thirty years afterwards these lands remained unmolested.

But the Shawnee did not find their new home as agreeable as they had, perhaps, imagined, and it was not long until they and their neighbors began to find the upper Ohio Valley more attractive than the valleys and streams of eastern Pennsylvania. In about 1720 a western migration began that eventually made the upper Ohio Valley the home of the three tribes known as the Shawnee, the Delaware, and the Mingo. It was the Shawnee, however, who settled in greatest numbers in

[3] Sipe, *Indian Wars,* 73.
[4] Hanna, *Wilderness Trail,* 1:150.

western Pennsylvania in the years from 1720 to 1745, and it is with them therefore that this chapter is principally concerned. It was the Shawnee, with whom trading conditions first became unsatisfactory, who led the futile but protracted agitation for reform. The main Shawnee town in western Pennsylvania was called Chartier's Town, after the half-breed trader, Peter Chartier, who had followed close on the heels of the migrating Indians, and it was located near what is now Tarentum in Allegheny County. It was at this town that trading tended to center and that most of the events to be described took place. Chartier's Town may well be called the capital of Allegania.[5]

It was a debatable land, from the standpoint of ownership, that these wanderers entered in the 1720's. It was debatable even before the white men came to contest its ownership, and it was debatable subsequently in a degree not to be measured merely by the strength and numbers of the actual red and white residents thereon. It was a land claimed and fought over by two non-resident powers, one the great British-supported Iroquois confederacy, and the other the French fur-trading empire with its backbone in the St. Lawrence Valley and the Great Lakes country. So important were these two factors in the history of the debatable land from 1720 to 1763 that the strugglings of the few thousand people inhabiting the country appear insignificant in proportion. But this appearance of course is entirely illusory.

When the first Delawares and Shawnee began to appear at the Allegheny Valley terminus of the Shamokin, Frankstown, and Raystown trails, they were indulging themselves in a solution of domestic troubles in which they were not altogether legally justified. The fact that they were helpless victims of the congestion of population on the Delaware, the Schuylkill, and the Susquehanna, was not sufficient grounds, from the Iroquois point of view, for them to desert their eastern homes for transmontane ones. The fact was that the Delawares,

[5] Hanna, *Wilderness Trail*, I:182-191.

Shawnee, and Mingo occupied their eastern homes as vassals of the Iroquois, that they had decided to vacate these homes without consulting their overlords, and that they had the effrontery to appropriate for their new homes lands that belonged by right of conquest to these same overlords. Nor was the conflict involved merely one concerning the abstract right of the Iroquois to the land. The occupation of the West by the Delaware, Shawnee, and Mingo was fraught with danger for the future, because if these tribes should become part of the fur-trading empire of the French, they would in effect convert the possession of the land to the French, thus limiting the British empire to the Atlantic plain and drastically circumscribing the domain on which the Iroquois could rely for the furs and skins required by the Albany trade.

Although trading complications arose among the Indians almost as soon as the first tribesmen arrived in the Allegheny country, for the first ten years the migration was not considered dangerous or offensive either by the Iroquois or by the Pennsylvania authorities. This was because until 1731 neither of these authorities was aware of any French tampering with the migrants. The normal course of trade had set in as Pennsylvania traders, including Peter Chartier, James Le Tort, Jonas Davenport, Edmund Cartlidge, and Peter Allen, followed the tribesmen to the new hunting grounds. It was the custom of Cartlidge and Davenport to give the Indians their supplies of guns, ammunition, clothing, and ornaments in the fall before they went out on the hunt and to receive their skins and furs in payment in the following spring. According to a statement of these gentlemen in 1730, the trade prior to that time was most productive and they "Gott Larger quantityes of Skins and furrs, and Dissposed of more Goods than had been for many years before." Productive as it was, however, the western Pennsylvania fur trade was not without its inherent weaknesses. Complications had appeared before 1730 that show that it might have been wiser had the English and the Iroquois forbidden the migration in the first place or else exerted greater efforts to keep it under control. As early as July, 1727, the Iroquois had been obliged to ask Governor Patrick Gordon of Pennsylvania "that none of the Traders be allowed to carry any Rum to the remoter Parts where James Le Tort trades, (that is Allegany on the Branches of Ohio)." This request is much more significant than it seems at first observation. It indicates the appearance in the West of an evil that had never before appeared among the trans-montane tribes living in the Iroquois sphere of influence. When the Iroquois were middlemen in the process of trading furs and skins for English goods, there was no danger of the presence of excessive supplies of spirits. But the Iroquois were not the trading power they once had been. They were not only obliged to let the Pennsylvania traders exploit the new field, but were also compelled, when dangerous practices appeared among those traders, to appeal to the governor of the colony to correct the evil instead of correcting it themselves.[6]

There was a law on the statute books at this time that had been passed in 1722, entitled "An Act to prohibit the selling of Rum and other Strong Liquors to the Indians, and to prevent the Abuses that may happen thereby." But where there were no enforcing officers this law had no effect. Just what the uncontrolled rum traffic meant was first indicated in 1730 when two groups of traders brought it to the attention of the Pennsylvania government. One group consisting of Cartlidge, Davenport, and one Henry Bailey complained to Governor Patrick Gordon that a set of irresponsible traders "Such as had been your petitioners Servants" were, by their use of rum, making it impossible for the Indians to pay their debts. These undesirable traders would meet the Indians in the spring before Davenport and his associates appeared and with "a Small percell of Goods and Large quantityes of Rum" deprive the red men of all their peltry. The result was that in 1730 the

---

[6] *Pennsylvania Archives,* first series, 1:261; *Pennsylvania Colonial Records,* 3:274. A discussion of the Pennsylvania traders is in Hanna, *Wilderness Trail,* 1:160-181, and in Donehoo, *Pennsylvania,* 1:331.

Indians were indebted for two thousand pounds, much to the dismay of the complainants. Another company of traders under the direction of one John Maddox complained that certain irresponsible Iroquois Indians in June, 1729, had brought fourteen kegs of rum from Albany and sold it to the Delawares on the Allegheny for all the furs that were in their possession. Seeking more rum, the Delawares demanded goods of Maddox on credit and upon the latter's refusal "beat and wounded him sorely," after which Maddox let them have some goods. Maddox desired Governor Gordon to see to it that the Indians made reparations.[7]

The most significant thing about the rum difficulty was the way in which the Pennsylvania authorities responded to the complaints of the Iroquois and the traders. In effect, these responses were that since there were laws on the Pennsylvania statute books curbing the rum traffic, it was up to the Indians to break all the rum kegs that were brought to their country. Said Governor Gordon to the Iroquois in July, 1727, "The sale of Rum shall be prohibited both there [*on the upper Susquehanna*] & at Alegany, but the Woods are so thick & dark we cannot see what is done in them. The Indians may stave any Rum they find in the Woods, but . . . they must not drink or carry any away." On October 4, 1729, the governor solemnly laid down several "Rules and Injunctions," the observance of which by the Allegheny traders would maintain "the friendship established by many Treaties and with the greatest Care between us and the Native Indians." The first of these read, "That, as it is prohibited by a Law provided for that purpose, to furnish the Indians with Rum and other Strong Liquors, from the excessive use of which Disorders have frequently ensued, You are carefully to avoid that pernicious Practice." And in response to the protests of Davenport and Cartlidge

---

[7] Pennsylvania, *Statutes at Large*, 1682-1809, vol. 3, p. 310-313; *Pennsylvania Archives*, first series, 1:261, 265. Excessive use of rum in the fur trade was no new thing in Pennsylvania in this period, but previous experience had been confined to the trade east of the mountains. See Hanna, *Wilderness Trail*, 2:304.

The Indians of Allegania

in 1730, Governor Gordon wrote a letter to "the Indians on Allegheny," dated May 27, which stated, "I therefore order all the Traders that when you have finished your hunting and return with your Skins to your ffamilies [sic], those you pay your Skins to shall give you Some Drink to chear you, but at all other times you should forbear it."[8]

This failure on the part of the Pennsylvania government to assume real responsibility in controlling the Indian trade in the West is of the most fundamental significance in the history of western Pennsylvania Indian affairs. Unwilling and unable to establish an Indian department, the eastern Pennsylvania authorities allowed matters to drift from bad to worse. In the French and Indian War and during the so-called Pontiac Conspiracy, the British imperial government was obliged to rush troops and supplies to the protection of the colony whose abdication of responsibility in controlling Indian relations was the most important reason for the revolt of the Indians.

From negligence in curbing the rum traffic it was but a short step to negligence in controlling other factors in Indian relations, such as the price and quality of trading goods. The Pennsylvania government adopted a policy based on the principles of rugged individualism when a policy of social control would have kept Indian relations peaceful and harmonious. The declaration of Governor Gordon to the Iroquois in 1727 had the ring of true eighteenth-century liberalism: "As to Trade, they [the Iroquois] know 'tis the Method of all that follow it to buy as Cheap and sell as dear as they can, and every Man must make the best Bargain he can; the Indians cheat the Indians & the English cheat the English, & every Men [sic] must be on his Guard."[9].

An excellent illustration of the Pennsylvania conception of how Indian trade should be managed is found in the fourth

[8] *Pennsylvania Colonial Records,* 3:274-276; *Pennsylvania Archives,* first series, 1:244, 262.
[9] *Pennsylvania Colonial Records,* 3:275.

of Governor Gordon's "Rules and Injunctions" of October 4, 1729. In this article the governor advised the fur traders to form a trade association for the control of prices. It proposed that "all persons of this Province having goods to dispose of . . . enter into a mutual Agreem^t to Sell and buy or receive at some one certain reasonable price, according to the value of the Goods, and that none attempt to undermine another in their Dealing, for from such Practices, Disgusts and Animosities amongst the Indians as well as others must inevitably arise, wch in so remote a Situation where no regular Governm^t is established, may in their consequences prove dangerous." Just how far the governor was willing to go in supporting these trade agreements was stated in a letter of James Logan, secretary of the Provincial Council, to the Allegheny traders informing them of the "Rules and Injunctions." "You must by no means," wrote he, "pretend to the Indians that the prices you sett are by the Goven^rs Appointm^t, for you may assure yourselves that the Governour will no way concern himself in this point otherwise than to caution you that none shall exact on the Indians on the one hand, and on the other that no Methods be used by any of you to provoke or incense any of them against others of the Traders."[10]

And so when an overt act occurred, as in the case of the robbery of John Maddox in 1729, the voice of government, through Governor Gordon, spoke to the offending Delawares directing them to undertake to bring the offenders to justice. "I desire," wrote the governor on August 20, 1730, "that you will call before you the Persons who took away the said Goods, whose Names Mattox will give you, and lett them know that I expect that they will make Satisfaction to him . . . I must insist that you make those Indians sensible of their Folly and Rashness, and that I will not allow any such Insults to be offered to our People, but in every such Case will expect that the Offenders shall not goe unpunished." Thus was the language of control read to the new inhabitants and traders in the

[10] *Pennsylvania Archives,* first series, 1:244, 245.

debatable land where, as Gordon confessed, "no regular Governm^t is established."[11]

Suddenly the problem of what to do about the western Pennsylvania trade assumed a new aspect that led the framers of policies and proclamations to drop their policy of attempted trade control and to adopt one of attempting to stop the migration and draw those who had migrated back to eastern Pennsylvania. The occasion for the change was the appearance in the summer of 1731 of the ogre of French interference with the western Shawnee and Delawares. At a meeting of Governor Gordon and his Council on August 4, the former announced with great solemnity that he had an "Affair of very great Importance to the Security of this Colony & all its Inhabitants" to lay before the members. Secretary James Logan then arose and produced to the horrified gaze of the governor and Council a map published in London in 1721 in which the French claims to the interior were represented as extending as far east as the Susquehanna River. Moreover, according to the secretary, the danger was not one of mere claims, but of the actual incorporation of western Pennsylvania in the French empire. He pointed out that some Shawnee Indians were "seated" on the Allegheny and "that the French have been using Endeavours to gain over those Indians to their Interest." He had been informed by traders, he said, that "some years since" a Frenchman, named Cavilier, had appeared among the Shawnee "sent as 'twas believed from the Governor of Montreal." This gentleman on his return to Montreal took several Shawnee chiefs, who later returned to their Allegheny homes "highly pleased." In the spring of 1731 this same gentleman with five or six others visited the Indians and brought an interpreter and a gunsmith

[11] *Pennsylvania Archives,* first series, 1:266. On August 20, 1731, as a result of the killing of his cousin by the Delaware king, Sassoonan, Governor Gordon issued a proclamation requiring all traders desiring licenses to appear before him personally and requiring all justices of the peace to invoke the law of 1700 against all unlicensed traders. This, however, could not have any effect where there were no justices of the peace. The law of 1700 concerning Indian traders is in Pennsylvania, *Statutes at Large,* 1682-1809, vol. 2, p. 140.

"to work for them gratis." According to the record, Logan "then went on to represent how destructive this Attempt of the French, if attended with Success, may prove to the English Interest on this Continent, and how deeply in its consequences it may affect this Province."[12]

As a matter of fact Logan was quite justified in his apprehensions about the Franco-Shawnee connection. From the very begininng of the Shawnee migration to western Pennsylvania it was part of French policy to win this tribe away from the English. Indeed it was to the French that the Shawnee turned early in the 1720's when life in eastern Pennsylvania began to be unbearable, and in 1724 the Marquis de Vaudreuil, governor of Canada, had adopted "measures" to bring the Shawnee nearer to the French. These measures included the sending of "a person capable of properly managing that negotiation to ascertain the dispositions of those Indians." Vaudreuil died in 1725, and his successor, the Marquis de Beauharnois, continued his predecessor's policy of encouraging the Shawnee to come under the French sphere of influence. On October 1, 1728, he and the intendant, M. de Clerambaut d'Aigremont, reported: "It would promote in a considerable degree the prosperity and security of the Colony, could these Indians settle between Lake Erie and the Ohio River. Naturally fond of the French, they would form a barrier between the Iroquois and us, and their numbers would make them respected. They would reinforce our domiciliated Indians, who are decreasing every day; and in case of war with the Iriquois, would, doubtless, be of very great assistance." Beauharnois, therefore, in 1728 sent Cavilier, the same person earlier sent by Vaudreuil, with instructions to bring some Shawnee to Montreal in order that the governor might "examine with those Chiefs the district that could be assigned them for the establishment of the new villages alongside the French." The French were satisfied with the settle-

---

[12] The proceedings of the council meeting of August 4, 1731, referred to in this and the following paragraphs, are in *Pennsylvania Colonial Records*, 3:402, 403.

ment already made by a part of the Shawnee on the Allegheny, but by having the Indians come to them for authorization of their new home, they hoped to remind them of French authority and to ascertain that those sections of the tribe that had not yet migrated from eastern Pennsylvania would make their new settlements with that authority in mind. When the Shawnee reached Montreal they confided in the French that "being unhappy with the English, and united formerly with the French, they had come to ascertain if he would receive them, and where he would wish to locate them." The governor replied that they were at liberty to select "a country where they might live conveniently and within the sound of their Father's voice." In the summer of 1731 the Shawnee repeated their request of the French. This time the French, still seeking to impress their authority on the Indians, sent Captain Chabert de Joncaire "to locate them on the north bank of the river Oyo [*Allegheny*]."[13]

Logan in reporting the French danger to the Pennsylvania Council judged rightly in giving it a position of major importance. And important dangers required drastic remedies. The remedy proposed to the Provincial Council by Logan was the bodily removal of the Indians back to the regions under British influence. But, as in the case of trade control, when it came to devising ways and means of actually bringing the Indians back, the Pennsylvania authorities adopted the maxim, "Let George do it." George, in this case, was the Iroquois. Logan moved that "a treaty should be sett on foot with the five Nations, who have an absolute authority as well over the Shawanese as all our Indians, that by their means the Shawanese may not only be kept firm to the English Interest, but likewise be induced to remove from Allegheney nearer to the English Settlements." The Council concurred in the recommendation, as the members believed with Logan that a treaty with the Iroquois was "absolutely necessary." Naturally desirous of knowing how far the money-granting body of the

[13] *New York Colonial Documents*, 9:1013, 1016, 1033.

colony would approve the scheme, Governor Gordon on November 23 recommended to the General Assembly the making of "proper Regulations" to control the trade. The Assembly politely sought to shelve responsibility and replied the next day, "This danger [*from the French*] now seems very eminent [*sic*], and tho' we have not the means in our hands to prevent it, yet we esteem it our duty to do everything in power to give our Superiors a true information of the ill state of the Northern Colonies in general, and of . . . Pennsylvania in particular, from the late bold attempts of our two [*too*] nigh neighbours, the French."[14]

If the object of the planners of the Pennsylvania-Iroquois treaty of 1732 was to remove the western Indians back to the Susquehanna, it quickly became apparent when the Indian and Pennsylvania delegates met in August of that year that this was not going to be the main result of the conference. Concerning that issue, however, the Iroquois said that they would do three things. First, they would settle the quarrel that, according to the Shawnee, had been the cause for the migration of the latter, and thus make it possible for the Shawnee to return to a region set aside for them on the upper Susquehanna. Secondly, they would send orders to the Shawnee and Delawares to return. Thirdly, they would compel the French traders to leave the Allegheny country. Further than that they could not go. They expected the Pennsylvanians to co-operate by forbidding their own traders from going to the Allegheny and by undertaking any other measures deemed necessary. In this agreement the Pennsylvanians acquiesced, but it must have been plain that the Iroquois could not stop the French traders any more than the Pennsylvanians could stop their own. Indeed, the Quaker authorities were to admit this inability in the Iroquois-Pennsylvania treaty of 1736 when the Indians had repeated their request for exclusion of the traders.[15] As a matter of fact, the trans-

[14] *Pennsylvania Colonial Records*, 3:419, 421.
[15] *Pennsylvania Colonial Records*, 4:90-95.

montane Indian problem was a minor one in the minds of both Iroquois and Pennsylvanians when the former saw that the latter wanted their friendship and when the latter saw that the Iroquois would remain friendly—for a price. Subsequent treaties between the two parties were given over to eastern matters such as those of land cessions, payments to the Iroquois for quitclaims, and the stopping of hostilities between the Iroquois and the Catawba.

The treaty council of 1732 lasted from August 23 to September 2 and was devoted mainly to the establishment of friendship between the two parties and the drawing up of articles for that purpose. The first days were devoted to a discussion of the French issue, with the Iroquois assuring the Pennsylvanians that the latter need not fear that the Six Nations would go over to the French. The Indians declared that they held under their influence many of the western tribes, including the Miami and the Ottawa, who traded with them and who would support the English in the event of an Anglo-French war. This relieved the minds of the Pennsylvanians. Gifts were presented to the Indians and the articles of friendship agreed upon. These included a pledge that each would let the other know of any danger from foreign enemies; the appointment of the official Pennsylvania Indian interpreter, Conrad Weiser, and the Iroquois vicegerent, Shikellamy, to act as agents or ministers of the two parties in administering friendly relations; the declaration of "an open Road between Philadelphia and the Towns of the Six Nations" over which Indians and whites could travel unmolested; and finally a solemn declaration of alliance or, in the words of the agreement, a "League and Chain of Friendship & Brotherhood" between the two parties "to continue so long as the Heavens, Sun, Moon, Stars & the Earth shall Endure."[16]

However significant the Iroquois-Pennsylvania alliance of 1732 may have been as the beginning of a new era in eastern

[16] The proceedings of the treaty council of 1732 are in *Pennsylvania Colonial Records*, 3:435-452.

Pennsylvania Indian affairs, the Shawnee reception of the attempts to remove them back to the East was even more significant in western Pennsylvania affairs. It would be inaccurate to say that the Shawnee refused to go east. They merely declined with thanks. To the request that they return to the Susquehanna, the two Shawnee chiefs, Opakethwa and Opakeita, told the Pennsylvania Council on September 30 that "the place where they are now Settled Suits them much better than to live nearer; that they thought they did a Service to this Province, in getting Skins for it in a place so far remote; that they can live much better there than they possibly can any where on Sasquehannah." To the threat that the traders would be forbidden to go to their country, they replied that "they had horses of their own, and could bring down their Skins to the Trader[s]." For the offer of a reservation on the Susquehanna they thanked the authorities kindly and desired "it may be secured to them."[17]

There is a significant note of independence in the talk of the Shawnee that shows that they intended to stay in western Pennsylvania. This same note is to be found in an exchange of sentiments with the Pennsylvanians earlier in the year 1732 on the subject of trade control. Edmund Cartlidge had delivered to the Shawnee a message from Governor Gordon inviting the tribe to a conference at Philadelphia and exhorting them to good behavior and less rum drinking. Cartlidge, in reporting the Shawnee reply to Gordon, wrote that with the French seeking to trade on the Allegheny it was more necessary than ever for the English to have "a Better Regulation of the Indian Trade" because "ye Eyes of the Indians are all now upon us, as weighing both us and the french In a Ballance to See which will bee found wanting." He said that the Shawnee were particularly impressed with the inability of the government of Pennsylvania to stop the traders, especially

---

[17] *Pennsylvania Colonial Records*, 3:462. Three of the four Shawnee who attended the conference contracted smallpox, and two of them died in Philadelphia. *Pennsylvania Colonial Records*, 3:463.

30

the licensed ones, from bringing out so much rum. Wrote Cartlidge, "Severall of our Indians Refflects on mee, and Says thatt I have Told them from time to Time thatt there Should nott Come Such Large quantity of Rum among them, butt they See no Truth In Itt, and admires thatt the Govern[r] Cannott Rule his own people." Cartlidge wrote also that news of the threats of the English to stop the traders and disperse the French "putt all ye Shawanise Into Such a Consternation thatt they thoughtt of nothing Else butt a warr," from which state of mind the Indians were rescued only by the assurances to the contrary of Peter Chartier and the French. Cartlidge warned that "the Consequence mightt have been fatall to Some, So thatt Care Should be Taken who Comes here on acc[tt] of Trade, and not Suffer Such Idle Lying Villans to Come among the Indians."[18]

Since the government of Pennsylvania was unable to control the rum trade to the western parts, the Shawnee finally hit upon the device of associating among themselves under the guidance of the licensed and approved traders in order to be rid of the evil. But before doing so they wanted express authorization from the Pennsylvania authorities. A group of four chiefs, therefore, on April 24, 1733, wrote Governor Gordon seeking the desired authority. "Dear Friends," they said, "There is yearly & monthly some new Upstart of a Trader without Licence, who comes amongst Us & brings with him nothing but Rum . . . but takes away with him those Skins which the old licens'd Traders who bring us every thing necessary ought to have in Return for their goods sold to us some years since. Wee therefore beg thou wou'd take it into Consideration and send Us two firm Orders, one for Peter Cheartier, th' other for Us to break in pieces all the Cags so brought, and by that Means the old Traders will have their Debts which otherwise never will be paid."[19]

The authorization did not come, and the next year, 1734,

[18] *Pennsylvania Archives,* first series, 1:327, 328.
[19] *Pennsylvania Archives,* first series, 1:394.

the Indians and the traders went one step further. They drew
up a list of desirable and undesirable traders. The latter, fifteen in number, the Indians wished excluded from the trade.
The former, seven in number, they designated as worthy of
licenses. These seven were Jonas Davenport, Lazarus Lowrey,
James Le Tort, Francis Stevens, James Patterson, Edmund
Cartlidge, and Peter Chartier. The last-named trader they
especially recommended and stated that they reckoned him
"one of us" who "is welcome to come as long as he pleases." It
was proposed that six of the seven traders (all but Chartier)
should not be allowed to bring into western Pennsylvania
"more than 30 Gallons of Rum, twice in a year." As for Chartier, he might bring "what quantity he pleases, for he trades
further y^n ye Rest." Each trader must bring his license with
him and bring all his rum to "ye Cabbin where he lives directly, & not . . . hide any in ye woods." It was provided also that
no hired man in the employ of any trader could bring rum into
the woods. In order to enforce these control measures it was
proposed that the Indians and the traders might, whenever
they saw undesirable traders, "stave their Cags, & seize their
goods." It was added, however, that if the Indians were indebted to any of these undesirables the latter might be allowed
to apply in person for payment, and if the Indians had the
wherewithal to pay they would do so. Another significant
proposal in this plan was that "every trader may be obliged
to bring good Powder."[20]

This proposal was naturally open to considerable criticism.
It struck at the basic principle of trade prevalent in those days
among English-speaking people, the principle of freedom of
competition. It might be said that the plan was one conceived
by a small coterie of traders seeking monopoly privileges, who
found in the Indians willing tools to aid them in their selfish
schemes. Granting, merely for the sake of argument, that this
criticism might be valid, the fact still remains that the proposal proves that Anglo-Indian relations in western Penn-

[20] *Pennsylvania Archives,* first series, 1:425.

sylvania in 1734 were not in a healthy condition. It was but ten years later that Peter Chartier, the most beloved and influential trader in the "monopolistic ring," led his Shawnee brothers to support the French in the first Anglo-French war to take place since the Indians had migrated to western Pennsylvania. The western Pennsylvania Indians, led by the Shawnee, were seeking homes where they could find safety and security and where they could live their lives according to normal Indian standards. It is evident that at no time from the beginning of the migration until 1734 were they assured of such safety and security by the English. And conditions were to grow worse instead of better in the years that followed.

Not long after 1734 the Shawnee in western Pennsylvania became conscious that unless something was done for them, they and the Pennsylvania authorities would come to the parting of the ways. From about 1737 to 1744 the Shawnee Indians on the Allegheny made it quite clear to the authorities that it depended on the Quaker government whether or not the Shawnee would cast their lot with the French in the next Anglo-French war. The first evidence of their attitude came in the summer of 1737 when the Shawnee chiefs in a message to the proprietor of Pennsylvania put it squarely before that distinguished gentleman that the time had come when the Shawnee must choose between the French and the English. They pointed out the helpfulness of the French toward them and, by inference, the negligence of the English. Every year, they said, the French sent them "some Powder, Lead, and Tobacco, to enable them to withstand their Enemies . . . they are gott so far back that they can goe no further without falling into their Enemies' hands or going over to the French, which they (the Shawanese) say they would willingly avoid." They could not return to the Susquehanna as the Pennsylvania government had repeatedly urged, because if they did so "they must starve, litle [*sic*] or no Game being to be mett with in those parts." Therefore the Shawnee asked the people of Pennsylvania as "Brethren and Allies" to "furnish them with some Arms and Amunition for their Defence against their Enemies, and to secure their Continuance at Allegheny."

The reply of the government of Pennsylvania to their plea was as unsatisfactory to the Indians as all other replies from that source had been. Indeed, considering the danger involved, the reply was close to being one of folly. The Provincial Council, headed by James Logan, who was now its president, advised the proprietor to say that it would "be very improper . . . to send Powder & Lead because they have thought fitt to ask them." Instead the Indians should be invited to a council being planned by the colonies of Pennsylvania, Maryland, and Virginia for the purpose of putting an end to the war between the northern and southern Indians. A message to the Shawnee to this effect, accompanied by a present worth ten pounds or less, was deemed by the Council sufficient "to prevent their Defection and to keep them attached to the British Interest." As a matter of fact, such a message was an evasion of the whole question and meant that the Indians could count neither on governmental control of trade nor on direct government relief in time of crisis.[21]

There was one thing that the western Pennsylvania Indians could still do to solve the trade problem without going over to the French. This was to do for themselves what they had been urging the Quaker government to do and what the Quaker government had been urging them to do; that is, to prohibit the sale and importation into western Pennsylvania of intoxicating liquors. If this could be done, it might reasonably be expected that organized control of other aspects of the trade might be undertaken by the Indians. At a council, probably held at Chartier's Town, it was decided "to Leve of[f] Drinking of Rum for the Space of four years." The Shawnee found justification for their action in the message sent to them in the

---

[21] The message of the Shawnee to the proprietor and the advice of Council are in *Pennsylvania Colonial Records,* 4:233-235. See also *Pennsylvania Archives,* first series, 1:551.

fall of 1737 by Governor Gordon, which evidently suggested, as other messages from the same source had done, that the Shawnee quit drinking rum and that they destroy the excessive supplies brought to them by the traders. The Shawnee chiefs, Loyparcowah, Newcheconer, and Coycacolenne, wrote to Governor Penn and James Logan that this measure was adopted because of "the ill Consequances that attend itt and what Disturbance itt makes" and in the hope that "we would Live in Peese and Quiettness and become another People." Only two of the traders, Chartier and George Miranda, were present at this fall council, but during the winter the rest were informed and "they where all willing." As soon as all the traders were informed and had expressed their willingness, a grand ceremony was held on March 15, 1738, at which all the rum available, about forty gallons, was "Staved and Spilt" and "Throwne in the streete." Moreover, the one hundred warriors present took a solemn oath not to permit for four years the importation of rum or other strong liquor into the Indian country. Four men were appointed to supervise the enforcement of this prohibition and to cause all liquors imported in violation of the agreement to be staved. The governor of Pennsylvania was asked to co-operate by giving "Strick orders" to prevent "Rum Comeing two the Hunting Cabins or two the Nabering Towns." The French, the Iroquois, the Delawares, and the Shawnee still living on the Susquehanna, were told of the decision and asked to inform all traders thereof, and it was made emphatically plain that all rum would be destroyed regardless of the circumstances.[22]

It is evident that the old question as to the return of the Indians to the East had been irrevocably settled in the negative. In the Philadelphia treaties of 1732 and 1736 the Pennsylvanians and the Iroquois had discussed at great length the enforcement of the removal of the Shawnee, but nothing had been done, and shortly afterwards it was seen to be a hopeless proposition. Conditions were becoming too crowded in the

[22] *Pennsylvania Archives,* first series, 1:549-552.

Susquehanna Valley, and the Iroquois found it more to their advantage to settle the Delawares there and to permit the tribes already in the region to move farther up the main stream and to sell claims to parts of these lands to Pennsylvania and Maryland. Indeed, it was during the years following the Iroquois cession to Pennsylvania in 1736 of the lower Susquehanna that most of the remaining Shawnee in eastern Pennsylvania left that region and received permission from the French to settle near Detroit. Obviously, therefore, the thing for Pennsylvania to do was openly to acquiesce in the settlement of the western part of the colony by the Shawnee and to do everything possible to keep them from succumbing to French influence. Pennsylvania was unwilling to go the whole way in this respect, but the authorities were willing to recognize the Shawnee right of settlement in the West and to make a paper alliance by which the Indians pledged not to support the French in case of war. This was done at the treaty of August 1, 1739, held in Philadelphia. The Shawnee thereby promised to "behave on their parts as true Friends & Brothers to the Christian Inhabitants of the said Province," and that they would "not by any Motives or persuasions be induced to join with any Nation whatsoever who shall be in Enmity with the Subjects of the Crown of Great Britain, in any Acts of Hostility against them."[23]

But paper alliances unbacked by improved trading conditions could not prevent the Shawnee from going over to the French. Events moved rapidly to the denouement of 1745. The Pennsylvanians were not without warnings of the danger of a Shawnee repudiation of the treaty of 1739. One of these was brought to the attention of Governor George Thomas in June, 1743, by one James Hendricks, a "servant to an Indian Trader at Alligheny." His story was of a general Indian uprising against English traders in that far country. He deposed "that he had seen the Indians there in pursuit of some of the

[23] *Pennsylvania Colonial Records,* 4:234, 346; *New York Colonial Documents,* 6:99, 103, 105, 107; 9:1059, 1097.

Traders, And that he had heard the discharge of two or more Guns, from whence he verily believ'd that the pursued Traders were murder'd, and at the same Time declared his Apprehensions that the Indians designed to cut off all the Traders in those parts." Hendricks reported that several inhabitants of Lancaster County had left their homes and had come as messengers to Philadelphia to inform the governor and have a hearing before the Provincial Council. Two depositions by Indian traders were read at this time, in which the writers said "that they were desired by some Indian ffriends [*sic*] of theirs to make the best of their Way out of the Indian Country, to avoid their being murder'd by the Indians, who were come to a Resolution to cut off all the white People." Other evidence to the same effect was presented in the form of what Governor Thomas called "some groundless insinuations of one Peter Chartier, an Indian Trader." After considering all the evidence, the governor informed the Council members that they had nothing to fear. "They might be assured," he said, "there was no Disposition in the Indians to begin a War, and that the Informations given by Hendrick's and the rest were the Effect of fear & Chartier's Villanous Reports." He advised the Lancastrians to go home and quiet the people and promised them that the secretary of the Council, Richard Peters, would be in their county in the near future to give them official assurance that there was no danger.[24]

It is evident that there was something brewing in western Pennsylvania in spite of Governor Thomas' assurances to the contrary. At the treaty held at Lancaster in June, 1744, to iron out difficulties between the Iroquois and the colonies of Pennsylvania, Maryland, and Virginia, most of the English traders to the Allegheny were present. The news of the French declaration of war with England had just been announced, and the traders hesitated to return to the West for fear of an unfavorable reception. The Pennsylvanians put it up to the Iroquois to decide whether or not the Allegheny country would be safe

[24] *Pennsylvania Colonial Records*, 4:655.

37

for traders. According to Conrad Weiser, the Iroquois had replied that they would not permit either party to the war "to March any Troops over nor to commit Hostilities" on any land under Iroquois jurisdiction. On the basis of this reassurance, Weiser said, the Allegheny traders "went immediately to Trade again to Ohio, thinking themselves secure from being molested either by the French or Indians."[25]

But with a state of war existing between his nation and the French, Governor Thomas was far more concerned about the danger in western Pennsylvania in 1744 than he had been in 1743. Although the treaty at Lancaster cemented the Anglo-Iroquois alliance strongly enough to prevent the Six Nations from aiding the French, and although the Iroquois had promised to preserve Indian neutrality in western Pennsylvania, the governor was worried. When the General Assembly met at Philadelphia on July 31, 1744, he observed to them that all was not well among the Shawnee. Only one Shawnee delegate, he said, was present at the Lancaster treaty. Moreover, Shawnee relations with other tribes were not satisfactory. These nations, he said, were trying to induce the whole Delaware nation to join them in the West and they were "far from being on Good Terms" with the Iroquois. The Iroquois-Pennsylvania alliance at the treaty of Lancaster had stimulated this antipathy. Alluding, no doubt, to the Shawnee migration itself, the governor said, "The Closer our Union has been with the Six Nations the greater distance they [*the Shawnee*] have kept from us."[26] But the most disconcerting of all the signs of unrest among the Shawnee was the rumor that they were considering joining the French and bringing some of the Delawares with them. "It is Whispered amongst them [*the Six Nations*]," Governor Thomas told the Assembly, "that should they be obliged to take part in the War between us and the French, they will have the Shawonese and perhaps

[25] *Pennsylvania Colonial Records,* 4:780.

[26] See the report of a Shawnee plot among the Lake tribes to form a confederacy against the Iroquois. *Pennsylvania Archives,* first series, 1:663.

the Delawares also to Oppose them." The governor's conclusions concerning the evidence available were in strong contrast to his conclusions on the evidence of the Lancastrians in 1743. He now stated, "I wish any method could be fallen upon to secure them [*the Shawnee*] effectually to the British Interest, as they lie upon one Part of our Frontiers, and our most valuable Trade for Skins is with them; but considering their Frequent intercourse with the French and their Inconstancy, I almost despair of it." So concerned was Governor Thomas that he advocated a measure that his predecessors had refused to entertain. This was government control of the Indian trade. He went even further. He admitted that the cause of the deplorable situation in 1744 was the lack of such control in the past. His confession deserves direct quotation:

"I cannot but be apprehensive that the Indian Trade as it is now carry'd on will involve us in some fatal Quarrel with the Indians. Our Traders in Defiance of the Law carry Spirituous Liquors amongst them, and take the Advantage of their inordinate Appetite for it to cheat them of their Skins and their Wampum, which is their Money, and often to debauch their Wives into the Bargain. Is it to be wondered at then, if when they Recover from the Drunken fit they should take severe Revenges. I shall do all that lies in my Power to prevent these Abuses by ordering a Strict Observance of the Law relating to Licenses, and the rigidest Prosecutions against such as shall be discovered to Sell Rum to the Indians. But I am Sensible these will avail but little, the ill practices of these people being carry'd on in the Woods, and at such a Distance from the Seat of Government that it will be very difficult to get Evidences to Convict them. If I am Rightly informed, the like abuses of the Traders in New England were the principal Causes of the Indian Wars there, and at length Obliged the Government to take the Trade into its own Hands. This is a matter that well deserves your Attention, and perhaps will soon require your imitation."[27]

[27] The governor's message is in *Pennsylvania Colonial Records*, 4:737-740.

To these suggestions the General Assembly gave an attentive ear. By no means did they deprecate the governor's fears, nor did they seek to controvert the evidence. They advised the governor to seek to prevent the migration of the Delawares to the Shawnee country and offered to appropriate such money as was reasonable for the purpose of keeping the Delawares under the British influence. As to trade, they agreed that Shawnee complaints were "not without just Grounds," and that the governor should seek to enforce the license and rum laws more rigidly. But when it came to passing a law to control the trade, the Assembly simply threw up its collective hands in dismay at the difficulty of preparing such a law. "To provide a Bill," they said, "for amending the Law in respect to Indian Traders would, we think, require longer time than will be convenient for us to stay together at this Season of the Year; and that, therefore, it will be best referred to the Consideration of the Succeeding Assembly."[28]

By the time the next Assembly met, the Shawnee, led by Peter Chartier, had gone over to the French. Exactly what happened and why, is hard to say. Weiser said that Chartier was angry at being reprimanded by the governor for spreading the reports of Shawnee defection in 1743. It is clear, however, that Shawnee discontent went deeper than that. The unregenerate Pennsylvania traders were the objects of hostility. It has been seen that it was only after the assurances given by the Iroquois at the treaty of Lancaster in 1744 that some of the traders returned to western Pennsylvania. When they did so they found the Shawnee waiting for them. Two traders, James Dunning and Peter Tostee, were ascending the Allegheny in the spring of 1745 with a load of furs and encountered, near Chartier's Town, four hundred armed Shawnee headed by Peter Chartier himself, who took them prisoners and robbed them of their effects, which they valued at sixteen hundred pounds. According to the Marquis de Beauharnois, governor of Canada, eight traders in all were treated

[28] *Pennsylvania Colonial Records*, 4:741.

in this manner. Then followed a migration. Whether the Shawnee feared English or Iroquois vengeance, whether they sought
better hunting, or whether they sought freedom from Pennsylvania rum, most of the Shawnee of western Pennsylvania
left their Allegheny towns to resume their wanderings.[29]

It is evident from these events that except for the plundering of the traders there was to be at this time no Indian war
on the frontiers. When Governor Thomas heard of the migration he was greatly relieved and informed the General Assembly that it was his opinion that "the Advantages of the Trade
Excepted, the further these People remove from our Borders,
the better it will be for Us."[30] But this was to prove only a
short-lived relief. Western Pennsylvania was not to be swept
clean of either Indians or the Indian problem. Some of the
Shawnee were to return. And even as the canoes of Chartier's
band disappeared in the distance down the Ohio, the trails
across the mountains to the east were being traveled by more
and more Delaware migrants who had found conditions unbearable on the Susquehanna and Juniata. Unless the government of Pennsylvania found better ways of treating the new
migrants to western Pennsylvania than had previously been
used, war was sure to come to the Quaker commonwealth.

[29] *Pennsylvania Colonial Records*, 4:758, 759, 780; Hanna, *Wilderness Trail*, 1:311;
New York Colonial Documents, 10:20.
[30] *Pennsylvania Colonial Records*, 4:758.

3

A Decade
of Iroquois Supremacy,
1745-1754

The history of Indian affairs in western Pennsylvania in the decade following the departure of the Shawnee is about as different from that of the decades preceding as it possibly could be. The period now under consideration is characterized by a marked improvement in the conditions of the fur trade, largely as a result of the activities and influence of George Croghan and his associates. Conditions did not become perfect, and Indian complaints did not disappear, but, considering the volume of the trade and the number of Indians involved, conditions were much better in the region than they had been for the Shawnee. The period is also characterized by a change in the Indian attitude toward the French and the English. Partly as a result of the dominance of the Iroquois and partly as a result of improved trading conditions, the Indians in general showed satisfaction in regard to the English and dissatisfaction in regard to the French. True, the decade closes with the French occupation, but, as the sequel will show, that occupation was not sought by the local Indians, and it produced an opposition to the French on the part of the Iroquois, which failed in its object not because the Indians did not want the expulsion of the French, but because the English were not able to raise forces quickly enough to effect that expulsion. The decade is also characterized by a slight increase in the interest of Pennsylvania and of Virginia in western Indian affairs. This increase was not enough, however, to enable either province to take a really effective part in helping the Indians to resist the French.

The migration of the Shawnee in 1745 was not a purge, but it was a sifting. Their departure meant a very drastic change in the population set-up of western Pennsylvania. It really meant a change in leadership from that of the Shawnee to that of the Iroquois. In the decade prior to 1745, Iroquois bands had begun to invade the country from two directions: from the northeast by way of the Allegheny River and from the northwest from the new Iroquois settlements on the Cuyahoga River in what is now Ohio. The latter group was the most numerous and settled in such numbers on the Beaver River and its tributaries that by 1747 the capital of the Iroquois in the upper Ohio Valley was Kuskuski (near modern New Castle), with Logstown on the Ohio as the port of entry for trade and as the scene of diplomatic contacts.[1]

The Iroquois were the dominant Indians in western Pennsylvania during the decade from 1745 to 1754, but they were by no means the only Indians. During this period a band of about one hundred Wyandot warriors and their families settled on and near the Shenango River. The Delawares continued to recruit new members from the East and to make their villages on the Allegheny River and its tributaries. Kit-

[1] Hanna, *Wilderness Trail,* 1:346, 348.

tanning was still the most important Delaware town. Most of the few Shawnee who returned after the migration under Chartier were to be found in or near Logstown. At Logstown in September, 1748, Conrad Weiser asked the deputies "of all the Nations of Indians settled on the Waters of Ohio" to give him a list of their "fighting Men." He received the following returns: Iroquois, 307; Delawares, 165; Shawnee, 162; Wyandot, 100; Chippewa, 40; Mahican, 15.[2]

Although the Iroquois in western Pennsylvania were looked upon merely as hunters by the grand Iroquois council at Onondaga, they assumed the air of overlords toward the non-Iroquois peoples settled on the upper Ohio. They had not been sent out deliberately by the New York Iroquois to keep the rest of the tribes in submission, but they had come as part of a natural migration because the hunting in the Cuyahoga and Beaver valleys was superior to that at home. Nevertheless they were the most numerous of the peoples collected in the new country, and their rights to ownership of the land were recognized by the other tribes. It is surprising to note how many non-Iroquois towns, especially Delaware towns, had a few Iroquois inhabitants. Delaware Jo, an emissary sent in 1755 to the upper Ohio by deputy Indian superintendent George Croghan, reported, "There are more or less of the Six Nations [Iroquois] living with the Shawonese and Delawares in their Towns." The Delaware subservience to the Iroquois is well known, and it is fair to say that the migration of the former to western Pennsylvania, at least after 1745, was conducted with the express permission and under the close supervision of the Iroquois. And after 1747 Tanacharison, or the Half King, the Iroquois vicegerent, exercised the prerogatives of his high office over the Iroquois and Delawares at Logstown, while his colleague, Scarouady, presided over the Shawnee Indians assembled there.[3]

[2] Hanna, *Wilderness Trail*, 1:311; *Pennsylvania Colonial Records*, 5:351.
[3] *Pennsylvania Colonial Records*, 5:478; 6:155, 159, 782; Hodge, *Handbook of American Indians*, 1:526.

A Decade of Iroquois Supremacy

This dominance of the upper Ohio Valley tribes by the Iroquois was a strong factor in making possible the revival of British influence in the West during the first part of the decade. It was the Iroquois around whom British policy centered in the attempts made during these years by the French to incorporate western Pennsylvania into New France. Finally, when it became apparent that the loyal Indians with the inadequate support they received from the English could not successfully resist the French, the Iroquois moved away and left the Shawnee, Delawares, and a few Iroquois renegades, the Mingo, to readjust their settlements and hunting grounds under the auspices of the French.

Another important factor concerning the population situation on the upper Ohio in the decade under consideration is the large increase in the numbers of Indians during a comparatively short period. The Frenchman, Céloron, who led the well-known French expedition down the Allegheny and the Ohio in 1749, expressed great surprise at the increase of the Indian population in the ten years since he had last been over that route. This fact is of great importance in accounting for both French and English policy in western Pennsylvania. It intensified the vigor with which the French sought to bring the newly settled Indians under their influence after 1749. Moreover, the newness itself of the population meant added strength to the British influence because the new tribes were either historically pro-British, as were the Iroquois, or but recently pro-French, as were the Wyandot and the Miami. The English traders, also, led by the indefatigable George Croghan, sought to bring the newly located tribes more and more into commercial and political accord with the English.[4]

The scene of the new population movement was not confined to western Pennsylvania alone, although the Iroquois and Delaware capitals and ports of entry were in that region. The scene also included practically all of what comprises the state of Ohio today. The Wyandot, who since 1700 had been

[4] Kellogg, *French Régime*, 412-415.

gradually migrating from the northern side of Lake Erie to the west and south thereof, found early in the 1740's that British goods were much cheaper than French. Hence during King George's War the Wyandot on the Sandusky under the leadership of Orontony (Nicholas) were definitely within the Croghan trading empire, much to the dismay of the French at Detroit. The news of the superior advantages of the English trade quickly spread to the Miami and resulted in a movement of part of that nation, led by La Demoiselle (Old Briton), from the Wabash-Maumee country in what is now Indiana to the upper waters of the Great Miami River in what is now Ohio, where the village of Pickawillanee was founded. By 1750 Croghan and many other Pennsylvania traders had an important station at this village, where they did a thriving business. The Scioto River was also part of the new scheme of things. Here most of the Shawnee had reunited from the Carolinas and from the Cumberland and Allegheny valleys. This tribe, too, had slipped away from its French proclivities under the irresistible pressure from the English traders, until the English at the council of Philadelphia in October, 1753, announced that the Shawnee and the English were perfectly reconciled.[5]

The ministering agent who tied together the English and Iroquois interests was George Croghan. It was largely through his action that the government of Pennsylvania was brought to bestir itself to recognize the necessity of taking a more active interest in western Indian affairs, although it must be confessed that this interest failed miserably in the French crisis of 1753-54. It was not that Croghan's opinion carried sufficient weight with the government to bring about this interest, but he was the medium by which the events that took place and the attitude of the Indians were transmitted to those in authority, and his advice was valuable. Conrad

[5] Kellogg, *French Régime*, 412, 413; Hanna, *Wilderness Trail*, 1:321-329; Volwiler, *George Croghan*, 36; W. M. Darlington, *Gist's Journals*, 48; *Pennsylvania Colonial Records*, 5:681.

A Decade of Iroquois Supremacy

Weiser, who, as the result of years of experience in Indian relations in the East, had gained the confidence and respect of the executives and legislators of Pennsylvania, brought Croghan to the attention of the authorities at the beginning of the colony's interest in trans-Appalachian affairs.[6]

The circumstances that brought the colony of Pennsylvania to a grudging and half-hearted abandonment of its policy of refraining from taking any positive measures on behalf of the western Indians were determined by the anti-French activities of the Ohio Valley and Lake Erie Iroquois and Wyandot during the latter years of King George's War. The Iroquois proper, that is, the Six Nations residing in New York state, managed for the most part to remain neutral in that controversy, although Sir William Johnson had influenced some of the warriors, mostly Mohawk, to take a more or less defensive part in the British interest.[7] To the west the Iroquois were less discreet, and Croghan seems to have been in some measure *particeps criminis*. By 1747 Croghan had brought the Iroquois and Wyandot of the Lake Erie streams, that is, the Cuyahoga and the Sandusky, into his trading system. So pleased were these Indians with the cheapness of the English goods that, taking their cue from the Albany council of August and September, 1746, in which the English had urged the Iroquois nation to take up arms against the French, they undertook to pursue the war against the French with great vigor.[8] The result was a series of murders of French traders. In a letter to Governor Thomas dated May 16, 1747, in Croghan's handwriting and on Croghan's paper, three Iroquois chiefs were made to say that their people had killed five French traders near Detroit. They ascribed their belligerent

[6] For a description of the establishment and growth of Croghan's fur-trading structure in the Ohio Valley, see Volwiler, *George Croghan*, 17-54.
[7] Arthur Pound and Richard E. Day, *Johnson of the Mohawks*, 115-118 (New York, 1930); *Pennsylvania Archives*, first series, 1:749.
[8] Volwiler, *George Croghan*, 35; *New York Colonial Documents*, 6:317-326. There were Wyandot towns on both the Muskingum and the Shenango. Croghan had a trading house at the Wyandot town on the upper Muskingum. W. M. Darlington, *Gist's Journals*, 37, 105, 161.

action to the urgings of the English at Albany and promised the capture of Detroit and the accession to the English interests of many of the western tribes, including the Chippewa and the Ottawa. They presented the governor with "one of those Frenchmen's Sculps" and assured him that "itt Shall not be yͤ Last of them," and they requested him to send them some powder and lead "to Carrey on yͤ Expedition with a Vigor." Ten days later Croghan himself wrote to Richard Peters, secretary of the Provincial Council, announcing that "allmost all the Ingans in the Woods, have Declared against yͤ French." The Iroquois desired to send the governor of the Quaker commonwealth "a Letter, a French Scalp, & some Wompom." Croghan advised that the presents be accepted and that the colony encourage the Indians to further hostilities by sending them powder and lead. Some time later another French trader, who had sought to compete with Croghan among the Wyandot, was killed by a Wyandot, because, according to Weiser, he offered "but one charge of Powder & one Bullet for a Beaver skin."[9]

It is significant of the new state of things in the West that the western Indians were more disposed for warfare in behalf of the English than were the New York Iroquois. It means that the Pennsylvania traders had made the Ohio Valley and Lake Erie tribes more satisfied with the English than were the Indians of New York, who found British trade much less satisfactory than in times gone by. It means that Pennsylvania was invited to take part in a war declared on the French by the King of England, urged on the Indians by the king's representatives, and made possible of successful prosecution by English traders. Under the circumstances it was hardly an unusual thing for the Indians and for Croghan to request the aid of the government of Pennsylvania.

[9] *Pennsylvania Archives*, first series, 1:741, 742; Volwiler, *George Croghan*, 59, 60; *Pennsylvania Colonial Records*, 5:87. In September, 1747, while at Thomas McKee's house on the Susquehanna, Weiser was offered a French scalp by some Ohio Indians. He, of course, refused to accept it. *Pennsylvania Colonial Records*, 5:138.

Pennsylvania was not, of course, to be forced into the king's or the Indians' or Croghan's war, but the commonwealth was for the first time to be forced to appropriate money to insure peace among the trans-Appalachian tribes. Croghan's letters had in June resulted in the grudging consent of the Provincial Council, evidently at the request of Thomas Lawrence, a member of that body and a business associate of Croghan's, to the expenditure of two hundred pounds for presents to the western tribes, but no deliveries had actually been made, because of delays and bickerings over the proper guarantees of the reliability of the carrier. It is interesting to note that this present was called a "handsome" one by the Council and a "small" one by Weiser. The occasion for the change in Pennsylvania's historic policy toward the western tribes and that led the authorities into definite action was the appearance in Philadelphia of the Ohio Indians themselves. Ten of these unexpected and unwanted callers appeared in the Quaker capital early in November. They demanded in picturesque language and in no uncertain terms that the British support them in the war that the British had begun and in which the British had involved the Indians.[10]

The request of the Indians was so pointed and so typical of Indian terminology that it deserves quotation at length. "This," they said, referring to the decision for war, "the Young Warriors have done—provoked to it by the repeated Applications of our Brethren the English. And we are now come to tell you that French have hard Heads, and that we have nothing strong enough to break them. We have only little Sticks & Hickeries . . . We therefore . . . desire that we may be furnished with better Weapons, such as will knock the French down . . . When once we, the Young Warriors, engaged we put a great deal of Fire under our Kettle, and the Kettle boil'd high, and so it does still . . . that the French Men's Heads might soon be boil'd; But when we looked about us to see how it

[10] Volwiler, *George Croghan*, 60; *Pennsylvania Colonial Records*, 5:121; *Pennsylvania Archives*, first series, 1:762.

was with the English Kettle, we saw the Fire was almost out, & that it hardly boil'd at all, & that no French men's heads were like to be in it. This truly surprizes us, & we are come down on purpose to know the reason of it. How comes it to pass that the English, who brought us into the War, will not fight themselves? This has not a good appearance, and . . . we . . . desire you wou'd put more Fire under your Kettle."[11]

There was no choice in the matter for Pennsylvania. Indians who had once taken part in the Anglo-French war might, if the English were ungrateful, go over to the French because that would be the only way for the Indians to square themselves with the French if the latter gained the ascendancy. "Providence," said Weiser, trying to put the matter in a mild light, "had furnished this Province with a fine opportunity of making all the Indians about the Lakes their Friends, & warm Friends too." He advised a preliminary present to be given to the warriors on their way back and a larger present to be delivered to them in their own country in the spring of 1748. The Council acquiesced. Through its president it praised the Indians for taking up the English cause, referred to the British victory in the capture of Louisbourg to show that the kettle was boiling high and that plenty of Frenchmen's heads were in it, and told them that gifts to the amount of two hundred pounds were waiting for them at John Harris' (Harrisburg) and that more would be ready in the spring. The question of whether or not the Indians were to continue to fight the French was adroitly avoided. The warriors were eminently pleased, danced the war dance as a sign of what they proposed to do to the French, and started on their return home. Although the Quaker Assembly in making the necessary appropriation sought to salve its conscience by saying that the money was to be used to supply the Indians with "Necessaries towards acquiring a Livelihood . . . and not to encourage their entring into War," the Indians themselves did not so interpret the gifts.[12]

[12] *Pennsylvania Colonial Records*, 5:148-152, 156, 185.   [11] *Ibid.*, 5:146.

However involuntary the new policy was, Pennsylvania, once embroiled in western Indian complications, was naturally obliged to continue the process. According to one estimate, the cost to the commonwealth of Indian affairs during the years from 1748 to 1752 equaled the cost for the entire thirty years preceding that period. The same threat of French influence that had forced the issue at Philadelphia in the fall of 1747 was also used by the Indians after the Philadelphia meeting to guarantee deliveries in the spring of 1748. Scarouady, Iroquois representative from Logstown, who had been one of the delegates at the Philadelphia meeting, told Conrad Weiser on the way back home, "Brother, I am very glad that our Brethren in Philadelphia took into their serious Consideration what we have said to them. The French Party is very strong among us, and if we had failed in our Journey to Philadelphia, or our Expectations wou'd not have been granted by our Brethren in Philadelphia, the Indians would have gone over to the French to a Man ... Let me desire You to set out early in the Spring with the Supplies our Brethren have been pleased to promise Us . . . pray don't miss."[13]

But Pennsylvania did miss, and in so doing, showed the half-hearted nature of its policy. From the autumn of 1747, when the commonwealth's officials at Philadelphia promised the Indians what the red men interpreted to mean support in war, to the treaty of Logstown a year later, Pennsylvania's interest in the Indians went through a period of decline. When Croghan, representing the Quaker commonwealth, met the tribes at Logstown in May, 1748, he did not have the larger presents that had been promised. He had goods, mostly powder and lead, amounting to somewhat less than two hundred pounds. The gift was just enough to keep the Indians from going over to the French. It was not until October, 1748, that the larger gift was made at Logstown by Conrad Weiser, assisted by Croghan, and the gift was accompanied by the information that the war was over and that the Indians were

[13] Volwiler, *George Croghan,* 56; *Pennsylvania Colonial Records,* 5:166.

not to attack the French. Indeed, Weiser's first instructions, which had been made in June when the Philadelphia officials had not yet received news of the end of the war, were to discourage the Indians from taking part in the conflict.[14]

It was more than the mere announcement of an end of hostilities that made the treaty of Logstown an anticlimax from the Indian point of view. With the danger of French attack over, the Pennsylvanians could afford to be less cordial to the western tribes. For one thing, Weiser demanded an explanation for Iroquois attacks made on whites in South Carolina in the course of an incursion on the Catawba, and he also rebuked the Indians for robbing Pennsylvania traders and for excessive drinking. This was the answer to Scarouady's request at Philadelphia that the rum trade be suppressed, and it was delivered by the man who had told the Provincial Council in seconding Scarouady's request, "Death, without Judge or Jury, to any Man that carrys Rum to sell to any Indian Town, is the only remedy to prevent that Trade . . . It is an abomination before God & Man." Only a year before, this same Conrad Weiser, in speaking of Indian relations on the Susquehanna, had said, "I shall be sick of Indian Affairs If no medium is found to do them Justice . . . I find it very hard sometimes to Excuse the Government . . . the Indians have just reason to Complain at the behaviour of some of our people." In May, 1748, the chief executive of Pennsylvania had advised the Assembly to "prepare a Bill for limiting the number of Indian Traders, and the putting them under proper Regulations," but it is apparent that trading conditions in the fall of that year were little better than in the days of the Shawnee ascendancy. In Pennsylvania between August 10, 1747, and August 10, 1748, there were nine licensed traders as against thirty unlicensed ones, and the disparity would no doubt be greater if the Virginia and Maryland traders were counted.[15]

[14] *Pennsylvania Colonial Records*, 5:292, 294.
[15] *Pennsylvania Colonial Records*, 5:167, 230, 351-353, 356; *Pennsylvania Archives*, first series, 1:751; 2:14.

A Decade of Iroquois Supremacy

It is fair to say that however lukewarm was Pennsylvania's interest in the Indians of the upper Ohio Valley, the Indians were not likely to prove a serious menace to the Quaker commonwealth, so long as peace was maintained between England and France. Croghan expected French machinations among the tribes and sent his agent, Andrew Montour, among the Lake Erie Indians in June, 1749, to look into the situation. But Croghan was not worried. "I Make no Doubt," he wrote in July, 1749, "butt the French will Make use of unfair Methods they Can to bring over all ye Indians they can to there Interest, But I am of opinion that ye Indians are So well grafted in ye English Interest that they will Nott be Esey Deceved by the French."[16] After all, English prices continued to be more attractive to the Indians, and Croghan himself was an influence for good in respect to trade control.

No one, after 1749, was more conscious of the preference of the Indians of western Pennsylvania and of the Ohio Valley for the English than were the French themselves. This consciousness was the result of the expedition down the Allegheny and Ohio of Pierre Joseph Céloron, sieur de Blainville, commandant of a detachment of some 250 French and Indians, sent early in the year by the governor of New France, the Marquis de la Galissonière, to overawe the Indians and to expel the English traders from French soil. Céloron, instead of overawing the Indians, was forced to bury his famous leaden plates lest the red men discover and destroy them, and he contented himself with verbal warnings to the English traders lest his plundering of them lead to his own destruction. When he reached the Shawnee and the Miami country he was forced to submit to the most unexpected humiliations. So discouraged was Céloron that he wrote at the end of his journey, "All that I can say is, that the nations of these localities are very badly disposed towards the French, and are entirely devoted to the English. . . . If our traders were sent there for traffic, they could not sell their merchandise at the same price

[16] *Pennsylvania Archives,* first series, 2:31.

as the English sell theirs, on account of the many expenses they would be obliged to incur.... A solid establishment would be useful in the colony, but there are a great many inconveniences in being able to sustain it, on the score of difficulties of the ways for transporting provisions and the other suitable requisites."[17]

If Céloron thought that the governor of New France was going to sit idly by while economic forces brought tribe after tribe into the British fur-trading system, he was profoundly mistaken. The governor might have saved his master, the king, a tremendous expense if he had done so, but it could hardly be expected that he would admit the advisability of such a move even if he had recognized it. The French naturally sought to renew the trade that King George's War had caused them to lose. The renewal was made difficult by the rise of competition from the Pennsylvania traders, by the shift of Indian population to the upper parts of the Ohio Valley, and by the increase of the Iroquois content of that population, but these factors did not seem to discourage the French. They continued to regard the English traders as intruders and to look forward to the day when French power would be strong enough to accomplish the expulsion of those intruders. Plans along these lines were gradually made after 1749, so that, by the time the Marquis Duquesne became governor of New France, in 1752, the stage was set for vigorous strokes. Governor James Hamilton of Pennsylvania described the situation fairly when he told the Assembly on August 8, 1750, "The French still continue their Threats against the Indians who carry on Commerce with our Traders ... they are frequently alarmed as if the French were approaching in a military Manner, and therefore keep themselves upon their Guard."[18]

The French restoration began with the tribes nearest to French power—the Miami, the Wyandot, and the Shawnee of the Scioto Valley, all of which, as has been pointed out, were

---

[17] Galbreath, *Expedition of Celoron,* 57.
[18] *Pennsylvania Colonial Records,* 5:455.

well within the system of the Pennsylvania traders by 1747. The Wyandot had been brought into the English political alliance along with the Iroquois as the result of the Philadelphia conference of 1747. The Miami and Shawnee had been brought in at the treaty of Lancaster in July, 1748, when representatives of these tribes thrust themselves upon the attentions of the Pennsylvania authorities as had the Iroquois and Wyandot the year before. The process of the Lancaster affair had been somewhat similar to that of the Philadelphia one, and the Miami and Shawnee had been sent back home with promises of goods to come. But while these two tribes were in a stage of great expectations, the Wyandot began to enter a stage of disillusionment. A delegation of them waited on Croghan at his home in Pennsboro Township on May 17, 1750, and declared that they were not satisfied with the peace, "for the French are always threatening Us." They requested, moreover, "that the English Governors would jointly apply to have Us included in the Peace, that we may not be subject to the Intimidations and Resentment of the French, but be in quiet as well as you." Seldom has the Indian point of view been more completely misunderstood by the English. Governor Hamilton, in discussing the Wyandot complaint, told Croghan to tell the Wyandot and the Iroquois that it was up to them to defend themselves against the French. "As we do not infringe upon the Liberties of the Indians," he was instructed to say, "so neither ought the French to do it, and if they do it ought to be the voice of one and all the Indians to resent and to put a stop to such unjust Proceedings."[19]

Soon the Miami also began to discover what it meant to have made the decision to ally with the English. At the conference with Croghan on May 17, 1750, the Twightwees, as the English called the Miami, had asked for more traders to supply their needs. The occasion for this request was the visit

[19] *Pennsylvania Colonial Records,* 5:308-316, 435, 521. On January 4, 1751, Christopher Gist while journeying down the Ohio picked up a report that the Indians of the Wyandot nation still under the French influence were expected to join their pro-English colleagues. W. M. Darlington, *Gist's Journals,* 40.

to the Pickawillanee country in the summer of 1749 of over two hundred French and Indians for the purpose of persuading the Miami to return to the Wabash and Maumee country. The Miami declined and at the same time refused a small present of two barrels of powder, four bags of bullets, some paint, and some needles and thread. The real reason that the Pickawillanee Miami did not receive the attentions of more English traders was that trading conditions were not safe. Hamilton therefore told the Miami that if they wanted more traders it was up to them "to preserve the road safe and commodious." This was practically impossible—fourteen people had recently been killed between Logstown and Pickawillanee, and two others had been captured. Thus the only hope for the Miami was to leave the Great Maumee Valley and to settle farther up in the Ohio Valley. They had broached the subject to Croghan in the summer of 1750, and he, on behalf of the Miami and the Shawnee, brought it to the attention of the Iroquois at Logstown and Kuskuski. A year later, in the spring of 1751, when Croghan and Christopher Gist were at Pickawillanee delivering to the Miami Pennsylvania's gift of one hundred pounds, Ottawa Indians under French instructions repeated the request that the Miami return, this time with a warning that if they did not, there would be war in the coming spring. But the Miami still cleaved to the English, and the French were publicly denounced. Articles of alliance were even drawn up with two more tribes, the Piankashaw and the Wea, and everybody was invited to Logstown in the spring of 1752 to receive more presents from Virginia and Pennsylvania.[20]

True to their promise, however, the French struck. The first attack took place in the summer of 1751, shortly after the visit of Croghan and Gist. The attack, led by Sieur de Bellestre, was a failure because of the smallness of the band,

[20] *Pennsylvania Colonial Records,* 5:433, 437, 450, 451, 472, 482, 485, 497, 522-524; *New York Colonial Documents,* 6:735; W. M. Darlington, *Gist's Journals,* 37, 52, 53, 55; Kellogg, *French Régime,* 417, 418. A price of one thousand dollars was at this time reported placed on Croghan's head by the French. *Pennsylvania Colonial Records,* 5:483; Volwiler, *George Croghan,* 78.

and resulted in the killing of only two Miami. But the reckoning came a year later. On June 21, 1752, the youthful Charles Langlade and his band of French and Ottawa captured the village of Pickawillanee and completely destroyed every vestige of the British trade. The Miami were convinced of French superiority and returned westward to the Maumee and to the French—less than two years after they had made it known to the English that it was their wish to move eastward nearer to English traders and protection.[21]

Much that has been said of the Pickawillanee Miami and of the unsatisfactory nature of trading conditions on the Great Miami River applies to the Shawnee also, because most of the country between Logstown and Pickawillanee was inhabited by that tribe. In the summer of 1750 a Franco-Indian attack on a Shawnee town, probably on the Scioto, was made, in which one Shawnee warrior was killed and three non-combatants were captured. In the pursuit that followed, five Frenchmen and several Indians were captured. By 1752 conditions were so bad in the Shawnee country that that tribe was forced to protest to the English. In a message to Governor Hamilton dated February 8, 1752, signed by four chiefs and five traders, they said that they were going to strike the French "and not suffer ourselves to be insulted any more," and they asked the English to support them, or, as they put it, that "you speak to us . . . and that you don't speak for nothing." It was beyond the power and the disposition of Hamilton to encourage them in war or to engage to assist them, and he delegated to Croghan the task of informing the Shawnee of his inability to aid them. Croghan was instructed to put the best face he could on the matter by referring the Shawnee to the Virginians, who by 1752 were beginning to take Pennsyl-

---

[21] Kellogg, *French Régime*, 418-422; *Pennsylvania Colonial Records*, 5:599, 600; "The Treaty of Logg's Town, 1752," in *Virginia Magazine of History and Biography*, 13:152 (1905-6). Some of the Miami remained friendly with the English until after the council of Carlisle in October, 1753, but by January, 1754, Croghan reported them all back with the French. *Pennsylvania Colonial Records*, 5:677, 681, 732; Goodman, *Journal of Captain William Trent*, 35.

vania's place in assuming responsibility for protecting the Indians against the French.[22]

Pennsylvania's side-stepping of the Shawnee problem is indicative of similar actions on her part in the field of western Indian problems in general. By 1750 the time had come for stronger action than the mere sending of gifts to the tribes. Military action of a defensive character was required. This was brought squarely to the attention of Governor Hamilton by Croghan in a letter from Logstown, dated November 16, 1750. He reported the presence of the French agent, Philippe Thomas de Joncaire, at the headwaters of the Allegheny with five canoeloads of goods, where he was lavishing presents on the tribesmen and promising to build a fort if he could get the Indians to consent. This so alarmed the Ohio Valley Iroquois in general that they demanded of Croghan that the British afford adequate protection in the form of an English fort. Hamilton placed Croghan's letter before the proprietor of the colony and received in reply the offer by the proprietor of a gift of four hundred pounds down and one hundred pounds a year for the erection and maintenance of a fort and garrison in western Pennsylvania. The Assembly would have to supplement the gift with appropriations. This, characteristically, the Assembly would not do. Croghan was therefore sent to Logstown with the usual presents for the year 1751 and with instructions to "sound the Indians in a private manner" on the subject. He was expressly forbidden to make any public mention of building a fort. But the fact that the Quaker authorities thought they could avoid discussion of a matter so vital to the Indians shows how completely the whites misunderstood the whole problem. The Indians took Croghan's silence at the conference at Logstown in May, 1751, to mean that Pennsylvania was going to build the fort. Hence when Croghan, in the presence of Joncaire, told the Indians to expel the French, the Iroquois trustingly accepted the English advice and told Joncaire to "go home directly off our

Lands." They told the English, moreover, that they would in the course of two months decide on a proper place for the fort and that they would then inform the governor of Pennsylvania.[23]

The Quaker Assembly made short shrift of the matter. Relying on information they said they had obtained from Conrad Weiser and from Andrew Montour, who had accompanied Croghan, they, on August 21, 1751, emphatically repudiated Croghan's report and said that he had "misunderstood or misrepresented" the feelings and wishes of the Indians. There was no need for a fort. "We have always found," they said, "that sincere, upright Dealing with the Indians, a friendly Treatment of them on all occasions, and particularly in relieving their Necessities at proper Times by suitable Presents, have been the best means of securing their Friendship." Governor Hamilton was clearly aware of the negligence of the Assembly. "I have little reason to expect," he wrote to Governor Clinton of New York on June 6, 1751, "they will ever act a proper part in Indian affairs, untill either some notable calamity befall our back inhabitants, or till they have such injunctions laid upon them from home as they will not venture to disobey."[24]

It was now up to Virginia to attempt to fill the breach. The first formal council between the Virginians and the Indians took place at Logstown in June, 1752. This council had been called to assist the struggling Ohio Company of Virginia to establish the fur-trading and settlement colony on the Virginia lands granted to it on the upper Ohio. Christopher Gist, the company's agent, had toured the Ohio Valley from October, 1750, to June, 1751, inspecting the lands and inviting the Indian tribes to a treaty to be held at Logstown.[25] The meeting was thus not planned by Virginia consciously and formally to take over the responsibilities of administering Indian rela-

---

[23] *Pennsylvania Colonial Records,* 5:497, 515, 522, 534-538.
[24] *Pennsylvania Colonial Records,* 5:547; *New York Colonial Documents,* 6:710.
[25] W. M. Darlington, *Gist's Journals,* 31-66.

tions that had been avoided by Pennsylvania. It was only a step in that direction.

The Ohio Company had been chartered by the king on the assumption that the Virginia lands bordering on the upper Ohio had been ceded by the Iroquois to Virginia by deed of July 2, 1744, made at the treaty of Lancaster, for which the Indians had received four hundred pounds.[26] According to the English, this deed recognized "the King's Right to all the Lands that are or shall be by his Majesty's Appointment in the Colony of Virginia."[27] According to the Iroquois, it recognized the king's rights to lands in Virginia "as far as it is settled, & back from thence to the Sun setting," which was intended to mean "the Hill on the other Side of the Allegany Hill." At the treaty at Logstown, according to Governor Robert Dinwiddie's instructions, dated April 26, 1752, the Virginia commissioners were to obtain a confirmation of this deed. The Indians were to be liberally compensated at the treaty and were to be assured that the Ohio Company's designs would not imperil the status of the Indians but would give them better trading conditions and protection from obstreperous English frontiersmen and from the French. "The chief point in view," said Dinwiddie, "is to carry on a Trade to the mutual benefit of them & the inhabitants of this Colony, and to make such a settlement, as may preserve them, our brethren and ourselves from any Injuries from the French in case of a future War."[28]

The result was that at the treaty of Logstown in return for a half-hearted consent to the reaffirmation of the Lancaster deed of 1744 the Indians obtained of the Virginians an equally half-hearted promise to build a "strong house" at the forks of the Ohio. In a document dated June 13, 1752, the Indians con-

[26] W. M. Darlington, *Gist's Journals*, 217-219, 726; Fernow, *Ohio Valley*, 253, 251, 252. In this source the reference to the treaty of Lancaster is interrupted in the middle of a sentence and completed on the pages immediately preceding.

[27] *Pennsylvania Colonial Records*, 4:726.

[28] "The Treaty of Logg's Town, 1752," in *Virginia Magazine of History and Biography*, 13:149, 167, 168 (1905-6).

firmed the deed "in as full & ample a Manner as if the same was here recited" and consented to "making a Settlement or Settlements of British Subjects on the southern or eastern Parts of the River Ohio," with a promise not to molest the settlement but to "assist and Protect" it. But they hoped the Virginians would "take care to send none among us but good Men" and that they would "advise them how to behave." Moreover, when the Virginians wanted to know whether the Indian request for a fort "implied a Settlement of People, as well as an House," Tanacharison, the Iroquois vicegerent on the Ohio, replied in the negative. When the Virginians insisted that it was too costly for the keepers of the "strong house" to import their food, Tanacharison replied that his people would take care that "there shall be no Scarcity of that Kind." The next year when William Trent on behalf of the Ohio Company agreed on the forks as the site of the "strong house," he pledged Virginia to form no settlements or improvements on the land and to evacuate when required to do so by the Six Nations. The sum and substance of what was done at Logstown in 1752 was described by Governor Dinwiddie in a letter of May 21, 1753, to Governor Hamilton as "Liberty of settling a fixed Trade to supply them with necessaries and Leave to build Two Forts."[29]

It is evident that the Virginians were in no rush to build a fort at the forks of the Ohio. Throughout 1752 and 1753 they met each new situation with the same old formula: gifts and negotiations. After the close of the treaty of Logstown on June 13, 1752, the next order of business was to placate the Pickawillanee Miami, some of whom after the disaster of June 21 had appealed to Governor Dinwiddie. "We must look on ourselves as lost, if our Brothers, the English, do not stand by us, and give us Powder and Lead and Arms." And so William Trent, an Ohio trader whose home was near Winchester, was

---

[29] "The Treaty of Logg's Town, 1752," in *Virginia Magazine of History and Biography*, 13:168-174 (1905-6); Virginia, *Calendar of Virginia State Papers*, 1:277; *Pennsylvania Colonial Records*, 5:630.

dispatched by the governor to the Great Miami with a present. When Trent reported to Dinwiddie in January, 1753, that part of the Pickawillanee Miami had returned to the French, the governor was chagrined, but he did not view the situation as alarming.[30]

In February, 1753, Dinwiddie did not feel that there was much danger of a great French army invading the Ohio Valley, and he therefore prepared for the delivery of another gift of powder and lead to the Iroquois at Winchester in April. Before this could happen, however, the French had occupied Presque Isle, and the Iroquois had appealed to Virginia for aid, which led Dinwiddie to send Trent with some of the desired goods direct to the Indian country. By this time Trent was alarmed. He wrote to Governor Hamilton on April 10, 1753, "The Indians are in such confusion that there is no knowing who to trust. I expect they will all join the French except the Delawares, as they expect no assistance from the English." In spite of this state of affairs, Trent had no other instructions than to promise the Indians the erection of a trading house on the Ohio where there would be kept a "Quantity of Warlike Stores . . . ready to supply you upon any Emergency." There was no suggestion of any white troops being sent to help in the defense of the Iroquois. Instead, Trent exhorted the Indians to defend themselves: "What, is the heroick Spirit of your Ancestors lost? Will the Six Nations, who were formerly a Terror to the French suffer themselves to become their Slaves? I desire you not to let them build any strong House in your Country, for they make a bad use of them." He told them that if they would ally with the Cherokee, Catawba, and Wyandot, the French would not dare to attack them. He told them that he expected each nation to state its intentions—"whether you intend to let the French finish their Forts and take your whole Country away from you

---

[30] "The Treaty of Logg's Town, 1752," in *Virginia Magazine of History and Biography*, 13:153 (1905-6); Goodman, *Journal of Captain William Trent*, 83-105; Dinwiddie, *Official Records*, 1:22.

and make Slaves of you all; or whether you intend to drive them off."[31]

Precious time was slipping away. The Iroquois accepted Trent's instructions and went through the process of giving the French three warnings, the last one of which was delivered by Tanacharison, who declared, "I will strike over all this Land with my Rod, let it hurt who it will." The Iroquois, in return, fully expected the immediate establishment of the "strong house" at the forks of the Ohio promised by Trent. The English trader, John Fraser, wrote from the forks on August 27, 1753, that Trent had visited there on the twenty-fifth and viewed the ground on which the fort was to be built. "They will begin," said Fraser, "in less than a month's time. The Money has been laid out for the building of it already, and the great Guns are lying at Williamsburg ready to bring up." It was not begun in a month's time. Instead, more promises had been made at the treaty of Winchester in September, 1753, of goods to be delivered to the Indians by Gist, Trent, and Montour after the fort was constructed.[32]

By the fall of 1753 the French had proceeded as far south as Venango, where their advance was halted for the winter season. Now was the time for the Virginians to fortify the forks of the Ohio. But the Ohio Company was merely a trading company and could hardly be expected to turn a trading house into a fort and to sustain it with a well-equipped garrison, and the colony of Virginia was not disposed to sustain such an enterprise without authorization and support from the king. This authorization and support did not come until early in November in the form of practically identical letters from the Earl of Holderness, secretary of state, to all the governors of North America. The letters were dated August 28, 1753, and specified that, before any military action was taken, the French be requested to withdraw. In the event of

---

[31] Dinwiddie, *Official Records*, 1:22, 23, 39; M. C. Darlington, *Henry Bouquet*, 28-33; Volwiler, *George Croghan*, 80.

[32] *Pennsylvania Colonial Records*, 5:660, 666-668; Volwiler, *George Croghan*, 81.

a refusal the colonies were then authorized to resort to arms. Thus more delay ensued while Washington and Gist visited the French commandant at Le Bœuf and received the official refusal of Legardeur de St. Pierre to withdraw. At last, however, the signal for the construction of the fort was given. On January 27, 1754, William Trent was commissioned a militia captain by Dinwiddie and authorized to raise one hundred men in his county. He was to proceed to the forks of the Ohio and to assist the agents of the Ohio Company, who Dinwiddie assumed had started to build, in finishing their fort. Washington was to join him at the fort with a hundred more men from Frederick and Augusta counties. Major John Carlyle was appointed commissary with instructions to raise provisions for five hundred men for six months. He was also instructed to deliver to the fort ten cannon and two hundred small arms with the necessary ammunition, and he was given authority to impress, if necessary, the means of transporting these supplies to the West.[33]

It was not until about February 1, with the winter all but gone, that Trent arrived at the forks and began his work. He arrived, not with one hundred men, as was planned, but with thirty-three, and from then until April 17, the day of the surrender to the French, the number of men at the fort never exceeded fifty. It was really due to the efforts of just one man that a complete disillusionment of the Indians in regard to the British was prevented on the approach of the French. This was Ensign Edward Ward, third in command of Trent's company and commandant on April 17 in the absence of Trent and the second-in-command, Lieutenant John Fraser. Trent's absence was a legitimate one—he was at Wills Creek on the Potomac seeking to hasten the necessary supplies—but Fraser's was not; for this gentleman was busying himself at his home at the mouth of Turtle Creek preparing to save his fur-trading effects from the certain vengeance of the French. Thus Ward, follow-

---

[33] *Pennsylvania Colonial Records*, 5:689; Washington, *Diaries . . . 1748-1799*, 1:43-67; Dinwiddie, *Official Records*, 1:49, 53, 55.

ing Tanacharison's counsel to hasten to throw up the stockade around the fort and adhering to the same chief's advice to try to put the French off until the return of Trent, stuck to his post to the last, knowing, as he said, that "the bad consequences of his leaveing it as the rest had done would give the Indians a very indifferent opinion of the English ever after."[34]

On so small a matter as the insight and ingenuity of one man did British control of the Indians balance on April 17, 1754, when Ward surrendered to the French captain, Claude Pierre Pecaudy de Contrecœur. The affair is indicative of the general level to which English prestige had declined in the Ohio Valley at this time. The return of the Pickawillanee Miami to the Maumee country and to the French had been compleied, and British trade with the Indians was at a standstill. On April 10, 1753, Trent reported that disaster had overtaken three British trading parties. One of these parties was attacked in Kentucky by a band made up mostly of Ottawa, and eight prisoners were taken, five of them employees of Croghan and Trent and three of the trader Lazarus Lowrey. In this raid Croghan and Trent lost goods to the value of three or four hundred pounds. Another disaster occurred to the trader John Findlay, who had three men killed in an attack by French Miami on one of his trading parties; and a third disaster occurred when Michael Teaffe, one of Croghan's employees, was robbed near Lake Erie of five horseloads of skins by a party of French Wyandot. By fall the demoralization of the British Indian trade had spread so far that John Fraser, whose main trading post was at Venango, declared on August 27, "I have not got any Skins this Summer, for there has not been an Indian between Weningo [*Venango*] and the Pict Country [*Great Miami*] hunting this Summer, by reason of the French."[35]

[34] *Pennsylvania Archives,* first series, 2:118; Virginia, *Calendar of Virginia State Papers,* 1:278; W. M. Darlington, *Gist's Journals,* 277, 278.
[35] W. M. Darlington, *Gist's Journals,* 192; *Pennsylvania Colonial Records,* 5:659. See also deposition of John Trotter, trader at Venango, dated March 22, 1754, in *Pennsylvania Archives,* first series, 2:131.

The situation was further aggravated by Pennsylvania's almost complete neglect of the Indians during the crucial days from the fall of 1753 to the spring of 1754. As in the days of the war menace of 1747 to 1748, the Iroquois had turned to the English, first by going to Winchester in September, 1753, and then by turning north to Pennsylvania when they heard that the Quaker government had six hundred pounds' worth of goods for them. Benjamin Franklin, Richard Peters, secretary of the Provincial Council, and Isaac Norris, speaker of the General Assembly, were hastily constituted a commission to meet the Indians at Carlisle. On October 1 the Council opened, and the Indians presented a complete program for the control of the Indian situation. Settlers were to stay off the Ohio lands, but trade was to be purged of the sale of rum and ordered in such a manner that at only three places, Logstown, the forks of the Ohio, and the mouth of the Kanawha, could it be carried on, and in these districts only under the strictest supervision to insure honest traders and reasonable and uniform prices. But to the consternation of the Indians, not only were these matters of trade set aside by the promise of referring them to the governor, but also the goods that the red men had come to receive were withheld from them, because news had come during the conference that the French had occupied Venango, and it was feared that the arms and ammunition might be captured by the enemy. The goods were to be placed in the keeping of Croghan at Aughwick to be distributed upon the governor's orders. Action of this kind was tantamount to a confession by the Quaker government that affairs in western Pennsylvania were beyond its control. There would have been no danger to the arms and ammunition if there had been a fort and garrison on the Ohio. The Iroquois specifically asked Governor Hamilton for the construction of such a fort, in a meeting at Logstown on October 27, but Hamilton in his reply, dated November 20, ignored the request. The truth was that he knew the Quaker Assembly would not sustain such an action. Hamilton addressed that body on the western crisis, and he exhorted them to raise troops to co-operate with Virginia, to appoint a government agent to reside on the Ohio, and to reform the law and administration of Indian trade. But on March 2 he met with a flat refusal on all points, and the whole business bogged down into a futile and bitter wrangle between the governor and the Assembly as to his right to call out troops when there was no assurance that the disputed lands were in the jurisdiction of the colony. These disputations were not known at once to the Indians, who were kept in hopes of favorable action from Pennsylvania by the delivery at Logstown in January, 1754, by Croghan, Montour, and John Patten, of the goods withheld from the Indians at Carlisle in October.[36]

By the middle of May, 1754, the Ohio Valley Iroquois and their dependents, who in February and March had been in high spirits because of the coming of Trent to start the "big house," were bewildered. Croghan, who, with Andrew Montour, was now an official Pennsylvania agent residing in the Indian country, wrote to Governor Hamilton on May 14, "The whole of ye Ohio Indians Does Nott No what to think, they Imagine by this Government Doing Nothing towards ye Expedition that ye Virginians and ye French Intend to Divide ye Land of Ohio between them, and if they should putt that Construction on ye Delays of this Government, itt will Certainly be of ill Consequence to the English in gineral."[37] The Iroquois were still loyal and were still able to keep the Delawares, Shawnee, and some of the Wyandot loyal also, although all the Indians residing in the towns between Presque Isle and the forks of the Ohio had acquiesced in the French occupation. Many of the Delawares had, however, deserted these towns and had joined their brethren beyond the French sphere of occupation. The further spread of French influence after the capitulation of Ward at the forks would depend upon

[36] *Pennsylvania Colonial Records*, 5:674-676, 680, 682, 691, 693-696, 719-722, 731-735, 747-749, 751-755, 758-764; *Pennsylvania Archives*, first series, 2:132-136.

[37] *Pennsylvania Colonial Records*, 6:21; *Pennsylvania Archives*, first series, 2:144.

the outcome of the appeal of the Indians for English aid. The Iroquois and their dependents would remain loyal so long as the English held the upper hand over the French. But if the British were defeated in the first encounters, the Iroquois would depart from western Pennsylvania and leave the dependent tribes to go over to the French.

The Virginia military operations immediately following Ward's surrender were thus of extreme importance to the Indians. As has been previously pointed out, Ward had remained at the English fort in the face of overwhelming odds mainly to sustain Iroquois faith in British arms. His action had the desired effect, and after he had left the fort to the French, he reported to Washington that the Indians remained "steadfastly attached to our Interest." Tanacharison himself wrote to the governor of Virginia on April 18, the day after the evacuation, in great spirit, saying he was ready to fight at any time. "Have good courage," he said, "and come as soon as possible; you will find us as ready to fight them [*the French*] as you are yourself. . . . If you do not come to our assistance now, we are entirely undone, and I think we shall never meet together again."[38]

This message had a strangely unfortunate result. It led Major George Washington to take his little detachment into the wilderness before he was really warranted in doing so, considering the great superiority of the French in men and arms. A council of war was held at Washington's headquarters at Wills Creek on April 23, where the fatal decision was made to advance the 180 odd troops to Redstone on the Monongahela, there to await the reinforcements necessary before laying siege to Fort Duquesne, as the French called the fort they had built on the site of the one captured from the English. "It was thought a thing impracticable," Washington admitted in his diary, "to march towards the Fort without sufficient strength; however, being strongly invited by the Indians, and particularly by the speeches of the Half-King [*Tanacharison*], the

[38] Washington, *Diaries . . . 1748-1799*, 1:75, 76.

president [*of the council of war*] gave his opinion that it would be proper to advance, as far as Red-Stone Creek . . . and encourage the Indians our Allies, to remain in our interests." Washington thereupon sent an express to Governor Dinwiddie to hasten with the supporting troops, ammunition, arms, and artillery. At the same time he sent an express in the opposite direction to ask Tanacharison to join forces with him as soon as possible.[39]

True to his word, Tanacharison and his colleague, Scarouady, gathered together a small band of Iroquois and a few Shawnee and Delawares. By May 27 the French and English forces had converged near the Great Meadows in Fayette County, Pennsylvania. Tanacharison discovered the location of a French reconnoitering party in the evening, and word of his discovery was sent to Washington. In the morning of May 28 the red and white allies met and defeated the French. Ten Frenchmen, including the commander, Ensign Coulon de Jumonville, were killed, and twenty-one prisoners were taken. Blood had now been shed, and unless Washington and the Virginians were successful in sustaining themselves against the French, the days of the Iroquois in the Ohio Valley were numbered. A migration of Iroquois to Washington's camp at Great Meadows soon set in; among the first arrivals was Queen Allaquippa, who, on June 1, brought about thirty families from her town on the Monongahela. News of the Anglo-Iroquois victory spread quickly, and on June 18 a group of about forty French Iroquois, Delawares, and Shawnee asked Washington for a conference. This conference was clearly designed to prepare the way for a British restoration. The Indians wanted to know if the Virginians would attack the Ohio Valley Indians in the event of a reconquest and also sought to find out if the Virginians were really strong enough to defeat the French. Washington, of course, reassured the Indians as to their safety in case of a reconquest and put on a bold front in regard to his strength and the reinforcements

[39] Washington, *Diaries . . . 1748-1799*, 1:77-79.

that were on the way. It is doubtful, however, that the Indians were impressed. Washington also used the occasion to plant among the Delawares and Shawnee near Fort Duquesne the seeds of an Indian uprising to accompany the British restoration. The conference broke up amicably on June 24, and the Indians returned to the Ohio.[40]

For Tanacharison and Scarouady and his band of Iroquois, the die had been cast. On June 26 news was brought to Washington that Scarouady had burned his beloved Logstown to the ground and had started with his people to join the Virginians.[41] Little did the Indians know that they were never to return to their council fire. But they must have had some idea of their position shortly afterwards, as Washington's advance reaped the results of its prematurity. After the defeat of Jumonville, Washington remained at the Great Meadows, engaged in building a fort and in scouting about looking for the larger French force that he expected. On June 16 he started forward and in the next two weeks he had advanced his forces exactly thirteen miles, to Gist's Plantation (Mount Braddock), where he received word that a large French detachment was near at hand. A council of war hurriedly decided to order a retreat, but the best that could be done was to get the exhausted and half-starved band back to Fort Necessity at the Great Meadows, where they awaited the French. On July 4 the inevitable surrender of the English took place. Tanacharison and his Iroquois were disgusted and refused to take part in the useless resistance. The whole affair was a disillusionment to the Indians such as they had not yet experienced. Tanacharison told the story to Conrad Weiser a few weeks later at Croghan's home at Aughwick. Weiser related on August 3 that Tanacharison "complained very much of

[40] Washington, *Diaries . . . 1748-1799,* 1:87, 90, 93-101.

[41] Washington, *Diaries . . . 1748-1799,* 1:101. Logstown was restored as a Mingo town under French auspices but was abandoned in 1758 after the English had captured Fort Duquesne from the French. Hodge, *Handbook of American Indians,* 1:773.

the Behaviour of Col. Washington to him (tho' in a very moderate way, saying the Col. was a good-natured man but had no Experience), saying that . . . he would by no means take Advice from the Indians; that he lay at one Place [*Great Meadows*] from one full Moon to the other and made no Fortifications at all, but that little thing upon the Meadow, where he thought the French would come up to him in open Field; that had he taken the Half King's [*Tanacharison's*] advice . . . he would certainly have beat the French off; that the French had acted as great Cowards, and the English as Fools in that Engagement."[42]

Tanacharison and Scarouady had made a terrible mistake. They had vastly overestimated the strength of the English. Washington's attempt to impress the Indians had been only too successful in so far as these Iroquois leaders were concerned. It marked the end of their leadership among their own people and led straight to their repudiation by the Iroquois council at Onondaga that they represented. Their mistake was made at a time when the Indians of the Ohio Valley, especially the Iroquois, were ready to acquiesce in the fact of French supremacy if the English were unable to drive the French away. The fact that Tanacharison and his small band had made the mistake of taking up the hatchet on the assumption that Washington's advance meant the immediate expulsion of the French, did not commit the Iroquois nation as a whole, whose voice still came from the ancient council fire at Onondaga. That voice declared that the Shawnee and Delawares should "meddle with the French neither in one way nor the other, but stand Neuter and keep their Ears and Eyes towards the Six United Nations." And the Delawares, the Shawnee, and the few Iroquois who stayed on the Ohio after the departure of Tanacharison, Scarouady, and their band, still listened to the voice from Onondaga. Before Washington's surrender, the Delawares on the Ohio had plotted against the Onondaga council in strict secrecy; but after the surrender

[42] *Pennsylvania Colonial Records,* 6:151.

these plots were forgotten, and the Onondaga counsels for neutrality were strictly adhered to.[43]

Iroquois supremacy upon the upper Ohio had undergone a basic change. After the burning of Logstown in June, 1754, it was of an absentee nature, and this was a prelude to its disappearance. After Washington's defeat, Tanacharison fled with his two or three hundred followers in unregal haste, first to the Virginia base at Wills Creek and then to the more generous care of George Croghan at Aughwick. There on September 3 Tanacharison received Delaware emissaries from the Ohio, who, ever faithful to their ancient pledge of subjection to the Iroquois, sought advice and counsel from him, who was still vicegerent over the Ohio tribes. At Aughwick, far from their beloved towns and hunting grounds, perplexed Indian vassals turned to their equally bewildered overlords and asked for a renewal of that protection that the Iroquois were bound to provide the Delawares. "We have hitherto followed your directions and lived very easy under your Protection," said Beaver, spokesman of the Delawares, "and no high Wind did blow to make Us uneasy; but now Things seem to take another turn, and a high Wind is rising. We desire You, therefore, Uncle, to have your Eyes open and be watchful over Us, your Cousins, as you have always been heretofore." The reply of Tanacharison was as guileless as was Beaver's plea. He could not give the protection asked for but must submit the whole matter to Onondaga "where it ought to be." The Shawnee were less considerate of Tanacharison at the Aughwick council. At no time during the proceedings did they address themselves to him or recognize him as the Iroquois vicegerent. Moreover, the Shawnee announced at this council that they had been approached by the remnants of the Pickawillanee Miami to strike the French and that they had refused to do so without even bringing the matter to Tanacharison's attention. They had completely ignored the vicegerent's decision to oppose the French and had declared in favor of the neu-

[43] *Pennsylvania Colonial Records,* 6:158; Washington, *Diaries . . . 1748-1799,* 1:99.

trality policy of the Onondaga council. As the result, said Conrad Weiser, "Tanacarisson and Scarrooyady are out of humour with the Shawonese for not consulting them about an answer to the Twightwees [*Miami*]."[44]

After this humiliating council, Tanacharison went off to John Harris at Harris' Ferry (Harrisburg) to die, while his successor as Half King, Scarouady, went north to the headquarters of his nation at Onondaga, to attempt to placate the Iroquois and to win support for the English expedition under General Braddock that was then being planned. The result was indicative of a new order of things upon the upper Ohio. Scarouady was repudiated, and the Delawares and Shawnee were again told to remain neutral and to bide their time until the Indians could discover who was to gain the ascendancy. Scarouady reported the Onondaga decision to the Provincial Council of Pennsylvania at Philadelphia on March 31, 1755, and although he presented the facts in a light that was designed to save his face he could not conceal the basic fact that his superiors were for neutrality. He said that the council wanted the Shawnee and Delawares "to consider themselves as under the Protection of the Six Nations, and that they are well affected towards them. . . . In the mean Time as the English were their Brethren, and their Cause was much favoured by the Indians, they desired them to have their Eyes and Ears towards the Six Nations and their Brethren the English as they had hitherto done, and not to look towards the French. . . . this will not hinder them from coming and appearing for the English at a proper Time, that is to say, when they appear to be capable of protecting Us against the French."[45]

This decision of the Onondaga Iroquois was a repudiation of their vicegerent's policy of taking up the hatchet at Washington's request against the French. It made of Scarouady and his followers a band that did not have the backing of the tribe to which its members belonged.[46] The subsequent activ-

[44] *Pennsylvania Colonial Records,* 6:140, 150-160, 181.
[45] *Pennsylvania Colonial Records,* 6:342.
[46] The fallen position of Scarouady was well illustrated at a conference in August,

ity of this band, including the scouting a few of them did for Braddock, was not significant. These Indians were gradually reabsorbed into the ranks of their people and thus lost their identity as a factor in the Indian history of the Ohio Valley. The few Iroquois left in the Ohio Valley, the Mingo, supported the French. They were to play an important role in the subsequent history of Indian affairs.

The Onondaga decision was the prelude to an era of confusion. The Iroquois furthered the idea of neutrality because they did not wish to involve their nation in unnecessary war. They were convinced that the English were too powerful for the French and would be easy victors without aid from the Indians. If their belief in the eventual triumph of the English should be fulfilled, the old Anglo-Iroquois stabilization of the upper Ohio Valley would be restored. But unfortunately Braddock's defeat in July, 1755, was to cause so many Ohio Valley Indians to believe that the French were destined to be the victors that the Indian situation was thrown into a state of near chaos that lasted from 1755 to 1763. This new situation forms the burden of the ensuing chapter.

1755, when the pro-English Wyandot sought the aid of Pennsylvania. Scarouady was present but was not addressed and did not speak throughout the whole council. *Pennsylvania Colonial Records,* 6:522-524.

4

The Breakdown
of French Ascendancy,
1755-1758

W E ARE ALLEGHANY INDIANS, and your enemies. You must all die." Thus spoke the leader of the band of Delaware Indians from the Ohio who entered the home of Barbara Leininger on Penn's Creek in what is now Snyder County, Pennsylvania, in the early morning hours of October 16, 1755. The band then shot her father, tomahawked her brother, and took her and her sister Regina prisoners. A similar tragedy was enacted at the near-by Le Roy home. When the three days' slaughter in the neighborhood was over, nineteen scalps had been collected, more than ten prisoners taken, farmhouses burned, and livestock captured or killed. Barbara and her friend, Marie Le Roy, and two of the captured horses were assigned to a Delaware named Galasko and led off to the Allegheny.[1] Thus was broken for the first time since 1682 the league of peace and amity made under the famous elm at Shackamaxon between William Penn and the Delaware Indians.

This "Penn's Creek Massacre" was the signal for a scourging of the eastern Pennsylvania frontier by both eastern and western Pennsylvania Indians that makes the annals of the French and Indian War the bloodiest in the history of Anglo-Indian relations.[2] It introduced a period of confusion in Indian relations marked by two wars, in which the Indians of western Pennsylvania sought, against their own better judgment, to push back to the seaboard the representatives of the English race. The action of the Indians was not, however, a voluntary one but was brought on by the inability of the English to sustain them. The true Indian had little more love for the French than he had for the English. He would have preferred to have been left entirely alone.

It has been said that Braddock's defeat on July 9, 1755, was the occasion for this bloody turn of events. It would be more accurate to say that Braddock's defeat was the occasion for the French forcing the western Pennsylvania Delawares and Shawnee, against their will, to take up the hatchet against the English.[3] The truth of this is well illustrated by the debate between English and French Indians that took place at the Delaware village of Assarugheny on the Susquehanna in what is now Lackawanna County, where the belligerently disposed Indians of eastern Pennsylvania had concentrated after Braddock's defeat. These Indians had told Paxinosa, the leader of

[1] Le Roy and Leininger, "Narrative," in *Pennsylvania Archives,* second series, 7:427-438.
[2] The best account of the scourging of the Pennsylvania frontiers from 1755 to 1757 is in Sipe, *Indian Wars,* 203-355.
[3] There were very few Pennsylvania Indians in the force that attacked Braddock. James Kenny, Pennsylvania Indian factor at Pittsburgh from 1759 to 1763, was told by a Delaware on January 13, 1763, that at Braddock's defeat there was "not One of y[e] Delawares & only four Mingoes & three Shawanas, all y[e] Rest Northr[n] Indians." Kenny, "Journal," 1761-63, in *Pennsylvania Magazine of History and Biography,* 37:183 (1913).

the few Shawnee still remaining in the East, that the main reason for their revolt was the general ill treatment of the Indians by the English, as evidenced especially by the means employed at the treaty of Albany in 1754 to accomplish the Iroquois cession of the Delaware lands west of the Susquehanna to the Ohio River. In reply Paxinosa declared, "If the English or the People of Pennsylvania had cheated them out of any Lands it would have been prudent to have asked or demanded Satisfaction first, and not to have used violent means immediately . . . it was altogether the Craftiness, Power, and Bribery of the French that had brought the Delawares over to them."[4]

Although the Iroquois cession of Delaware lands at the treaty of Albany was a real grievance and stirred many a Delaware on to bloody reprisal, it would not of itself have produced a general state of belligerency on the part of the aggrieved Indians.[5] This fact is illustrated by the description of the Indian reasons for siding with the French given by the Delaware chief, Shingas, to his captive, Charles Stuart, on November 3, 1755, at Kickenapaulin's town on the Kiskiminetas after the return from the October massacres. Shingas said that he had been one of a delegation of six western Pennsylvania Indians, two each from the Delaware, Shawnee, and Mingo tribes, that had met Braddock on the road to Fort Duquesne to see if peace might not be possible if the British conquered the French, and that they had pleaded with Braddock not to rob them of their lands. "Gen¹ Braddock replied," said Shingas, "that the English Shoud Inhabit & Inherit the Land." Shingas then asked him "whether the Indians that were Freinds to the English might not be Permitted to Live and Trade Among the English and have Hunting Ground

---

[4] *Pennsylvania Colonial Records*, 7:53.

[5] The Delaware attacks are described in *New York Colonial Documents*, 7:331. The cession of 1754 was much more of a grievance with the eastern Delawares than it was with their western brethren, although the result of the first months of the war was to cause many of the belligerent Delawares in the East to go to the Ohio. *Pennsylvania Colonial Records*, 7:324-326.

sufficient To Support themselves and Familys." Braddock replied, "No Savage Shou^d Inherit the Land." After another council on the following day with similar results, Shingas and his colleagues returned to their people, who, upon learning of Braddock's haughty attitude, became "very Much Enraged." A party of them at once resolved to join the French, but, according to Shingas, "the Greater Part remained neuter till they saw How Things wou'd go . . . and were still in hopes that the English wou'd Be Victorious . . . but after the French had ruined Braddocks Army they immediately compell^d the Indians To join them and let them know that if they refused they wou'd Immediately cut them off, On wch the Indians Join^d the French for their Own Safety."[6] A similar view of the causes of Indian grievances was expressed by the Iroquois, Thomas King, on October 18, 1758, at a council at Easton. The Iroquois, it should be noted, remained officially neutral during the war, although they traded with the French. Said King, "When we first heard of the French coming to the Ohio we immediately sent Word to the Governors of Virginia and Pennsylvania; we desired them to come, and likewise to supply us with such Things as were proper for War, intending to defend our Lands, and hinder the French from taking the Possession of them; but these Governors did not attend to our Message. . . . The French however came and became our Neighbours, and you neither coming yourselves, nor assisting us with Warlike Stores, our People, of necessity, were obliged to Trade with them for what we Wanted, as your Traders had left the Country."[7]

The involuntary nature of the acceptance of the French hatchet by the western Pennsylvania Indians indicates a

<hr/>

[6] Stuart, "Captivity," in *Mississippi Valley Historical Review*, 13:63 (1926). As late as May 19, 1755, Conrad Weiser received word that the Ohio and Allegheny River Indians "say they will be glad to see the French drove away from Ohio." *Pennsylvania Archives*, first series, 2:319. For the negligence of the English in regard to the Indians during Braddock's expedition, see *Pennsylvania Archives*, first series, 2:308, and *New York Colonial Documents*, 7:270. For Scarouady's opinion of Braddock, see *Pennsylvania Colonial Records*, 6:589.

[7] *Pennsylvania Colonial Records*, 8:198.

fundamental skepticism held by the Indians toward both French and English. The Indians sensed correctly that France and England were not going to all the expense of carrying on a great war without expecting some compensating benefit. And the leaders of the red men were astute enough to know that the fur trade was not the only one of these benefits, but that land was fully as important. Peter Wraxall, secretary to the Indians for the government of New York and personal secretary on occasion to Sir William Johnson, British superintendent of Indian affairs, called Johnson's attention to this fact in his "Thoughts upon the British Indian Interest in North America," prepared at Johnson's request and submitted to him on January 9, 1756. "Our Six Nations and their Allies," wrote Wraxall, "at least the Politicians amongst them look upon the present disputes betw^n the English and French . . . notwithstanding our plausible pretences of rescuing their Lands . . . as a point of selfish Ambition in us both and are apprehensive that which ever Nation gains their Point will become their Masters not their deliverers—They dread the success of either and their ablest Politicians would very probably rather wish us to continue destroying each other than that either should be absolute conquerors . . . Could they depend upon our destroying the French Forts & Settlements and erecting none of our own in their room but leave those Lands quite free to them, I am inclined to beleive [*sic*], that not only the Six Nations, but most nations of Indians in those parts might be brought to join us upon this plan . . . But the Indians suspect we have different views; that to restore their Lands to their natural state and deliver 'em over to them as Proprietors of the soil are not the ends we aim at."[8]

Being thus forced to support the French, the western Pennsylvania tribes, especially the Delawares, found plenty of grievances to justify their action. The commerce in rum, unscrupulous traders, land robbing, murders of their tribesmen that went unpunished, and the general insolence of the

[8] *New York Colonial Documents*, 7:18.

frontiersmen toward them were all raked up and used to inflame the savage mind. The Delawares also found a justification for their belligerency toward the English in the fact that many of the Iroquois, especially the Seneca, had accepted the French hatchet. In January, 1756, George Croghan related an interesting story of the visit of one of his spies, Delaware Jo, to Kittanning late in 1755. The Delaware chief, Beaver, told Delaware Jo that Contrecœur at Fort Duquesne had often offered him the hatchet but that he had refused, saying he "should be advised by the Six Nations." Finally in April or May, 1755, a party of Iroquois called at the fort on their way to war against the southern Indians. Beaver said that Contrecœur was able to prevail on these to give the Delawares and Shawnee the hatchet. At Logstown the Shawnee told Delaware Jo the same thing. He was also informed that some Iroquois "always accompanied them in their Incursions upon the English and took Part with them in the War."[9]

Having committed themselves to war, the young Delaware, Shawnee, and Mingo warriors worked themselves up into a frenzy that resulted in acts of the most revolting cruelty. These slaughterings, slow tortures, and indiscriminate massacres of old and young men and women, were perpetrated in the knowledge that the lands the Indians reconquered were to be guaranteed by the French to their perpetual use for hunting. Indeed it seems to have been the opinion of a majority of the young braves that they could actually remove the English from the continent of North America. James Smith, who was captured near Bedford before Braddock's defeat and who spent most of the subsequent years of the war among the Indians, said that this view was particularly dominant in 1756, as the result of the fact that the Indians had cleared the Pennsylvania, Maryland, and Virginia frontiers of settlers. "The Americans," they said, "were altogether unacquainted

[9] *Pennsylvania Colonial Records*, 6:782. The belligerent eastern Pennsylvania Delawares gave the Shawnee Paxinosa the same explanation. *Pennsylvania Colonial Records*, 7:66.

with war of any kind, and consequently very unfit to stand their hand with such subtil enemies as the Indians were. . . . the white people appeared to them like fools; they could neither guard against surprise, run, or fight." Smith found, however, that this view was not held by the old men of the tribes, who nevertheless "were willing to propagate the idea, in order to encourage the young men to go to war." The Indians thus fell victims to their greatest weakness, their depth of feeling, and established for themselves a reputation for barbarous cruelty that gave white men of the day and of generations to follow an effective formula of justification for treating the red men as beasts. M. Pouchot, a French officer in western Pennsylvania during the war, wrote in his memoirs, with rare understanding, "The Indian abuses himself, because he feels too much. He yields without difficulty to the impulses of vengeance, and raises the cry of arms, which he always takes to destroy, and never to acquire or to preserve. His appetite is tyrannical and his wants urgent. Both have been multiplied since the discovery of the new world. To satisfy these, he has forgotten his dearest interests, and has become the instrument of hatred between two powerful rivals, as also that of his own destruction."[10]

The murderous warfare of 1755 to 1757 was thus a thing the French could not stop even if they had wished to. And if the truth be known, it is probable that they did not wish to, in spite of the fact that they often urged moderation on the red men. The exigencies of the situation for the French required that the Indians keep the English at a distance. Captain Dumas, the commandant at Fort Duquesne, reported as early as the spring of 1756 that the fort was in no condition to resist an attack with artillery. Montcalm wrote from Quebec on June 12, "Fort Duquesne is not worth a straw. A freshet nearly carried it off a short time ago." Vaudreuil reported home that Dumas' policy was "to harass the enemy by trying

---

[10] J. Smith, *An Account of the . . . Life and Travels*, 47; Pouchot, *Memoir upon the Late War*, 2:261.

to oblige them to keep on the defensive." If a British force should march against him he was to call his Indians to him and meet them in the wilderness, since "in the present state of the fort, it would be impossible to make any resistance for any length of time, were he to allow himself to be besieged in it."[11]

This policy on the part of the French and these tactics on the part of the Indians could not serve to establish and maintain French military control in Pennsylvania, unless France was able to outdo the British in pouring money into the defense of the Ohio Valley. This she was unable to do. England elected to make it a fight to a finish, and France did not have the resources to send troops and supplies to such a remote point as Fort Duquesne, which could only be reached by a most circuitous route. This meant a continued dependence upon the Indians for the task of keeping the English at a distance. And with the thousands of troops that England was able to send out in 1758 under General John Forbes, it was utterly impossible to expect the Indians to do the job alone. Indeed, early in 1758 the French were unable even to sustain the bands that had kept the frontier unpopulated throughout 1756 and 1757. As early as May 9, 1757, Croghan's emissaries brought back news that the Indians in western Pennsylvania were "very much distressed for Provisions," and on January 28, 1758, it was reported from Fort Duquesne that "the Indians, to whom large presents cannot be made, as the stores are empty, begin to dislike going out to fight."[12]

Under these circumstances it was natural that the English, profiting by their experience in regard to their negligence of the Indians on the Braddock expedition, should renew negotiations with the Indians preparatory to the English restoration in western Pennsylvania. And, as might be expected, the Indians were quite ready to receive them. Enough has been said to show that the Delawares, Shawnee, and Mingo, cruel and savage as their attacks on the English had been, were

[11] *New York Colonial Documents*, 10:416, 425.
[12] *Pennsylvania Colonial Records*, 7:515; *New York Colonial Documents*, 10:837.

always ready to acquiesce in something they could not prevent and to lose confidence in the power that was unable to sustain itself in the field of battle. It is quite in keeping with this Indian trait that the Delaware, Beaver, in the fall of 1755, shortly after his people had declared war on the English, should tell Croghan's emissary, Delaware Jo, that some of those who had taken up the hatchet were already sorry for what they had done "and would be glad to make up Matters with the English."[13] But Indian acquiescence in a British restoration did not mean that the tribesmen expected to be punished for their bloody outrages. In the negotiations with the English they assumed the attitude that they would permit the English to return on conditions that the Indians be not deprived of their hunting grounds and that every effort be made to restore the *status quo ante bellum,* if not to improve that status.

The clearest statement by the Delawares of what they wanted from the English was made by Shingas to captive Charles Stuart at Kickenapaulin's town in November, 1756. Stuart, reporting Shingas' talk, said that the Delawares "were now willing again To make Peace with them and restore all their Captives and Everything Else they had from them Provided the English wou'd Comply with the Following Proposals Viz^t 1st the English shou'd send 5 Men among the Indians who shou^d live well at the Indians expence with them, But [should] work for them without any other Pay from the Indians than Supporting Said Workmen and their Familys with Proviss^s and all other necessaries that they stood in need off— the Business said men were to Be Employ^d in were—Making of Powder, Smelting of Lead from the Ore, and Indians wou^d Engage not only to find them Lead Mines But mines of Every other Metal that was necessary—Weaveing of Blanketts— Makeing and Mending Guns for them—and Mr Stuart thinks the Other Man was to Be Employ^d in Makeing of Iron —The 2^d Condition was that the English shou^d Come and Settle among them with their Families and Promote Spinning

[13] *Pennsylvania Colonial Records,* 6:782.

for Shirts and In Genl shou^d Bring all Kinds of Trades among them that they might be Supplied with what they want near home, and that they and the English shou'd Live Together in Love and Freindship and Become one people   But the Indians did not Insist nor Desire that the English sho^d Be obliged to Intermarry with them."[14]

Indian expectations were high, and the first negotiations with the English did not discourage them. Word had come in from time to time that the Ohio Indians were not altogether satisfied with the French, mainly because of the growing shortage of provisions. George Croghan, who had been appointed deputy superintendent of Indian affairs in Pennsylvania under the superintendent, Sir William Johnson, sent Indian emissaries to visit the Ohio Indians in the spring of 1757. These had reported back in May that if accredited agents of the Indian department should extend the invitation and make the necessary assurances of justice to the Indians, or, as the Indians put it, "send proper Belts, and Wise Men," the Ohio Valley tribes would send delegates east to "settle all differences subsisting between us." At about the same time an Ohio Indian named Wauntaupenny, captured near Raystown (Bedford), reported to the commandant at Fort Littleton that "the Delawares say that all their People wou'd lay down the Hatchet upon a Flag of Truce from the English." This Indian made other observations that indicate a surprising degree of Indian impatience with the French. Confirmation of this information was obtained by Croghan at the treaty of Easton in July, 1757, with the eastern Pennsylvania Indians.[15]

By the spring of 1758 the western Pennsylvania Indians seem to have had enough of the French. This came out as the result of the visit, in June, of Christian Frederick Post, the Moravian missionary, to the town of the Delaware chief, Tedyuscung, at Wyoming. Here Post met Kittiuskund and another chief, Pisquetomen, who was the brother of Shingas

[14] Stuart, "Captivity," in *Mississippi Valley Historical Review,* 13:64 (1926).
[15] *Pennsylvania Colonial Records,* 7:516, 531; Volwiler, *George Croghan,* 136.

and Beaver, and several other Indians "from Allegheny" who had "purposed to go down to Philadelphia" but, having become suspicious and afraid for their personal safety from having talked with eastern Indians, had decided not to complete their journey. They did, however, unburden themselves to Post and told him that "they were sorry that they had gone to War against the English, and wished often to have seen some Messengers from the Government with whom they could have spoken, for then they had long left off the War against them." It is evident that the Ohio Indians were extremely worried. According to Post, one of them, "Lifting up his Hands to Heaven, wished that God would have Mercy upon them and help them and bring them and the English together again, and establish an everlasting Ground and Foundation for Peace between them." The Delawares urged Post to advise Governor William Denny of Pennsylvania to send an official agent back to the Ohio with them. Such an action "would be of great consequence to them, who live above Allegheny." The French, they said, were a broken reed and were ready to evacuate Fort Duquesne upon the approach of a large English force. The French had told them, "Children: the English have almost beat me. I have nothing to live on . . . If the English come too strong upon me I will Leave the Place. I am but weak, and I should loose a great Many Men." Realizing the importance of what had been suggested, Post prevailed on these Delawares to set aside their fears and to present their petition to Governor Denny and the Provincial Council at Philadelphia. The result was that on July 14 Post was authorized to go with Pisquetomen and on the fifteenth received his instructions from Governor Denny.[16]

Ushered into the Delaware country by a chief of the nation, Post accomplished the remarkable feat of undermining Indian support of the French in the very presence of the French themselves. He could do this with impunity because he was at all times closely guarded by Indians who forbade the French and

---

[16] *Pennsylvania Colonial Records*, 8:144, 147.

enemy Indians to molest him. To have done so would have been suicide for the French. The Delawares, who were his protectors, never once wavered in their insistence upon Post's safety. From August 13, when he entered Kuskuski, which was now a Delaware instead of an Iroquois capital, until September 8, when he took his departure from the town, the Indians never relinquished their vigilance in his behalf, even though they could not quite bring themselves to believe that Post truly represented British policy.[17]

The main thing that happened at Post's conferences with the Indians was the disillusionment of the Indians as to the English attitude toward them. When Post first arrived at Kuskuski, the Delaware chiefs repeated over and over again how surprised they were and that they had never expected to see the English again. They insisted that Post speak to all the nations assembled at Fort Duquesne and accompanied him to the bank of the Allegheny across from the fort, where on August 26 he delivered his simple message of peace. There he told the assembled representatives of all the western tribes that peace had been made in July at Easton with Tedyuscung and the eastern Delawares, who had been given ample assurances of justice in regard to their land difficulties. He then invited the western nations to make peace with the English and to withdraw from the French. All who did so would be treated as friends by Forbes's army, which was then advancing upon Fort Duquesne. The only other condition Post attached to the reconciliation was the return of the white captives taken during the war. No definite reply was made to Post at this time. He was taken back to Kuskuski, and it is significant that on his return he was treated cordially by the Indians through whose towns he passed—a treatment that was quite the reverse of what he had experienced on his trip to Fort Duquesne. On the road to Kuskuski, Shingas inquired of him if the English would hang him for his part in the war. Post

[17] The account in this and the following paragraphs of Post's visit to the Ohio country is based on his "Journal," in Thwaites, *Early Western Travels*, 1:193-226.

replied, "That was a great while ago, it was all forgotten and wiped clean away."

At Kuskuski the Delawares made known the Indian decision in regard to Post's proposals of reconciliation. It was made by the Delawares in behalf of all the nations to which he had spoken at Fort Duquesne. It was a decision remarkable for its restraint. The Indians did not rush to accept Post's proposition. Instead they told him to return and get all the English to support his plan. They knew that Post represented only the government of Pennsylvania and that he did not speak for the other colonies, for Forbes, or for the British Indian department. The reply was addressed to the "Governor and people of *Pennsylvania.*" "If you will be strong," the Delawares said, "it is in your power to finish that peace and friendship well. Therefore, brethren, we desire you to be strong and establish it, and make known to all the *English* this peace and friendship, that it may embrace all and cover all. As you are of one nation and colour, in all the *English* governments, so let the peace be the same with all. Brethren, when you have finished this peace, which you have begun; when it is known every where amongst your brethren, and you have every where agreed together on this peace and friendship, then you will be pleased to send the great peace belt to us at *Allegheny.*"

This was a significant reply. It shows how cautious the Indians had to be lest they give themselves over to English vengeance of an open or of a subtle nature. Events were to prove that they were not cautious enough. For the moment they were rightly skeptical. One thing that made them suspicious was that Post did not make his appearance until after Forbes had started. "If you had brought the news of peace," they said, "before your army had begun to march, it would have caused a great deal more good." Moreover, they feared that the English would take more lands away from them. They could not understand how the English could go to all the expense of conducting a great war against the French on Indian land without using the reconquered lands for themselves. "Now, Brother," they said to Post, "we love you, but cannot help wondering why the *English* and *French* do not make up with one another, and tell one another not to fight on our land." Or, as Shamokin Daniel, Post's guide from the East, said, after he had had some French liquor, "D—n you, why do not you and the *French* fight on the sea? You come here only to cheat the poor *Indians*, and take their land from them." Shingas rebuked Daniel for his ill-chosen language, but his own sentiments were not exactly the reverse of Daniel's.

It is evident that the Ohio Valley Indians had not yet been won back to the English. Indeed, during July, 1758, several hundred Ottawa, Chippewa, Potawatomi, and Wyandot, rendezvoused at Detroit at the call of the French and proceeded to Fort Duquesne to oppose Forbes, convinced, as the Wyandot captive, James Smith, said, "that they would serve him as they did General Braddock, and obtain much plunder." The Indians could not know that the fall of Louisbourg on July 26, 1758, forecast the downfall of the French American empire; indeed, even the English could not count on the effect of the victory, especially when the invasion of Canada failed ingloriously in the same month at Ticonderoga. To be sure, the enthusiasm of the Indians had declined as the result of the shortage of supplies given them by the French, whose resources were diverted to frontiers in Europe and India as well as in America. A sullenness was observed by Charles Stuart and James Smith in 1757 among the Indians about Detroit, and Croghan told Forbes in August, 1758, that the Detroit Indians would certainly desert the French soon. But orders had not been sent for the abandonment of Fort Duquesne, and the Indians still relied on the French for food, clothing, guns, and ammunition. And it was more than a remote possibility that Franco-Indian attacks might force Forbes and his army to spend the winter in the western Pennsylvania mountains.[18]

[18] J. Smith, *An Account of the . . . Life and Travels,* 102; Stuart, "Captivity," in *Mississippi Valley Historical Review,* 13:77 (1926); Forbes, *Letters . . . Relating to . . . Fort Duquesne,* 35.

It is thus evident that if the English were to make the most profit out of Post's mission they should speed up the process of peacemaking. "Any Indian friendship," wrote Forbes to Governor Horatio Sharpe of Maryland on September 3, 1758, "at this critical time might prove a great dimunition [*sic*] to the strength of the French." By September 6 Forbes was unable to delay his advance any longer to wait upon the outcome of peace negotiations. On that day he wrote to William Pitt that he wished that a preliminary settlement had been made at Easton sooner, so that the Indians could withdraw from the scene of the approaching hostilities. "Now," he wrote, "my scene of offensive Operations must imediately be put in Execution, when it will be hard for me to distinguish betwixt our friendly disposed Indians, and our real Enemies." He wrote to Governor Denny on the ninth asking him to tell the Indians at Easton of his advance. In the meantime Post and Pisquetomen had left Kuskuski on September 8, and on October 3 Pisquetomen laid the Indian message before the Provincial Council at Philadelphia. Governor Denny at once set the wheels in motion for the resumption of the general council at Easton, and it was resumed on October 7. Here the governor and the council publicly repudiated the treaty of Albany and relinquished to the Indians all the lands beyond the mountains.[19]

A new day seemed to be dawning for the western Pennsylvania Indians. This agreement at Easton constituted a guarantee to the Ohio Valley tribes that the colony of Pennsylvania had no designs on their lands. According to Colonel Henry Bouquet, second-in-command under Forbes, it was "the blow which has knocked the French on the head."[20] So far as the Delawares were concerned, the action went a long way toward making the peace "stronger," to use Indian terminology. With the news of this agreement and an invitation to the Indians to

[19] Forbes, *Letters . . . Relating to . . . Fort Duquesne,* 35, 36, 40; *Pennsylvania Colonial Records,* 8:169, 174, 199, 203, 220.

[20] Forbes, *Letters . . . Relating to . . . Fort Duquesne,* 69.

attend a grand council of ratification at Philadelphia, Post and Pisquetomen and two Iroquois were sent back to the Ohio in the hope of preventing the spreading of hostilities between Forbes and the Indians. On November 7 they caught up with Forbes at Loyalhanna (Ligonier), where Post and his Indian companions were greeted with great hospitality and entrusted with messages to the Delawares and Shawnee to the effect that all was forgiven and that the Indians should stay out of the way while the English whipped the French. Post's little band resumed its journey on November 11 and was escorted as far as the Allegheny by Lieutenant Williams Hays and fourteen men. It reached Kuskuski on the sixteenth and found it deserted of warriors.[21]

The days from November 16 to 20 were precarious ones for Post. On the day after his arrival at Kuskuski the Delaware warrior Kickenapaulin came in with news that his people had fallen on Lieutenant Hays's party that had conducted Post to the Allegheny and had killed five and taken five prisoners, one of whom they were to burn at the stake. Letters had been taken from Hays which the French told the Indians contained statements to the effect that after the English had conquered the French they would destroy the Indians. It also appeared that many Delawares had been in the French band that attacked Fort Ligonier on October 12, but the Indians told Post that they had started out with the intention of seeking a parley with Forbes and had been prevented by the fact that the French in the band insisted on attacking Forbes. Post was guarded closely, however, and was promised an immediate opportunity to deliver his messages to the assembled tribesmen, who in the meantime refused the urgings of the French to take up the hatchet.[22]

---

[21] Post, "Journal," 1758-59, in Thwaites, *Early Western Travels*, 1:242-245, 264-267; Forbes, *Letters . . . Relating to . . . Fort Duquesne*, 64-66.

[22] Post, "Journal," 1758-59, in Thwaites, *Early Western Travels*, 1:250-252. Four years later the same explanation of the attack on Fort Ligonier, but with more detail, was made to James Kenny at Pittsburgh. Kenny, "Journal," 1761-63, in *Pennsylvania Magazine of History and Biography*, 37:159 (1913). Kenny's Dela-

The Breakdown of French Ascendancy

The fate of Fort Duquesne was in the balance. The tribes-men from the regions about Detroit who had rallied to the French in July were gradually forced to go home to provide for their families. Those that stayed on after Grant's defeat on September 14 went home after the repulse of the French and Indian attack on Fort Ligonier. This repulse had a tre-mendous effect on the Indians. It convinced them that they had no Braddock to deal with, but seasoned frontiersmen. According to James Smith, "They said that Forbes's men were beginning to learn the art of war, and that there were a great number of American riflemen along with the red-coats, who scattered out, took trees, and were good marks-men; therefore they found they could not accomplish their design, and were obliged to retreat. . . . The Indians said if it was only the red-coats they had to do with, they could soon subdue them, but they could not withstand *Ashalecoa,* or the Great Knife."[23] It was clear then that if the French were going to have Indian help in repulsing Forbes, it would have to come from the western Pennsylvania Indians.

On November 20, 1758, the great decision was made that sealed the doom of Fort Duquesne. On the afternoon of that day, Post, at Kuskuski, read the news of the treaty of Easton as contained in the message of Governor Denny. In the eve-ning a French captain from Fort Duquesne arrived and de-clared to the Indians: "The *English* are coming with an army to destroy both you and me. I therefore desire you immedi-ately, my children, to hasten with all the young men; we will drive the *English* and destroy them." The French officer then offered a string of wampum to one of the leaders, who declined to take it, saying, "I have just heard something of our brethren the *English,* which pleaseth me much better. I will not go. Give it to the others, may be they will go." The Frenchman

ware informant also told him that there were no Delawares with the French at the time of Grant's disastrous attempt to occupy Fort Duquesne on September 14. Kenny, "Journal," 1761-63, p. 183.

[23] J. Smith, *An Account of the . . . Life and Travels,* 103.

then threw it to a fireplace before which several warriors stood. But they would not touch it and kicked it from them "as if it was a snake." One of them, Captain Peter, took a stick and flung the string to the other side of the room. He then declared, "Give it to the *French* captain, and let him go with his young men; he boasted much of his fighting; now let us see his fighting. We have often ventured our lives for him; and had hardly a loaf of bread, when we came to him; and now he thinks we should jump to serve him." Then, said Post, was the captain mortified, and his countenance became "as pale as death." Until midnight the Indians "discoursed and joked." At the same midnight hour the French captain sent his messengers to Fort Duquesne, but to no avail. Four days later, on November 24, the English flag was raised at Kuskuski, an event that preceded by one day the English flag-raising at Fort Duquesne.[24]

[24] Post, "Journal," 1758-59, in Thwaites, *Early Western Travels,* 1:255-258.

5

Indian Revolt
Against British Economy,
1758-1765

THE INDIAN enthusiasm for a change from French to English rule should not be misunderstood. No sooner had the English flag been raised in the Ohio Valley than the Indians sought to have it hauled down and the country left to the undisturbed possession of the Delawares, Shawnee, and the rest of the tribes. The dominant thought in the minds of these Indians after the days of rejoicing over the fall of Fort Duquesne had passed was that the British would soon imitate the French and depart from the Ohio. Such a thought was clearly an unreasonable one from the military point of view, because the French still lingered on the upper Allegheny and the lower Ohio and would have sought to reoccupy the fort if the English had completely withdrawn. But the fact that the thought came to the Indians' minds shows that to them Forbes's expedition meant the complete restoration of the West to the dominion of the Indian tribes and that their rejoicing was more on their own account than it was on the account of the British. After several days of negotiations with the Iroquois, by which Kuskuski was officially transferred to the Delawares, and the Iroquois supremacy over them and over the Shawnee was acknowledged, the nations turned to Christian Frederick Post and politely asked him to leave. On November 28 Chief Beaver said to him, "I would tell you, in a most soft, loving and friendly manner, to go back over the mountain, and to stay there; for, if you will do that, I will use it for an argument, to argue with other nations of *Indians.*" It appeared in the course of the discussion that there was a definite understanding on this point among all the Ohio Valley Indians. One of the chief Delaware counselors, Kittiuskund, told Post secretly, "All the nations had jointly agreed to defend their hunting place at *Alleghenny,* and suffer nobody to settle there . . . if the *English* would draw back over the mountain, they would get all the other nations into their interest; but if they staid and settled there, all the nations would be against them; and he was afraid it would be a great war, and never come to a peace again."[1]

At Post's suggestion, the discussion over the withdrawal of the British was transferred to Pittsburgh. On December 4, at the first meeting to consider the matter, Colonel Henry Bouquet, in command at Fort Pitt after the departure of Forbes on the previous day, expressed great disappointment that the Indians should demand his withdrawal. Bouquet insisted that troops be left at Pittsburgh, not only because of the French danger, but also because they would be necessary to supervise the Indian trade. He sought to mollify the Indians by promising the resumption of trade in the near future, and he invited them to Philadelphia so that they could cement the new friendship "and the prices of goods fixed on to your

[1] Post, "Journal," 1758-59, in Thwaites, *Early Western Travels,* 1:274, 278.

satisfaction." After this meeting the Indians held a conference among themselves, which resulted in their refusal to make any concessions; but the agents of the British Indian department, Croghan and Andrew Montour, would not tell Bouquet of the refusal. The next day, under the influence of Croghan, a document was drawn up by which the Indians consented to allow Bouquet to leave two hundred men at the fort; but on December 6 Shingas and his fellow counselors denied to Post that they had done so. According to Post, they said, "Now you will let the governor, general, and all people know, that our desire is, that they should go back, till the other nations have joined in the peace, and then they may come and build a trading house." Whether or not the Delawares were merely being petulant is hard to say, although it would seem that the major issue of the keeping of settlers from their lands had been pretty well settled in the Indians' favor. It is probable that they did not take Bouquet's refusal to leave very seriously, because on December 23, on his way home, Post heard that the Delawares had refused to let the French from Venango march on Colonel Hugh Mercer, who had been left with the two hundred men at Pittsburgh.[2]

It is clear that the Ohio Valley Indians supported the British in the restoration following the fall of Fort Duquesne in the same involuntary manner that they had supported the French in the occupation of the Ohio Valley in the years from 1753 to 1758. The Indian insistence upon the immediate withdrawal of British troops is ample proof of the fact. And the actions of the Indians during the spring and summer of 1759 show further that the red men of western Pennsylvania were not altogether sure that the French were to be completely expelled from the country. They had good reasons for their doubts. The French still maintained their garrisons at Venango, Le Bœuf, and Presque Isle, and preparations were under way for a reoccupation of Fort Duquesne in the year 1759.

[2] Post, "Journal," 1758-59, in Thwaites, *Early Western Travels*, 1:282, 285, 288; *Pennsylvania Archives*, first series, 3:572-574.

Council Fires on the Upper Ohio

French officers and traders continued to circulate among the Indians in all the towns north and west of Pittsburgh, and French Indians kept a constant watch on the activities at the English garrison. Everything was in readiness for an attack, and magazines of arms and ammunition were established at Kuskuski and at other strategic points.[3]

During the winter of 1758-59 the northern or Lake Indians (Ottawa, Chippewa, Potawatomi, and Wyandot) began to gather near Kuskuski for the impending attack, and it was reported at Pittsburgh in March that preparations were being made at Presque Isle to accommodate an army of fifteen hundred. Beginning in mid-April, sporadic attacks on whites by Indians began; these increased in frequency throughout May, June, and July, and reached a climax with an attack on Fort Ligonier on July 6. On June 17 and again on July 13 all the inhabitants of Pittsburgh were summoned inside the fortifications as a Franco-Indian attack was expected. On the second of these occasions, the people stayed in the fort for three days, all valuables including tradesmen's goods were brought within the walls, several cows were killed, and houses and stores were burned or torn down. This was the result of the report of two of Croghan's spies who had been to Venango that an army of well over a thousand French and Indians was assembling at Venango for a descent upon Pittsburgh. The only thing that saved Pittsburgh from a French reoccupation was the news that arrived at Venango on July 12 that the army should go at once to the relief of the French and Indians at Niagara, who were about to succumb to Sir William Johnson and his Iroquois hordes.[4]

The lack of Indian enthusiasm for the British during these first months of 1759 is most noticeable. A party of Iroquois representing the Seneca of the upper Allegheny at Buckaloon, after failing to find Forbes at Pittsburgh in December, 1758,

[3] *Pennsylvania Colonial Records,* 8:284, 295, 310.
[4] *Pennsylvania Colonial Records,* 8:292, 311; Kenny, "Journal," 1761-63, in *Pennsylvania Magazine of History and Biography,* 37:417-431 (1913); *Pennsylvania Archives,* first series, 3:669, 671.

had, after a conference with Mercer, sent two of their number to Philadelphia. Through Andrew Montour they told the English at Philadelphia on February 20, 1759, that the Indians on the upper Allegheny, "if kept any Longer in this State of uncertainty, will be constrained to join the French, which they have no mind to do, provided the English General will engage their Services by open and affectionate Messages." As for the Delawares and Shawnee, Mercer wrote to Governor Denny on January 8 that they knew all that the French were doing but would tell the English nothing. "And these Scoundrels," he said, "come in Shoals every Day, to live upon us, pretending the utmost Friendship." On March 1 Mercer wrote that the old men of the Delawares would remain neutral in the expected attack and that the "young Villains who have swilled so much of our Blood, and grown rich by the plunder of the Frontiers, have still some French Poison lurking in their Veins." On June 30 some Delawares who brought in news of the French advance behaved "very saucy," according to James Kenny, the Quaker factor of the Pennsylvania government store at Pittsburgh. Finally, on August 14, when news came in of the fall of Niagara and Ticonderoga and the resulting evacuation of Presque Isle, Le Bœuf, and Venango, there was great rejoicing among the whites, but, said Kenny, "Many of ye Indians seem more sober, their practice of singing & dancing was remarked to have ceased last night."[5]

The capture of Niagara by Sir William Johnson on July 24, 1759, was as much of a milestone in the development of British Indian policy in western Pennsylvania as was the capture of Fort Duquesne on November 25, 1758. It meant a somewhat haughtier tone in the British pronouncements to the Indians. Colonel Mercer gave voice to the new feeling pervading British military circles when he wrote to Governor Denny on August 12, "We can now talk to our new Allies in a proper Stile, as their Services are not Necessary." He added, how-

[5] *Pennsylvania Colonial Records*, 8:270, 292-297, 305; Kenny, "Journal," 1758-59, in *Pennsylvania Magazine of History and Biography*, 37:426, 437 (1913).

ever, "Tho' the Consistency of our Plan in bringing them entirely over to the British Interest, ought to be preserved by treating them with a great kindness, but suffering none of their insults."[6]

What was this British plan of which Mercer wrote? It consisted of many parts, which were determined by the exigencies of the situation. First, there was the necessity of expelling the French from Detroit and the Wabash-Maumee country. While this was going on, peace with the Indians in the lands already reconquered was to be established. The Indians' temporary needs were to be met by gifts of guns, ammunition, and clothing. They were to be promised the return of normal trading conditions by the erection of military posts throughout the Northwest where private traders might carry on the commerce under rules, regulations, and protection provided by the Indian department and the military authorities. Councils with sections of the tribes were to be held from time to time as necessity arose, to make clear to the Indians what was expected of them and what they in turn had a right to expect. A requirement of the whites, which at first appeared rather trivial but which was really of great importance to the Indians and out of which arose one of the controversies that brought about the revolt under Pontiac, was the demand that the Indians restore all white captives taken since 1755. The plan that was formulated to take care of these issues was not drawn up in one document nor presented to all the tribes at one time. It grew out of instructions sent by Sir William Johnson to his deputy in the West, George Croghan, and out of instructions sent by the military commander-in-chief, Jeffery Amherst, or his immediate subordinates, to the commandants of the western posts.

The British plan had elements of weakness that gradually became apparent. Every measure either contained qualities that were displeasing to the Indians or, when carried out, developed such qualities. The British conquest of the Detroit,

[6] *Pennsylvania Colonial Records*, 8:394.

Indian Revolt Against British Economy

Mackinaw, and St. Joseph River country was offensive to the tribes in that region because they had never known any trade or rule that was not French. The temporary nature of gifts to the Indians, especially of guns and ammunition, became too soon apparent as the necessity for economy made the Indians the first sufferers. The lack of adequate supplies for such purposes was most noticeable at subsequent treaties with the Indians, especially in the unfortunate distribution of goods at the treaty of Lancaster in 1762. Normal trade was slow in returning, because the English refused to give the traders unrestricted access to the Indian country and insisted that all trade be carried on only where English military posts were established. Some tribes considered that prices of furs and skins were too low. And the requirement in regard to the return of white prisoners soon became a source of discontent when, in spite of the preference of many of these for the Indian life, the British authorities insisted upon their complete restoration. These weaknesses did not, however, become painfully onerous to the Indians until the year 1762. To say that Pontiac's War was inevitable before then is to add a fatalistic tinge to the events from 1759 to 1762 that gives a false color to the facts.

In 1759 Indian affairs in the Ohio Valley naturally centered at Pittsburgh, which was the only point on the Ohio or on the Allegheny in that year at which there was a British garrison. A series of conferences between the British and the Indians took place there that were obviously of a preliminary nature and the principal effect of which was the circulation among the tribes of the elements of the British plan. The first conference was held in February on the occasion of Beaver's return from carrying Post's peace message to the West. Beaver brought with him two Ottawa warriors, whose nation was still under the influence of the French. Colonel Mercer told these warriors that England would be willing to call the Ottawa friends if the captives were returned and the French deserted. He warned them, however, that the English did not seek peace "thro' any apprehensions of their Power joined to the French, for we have this last Year defeated their United Forces in different Places." To Beaver, Mercer promised a complete opening of trade. "The Goods for opening a Trade," he said, "are upon the Road, and will be up as soon as the Waggons can come along. This and every other Engagement your Brothers, the English, have come under will be fulfilled in the most sacred manner, to your ample Satisfaction."[7]

A more formal conference was held at Pittsburgh in July, at which the Iroquois and all the tribes of the Old Northwest were represented to the number of five hundred and at which George Croghan, as official agent of the British Indian department, extended the olive branch to them all. Here Croghan read to them the maximum prices under which the fur trade was to be carried on. The Indians were also informed of the action of the council at Easton in 1758 in restoring to the Indians part of the land ceded at Albany in 1754. They were told that the English could "never taste true Satisfaction" until all the captives were restored. The remote nations were told that the English could do nothing for them in the way of restoration of trade until the French were removed, and it was pointed out that General John Stanwix was already on his way to Pittsburgh "to build a Trading House, to secure the Goods brought by the English Traders." A message was drawn up to send to the hostile French Indians then at Venango who were in the process of changing their objective from Pittsburgh to Niagara, which informed them that the English "are not Come here to War with the Indians, but to carry on Trade and Commerce with all Nations of them as far as the Sun setting." The conference was not a complete success, however, because the Delawares expressed strong discontent at the prices set up by Croghan and refused to consider any great council in the East while war continued with the French.

Another conference was held in October, at which were

---

[7] For the 1759 Indian conferences at Pittsburgh, see *Pennsylvania Colonial Records,* 8:308, 309, 382-391, 429-435.

present General Stanwix, Croghan, his agents, Andrew Montour and William Trent, and representatives of the Iroquois, Delawares, Shawnee, Wyandot, and Miami. This was the first meeting the Ohio Valley Indians had had with an English general, and the occasion was no doubt very impressive. Stanwix spoke to them in general terms and reminded them that they had not yet delivered up all the prisoners. Attention was called to the construction of Fort Pitt then in process, and Montour announced the fall of Quebec. But in spite of assurances, the Indians showed their suspicion of the English. The Wyandot speaker desired them not to extend the conquest to Detroit. "We have," he said, "repeatedly heard you intended to pursue the War against the French over the Lakes in our Country; we have been constantly alarmed with your coming, but now we are come here we find you are not gone; we should be glad you would not pursue them, they are a parcel of poor people, destitute of every thing, besides we do not know how the several Nations there might take it." Beaver then seized upon the occasion to repeat his complaint about high prices. "Be strong," he said, "and perform your Promises; don't make me ashamed."

The Indian situation during 1760 was much the same as it had been during 1759. The conquest of the French continued, and the business of circulating and enforcing the British plan of reconciliation with the tribesmen went on with few signs of discontent. At Pittsburgh, where the new Fort Pitt then stood, George Croghan, as deputy Indian superintendent, carried out the British plan in a most lavish way. His generosity, resulting from his great sympathy for the Indians and interest in the fur trade, was to have an unfortunate effect later when retrenchment was forced on him. After General Stanwix had left for the East, Croghan took the unusual step of fitting out at government expense, but without any orders except those of the commandant at Fort Pitt, a party of one hundred Indians, mostly Shawnee, to fight against the Cherokee, who had taken up the hatchet on the frontiers of Virginia and the Carolinas. He justified his action on the ground that the Indians were needed to protect these southern frontiers and also as "taking off that great Burthen of maintaining so many Indians as we have been hitherto obliged to do." Croghan also took the liberty of sending some traders into the Indian country. He continued the policy begun by Stanwix of rewarding the Indians with rum whenever they brought in white prisoners, although he admitted that this was a very expensive practice. But however extravagant his administration of British policy may have been, he took great pride in reporting that "the Indians of all Nations are gone home well satisfied, and quite easy in their minds to all appearances."[8]

The next step in the 1760 Indian operations was the establishment of British posts at Venango and Presque Isle and the extension of British influence over the tribes along the way. Accordingly, on July 7, under the direction of Brigadier General Robert Monckton, who replaced Stanwix at Fort Pitt in June, Croghan was sent north with Colonel Bouquet and a detachment of soldiers, and their purpose was accomplished with ease. The amusing situation was presented of French Indians, mostly Ottawa and Wyandot, supposedly in the role of spies, openly visiting Croghan and telling him that they had been sent to capture an Englishman and take him back to Detroit in order that information might be extracted from him.[9] Croghan made this trip the occasion to invite all the Indians he met to a conference at Fort Pitt, and his invitation was eminently successful because it brought down to the meeting in August representatives not only of the Delawares and Iroquois of the Allegheny, but also of the Ottawa, Chippewa, Potawatomi, Miami, Wyandot, Shawnee, and even of the far-off Kickapoo from the country west of the Wabash. Indeed the French spies were being given plenty of opportunity to observe British strength by being invited as friends to the British stronghold itself.

[8] *Massachusetts Historical Collections,* fourth series, 9:246-249.
[9] *Massachusetts Historical Colections,* fourth series, 9:287.

Indian Revolt Against British Economy

This Fort Pitt conference, lasting from August 12 to 20, was much like those of the previous year but was by far the most heavily attended, no less than one thousand Indians being present. The affair was little more than a good-will meeting and consisted mainly of the reading of a message from the commander-in-chief, General Amherst, outlining the British plan of reconciliation, with strong emphasis on the fact that the British had no designs on the Indians' lands. The various delegations of Indians replied in general terms and expressed the hope that the policy would be applied effectively and at an early date. They all emphasized that the most important part of the plan from the Indian point of view was that providing for the restoration of trade. It was made clear that the abnormal conditions resulting from the war and the departure of the French meant that the Indians' guns had fallen into disrepair and that they had no powder and lead. They were thus not yet able even to sustain themselves by the hunt, to say nothing of securing enough furs and skins to carry on trade.[10] The exchange of ideas at the council brought both to the Indians and to the British an insight into the other's point of view, and the British were able to observe the needs of the Indians and to study the way in which the plan should be administered to meet those needs. The Indians were unable to foresee, of course, that because of the requirements of economy the British would be unable to meet those needs in a manner necessary for the restoration of normal Indian life.

The establishment of English garrisons at Venango and Presque Isle and the establishment of communication between the latter place and both Pittsburgh and Niagara made the occupation of Detroit possible in the fall of 1760. This was carried out by troops commanded by Major Robert Rogers. The French commandant, Captain Bellestre, surrendered on November 29, two years after Forbes had entered Fort Duquesne. So far as the Indians were concerned, the occupation

---

[10] *Pennsylvania Archives,* first series, 3:744-752; 4:48, 49; *Massachusetts Historical Collections,* fourth series, 9:240-242.

was looked upon with passive acquiescence, as it was the first change of masters these tribes had ever known. The situation is well described by Major Rogers in his own account of his meeting on November 7, at the mouth of the Cuyahoga, with the Ottawa leader, Pontiac. "He demanded," said Rogers, "my business into his country, and how it happened that I dared to enter it without his leave? . . . I informed him that it was not with any design against the Indians that I came, but to remove the French out of his country, who had been an obstacle in our way to mutual peace and commerce, and acquainted him with my instructions for that purpose." Pontiac replied that Rogers must not march any farther without the Indians' consent. After he had consulted his fellow tribesmen, however, the great Ottawa leader gave Rogers his permission to advance, offered to supply him with food, and promised to prevent the Indians from attacking him at Detroit as Captain Bellestre had persuaded them to do, a promise that it became quite necessary for him to fulfill. "He assured me," said Rogers, "that he was inclined to live peaceably with the English while they used him as he deserved, and to encourage their settling in his country; but intimated, that, if they treated him with neglect, he should shut up the way, and exclude them from it; in short, his whole conversation sufficiently indicated that he was far from considering himself as a conquered Prince, and that he expected to be treated with the respect and honour due to a King or Emperor, by all who came into his country, or treated with him."[11]

After the capitulation at Detroit, Croghan, who had accompanied the expedition, met representatives of the Ottawa, Potawatomi, and Wyandot in council at the French fort on December 4. There he informed them of the complete reduction of Canada by the English and of the fact that all French Canadians would now become British subjects. The main outlines of the English plan of restoration were presented to them, and they were especially reminded that the delivery of the

[11] Rogers, *Account of North America*, 240-243; Rogers, *Journals,* 184-198.

white captives was "the only way you can convince us of your sincerity and future intentions of living in Friendship with all his Majestys Subjects." They were offered powder and lead in return for bringing in game for the British garrison and were granted a gunsmith to mend their firearms and a doctor to attend their sick. In their replies the tribes stressed, as the others had done in previous councils, the necessity for trade and for low prices of goods. In regard to the captives, the Wyandot speaker said that they would be returned but that the tribe did "not choose to force them that have a mind to live with us." "Be strong," said the Potawatomi speaker, "and bring large quantitys of goods to supply us & we will bring all our Furs to this place."[12]

Thus by the beginning of 1761 all the tribes of the Ohio Valley and the Lakes country, except what may be called the Illinois and Wisconsin country, had been brought within the English sphere of influence.[13] Croghan wrote from Fort Pitt on January 13, 1761, to his chief, Sir William Johnson, that he was greatly pleased at the prospects for the Indian trade. He was, however, apprehensive that unless there could be better regulation and control of the trade, the Indians would be rendered discontented. He wrote that he had persuaded General Monckton to prohibit the sale of liquor to Indians in large quantities, and he deplored the fact that the Pennsylvania government trading store at Pittsburgh, run by Quakers, should include rum in its wares.[14]

The moment that the French danger was completely gone and that all the Indians east of the Wisconsin-Illinois country seemed to be under the English influence, a change began in

[12] *Massachusetts Historical Collections,* fourth series, 9:370-377.

[13] After the capture of Detroit, Major Rogers and Andrew Montour started for Michilimackinac, and Lieutenant John Butler set out to take over the French post on the Maumee. Alexander McKee, one of Croghan's assistants, was sent along to remove French traders from the Shawnee country, and Croghan himself made arrangements with the Wyandot on the Sandusky for the erection of a fort. An officer was also sent to the Potawatomi country on the St. Joseph River in what is now southwestern Michigan. Johnson, *Papers,* 3:301, 316.

[14] Johnson, *Papers,* 3:303.

British policy that was to modify the English plan of reconciliation in such a way as to lead directly to the Indian revolt under Pontiac. This change was caused by the decision of the commander-in-chief, Lord Jeffery Amherst, and of his next in command, General Robert Monckton, to economize. The first announcement of the decision came on February 22, 1761, when Amherst wrote to Sir William Johnson announcing that the time had come to cut down on gifts to the Indians and to see to it that the red men returned quickly to their normal business of hunting. Amherst had no objection to furnishing the Indians with a little clothing and some arms and ammunition "in Cases of Necessity; but as," he continued, "when the Intended Trade is once Established they will be able to supply themselves with these [*goods*], from the Traders, for their furrs, I do not see why the Crown should be put to that Expence.—I am not neither for giving them any Provisions; when they find they can get it on Asking for, they will grow remiss in tl.eir hunting, which Should Industriously be avoided; for so long as their minds are Intent on business they will not have leisure to hatch mischief." He asked that particular care be taken in scrutinizing Croghan's account. "It Appears to me," said Amherst, "he has been bery [*sic*] bountifull." He warned Johnson against purchasing the good behavior of the Indians. "When men of what race soever behave ill," he declared, "they must be punished but not bribed."[15] These sentiments were echoed by Monckton, who informed Bouquet at Fort Pitt on April 5, 1761, "The Indian Expence is Immense ... It is time now that the Indians, should live by their Hunting, & not think that they are always to be receiving Presents."[16]

One of the unfortunate aspects of this enforced economy, from the Indian point of view, was that it was imposed on the

[15] Johnson, *Papers*, 3:345. Amherst had no idea of abandoning trade regulation and was willing to administer it until such time as the civil authorities either in England or in the colonies took it over. Johnson, *Papers*, 3:344. See Johnson's regulations (with Amherst's approval) in Johnson, *Papers*, 3:527-535.

[16] Bouquet Papers, Additional Manuscripts, 21638:205.

tribes before the traders had had an opportunity to re-establish normal trade relations throughout all the Indian towns. Croghan, as has been pointed out, began to let the traders go into the Indian country in 1760; but Bouquet put an end to that practice early in 1761. He announced to Monckton on March 23 of that year, "To prevent differences with the Indians, I have not permitted any Traders to deal at any other Places but where we have Posts." The reasons given for this policy were that there was too much horse stealing being done by certain tribes and that they had not yet returned enough captives. The Shawnee were particularly vulnerable on these two points. Much of the difficulty over horse stealing was traceable to the attempts of the whites to make settlements on Indian lands on the Monongahela, and much of the difficulty over the captives was traceable to Croghan's previously lenient policy and to the sincere unwillingness of the Indians to cause the heartbreaks resulting from the forced return of those who had learned to love the Indian ways and had become members of Indian families by marriage or adoption. Indian negligence on these two matters so irritated Bouquet that, instead of seeking to get at the root of the difficulty or abandoning Croghan's liberal policy gradually, he followed his military instincts and sought to force the Indians into action. On July 10, 1761, he wrote to Monckton, "I take this to be the time to put a stop to these Robberies, and the double dealing of the Indians . . . and if you would permit to take all Trade from them, they . . . would soon tire of it, and in the mean time they cannot do us any dammage but what we may retort upon them." Two weeks later he repeated these sentiments: "Those [*Indians*] in this District do not complain of any thing except that the Traders are not permitted to go to their Towns: But when they are told that the Reasons are their not delivering the Prisoners & continuing to steal our Horses, they have nothing to say, but repeat Promises they will not perform, till forced to it by keeping the Trade from them." Monckton fully endorsed Bouquet's policy: "You

doo verry Right," he wrote on August 24, 1761, "in not permitting the Traders to go to the Shawanese, & other Towns,
that Steal our Horses, till they leave it off; & bring in some of
our Prisoners; for they will never doo it till necessity Obliges
them."[17]

The pinch caused by military economy was also felt among
the more western tribes, where Pontiac's influence was strong.
The tribes centering around Detroit, the St. Joseph River, the
Sandusky, and the Wabash and Maumee rivers were so numerous and so remote from the sources of British trading supplies that it would have required a far greater expenditure
than England was capable of making to satisfy even the nearer
tribes. It was among these tribes that the French had recruited most of their Indian warriors during the French and Indian
War, and it was a confederation of these tribes that was to
provide the backbone of the forces that took part in Pontiac's
War. The underlying situation was revealed as the result of
the discovery of a premature plot among these tribes to revolt
against the English, evidently instigated by Guyasuta and
certain other Seneca leaders and probably encouraged by their
friend, Chabert de Joncaire. The plot was discovered in June,
1761, by the British commandant at Detroit, Captain Donald
Campbell, and action of a violent nature was prevented.[18]

The affair led to the holding of a great council at Detroit in
September, at which both Johnson and Croghan were present.
Much of the speechmaking had to do with the Indians' dis-
avowal of guilt in the plot and their promises to be good in the
future, and with Johnson's exhortations to good conduct and
pledges of the restoration of normal conditions. Especially out-

[17] *Massachusetts Historical Collections,* fourth series, 9:401, 433-435; Bouquet
Papers, Add. MSS., 21638:248.

[18] Bouquet Collection, Calendar, in Canadian Archives, *Report,* 1889, p. 299, 326;
Massachusetts Historical Collections, fourth series, 9:423-429; Johnson, *Papers,*
3:448-453, 456, 695, 696. The condition that led the Seneca to be part of this
movement was indicated during a conference held at Niagara early in August, 1761,
when one of them begged Sir William to "consider their poverty, & allow . . .
some ammunition to kill game for their support, as also to have pity on our Women
who have scarcely cloathing to cover their nakedness." Johnson, *Papers,* 3:464.

spoken was one of the Wyandot representatives: "Many articles," he told Johnson, "are very scarce & in particular powder is sold so sparingly & is so hard to be got that we are all apprehensive we must shortly be obliged to leave off hunting entirely, as our Young Men cannot procure sufficient to cloath themselves or provide for their Wives & Children." He asked that some arrangements be made to extend them guns and ammunition on credit as the French had done whenever the Indians were in difficulties. It is important to recognize that the need of the Indians for powder was a real one; for they had just participated in a war in which their domestic economy had been thrown quite out of balance, particularly in regard to their food supply. Sir William Johnson pointed out in October, 1764, that after the French war the tribes "did not Immediately return to hunting, their best Hunters having been generally concerned in the war." It is probably also true that these warrior-hunters, not being sure of what England intended to do to them, were hoarding their powder for use in the event that their fears of evil from the English were justified.[19]

What England should have done in this unusual situation was to have erred on the side of generosity. But the answer to the Indians' urgent requests was an uncompromising refusal. To economize was the order of the commander-in-chief. Johnson, in replying to the Indians at Detroit, stated that he was willing to help them in many ways, but as for credit, "it is absolutely out of my power to satisfy you." But Johnson did not dare to tell the Indians the nature of the instructions given to him by Amherst at Niagara before going to Detroit. These instructions, dated August 9, 1761, read, "You are sensible how averse I am, to purchasing the good behavior of Indians, by presents, the more they get the more they ask, and yet are never satisfied . . . I think it much better to avoid all presents in future, since that will oblige them to Supply themselves by barter, & of course keep them more Constantly Em-

[19] Johnson, *Papers*, 3:486, 487, 496; 4:557.

ployed by means of which they will have less time to concert, or Carry into Execution any Schemes prejudicial to His Majestys Interests." As the months passed, economy became a fetish to Amherst, who insisted upon it with all the zeal of his military heart. He deplored Croghan's extravagance, praised Bouquet for his policy of retrenchment, and urged further economies. As it appeared to him that the Indians had had plenty of time to deliver their prisoners, on July 25 he proclaimed an absolute embargo on all presents to them until all the captives were delivered.[20]

As a good soldier of the king, Amherst believed that he could force the Indians to a more industrious manner of living by the crude method of discipline. As a commander-in-chief over his officers, he insisted upon implicit obedience to his orders. But he would have been interested to know something of the correspondence that his orders caused to pass between two of his most trusted officers, Captain Donald Campbell, commandant at Detroit, and Colonel Henry Bouquet, commandant at Fort Pitt. On October 12, 1761, Campbell wrote to Bouquet, "We have got Peaceabl[e] Possession of the Fort, and every Thing is now quiet, tho I am certain if the Indians knew General Amherst['s] sentiments about keeping them short of Powder it would be impossible to keep them in temper." On November 28 Campbell again wrote to Bouquet, "All the Indian Nations have gone to their Hunting, and by that means will be quiet here 'till Spring. I hope the Gen[ll] will change [h]is present way of thinking, with regard to Indian Affairs, as I am of Opinion if they were supplyed with Ammunition it would prevent their doing Mischief."[21]

The year 1762 was to tell the tale. It was the year in which the Indians gradually learned what Johnson and Campbell dared not tell them. And they learned it not only in the Detroit country, but also in all the centers of British influence, so that

[20] Johnson, *Papers*, 3:498, 515, 520, 597; Bouquet Collection, Calendar, in Canadian Archives, *Report*, 1889, p. 16, 18. See also Johnson's economy order to Croghan of January 8, 1762, in Johnson, *Papers*, 3:604, 605.
[21] Bouquet Papers, Add. MSS., 21647:207, 259.

when the spring of 1763 came they were ready for a general uprising. It was a year during which reports constantly poured in from every British post that the Indians were complaining of a shortage of powder and of other matters. On the Fort Pitt sector Croghan was using his salary to buy gifts for the Indians and at the same time was threatening to resign. By the spring of 1763 he had spent all his salary on gifts to the Indians and was able to report to Johnson, "I Can say Now I Serve the King for nothing." His reports during 1762 as to the sentiments of the tribes in western Pennsylvania were increasingly pessimistic. In March he reported that the Seneca "seem Ripe for some Mischiff." In May he reported that all the tribes on the upper Ohio were uneasy. "Yᵉ Most Sensable of them ask Me what is yᵉ Reason that we allways was Calling them to Council During yᵉ Warr & giveing them presents & Now Take No Notice of them. They say yᵉ French was butt a poor peple butt they allways Cloathed any Indians that was poor or Naked when they Come to see them." By December he reported to Johnson that the situation was very bad indeed and that plots of war were circulating among the Delawares, Shawnee, and Seneca. The embargo on powder that Amherst looked upon as a preventative of Indian war was interpreted by the Indians as part of the British preparation for war. They therefore drew together to prepare themselves for defense and hoarded what powder they had, thus aggravating their own suffering by refraining from the hunt. They told Croghan "that they have No Intensions to Make Warr with yᵉ English Butt say itt is full Time for them to prepair to defend themselves."[22]

Croghan summed up the situation among the Indians in 1762 in an opinion that, being based on a real knowledge of Indian character, was most accurately prophetic. He said, "They begin more and more to dread our growing power. . . . The Indians are a very Jelous peple & they had great Expectations of being very Ginerally Supplyᵈ by us & from their

[22] Volwiler, *George Croghan*, 160; Johnson, *Papers*, 3:663, 733, 964.

poverty & Mercenery Disposion they cant Bear such a Disapointment. Undoubtedly yᵉ Gineral has his own Rason for Nott allowing any presents or amunision to be given them, & I wish itt may have its Desirᵈ Effect Butt I take this opertunity to acquaint you that I Dread the Event as I know Indians cant long persevere. They are a Rash Inconsistent peple & Inclinᵈ to Mischiff & will never Consider Consequences tho itt May End in thire Ruen. Thire Success yᵉ beginning of this Warr on our fronteers is to[o] Recent in thire Memery to Suffer them to Consider thire present Inability to make Warr with us and if yᵉ Sinecas Dellaways & Shawnas Should Brake with us it will End in a ginerall Warr with all yᵉ Western Nations tho they att present Seem Jelous of Each Other."[23]

Croghan's December statement was based largely on the report of adverse conditions brought in by his deputy, Thomas Hutchins, whom Croghan had sent out in April to tour the Indian country. Hutchins visited the Delawares, Wyandot, Chippewa, Ottawa; the Sauk and Foxes and Menominee in the Wisconsin country; and the Potawatomi, Miami, Wea, Kickapoo, Mascoutens, Piankashaw, and Shawnee. He arrived back at Fort Pitt on September 24. His tour only served to remind these tribes of the cruelty of the English policy of economy. "They were disappointed," reported Hutchins, "in their Expectations of my having Presents for them; and as the French has always Accustomed themselves, both in time of Peace and during the late War, to make these People great Presents, three or four times a year, and always allowed them a Sufficient Quantity of Ammunition at the Posts, they think it very strange that this Custom should be so immediately broke off by the English, and the Traders not allowed even to take so much Ammunition with them as to enable those Indians to Kill game sufficient for the support of their families."[24]

[23] Johnson, *Papers*, 3:964.
[24] Hanna, *Wilderness Trail*, 2:367. Also in *Michigan Historical Magazine*, 10:365-373 (1926).

Indian Revolt Against British Economy

Although the British policy of economy was by far the most weighty grievance in creating discontent among the tribes, the Indians also complained of land encroachments, and not without cause. The treaty of Albany of 1754 had been modified at Easton in 1758 so as to return to the tribes the lands west of the mountains. Hence any settlements made or any hunting done by individuals, other than that necessary to maintain the military posts, were invasions of Indian rights. Such invasions began immediately after Forbes took Fort Duquesne on November 25, 1758, when the people who had settled on the waters of the Monongahela before the war returned to their homes. From then on, settlements increased to such an extent that an Iroquois visitor to western Pennsylvania told Croghan in November, 1762, that the Indian users of these lands were "Mutering & Grumbling on account of their Lands & Complaining that y^r honour Did Nott order ye boundary Line between, them and the proprietors of Pensilvania to be Run." During 1760 and 1761 the squatter invasion of the Monongahela Valley was particularly heavy. Bouquet wrote to Governor Francis Fauquier of Virginia on February 8, 1762, "For two years past these Lands have been over run by a Number of Vagabonds, who under pretence of hunting, were Making Settlements in several parts of them." Bouquet called the attention of General Monckton to this practice in March, 1761, and asked for leave to issue a proclamation forbidding hunting or settling west of the mountains. In reply Monckton authorized Bouquet to expel the settlers, and in April Sergeant Angus MacDonald, commandant at Fort Burd (Redstone, later Brownsville) was ordered to drive the intruders off. But MacDonald could do nothing. On October 25, 1761, he informed Bouquet, "Here Comes Such Crowds of Hunters out of the Inhabitence as fills those woods at which the Indians seems Very much Disturbed and say the white people Kills all there Deer yet those hunters Keeps so far from the fort That I Cannot See Them nor Can I send after Them I have taken Some of there horses but Cannot take themselves If your Honour would be pleasᵈ to Send an Advertisement which I Could Set up at the Great Crossings to give them Notice Then I Could Handle them more Ruffer if they Should Come again." Bouquet acted at once and issued his famous proclamation of October 30, 1761, forbidding hunting or settling west of the mountains and ordering all officers discovering violators of the proclamation to deliver the culprits to Fort Pitt for trial by court martial.[25]

The only effect of Bouquet's proclamation was to make the hunters more wary. James Livingstone at Fort Cumberland in Maryland wrote to Bouquet on February 14, 1762, that it was impossible to stop them because they kept away from the forts on account of the proclamation. On April 1 Bouquet was optimistic enough to think that his measures of burning the cabins had disgusted the settlers. But within ten days, news came in to Pittsburgh that two settlers above Redstone, "One Tumblestone & another," were barbarously murdered in their houses. James Kenny in commenting on the affair said, "It Greives yᵉ Indians to see yᵉ White People Settle on these Lands & follow Hunting or Planting, especially in Virginia side & off yᵉ Road too." The hunting ground affected was used particularly by the Mingo, whose towns were located a little to the west. So far as these Indians were concerned, land aggression was the main grievance in determining their participation in Pontiac's War. In November, 1762, Kenny learned from Alexander McKee "that yᵉ Mingoes has a War Belt & Bloody Tomhock now offering to yᵉ Shawanas, requesting thier help as they are Going to Strike yᵉ English & drive them off their Lands."[26]

[25] Johnson, *Papers,* 3:931; "The Reservation of Indian Lands," in Canadian Archives, *Report,* 1889, p. 74; *Massachusetts Historical Collections,* fourth series, 9:397, 407; Bouquet Papers, Add. MSS., 21647:217. The best analysis of settlement in western Pennsylvania from 1758 to 1763 is in James, "The First English-speaking Trans-Appalachian Frontier," in *Mississippi Valley Historical Review,* 17:59-63 (1930).
[26] Bouquet Collection, Calendar, in Canadian Archives, *Report,* 1889, p. 199; "The Reservation of Indian Lands," in Canadian Archives, *Report,* 1889, p. 76; Kenny, "Journal," 1761-63, in *Pennsylvania Magazine of History and Biography,* 37:40, 152, 174 (1913).

It was not merely the privation and starvation[27] brought on by Amherst's zeal for economy and the encroachments on their hunting grounds that drove the Indians to despair. It was also the maddening effect on Indian pride of the insulting treatment from the white people, whom the Indians in their hearts despised. Kenny perceived this feeling and confided in his journal in January, 1763, that the Indians could not be blamed for resenting the treatment they received from the frontier rabble. Kenny's remarks, conditioned as they were by a desire to Christianize the red men, are most revealing, considering the time and place at which they were made. He said of the English, "Those that are most conversant amongst them, are mostly Men of Base principles, rather joyning with ye Indian customs & abominations, or shewing 'em worse Examples than they Naturaly are prone too, & its in Vain to pretend to Endeavour to turn them [*the Indians*] to the English Customs, Religions or Manners, Whilst they see frequently better & honester Men amongst themselves then [*than*] Most English People going by that Name amongst them . . . they are more Excited to abhore ye Name of a Christian by ye Vile Pretenders to that name resorting wt them & at this place which is Called an English Town [*Pittsburgh*]."[28]

Indian pride was particularly offended by the British insistence on the return of the captives. This matter reached a climax in 1762 as the result of an order forbidding British officers to give presents to the Indians when captives were brought to the posts. On July 7 there appeared at Fort Pitt a band of Delawares with fifty captives, about half the total number then held by that tribe. Since the king's officers could

[27] The Shawnee were afflicted during 1762 by a plague that cut them down by the score. Kenny received reports in which the number of dead varied from 100 to "150 men besids Women." Kenny, "Journal," 1761-63, in *Pennsylvania Magazine of History and Biography*, 37:168, 172, 178 (1913). Thomas Hutchins visited the Shawnee country in September, 1762, and found the people "Sick and Dying every day." Hanna, *Wilderness Trail*, 2:367.

[28] Kenny, "Journal," 1761-63, in *Pennsylvania Magazine of History and Biography*, 37:166, 182 (1913).

not give the Indians presents, the commandant tried to get the representatives of Pennsylvania then in Pittsburgh, Kenny and Christian Frederick Post, to buy a few kettles for the Indians. Kenny and Post refused but loaned the commandant some. This aid enabled the Delawares to go on, but their party had to be cut to thirty Indians and only eighteen prisoners, "chiefly Women & Children." After the captives had been given up at Lancaster, James Hamilton, governor of Pennsylvania, told them on August 26, "There yet remain a great many of our people, as prisoners, in some of your Towns . . . we expect . . . that they Shall all be delivered up . . . As to what you say about our promises of paying you for our Flesh and Blood, You must have been mistaken . . . it is never our Custom to purchase our Flesh and Blood of any Nation, whatsoever." They were then given money and presents to compensate them for their services in bringing the captives to Lancaster. Sick at heart, the Delawares along with some Shawnee set out for the West, after having promised to deliver up the rest of their captives by the first of October. As they traveled, their resentment mounted. According to the trader, Thomas McKee, they finally left most of their presents on the road and sent word to Governor Hamilton that "he might send for them to give to the Indians the next Treaty." They even muttered among themselves threats to turn north when they reached the Susquehanna and destroy Fort Augusta near what is now Wyoming, Pennsylvania, "alledging," according to Kenny, "as much reason for it as for them to deliver up ye Prisoners, for nothing."[29]

It is true, of course, that the Indians had originally wrested the captives from their families and taken them off as prisoners. But it was argued by the Indians that they had been

[29] Kenny, "Journal," 1761-63, in *Pennsylvania Magazine of History and Biography*, 37:161, 168 (1913); *Pennsylvania Colonial Records*, 8:760; Johnson, *Papers*, 3:921, 986. Provision for the hundreds of Indians assembled at Lancaster was far inferior to that for the Indians at all preceding treaties. The Oneida chief, Thomas King, said, "At Easton . . . I could have my Belly full of Victuals and plenty of Drink, but now I come here, I have little to eat; I am sure I have no other Drink than dirty water, which almost choaks me." *Pennsylvania Colonial Records*, 8:747.

taken in the course of war, that their lives had been spared, and that they had been treated well ever since. They pointed to the fact that the captives did not wish to return—"No wonder why they are so loath to come," said the Iroquois spokesman, Thomas King, at Lancaster, "when you make Servants of them." A Wyandot chief at the council of Detroit in 1761 had said of the prisoners, "We must observe that they are no Slaves with us, being at their free liberty to go anywhere, or act as they please, neither is it our Custom to Exercise any Authority over them, they having the same priviledges with ourselves—We beg you will not suppose that we ever illtreated any, or detained them a moment longer than they chose to stay." Another point that must be considered in viewing the negligence of the Indians in this matter is the difficulty of preventing the escape of captives while conducting a large band of them through the forests. The Iroquois had collected all the captives taken by the Seneca, but by the time they got to Lancaster most of them had disappeared. Many of them returned home to the Indians. King related the story of an Iroquois brave who had delivered up to the English a captive white woman whom he had married. Upon returning to his tribe he found that his wife had returned ahead of him. Whereupon he took her a second time to the English and told them, "Take care of her, and keep her safe, that she don't make her escape."[30]

The depth to which Indian pride was offended in 1762 is indicated by the rise of a religious revival movement among the Delawares traceable directly to their discontent with British rule. The movement was led by a prophet whose name is unknown but who resided at the town of Tuscarawas on the river of that name in what is now the state of Ohio. This

---

[30] Johnson, *Papers*, 3:486; *Pennsylvania Colonial Records*, 8:744, 745. It may be said that a great majority of the captives were returned to the English. See *Pennsylvania Colonial Records*, 8:735; Volwiler, *George Croghan*, 145. The Shawnee seem to have been the most delinquent in making deliveries and brought in only a few during 1761 and 1762. Through the efforts, however, of Croghan's deputy, Alexander McKee, who visited the Shawnee country in the fall of 1762, this nation was persuaded to promise to give up all captives.

prophet taught that by following the instructions of the great creator the Indians would in a few years be able to drive the whites out of their country. These instructions were based entirely on the idea of purging the tribesmen of all things they had learned from the whites and, as the captive, John McCullough, described in his narrative, of attempting "to live entirely in the original state that they were in before the white people found out their country." The thoroughness with which they sought to cleanse themselves of the white man's sins is most significant. They gave up the use of firearms and hunted exclusively with the bow and arrow. They lived entirely on dried meat and a bitter drink whose purgative quality was supposed to rid them of poisons absorbed by years of white contamination. They abandoned all commerce with the whites, clothed themselves in nothing but furs and skins, and would not even use flint and steel to make fire but required the bow and drill. The prophet predicted a war in the near future in which the whites would be entirely defeated. The movement began in 1759 or 1760 and by the spring of 1763, according to an informant of James Kenny, embraced the whole Delaware nation.[31]

It is probable that it was this forgotten Delaware prophet from whom the Ottawa leader, Pontiac, got the words of the Great Spirit's command with which he stirred to action the council of the Indian confederacy at the River Ecorces near Detroit on that fateful April 27, 1763. A Delaware Indian, Pontiac told the tribesmen, had visited the celestial realms and received this address from the Great Spirit: "I am the Maker of Mankind; and because I love you, you must do my will. The land on which you live I have made for you, and not for others. Why do you suffer the white men to dwell among you? My children, you have forgotten the customs and traditions of your forefathers. Why do you not clothe yourselves in skins, as they did, and use the bows and arrows, and the

[31] Kenny, "Journal," 1761-63, in *Pennsylvania Magazine of History and Biography*, 37:171-173, 175, 188 (1913); Pritts, *Incidents of Border Life*, 98, 99.

stone-pointed lances, which they used? You have bought guns, knives, kettles, and blankets, from the white men, until you can no longer do without them; and, what is worse, you have drunk the poison fire-water, which turns you into fools. Fling all these things away; live as your wise forefathers lived before you. And as for these English,—these dogs dressed in red, who have come to rob you of your hunting-grounds, and drive away the game,—you must lift the hatchet against them. Wipe them from the face of the earth, and then you will win my favor back again, and once more be happy and prosperous."[32]

The last straw for the Indians came in January, 1763, with the announcement of the formal treaty of peace between France and England. To Amherst it meant the end of danger, and he told Bouquet on March 13 that it would cause the Indians to give up all hope of aid from France and would bring about the return of all captives. On May 10 he instructed Croghan to prepare for a general council with all the tribes, at which the cession of Canada to England would be announced and all remaining captives turned over to the English. Amherst deprecated all suggestions of Indian disaffection and felt that the Indians had enough sense not to take up arms in the face of the British power now freed of French opposition. What the Indians thought, Amherst told Croghan, was of little consequence, because it was to their interest to keep quiet. But to the Indians the news of the cession of New France was the signal for revolt. On March 12, 1763, Croghan wrote to Johnson from Fort Pitt, "Ever Sence ye Reduction of Canada the Indians in those parts apeard very Jelous of our Growing power Butt Sence I acquainted them of ye paice & Lett them know that all North America was Ceaded to Greatt Britian they Seem Much More So." The way in which this news affected Newcomer, head king of the Delawares, was relayed to Kenny by Post, who witnessed the scene at which the Delawares were informed. "Newcomer," said Post, "was

[32] Parkman, *Conspiracy of Pontiac*, 1:206.

Struck dumb for a considerable time & at last s^d he did not know whether ye News was true but if they could hear it from their fathers i. e. ye French he would believe it . . . He s^d ye English was grown too powerfull & seem^d as if they would be too Strong for God himself."[33]

From such causes as these arose Pontiac's War. The story of the secret councils held during the early months of 1763 throughout the country by Pontiac and his emissaries; of the daring plot on May 8 against Major Henry Gladwin, commandant at Detroit, and its betrayal; of the defeat of Lieutenant Cuyler's relief expedition to Detroit; of the Indian capture of Fort Sandusky, Fort St. Joseph, Michilimackinac, Green Bay, Fort Miamis, Fort Presque Isle, Fort Le Bœuf, and Fort Venango; of the unsuccessful attacks on Detroit, Fort Pitt, Fort Ligonier, Fort Bedford, Fort Augusta, and Carlisle; of the battle of Bushy Run on August 5 and 6; of the shameful Paxton riots; and of the general desolation of the frontier, has been too well told by Francis Parkman to need repeating here.[34] Suffice it to say that even had the Indians not been betrayed at Detroit, the British would not have been swept from beyond the mountains, much less "from the face of the earth." The war would have been bloodier, to be sure, but the result would have been the same. Colonel John Bradstreet, who relieved Detroit in 1764, and Bouquet, who relieved Fort

[33] Bouquet Collection, Calendar, in Canadian Archives, *Report*, 1889, p. 20, 21; Johnson, *Papers*, 4:62; Kenny, "Journal," 1761-63, in *Pennsylvania Magazine of History and Biography*, 37:187, 192 (1913). An interesting direct effect on the Delawares and Shawnee of the news of the cesssion of Canada was the advice sent by the former to the latter in April, 1763, to hold up the delivery of all captives "till it was seen what turn things will take by the peace." Considering the sufferings and ugly feelings dominant among the Shawnee in 1761 and 1762, the work of Alexander McKee in the fall of 1762 in persuading them to return all the captives had been quite an achievement. Bouquet Collection, Calendar, in Canadian Archives, *Report*, 1889, p. 217, 218, 221, 224, 225; Kenny, "Journal," 1761-63, in *Pennsylvania Magazine of History and Biography*, 37:156, 169, 172, 174, 177, 186, 188, 194 (1913).

[34] Parkman, *Conspiracy of Pontiac*, 1:212-307; 2:1-155. An interesting exposition of the betrayal of the plot against Gladwin is in Helen F. Humphrey, "The Identity of Gladwin's Informant," in *Mississippi Valley Historical Review*, 21:147-162 (1934).

Pitt and subdued the Shawnee and Delawares in the same year, would have needed, and would have had, larger armies to force the Indians into subjection.

The defeated Indians were treated with the utmost contempt. The single gesture of friendship, the king's proclamation of October 7, 1763, forbidding white settlement beyond the mountains, meant nothing to the Indians, acquainted as they were with the facts of war. When by the fall of 1764 the Delawares, Shawnee, and Mingo failed to deliver all the captives at Sandusky on September 8 in accordance with the promise made to Bradstreet on August 14, Bouquet proceeded at once with an army to the town of Tuscarawas, where he arrived on October 13. On the twentieth, after informing the Indians that they had begun the war "without the least reason or provocation whatsoever," he demanded that all captives be delivered at Wakatomica on or before November 1. On November 9 Bouquet announced himself satisfied with the results of this order, but he required that hostages be left with him until terms of peace could be made between the Indians and Sir William Johnson. With about two hundred restored captives and with the promise that the rest would be delivered in the spring, Bouquet returned to Fort Pitt. It is recorded by John McCullough that on the way back, two of these captives made their escape "and went back to the Indians." Their names were Rhoda Boyd and Elizabeth Studebaker.[35]

In the spring of 1765 the Delawares dutifully made their appearance before Sir William Johnson at his home, Johnson Hall, near Johnstown, New York, and submitted to a treaty that represented a complete surrender. In this treaty, dated May 8, 1765, the Delawares agreed to permit the free passage through their country of all accredited British troops and traders; to do their utmost to assist the English to win the Illinois country from the Franco-Indian influence; to endeavor to cause the Shawnee, who were not represented at Johnson Hall, to return all their white captives; to restore the seven

[35] *Pennsylvania Colonial Records*, 9:207-233; Pritts, *Incidents of Border Life*, 104.

captives still left in their own country; never to harbor fugitives to their country; never to take revenge for injuries suffered; to turn over all Indians who in the future should rob or murder white men; not to molest squatters but to appeal to the officers of the Indian department; to agree to a cession of land in reparation for the losses caused by Indian attacks in 1763; to abide by any cession of their lands made by the Iroquois; to communicate the terms of the treaty to all other tribes; and to enter into no engagement with any nation without the knowledge of the superintendent of Indian affairs.[36]

Meanwhile the Shawnee, making preparations for their submission at Fort Pitt, assembled their tribesmen in a camp across the river from the fort. On May 10, in an impressive setting, the Shawnee, beating drums and singing their peace song, came across the river in their canoes with all the English captives. When all had assembled in the council house within the fort, Lawoughgua, the Shawnee spokesman, arose and, addressing the English as "Father" for the first time, recounted what it meant to them to restore the captives. "Father," said he, "Here is your Flesh and Blood, except . . . a few that was out with some of our hunting parties, & those will be brought here as soon as they return. They have been all tied to us by adoption, and altho' we now deliver them up to you, we will always look upon them as our relations whenever the great Spirit is pleased that we may visit them. . . . We have taken as much care of these prisoners as if they were our own Flesh and Blood; they are now become unacquainted with your Customs & manners, & therefore, Fathers, we request you will use them tenderly & kindly, which will be a means of inducing them to live contentedly with you. . . . Here is a Belt [of peace] . . . we hope that neither side will slip their hands from it so long as the Sun and Moon gives light."[37]

[36] *New York Colonial Documents*, 7:738-741.
[37] *Pennsylvania Colonial Records*, 9:259, 260. Two months later the Shawnee, together with some Delawares and Mingo, made their final peace with Sir William Johnson and ratified the treaty of May 8. *New York Colonial Documents*, 7:750-758.

6
A Decade
of British Muddling,
1765-1774

WITH the close of the military phases of the suppression of Pontiac's Conspiracy, the English government was again presented with the problem of restoring its influence to the French-ridden and war-ridden Indians of the Northwest. It did not fumble the problem as badly, perhaps, as it had in the days of Amherst, who had returned to England in the fall of 1763, but neither did it handle the matter in a way satisfactory to the Indians or to the people of America. What the government did was to drop the Amherst policy of economy long enough to give most of the tribes a few rounds of gifts, and then to refuse to build up a well-organized Indian department because the fur trade did not prosper as was expected and because the American colonies would not contribute

123

to the support of such a department. The policy of King George III of discrediting ministries contributed to the difficulties of the government because it did not admit of the enforcement of any permanent measures. The result was that although an approximation of normal trade returned under the auspices of private traders, by 1774 it was entirely uncontrolled, and the Indians in all quarters were complaining of the abuses of traders or of land grabbers or of both. This was not the only grievance of the Indians—a land cession was forced from certain tribes at the treaty of Fort Stanwix in 1768 that produced a bitter discontent among them and was one of the fundamental causes of the conflict in 1774 known as Dunmore's War.

During the Pontiac War the Indian "managers," who had been the subject of ridicule by Bouquet and by his fellow militarists in the years before the conspiracy,[1] retired from the scene, or, as in the case of Sir William Johnson, worked to keep five of the Six Nations neutral. But they did not retire from power. In fact one of them, George Croghan, went to England and became most influential in producing a temporary policy that was entirely the reverse of that sponsored by Amherst. It must have given Croghan a great deal of satisfaction to view the disgrace of Amherst while he himself was being continually consulted by members of the British Cabinet. The "illerate" Indian agent, as Bouquet contemptuously called him, described Amherst's fate in a letter to Johnson dated February 24, 1764: "Gincral Amhirsts Conduct is Condem^d by Everybody and [he] has been pelted away in ye papers ye army Curse him in publick as well as the Merchants . . . in Short he is No body heer Nor has he been askt aqustion [*sic*] with Respect to ye affairs of amerrica Sence he Came over which a gentelman might nott ask his footman."[2]

Croghan's advice centered about two main points: the guaranteeing to the Indians of the permanent possession of

---

[1] *Massachusetts Historical Collections,* fourth series, 9:321, 327.
[2] Johnson, *Papers,* 4:341.

their hunting grounds and the establishing of trade with them on a basis that would be agreeable to both the Indians and the British trading interest. In a letter written in January, 1764, Croghan submitted his proposals to the Board of Trade and brought home to these Englishmen the importance of following the policy outlined. Several factors worked to his advantage in the matter of getting his plan adopted. For one thing, he represented a large body of the merchants of Philadelphia, including the houses of Baynton & Wharton, and Franks, Simon, Trent & Company, who had made him their delegate in presenting their memorial before the Board of Trade for compensation for their losses in the Indian wars. He also spoke in the interest of the London merchants, who had obviously much to gain from the marketing of their goods in the Indian country. Still another advantage he had was a political one. British political circles were much agitated by the issue of "Wilkes and Liberty" in 1764, and the Whig party, then in power, was much embarrassed by the Wilkes opposition. It was the ministry's desire to prevent the Amherst policy that had brought about the Pontiac War from getting into public discussion. Hence action was delayed on Croghan's Indian proposals until Parliament had adjourned. After the adjournment the Board of Trade soon took up Croghan's matter. On July 12 Croghan wrote in triumph to Sir William Johnson announcing the agreement of the Board on "a plan for ye futer Manidgement of yr Departments & the Indian Trade." The plan made the despised "managers" completely independent of the military officers, and Croghan had no doubt that this fact would "be no small mortification to some people." It was an elaborate plan centralizing Indian management in the hands of the superintendent and his deputies. There were to be thirteen trading posts in the northern department at which all trade must be carried on under the supervision of an interpreter, a gunsmith, a commissary, and a deputy, who was to visit and inspect each post at least once a year. Prices were to be fixed by the superintendent and enforced by the commissary. Military officials were not to deal with the Indians except through the Indian department officials.[3]

The execution of this plan depended entirely on the securing of adequate funds, and since Parliament had adjourned, money from that source was not available. For reasons that give rise to speculation as to their motives, the signal was given to the military department to set aside some of its funds for the inauguration of the program. The first step in this inauguration was the distribution of presents to the Indians where such presents would do the most good. At the time that Croghan reported the Board of Trade's action to Sir William he also announced something that is not to be found in the published versions of the plan itself, that is, that the northern Indian department was to be given seven thousand pounds a year out of the appropriations for military expenditures "for presents to ye Indians & other Expences." "Thire Lordshipes Say," continued Croghan, "that ye Commander in Cheeffe will furnish you with what presents is Nesesary att present for ye Indians." This method of supplying funds was to last, however, only as long as the Indians continued to be hostile, and after that it was hoped that a tax on the Indian trade, to be approved by Parliament, would provide the necessary funds.[4]

It is clear that the application of the plan was on a quite temporary, not to say precarious, footing. Indeed Parliament never was to supply money for it and insisted that it was the duty of the colonies to provide the necessary funds. The fact that the colonies would not permit taxation without representation meant that the whole thing was eventually to be abandoned. But the actual though temporary application of the plan under military auspices was sufficient to provide the assurances necessary to get the Indians back to more normal hunting activity and to give the traders an opportunity to cater to the Indians' needs.

[3] *New York Colonial Documents,* 7:603, 604, 637-641; Johnson, *Papers,* 4:264-266, 267-271, 397, 462; Volwiler, *George Croghan,* 172, 175; Alvord, *Mississippi Valley in British Politics,* 1:221-223.

[4] Johnson, *Papers,* 4:463.

A Decade of British Muddling

Croghan returned to American shores late in 1764 filled with enthusiasm for the future—an enthusiasm that had more to do with his hopes for participation in the land and fur business in the Illinois country than it did with the hopes for the improvement of the upper Ohio Valley Indians. On December 4 he wrote to his deputy at Pittsburgh, Alexander McKee, desiring him to tell the Indians that he would soon be at Fort Pitt to open the fur trade and that they should be ready to bring in peltry on his arrival.[5]

With the good wishes of Johnson, of General Thomas Gage, the new commander-in-chief, and of the leading merchants of Philadelphia, Croghan arrived at Fort Pitt on February 28, 1765. Presents for the Indians, valued at twelve hundred pounds, and two thousand pounds in cash were sent with him. By holding back his presents during March and April he was able on May 10 to effect the return of all the white captives in the Shawnee country. On May 11 the first presents given to Indians by the British in over two years were distributed to the Shawnee, Delaware, and Mingo chiefs, and trade was declared formally opened. The tribes were so well satisfied that they appointed some of their members to accompany Croghan on a perilous mission to extend English power among the French-controlled tribes of the Wabash and Illinois country. Upon being informed of Croghan's success at Pittsburgh and of Johnson's success with the Delawares at Johnson Hall, Gage sought the co-operation of Governor John Penn of Pennsylvania in guaranteeing the safety of Indian goods from ravages such as the "Black Boys" of Cumberland County had committed on the goods of Croghan and others during the spring of 1765.[6]

A full application on the upper Ohio of the Board of Trade's plan for the control of commerce with the Indians was not to be made until it was felt sure that Croghan was to be success-

[5] Volwiler, *George Croghan*, 261-267; Bouquet Collection, Calendar, in Canadian Archives, *Report*, 1889, p. 312.
[6] Volwiler, *George Croghan*, 178-180; Carter, *Correspondence of General Thomas Gage*, 1:49, 59; *Pennsylvania Colonial Records*, 9:249, 263, 266.

ful in bringing the Wabash and Illinois Indian trade into the English system. In fact, so far as the British merchants and political imperialists were concerned, Fort Pitt and the upper Ohio Valley were interesting only as essential stepping-stones to the Illinois country, and when it finally became apparent by 1768 that the Illinois trade could never become part of an upstream transmontane system, interest in Pittsburgh lagged. Thus during the summer of 1765, trade was held under strict control by the Fort Pitt commandant, Captain William Murray, in conformity with orders from General Gage not to let any traders go into the Indian country. The Indians complained, but, according to Gage, in his report to Johnson of September 30, "they were told the Inconvenience of it, and seemed to be satisfied." Then when news came in of Croghan's favorable reception on the Wabash and the Illinois and of Captain Thomas Stirling's impending occupation of Fort de Chartres, Sir William Johnson decided to put the Board of Trade's plan into complete operation at Fort Pitt. Alexander McKee was thereupon appointed commissary for Fort Pitt at a salary of 150 pounds a year, and two permanent interpreters and a gunsmith were appointed. Similar establishments were made at Fort de Chartres, Detroit, Niagara, and Oswego.[7]

The British had no sooner muddled into this system of trade control than they began to muddle out again. The system was on a false basis to begin with, since it had not received the approval of Parliament. Moreover, it was simply inconceivable to the Indians that the whole Indian trade of the upper Ohio Valley sould be confined to Fort Pitt. The Indians wanted traders to come to their own country, and the British military forces were not powerful enough to stop traders from catering to the Indians' wishes. As early as July 6, 1766, Croghan wrote to Gage from the Shawnee country on the Scioto that he had been obliged to send the Shawnee a consignment of goods "as they [com]plained of the Distance to Fort Pitt

[7] Johnson, *Papers*, 4:848, 852; 5:76, 442-445; Volwiler, *George Croghan*, 182-188; Carter, *Correspondence of General Thomas Gage*, 2:385-387.

. . . and our not suffering any French [to] come amongst them." This transaction involved permitting a trader connected with the mercantile house of Baynton, Wharton, and Morgan to go to the Shawnee country and erect a store, much to the embarrassment of General Gage and more so to the Pittsburgh traders who had set up their stores in conformity with the regulations. The Pittsburghers demanded that something be done to protect them from the losses threatened by this unfair competition. Gage was evidently uncertain as to whether Croghan's measure was essential to the success of the latter's second visit, in 1766, to the Illinois country, and he therefore let the matter drop with an inquiry to Johnson.[8]

However temporary was the Baynton store in 1766, there was nothing temporary about the traders who, according to Croghan's report in the fall of 1767, "went from this last Winter to Trade in the Indian Countrys unknown to Capt Murray" and who "are still amongst them." And in that same fall, Baynton, Wharton, and Morgan joined the clamor against those trading outside of Pittsburgh. Through their Pittsburgh agent, John Campbell, they complained to Croghan on December 18, 1767, of a "Number of Lawless persons" at Redstone who "have lately forced a Settle[ment and opened] a Trade at one half the Rates agreed upon by the Com[missary of] Indian Affairs and the chiefs of the Indian Tribes." Campbell claimed that the leader of these outlaws, Colonel Michael Cresap of Maryland, was entirely responsible for the murdering of a Delaware chief there earlier in the year.[9]

How the Indians felt about the situation was indicated by the message of the Delaware chief, Netawatwees, entrusted to two white men for delivery to Captain Murray at Pittsburgh. "I desire," said Netawatwees, "you wou'd inform the great [general that] we are very desirous of having some Traders to [come] & Trade . . . [There are] traders both English &

[8] Johnson, *Papers,* 5:307, 346, 384, 399.
[9] Johnson, *Papers,* 5:738; 6:19. The murder referred to was of a Delaware chief named Captain Peter, who was killed in a quarrel over rum at the mouth of the Cheat River in the spring of 1767. Johnson, *Papers,* 6:524.

French in other Towns for [we know] them & know that they are there, & do trade there   [We do not] see any Reason why that which is allowed to them [is]refused to us. We have done every thing as we promised [to] Sir William Johnson, & think that we deserve these things [as] well as others. I desire, you would also tell him . . . that if no traders are allowed to come to our Towns it will hurt the trade of the Fort [*Pitt*] very much   when our Hunters comes in [*to the Delaware towns*] they will not go to the Fort, but . . . [will keep] their Skins by them to see what will be done and if no Traders are sent, they will carry them to the Traders that are in the other Towns; or will get some of them [to] come here & Trade. And particular we desire that John Gibson be sent to this Town; as we know him, & that he is a Good Man."¹⁰

The practices of the traders, both the English ones that "rove at Pleasure" and the French from St. Louis, caused Gage, who had once expected great things of the English system, to declare to Lord Shelburne on February 22, 1767, that it "is found upon Tryal not to Answer." "It would be a good Plan," said Gage, "if it could be executed universaly, but the Posts cannot be multiplied to the Degree Necessary to compleat it. . . . the Traders complain that they are prevented from getting the Quantitys of Furrs, they could procure from Nations who live at a great Distance from the Posts, were they not restrained from going to them; which gives the French Traders an advantage over them who go and reside amongst such Tribes . . . It is also so contrary to the old Custom of Trade . . . and they [*the Indians*] find so much more Trouble than formerly to procure their Necessarys, that the Indians are in general very averse to the Plan; are desirous that all Traders should come amongst them, and encourage them to act contrary to their Regulations."¹¹

The British government was not disposed to undertake the establishment of the posts that were, in Gage's opinion, neces-

¹⁰ Johnson, *Papers*, 5:381.
¹¹ Carter, *Correspondence of General Thomas Gage*, 1:113, 123.

sary to make the plan a good one. Parliament was less than ever inclined to undertake to appropriate money for the expenses, since the partial application of the funds in use had not produced the expected trade boom in the Illinois country. Moreover, by 1768 the American colonies had shown themselves averse to submitting to any and all types of taxation imposed by the British Parliament and were not disposed to tax themselves effectively. Thus on April 15, 1768, there were issued from Whitehall the king's official orders to abandon the control of the Indian trade. The order came in the form of a lengthy communication issued to General Gage and to all the governors of the American colonies, informing them of His Majesty's pleasure in turning the control of Indian trade over to them. The king also felt called upon to remind the colonies that it was his royal consideration and generosity that had led him to protect them against the Indians since 1763, when the colonies might have taken care of themselves "at no other Expence than the temporary Abandonment of a few straggling Settlements upon the Frontiers." What the colonists thought of His Majesty's suggestion is well known. No colony, save New York, appropriated a penny for assuming the burdens imposed. The official attitude of the General Assembly of Pennsylvania is typical. Gage proposed to Governor Penn on March 24, 1769, that the colony replace the commissaries, interpreters, and gunsmiths, about to be dismissed. Penn passed the matter along to the Assembly, which replied on May 24, "We ... are cheerfully disposed to give the utmost Attention to maintaining and preserving the Peace . . . and where our Laws for regulating the Trade . . . appear to be deficient, to alter and amend them; but as our attempting to extend the Laws of this Province beyond the Limits thereof, would be vain and ineffectual to regulate and restrain the Traders from the adjacent Colonies, We conceive it is not in our Power to apply a Remedy adequate to the Occasion."[12]

[12] Carter, *Correspondence of General Thomas Gage*, 2:61, 62; *Pennsylvania Colonial Records*, 9:582, 592; Alvord, *Mississippi Valley in British Politics*, 2:43-60.

Thus from 1768 to 1774, trade regulation in the upper Ohio Valley went from one extreme to another, and Indians who once complained of too much restriction were soon complaining of too little. This abandonment of control left trading transactions in a chaotic condition and subject to the practices of profit-mad and rapacious private traders. By the removal from the Indian department of the official overseers of trade, Indian administration was made dependent on the military arm, represented by the commandants and their forces at the various posts. The resulting military control of Indian affairs, a slender reed on which to rely for the preservation of peace, was rendered even more ineffectual by the gradual withdrawal of troops from the frontiers, which were to be used to awe the rebellious colonists in the East, and by the abandonment of certain frontier posts, including Fort Pitt. In 1772 the only forts left between the Ohio and the Lakes were Niagara, Detroit, and Michilimackinac, in contrast to the once highly organized and most effectual network of defenses established by the French. At these three posts were the only military forces, interpreters, and gunsmiths available to keep order among all the Indians of that vast region. In this connection it should be remembered that the Indians were entirely dependent upon the white men for firearms and their repair and for the needed ammunition. Moreover, the effect of the agreements of the rebellious colonists not to import goods from England augmented the prices of Indian supplies to a point that left the suspicious Indians without some of the necessaries to which they had become accustomed in payment for the products of their hunting. The general result was, according to one historian, that from 1763 to 1775, "instead of an increase in the number and value of furs and skins imported into England as a result of the French cession of the great fur-bearing regions of Canada and the Northwest," there was "a decided decrease each year."[13]

[13] Volwiler, *George Croghan*, 226; Carter, *Great Britain and the Illinois Country*, 94; Alvord, *Illinois Country*, 274-277.

A Decade of British Muddling

Repeatedly did the tribes recall to the English the lamentable state to which trading conditions had been reduced since the days of the French. In 1769 Sir William wrote of the Seneca that they had expected to receive the same treatment from the English that they had from the French, "that the latter repeatedly told them they would not, that they found it too true & that they were full of resentment thro' disappointment." At German Flats in New York at a congress in July, 1770, the Six Nations complained that the British had promised them that peace would assure them trade but that instead, "it is now worse, than it was before, for we cannot get goods at all at present, and we hear from all Traders, that nobody will bring in any, and that you have none for yourselves." Confusion and chaos, moreover, were reported from every quarter. Many of the traders who had wished the British commissarial system to be replaced by the older and less restrained method, now saw the necessity of a strict policy in order to control the increasing numbers of unprincipled and ruthless American traders. Rum had become one of the most important articles of trade, and Indian villages became scenes of drunkenness, debauchery, and riot, where the proud and virile representatives of a stoic race threw tradition to the wind and sold all their goods to experience the wild abandonment of joy which this strange firewater brought to them. After the congress of German Flats in July, 1770, Sir William Johnson reported that the Indians complained of the "great cargoes of Rum, which (of late in particular) are sent amongst them to their ruin as they call it; many Traders carry little or nothing else, because their profits upon it are so considerable," and he stated that it gave "encouragement to the meanest and most profligate Traders to go amongst them; in that, neither capacity or knowledge of the Indians, or their language is necessary for the sale of it."[14]

While the British muddled and the Indians suffered in the field of trade, a similar development was taking place in the

[14] *New York Colonial Documents*, 8:184, 226, 239.

matter of land.[15] In spite of the fact that the proclamation of October 7, 1763, pledged the English to no further transmontane encroachments on Indian lands, little more than a year had passed before official plans were being made for a cession beyond the mountains. The particular sufferers in this respect were the Shawnee and Delawares, who from 1765 to 1774 were forced to go through the painful process of seeing a great part of their hunting grounds torn from them by the superior power of the British and the overbearing Iroquois. The former tribes, it will be remembered, had been forced as a penalty for their part in Pontiac's War to forfeit their right to and use of the lands south and east of the Ohio River and had had notice to that effect served on them by their Iroquois overlords at Johnson Hall in 1765. The treaty of May 8, 1765, signed by the Delawares at that time and by the Shawnee and Mingo on July 4, specifically stated "that whenever His Majesty shall be pleased to direct that Limits shall be settled between his subjects and the Indians with their consent, The Delawares engage to abide by whatever Limits shall be agreed upon between the English and the Six Nations, and shall never disturb His Majesty's Subjects on that Account." The difficulty was, of course, that it was the Six Nations, or Iroquois, who were to make the decision on the boundary, for the obvious reasons that the lands belonged to the Iroquois and that they had remained neutral (with the exception of part of the Seneca) in Pontiac's War while the other tribes had taken up the hatchet.

There was no doubt in the minds of the Delawares, Shawnee, and Mingo that the Ohio River would be chosen by the Iroquois as the western boundary of the cession. In the very presence of the Delaware delegates at Johnson Hall on May 2, 1765, Sir William had asked the Iroquois what boundary they would like. The Iroquois at first named a boundary entirely east of the mountains, but when Sir William rebuked them for it they described a line the western part of which ran

[15] The establishment of a boundary line was part of the plan of the Board of Trade in 1764 for the management of Indian affairs. *New York Colonial Documents,* 7:641.

up the west branch of the Susquehanna to Kittanning and down the Ohio to the Tennessee River. Sir William, of course, perceived that this meant the loss to the Shawnee of their hunting grounds south of the Ohio, and in order to make sure that the Delawares and Shawnee were conscious of what the Iroquois were doing, he warned the Six Nations in words that could not be mistaken. "As what you have proposed about the Boundary," he stated, "is your own free proposition, and since you say you are the Owners of all the land you spoke about, I expect never to hear any grumbling about it." The Iroquois replied that the whole confederacy had agreed to the cession and that all the Indians concerned would be informed of it "at a Publick meeting in the Shawanese Country, where all the Western Nations often hold their Councils." Nothing was said about compensation, but time was to show that the Shawnee and Delawares were not going to sit idly by while the absentee overlords pocketed all the proceeds from the sale of Kentucky. It should be stated, however, that the Delawares were not as interested in the boundary settlement as the Shawnee. Their interest in the Kentucky grounds had always been negligible, and the cession did not include most of the Allegheny Valley lands that had until recently been used by them. Although many of them still lived on the Beaver River, the main part of their western population had migrated to the waters of the Muskingum, the Tuscarawas, and the Cuyahoga during the years of warfare.[16]

Although the British let their plans for a boundary settlement lapse after 1765, there was no such lapse on the part of the frontiersmen. Beginning in the summer of 1765, white settlers poured into the Monongahela Valley. This produced a

---

[16] *New York Colonial Documents,* 7:725-728, 734, 735, 740. A list of the different nations and tribes is in "A Selection of George Croghan's Letters," in Thwaites, *Early Western Travels,* 1:168. Although the Shawnee depended largely on Kentucky for their hunting, they had left western Pennsylvania entirely and in 1765 lived in the valley of the Scioto and on some of the western affluents of the Muskingum River. In defense of the Iroquois it must be said that they had on their hands a quarrel of their own with the Albany land grabbers and were seeking to appease Johnson.

feeling of desperation among the Indians, especially the Shawnee and Delawares, that all but precipitated an Indian war in 1768. Such a war was prevented chiefly by a belated willingness on the part of Pennsylvania to distribute presents to these tribes in a crisis and by the fact that the powerful Iroquois could be brought to frown upon the discontented ones. The squatters started their work in the spring of 1765 as soon as peace had been declared at the council at Fort Pitt on May 11. At a conference at Fort Pitt a year later, on May 24, 1766, the Shawnee, Delawares, Mingo, and Wyandot complained of this sudden invasion. Croghan, in reporting the conference to Gage, said, "As soon as the peace was made last Year, contrary to our Engagements to them [*the Indians*], a number of our people came over the Great Mountain and settled at Redstone Creek & upon the Monongahela, before they had given the Country to the King." This conduct, along with several murders of Indians by whites in the same region, led the Indians "to dread the consequences that may attend our Inhabitants and their young Warriors mixing so soon together." They declared that if the whites continued in this conduct the Indian nations would not be accountable for the future conduct of their warriors. Croghan told Gage that if effectual measures could not be found to remove the Redstone squatters and protect the Indians from being murdered till a boundary could be settled, "the Consequences may be dreadful, & We involved in all the Calamitys of another general War."[17]

The result was a veritable flood of proclamations. Captain Murray at Fort Pitt dispatched a subordinate, Alexander Mackey, to Redstone along with some Indians and posted a notice requiring all settlers to return at once to their "several Provinces," on pain of having all their goods seized and their persons driven off the land by armed force. Next on the list of

[17] The discussion of the settlers and of the measures taken against them in this and the two following paragraphs is based on *Pennsylvania Colonial Records*, 9:322, 323, 327, 349, 353; *Pennsylvania Archives*, first series, 4:251, 255; Carter, *Correspondence of General Thomas Gage*, 1:95, 100, 133, 147, 148; Johnson, *Papers*, 5:374, 560, 574.

those issuing proclamations was Governor Francis Fauquier of Virginia, who, on July 31, 1766, proclaimed that all the intruders were "immediately to evacuate" the Monongahela lands and if they failed to do so, "they must expect no protection or mercy from Government, and be exposed to the revenge of the exasperated Indians." On September 23 Governor John Penn of Pennsylvania decreed that all intruders on lands beyond the mountains were "immediately to evacuate & abandon them" and that all such intruders in the future were to be subject to "the severest Penalties of the Law" and to a denial of any settlement rights normally accruing to first comers. General Gage added his voice to the clamor and on July 2 offered to assist the governors of New Jersey, Pennsylvania, and Virginia with troops to evict the settlers. On September 13 none other than Lord Shelburne, British secretary of state for the southern department, took cognizance of the Redstone settlers and demanded that severe measures be taken against them by both Johnson and Gage. By December Governor Fauquier had issued three proclamations of banishment and despaired of their efficacy. To Governor Penn he wrote on December 11, "I find with you, no Regard is paid to Proclamations, and I can expect no great good from them."

The effect of these proclamations was negligible. The spring of 1767 brought a renewal of complaints by the Indians and a recognition by Gage and others that something besides proclamations was needed. In June Croghan and Murray had their hands full at Fort Pitt placating the Indians with promises and without presents. The tribes complained bitterly of more murders by the Redstone people and of the driving of game away from their hunting grounds. They said that the squatters told them that "They had the King's orders for making settlements there, and that they would not suffer any Indians whatever to Pass over or hunt on them." Croghan finally got the Indians to promise to keep the peace and to go home. The danger was so great, however, that Murray at once led a detachment to Redstone and in the presence of a hundred settlers commanded them to disperse. He resorted to the unusual practice of having the Indians themselves tell the settlers what would happen if they remained. According to Murray, the whites promised to remove immediately. On the way back to Fort Pitt the troops destroyed "as many Hutts as they could find."

But even troops were of no avail. Croghan reported to Johnson on October 18, 1767, from Fort Pitt, "Notwithstanding all the trouble that has been taken [to re]moove the People settled on Redstone Creek, & Cheat [River] I am well Assured there are double the Number of Inhabi[tants] in those two Settlements that ever was before." Even Gage admitted the futility of mere eviction when he wrote to Governor Penn on December 7, "As they [*the settlers*] met with no Punishment, we learn they are returned again to the same Encroachments on Red Stone Creek and Cheat River, in greater numbers than ever." The attitude of the whites is reflected in the rescue by white sympathizers of some settlers whom Governor Fauquier had caused to be jailed for murdering Indians. "All the People of the Frontiers," reported Gage to Shelburne on October 10, "from Pensylvania to Virginia inclusive, openly avow, that they will never find a Man guilty of Murther, for killing an Indian."[18]

War was fully expected to come with the spring of 1768. "Allmost [every] Body," wrote Croghan to Johnson on September 25, 1767, from Fort Pitt, "in this part of the Cuntry Expect [an] Indian Warr Next Spring Except y^r hono[ur] Can prevent itt." A month later he again wrote, "Nothing now, will in my opinion prevent a War [except] taking a Cession from them [*the Indians*], & paying them for their Lands." In December at Fort Pitt Croghan again had to go through the

[18] Johnson, *Papers,* 5:737; *Pennsylvania Colonial Records,* 9:403; Carter, *Correspondence of General Thomas Gage,* 1:152. See Johnson's expression of the frontier feeling, in *New York Colonial Documents,* 7:852. In the early spring of 1767 Johnson also reported rumors of a group of Virginians, apparently led by Michael Cresap, who were organizing a company to make "a large settlement near *to Ohio.*" It was reported that if the Indians made any opposition, the settlers would "cut off some of the nearest Indian Villages." *New York Colonial Documents,* 7:895, 914.

ordeal of placating the Indians with many words and few presents. He denounced the squatters and said the king would surely compensate the Indians in the spring of 1768. He then withdrew from the scene of impending hostilities as he had done in the months preceding the outbreak of the Pontiac War. A month had not elapsed after the making of these promises before an event took place that might well have been the signal for the outbreak of Indian war. This was the famous one-man murder of ten Iroquois on January 10 and 11, 1768, by Frederick Stump on what is now Stump's Run near Middleburg in Snyder County. This outrageous crime so shocked the Iroquois nation that these Indians descended at once on Johnson Hall to demand immediate and complete satisfaction.[19]

Although the murder was in eastern Pennsylvania and although the victims were Iroquois, the Shawnee and Delawares were highly incensed. Alexander McKee reported from Fort Pitt on February 13, 1768, "They were [suspicious] enough of us before, and very discontented; but this [affair] of Stumps, has made the Warriors of the different nations [jeal]ous." The settlers in the Monongahela Valley, fearing an Indian war, began at once to abandon their settlements. By March 1 Croghan was so alarmed by McKee's reports from Fort Pitt that he wrote to Johnson saying that a conference must be held there at once at which considerable presents must be made. If this was not done the Delawares and Shawnee would "attend a Meeting of thire own which [they] Cartainly have in agitation & if that [Meeting] Takes place I fair Hostilitys will [be the] Consequences." Johnson, however, had already advised Croghan on February 29 to set out for Fort Pitt at once to meet the Indians in that area, while he himself took care of the Iroquois. But the question still remained: where was Croghan to get the money to placate the

[19] Johnson, *Papers*, 5:701, 737; 6:10; Sipe, *Indian Wars*, 404-486. Although Stump was apprehended and jailed in Carlisle, he was rescued by a mob on March 23, 1768. He was never tried.

tribes now that the English had turned over Indian control to the colonies? The answer to this came from the colony of Pennsylvania. The Stump affair so thoroughly frightened the Quaker legislators that they suddenly took drastic measures to prevent the outbreak of war. On February 3, 1768, a law was passed and a proclamation issued ordering the evacuation of the Indian country by the Monongahela squatters on penalty of death, and commissioners were subsequently dispatched to order them off. In the same month three thousand pounds were appropriated by the Assembly, thirteen hundred to be sent to Johnson as a present of condolence to the Iroquois, and twelve hundred to be sent to Pittsburgh to be distributed by specially appointed commissioners to the Delawares, the Shawnee, and the Iroquois of the Ohio. The spectacle of the parsimonious Pennsylvania legislature thus thoroughly stirred from its traditional lethargy is an astonishing one.[20]

But it was not merely the unexpected generosity of Pennsylvania that averted war. It was also the fact that in the 1768 proceedings at Redstone and Pittsburgh, the power of the Iroquois was brought to bear on the upper Ohio Valley Indians. The reason was that, although the Iroquois were discontented during the years from 1765 to 1768, their discontent was caused by the fact that the lands were being occupied without being paid for; while the Shawnee and Delawares were discontented because they were the users of the invaded lands. One of the early examples of Iroquois tampering with the situation is seen in the fact that when the Pennsylvania commissioners assigned to the job of removing the Monongahela squatters performed their task faithfully, their work was almost entirely nullified by pleas of Mingo Indians to let the squatters stay till the pending treaty council at Fort Pitt.[21] At that council, held from April 26 to May 9, 1768, the same

[20] Johnson, *Papers*, 6:101, 110, 122, 129; *Pennsylvania Archives*, first series, 4:283; *Pennsylvania Colonial Records*, 9:481, 483; Volwiler, *George Croghan*, 219.
[21] *Pennsylvania Colonial Records*, 9:507. The commissioners were John Steel, John Allison, Christopher Lemes, and James Potter.

thing happened. Over eleven hundred Indians of the Iroquois, Delaware, Shawnee, Mahican, and Wyandot nations, not counting the women and children, were present. After an exchange of condolences, an airing of grievances, especially by the Shawnee, the presentation of over one thousand pounds' worth of presents, and the declaration that white messengers would proceed to Redstone to order the squatters to remove if four Indians would accompany them and order them off in the name of the Iroquois, the latter, who had dominated the proceedings, declined to send the Indian messengers on so "disagreeable" an errand. As has been seen, the Indians that had been with Captain Murray at Redstone in the spring of 1767, who were probably Shawnee or Delawares, had not had these same compunctions. The reasons for the scruples of the Six Nations in 1768 in regard to the settlers were given by the Iroquois, Guyasuta, who showed that his people fully expected a treaty of cession in the near future. According to Guyasuta, the warriors who had been suggested as messengers to the Redstone did not wish to incur the squatters' ill will, because if these settlers should be removed they would only return to their settlements "when the English have purchased the Country from us." In other words, the Iroquois saw no reason for taking drastic measures in a matter that was to them merely one of principle. The Indians thus dispersed to their respective hunting grounds, the Pennsylvania treaty commissioners returned to the East, and the Redstone squatters remained where they were.[22]

To the upper Ohio Indians the council at Fort Pitt of April and May, 1768, was obviously a prelude to the treaty of Fort Stanwix, held later in the year, where the great cession of land tentatively agreed upon in the spring of 1765 was finally put through. Shelburne's notice of January 5, 1768, conveying the news of the king's authorization of a purchase, had arrived

[22] *Pennsylvania Colonial Records*, 9:514-543. The Pennsylvania treaty commissioners were John Allen and Joseph Shippen, Jr. In May, 1774, at the time of the murder of Logan's family by Daniel Greathouse, the Mingo were to have reason to regret their consideration for the Redstone settlers. See chapter vii.

in New York on April 18, and was no doubt known to the Indians at Fort Pitt before the adjournment of the council on May 9. But it was not a very joyful prelude for the Shawnee and Delawares. These tribes saw their frank expressions of discontent at Fort Pitt disavowed by the overbearing Iroquois. Thonissahgarawa, an Iroquois, on May 4 publicly rebuked the Shawnee for mentioning their desire that there be no English forts in the West, and Guyasuta followed with a rebuke to the same nation for requesting that there be no more expeditions like Croghan's and Stirling's to the Illinois. Chief Beaver of the Delawares on May 6 asked for trade reforms and the exclusion of white hunters from the lands between the Allegheny River and the mountains. But these requests were practically ignored. The most genuine sentiment expressed during the proceedings was that of the Shawnee, Kissinaughtha, who replied to the Iroquois rebuke, "Though you say we were the only Nation that has mentioned this to you, we know that all other Nations of Indians wish, as well as we, that there were no Forts in this Country." The treaty was a disappointment to these tribes, and after its adjournment they sent delegates among the Wabash and Illinois Indians to seek encouragement.[23]

The outcome of the treaty of Fort Stanwix of 1768 was just what the Shawnee and Delawares had expected. There were too many other important interests, represented by governors, land speculators, traders, and missionaries, to be satisfied at the council for the petty desires of two small tribes to be of any weight, especially when the above interests stood to gain what the Shawnee and Delawares were to lose. The master of ceremonies at this epochal treaty, Sir William Johnson, really did not care whether these tribes attended or not and relied on the fact that they had had to submit to the judgment of the Iroquois on the boundary matter in 1765. When he learned that they might not be present, he wrote to General Gage on

[23] Johnson, *Papers*, 6:200, 333; *New York Colonial Documents*, 8:2; *Pennsylvania Colonial Records*, 9:529, 530, 537, 539.

A Decade of British Muddling

August 24, "Altho' I should have been glad that they were present, I can see no particular necessity for it, as the Six Nations are the undoubted Owners, and as such Considered by all the rest, who at a former meeting with me promised to pay due submission to whatever the 6 Nations shod agree upon."[24]

Hence when the council commenced on October 24 and the Shawnee and Delawares actually attended, they were lost in the crowd. Some of the Iroquois told Sir William on October 29 that the news they had received from the Shawnee indicated considerable anti-English agitation among them and the tribes to the west. The Spaniards and the French, Sir William was told, had for a long time been urging these tribes to take up arms against the English and had invited them to a council on the Mississippi "for that purpose." Many had been upon the point of responding but were waiting to observe the outcome of the treaty of Fort Stanwix. Possessed of this information, Sir William waited until everything had been agreed upon with the Iroquois. Then, on November 4, turning to the Shawnee and Delawares, he told them all that he knew about their relations with the enemies of England and, having thus covered them with guilt and shame, told the unfortunate users of the Kentucky hunting grounds to behave themselves and to "pay due regard to the Boundary Line now made."[25]

As has been stated, the Indians most adversely affected by the treaty of Fort Stanwix were the Shawnee. Although the ministry had expected the Great Kanawha to be the western boundary line, Johnson had little difficulty in persuading the authorities to accept the larger cession offered by the Iroquois. The fact that the British ministry in 1769 announced that it would countenance no settlements west of the Great Kanawha was to mean little, as the events of 1774 were to prove. The treaty deprived the Shawnee of their most important hunting grounds, the Kentucky country. No other tribe received

[24] Johnson, *Papers*, 6:333.
[25] *New York Colonial Documents*, 8:123, 131. For the complete proceedings at Fort Stanwix, see *New York Colonial Documents*, 8:111-137. See also Alvord, *Mississippi Valley in British Politics*, 2:61-78.

such a setback by the provisions of this treaty. It was not merely that the Shawnee received no part of the proceeds. It was also that the tribe was in danger of being deprived of hunting that was necessary for its very existence. The country that had been the ancient home of the Shawnee now became the object of the white hunters, settlers, and land speculators. From 1769, when Daniel Boone led the vanguard of the white invasion, to 1774, when the first settlers began to come in, the Shawnee looked on in sullen disapproval, their anger gradually mounting. In 1769 they told Boone to go home and not to bother them.[26] In 1774 they found themselves obliged to resort to war. In the meantime they looked about for allies.

As soon as they had learned of the sale at Fort Stanwix (now Rome, New York), they sent messengers to the Iroquois seeking to get them to disavow the cession. A part of the Seneca led by a chief called Gaustarax favored the Shawnee's request, but the rest of the Seneca and Iroquois would not give ear to it. Thereupon Gaustarax secretly sent belts among the nations to the west of the Shawnee, as Pontiac had done before him, in the vain hope that conditions would lead other tribes to prepare for another revolt.[27] But conditions were not as universally bad in 1769 as they had been in 1762. Moreover, counterplots were going on under the official auspices of none other than the head of the British Indian department.

The discontent among the Shawnee was clearly recognized by General Gage in his report to Lord Hillsborough on January 6, 1770. Gage wrote, "The Cession . . . is the Cause of all the Commotions that have lately happened, among the Indians. Great part of the Lands ceded, were claimed by the Six Nations by Right of Antient Conquest, and tho' the Tribes who resided near them admitted the Right, they felt no Inconvenience from it further than being forced to acknowledge a Superiority in the Six Nations. But now that the Six Nations

[26] See chapter 1.
[27] New York Colonial Documents, 8:316.

have Sold the Lands as Lords of the Soil, kept all the Presents and Money arising from the Sale, to their own use, and that the White People are expected in Consequence of it, to Settle on their hunting Grounds; these dependent Indians, are exasperated to a great Degree."[28]

Sir William was, of course, aware of the unrest in the country beyond the Iroquois towns caused by the treaty of Fort Stanwix, and he decided in 1769 to find out personally what was going on. When he reached the Seneca, the westernmost nation of the Iroquois, he was informed by them in solemn council that they had done their best to keep order and had tried to dissuade their people from receiving certain belts that had been sent them but that they had not been entirely successful. These belts had their origin not only among the Shawnee, but among the more western tribes. The tribes on the Illinois and on the Wabash and elsewhere in the Ohio Valley, incensed at the new British trading tactics, were reported as having attacked and plundered several traders' boats, and Sir William was convinced from what he heard among the Seneca that they were only awaiting a favorable opportunity to commence hostilities against the whites. At about the same time General Gage reported news of a confederacy forming between the Ohio Indians and the tribes on the Miami and the Wabash. Sir William went no farther west than the Seneca country. He returned to Johnson Hall with a new idea.[29]

Confronted by tribal discontent in the West and unable to satisfy the Indians in regard to a trading policy, he now proposed to weaken Indian power by setting the tribes against each other—the policy of "divide and conquer." Sir William wrote to his superiors in England in February, 1770, that it was disagreeable to have to permit the Indians either "to cut each others throats, or risque their discharging their fury on our Traders and defenceless frontiers . . . but however disagreeable the alternative is, common policy and our own safety

[28] Carter, *Correspondence of General Thomas Gage*, 1:245.
[29] *New York Colonial Documents*, 8:173, 183, 184; Alvord and Carter, *Trade and Politics*, 59.

requires it." Nor did his superiors entirely disavow this policy; for he was informed by Hillsborough that "the King however unwillingly, cannot but approve of your adopting the alternative, and making the security of his subjects and the peace of the frontiers, the principal object of your attention . . . but it would be most pleasing to His Majesty, if it could be attained without encouraging the Savages in their barbarous attacks on each other."[30]

In the meanwhile the Cherokee and the Six Nations, perceiving the attitude of the officials toward the Indians of the Ohio Valley, immediately sought to turn the situation to their own advantage. The former nation proposed in the fall of 1769 to unite with the Six Nations "in order to attack several of the Southern & Western Nations who had acted as Enemys to both" and implied that British support would be expected. Delegations from both nations urged upon Sir William that the British had as much at stake as they had themselves and instanced recent attacks by the western tribes on British traders.[31]

This suggestion was a little too much even for Sir William. Alliances with the Indians would mean that in the case of war the British would be expected to do most of the fighting because of their greater strength, and the expense of such participation must be avoided at all costs. He therefore evaded giving a direct answer to the Six Nations and the Cherokee but promised to give his decision at the congress that was to assemble in July at German Flats. He counted on the Cherokee to check the ambitions of the more aggressive group of the Six Nations because he had received word that the Cherokee had denied that they were attempting to draw other tribes into war. He stated, however, that in the event that the Six Nations could not be diverted, "I shall in that case make it as much their own affair as possible."[32]

When the congress met at German Flats in July, 1770, the

[30] *New York Colonial Documents,* 8:204, 211.
[31] *New York Colonial Documents,* 8:203.
[32] *New York Colonial Documents,* 8:223, 224.

representatives of the Iroquois were strong for war. In public session their spokesmen announced that the principal reason for the calling of the assembly was to come to an agreement with the Cherokee, who were expected "to invite us to engage against their troublesome neighbours with whose conduct we are likewise much dissatisfied." At private conferences Sir William found that the majority of the warriors were "obstinately bent on a war" and would not listen to the older warriors who were under his influence. They insisted that they could no longer put up with the treatment accorded some of their tribes by the Wabash Indians and stated that, considering the grievances the English had against these same Indians and that they, the Six Nations, had heretofore aided the English in their projects, they felt that they could now expect full assistance from the whites. Sir William thus had a difficult problem to solve, but by appealing to the Indians' sense of fair play he was finally able to convince them that "war should never be carried on with any Nation without very sufficient reasons, and until all other measures have proved ineffectual." They therefore agreed to send a message to the Wabash and Illinois tribes, to be delivered by the Shawnee. In this message the Six Nations and the Cherokee reprimanded those tribes for their treatment of the British traders "which shews that you are not in your senses. Wherefore we now take you by the head, and shake you so, as to bring you to them, and also take that hatchet out of your hands, which you run about with, doing Mischief." They were warned that if they did not listen, "the consequence will prove fatal." The notification of the western tribes took place at a great council held at the Scioto plains in the heart of the Shawnee country. Johnson reported that the Indians in that quarter had planned to form a union as he had feared but that at the advice of the northern Indians and after "many debates in general resolutions for promoting peace amongst all the nations," they had decided to abandon their schemes.[33]

[33] The proceedings at German Flats in 1770 and Johnson's report to Hillsborough

The Shawnee also came in for their share of humiliation at German Flats in 1770. Knowing of their dissatisfaction with the treaty of Fort Stanwix, Johnson called the Shawnee into the presence of their Iroquois overlords and declared that the British king "did not require the Lands so far to the Southward, if it was of the least inconvenience to his Children." The Iroquois, said Sir William, had been well paid for this land. In spite of this, he declared, "I find that there are some of your Dependants who live by your toleration, and who never had any Title to the soil, who talk, as if they were dissatisfied with your Act, or doubted your authority." The purpose and effect of such talk was obvious. The Iroquois proudly protested that their title was not to be disputed, that they would take care of any nation that questioned it, and "that you may assure the King, that it was *our* property we justly disposed of, that we had full authority to do so."

Thus, behind the claims and ambitions of the Six Nations and the Cherokee for supremacy over other Indian tribes, did British policy seek to tame the western Indians. So successful did Sir William's finesse seem to Hillsborough that the latter congratulated the Indian superintendent and noted with approval "that those natural enmities and jealousies which subsist between one nation and another . . . are a full security against any hostilities which (they well know) must in the end terminate in their own destruction, & which therefore they will never attempt."[34]

It was not long before Sir William had again to resort to the use of his puppets, the Six Nations, to dispel a threatening confederacy. This time his efforts were directed against the plotters already referred to, the long-suffering Shawnee and the disaffected group of the Seneca under Gaustarax. In the summer of 1771 Sir William informed Hillsborough, from information received by George Croghan at Fort Pitt from a Shawnee Indian, that the Six Nations were "concerned in

are in *New York Colonial Documents,* 8:227-244, 262.
[34] *New York Colonial Documents,* 8:270.

exciting the Shawanese, Delawares, & many others to make war upon us." Whether or not the information was genuine cannot be determined. At any rate a congress of the Six Nations was immediately called for the purpose of demonstrating to the Indians that such matters could not be kept secret and with the hope that those who had instigated the trouble would be rendered suspicious of the others for having divulged their plans. When the congress was assembled, Sir William, reminding the Six Nations of their ancient obligations to transmit to him all important information, rebuked them sharply and told them that he had been surprised to hear from another source "of some dangerous transactions which might prove the ruin of those concerned."[35]

Sir William's action was emphatic and sweeping. The Six Nations were directed to assemble at Scioto plains all the nations involved and to collect and destroy every belt circulated by Gaustarax. A council was accordingly held in the summer of 1772, but the Wabash and Illinois tribes who had received the belts refused to attend. The Six Nations thereupon instructed them by messenger to bring the belts to the general council fire of the nation at Onondaga at a time named. Again the western tribes failed to appear. Whereupon Sir William warned the confederacy that either the offending tribes must be made to attend at once or the belts in question must be collected and delivered to him without delay. The Six Nations promised that they would comply with his demands and would also endeavor to "convince all Nations of their fidelity to Us . . . as a proof that they the Six Nations have no part in their designs." A second council was held at Onondaga in the spring of 1773 and once again the western tribes were absent. The Six Nations asked Sir William for one more chance. They had called them to Onondaga twice, they said, and wished to call them a third time "before we strike." Besides, they boldly asserted, the refusal of the tribes to attend "is much owing to

[35] For Johnson's efforts to maintain peace described in this and the two following paragraphs, see *New York Colonial Documents,* 8:280, 315, 364, 366.

the English themselves for these Nations were never hearty, and some of them, not even pretended friends to the English."

This was too much for Sir William. If the western Indians could not be tamed by the Six Nations, they could not be tamed at all, and the conquest of the Ohio Valley from the French would be fruitless because most of the Indians would still be under the influence of the French traders of Louisiana. He therefore demanded that more aggressive action be taken against these recalcitrant tribes. "There is no necessity," he said, "of your using so much delicacy with people, who so little deserve favor from your hands, especially as you are in a great measure accountable for the actions of those who have been always deemed your dependants:—and perhaps it were better that you brought them to reason, than by tollerating their depredations to expose them to the powerfull arm of the English, who will certainly no longer suffer them to Act as they have done with impunity."

But Sir William knew as well as anybody that the Iroquois were not going to war in behalf of the English if the English did not take the lead. Discontent was too widespread, even among the Six Nations, for the British to be justified in expecting them to attack the tribes of the West in behalf of British imperialism. Neither Great Britain nor the colonies were disposed to do anything in their own behalf, for financial and constitutional reasons. A turning point in American Indian affairs had been reached. The sphere of influence of the English so far as it depended upon their satellites, the Iroquois, had been permanently contracted. From now on, the British must either change their tactics and assume the responsibility of keeping the western Indians at peace, or leave them to the neglect of the American colonies and states, or return them to the benevolent care of their rivals, the French and Spanish. The better course seemed to be to leave the Wabash and Illinois Indians to the French influence, since this procedure would leave the Shawnee without friends to the west, and the proper manipulation of the Iroquois and the Delawares would leave them without friends to the east. For war with some of the Indians was inevitable and must be prepared for. The Earl of Dartmouth informed Sir William in 1773 that he feared that an Indian war was "an evil which sooner or later we must submit to; and the only comfort I have under this apprehension is . . . that you shall be able to convince those Indians who are endeavoring to create this Confederacy, that we have a sufficient number [of tribes] who are well attached to His Majestys Interest, and who will be eager on such an occasion to give testimony of their fidelity."[36] The fulfillment of this hope, which was "the only comfort" of his lordship, was to prove small comfort indeed to the Shawnee.

[36] *New York Colonial Documents,* 8:360.

7

Dunmore's War

THE SHAWNEE NATION, too remote from the French in Louisiana to benefit by their trade, was the most neglected and unfortunate tribe of the whole region of the Ohio Valley and the Great Lakes. The reader has followed these Indians through their unhappy vicissitudes from 1763 to 1774; he is now to witness them goaded into desperate warfare by the aggressions of American frontiersmen. This Shawnee war of 1774 is better known as Lord Dunmore's War.

At the close of his "Account of the Rise of the Indian War, 1774," Richard Butler, later Indian commissioner and agent of the United States and first superintendent of Indian affairs, wrote, "These Facts I think was sufficient to bring on a war with a Christian instead of a Savage People, and I do declare

it as my opinion that the Shawanese did not intend a war this
Season, let their future Intentions be what they might; and I
do likewise declare that I am afraid . . . that they will bring on
a general war, as there is so little pains taken to restrain the
common People whose prejudice leads them to greater lengths
than ought to be shown by civilized People, and their Superiors take too little if any pains, and I do really think is
much to blame themselves in the whole Affair."[1] This statement cannot, of course, be accepted at its face value without
making a careful examination of the circumstances of the outbreak. Butler was a trader to the Shawnee country and was,
therefore, partial. He also suffered severe losses as the result
of the war. Other sources must therefore be consulted.

As has been repeatedly pointed out, the main bone of contention between the whites and the Shawnee was the Kentucky country. In the fall of 1773 Sir William Johnson advised
Lord Dartmouth that the Shawnee were in a state of alarm
over the large numbers of people from Virginia who were
settling in this territory. That these settlers were "remote
from the influence and Seats of Government" tended to agi-
tate the fears of the Indians, as did also the fact that most of
the newcomers "set out with a general Prejudice against all
Indians and the young Indian Warriors or Hunters are too
often inclined to retaliate."[2]

Conscious that trouble was brewing and that war might
break out in the coming season, the British had the Shawnee
keep representatives at Fort Pitt from the fall of 1773 until
the spring of 1774. As spring approached, news of the intentions of a Kentucky surveying party organized by Colonel
William Preston, county surveyor of Fincastle County, and
his deputy, Captain John (Jack) Floyd, and of settlement
parties bound for that region, including such leaders as George
Rogers Clark and Michael Cresap, became current on the
frontiers. It is therefore not strange that on March 8 the

[1] *Pennsylvania Archives*, first series, 4:570.
[2] *New York Colonial Documents*, 8:396.

Shawnee took occasion to represent the situation as they saw
it to Alexander McKee, the deputy of Sir William Johnson, in
order that the British might be prepared to do them justice.
They referred to the fact that the king's orders restricted
settlement to the Great Kanawha River and pointed out that
the boundary agreement was being violated and that their
hunting grounds were being overrun. Although they disap-
proved of acts of retaliation committed by their young men,
they said it was out of their power to prevent such acts, "for
when they are disappointed in their hunting, and find the
woods covered with the White People . . . they are foolish
enough to make reprisals without waiting to apply to the great
men that shou'd redress their complaints and regulate the conduct of their White Brethren towards them."[3]

The Shawnee were on strong ground when they opposed
white intrusion by references to England's expressed wishes
on the subject. Johnson had been warned against allowing
settlement west of the Great Kanawha, and the British ministry had accepted the lands in that region in 1769 on condition
that no settlement be made thereon. Nobody could deny the
justice of the Shawnee argument, and the king's ministers
could not ignore it, for the prohibition had originated with
them. Lord Dunmore, governor of Virginia, was therefore
called on the carpet for permitting and encouraging these aggressions. His reply, addressed to Lord Dartmouth, consisted
of a confession of the inability of British authority to do anything whatever to protect the American Indian from the law-
lessness of the frontiersmen. He wrote that he still believed
that it was best not to allow any settlements beyond the
boundaries of the colonies as they were defined in 1770. He had
sought, he stated, to enforce the law against squatters, "but
My Lord I have learnt from experience that the established
Authority of any government in America, and the policy of
Government at home, are both insufficient to restrain the
Americans; and that they do and will remove as their avidity

[3] *New York Colonial Documents,* 8:462.

and restlessness incite them. . . . they do not conceive that Government has any right to forbid their taking possession of a Vast tract of Country, either uninhabited, or which Serves only as a Shelter to a few Scattered Tribes of Indians. Nor can they be easily brought to entertain any belief of the permanent obligation of Treaties made with those People, whom they consider, as but little removed from the brute Creation." Since the people could not be prevented from occupying the new country, there were in Dunmore's mind only three possible ways to handle the situation. One was "to Suffer these Emigrants to hold their Lands of, and incorporate with the Indians"; another was "to permit them to form a Set of Democratical Governments of their own, upon the backs of the old Colonies"; and the third way, the one finally adopted, was "to receive persons in their Circumstances, under the protection of Some of His Majesty's Governments already established."[4]

This statement shows that the frontiersmen were not only to have their own way in occupying the Indian lands, but were also to have the active support of government. In other words, the only real obligation that the British had assumed in respect to the Shawnee, which was to stop settlement and surveying at the Kanawha River, was shown to be worthless. Not only was this the case, but the British Indian department, at the same moment that it confessed the injustice of the attack on the Shawnee, proceeded to isolate them completely by deliberately forbidding the Delawares and the Six Nations to give them any aid. Officials were loud in condemnation of the frontiersmen, and, after the war was over and the Shawnee were crushed, Dunmore was rebuked for his policy, but nothing was done for this unfortunate tribe.[5] Power was left in the hands of the land-hungry frontiersmen and speculators. It was a new demonstration of the age-old fact that in human

[4] Thwaites and Kellogg, *Dunmore's War,* 368-372; Alvord, *Mississippi Valley,* 2:75, 76.
[5] *Pennsylvania Archives,* first series, 4:577.

affairs, might makes right. In 1772 William Crawford, frontier land speculator, wrote from the West that there were so many people eager for land that they were stealing it from one another when they could: "As soon as a man's back is turned another is on his land. The man that is strong and able to make others afraid of him seems to have the best chance as times go now."[6]

Foremost among the backers of surveyors and settlers in the Kentucky country was George Washington. Ever since 1767 Crawford had been working in northwestern Virginia in the interests of this future statesman, and Washington's instructions to him in that year typify the enterprising spirit of the pioneers. He wrote that he intended to make an attempt to secure some of the lands west of the mountains on which settlement had been forbidden by the king's proclamation of 1763, "notwithstanding the proclamation that restrains it at present ... for I can never look upon that proclamation in any other light (but this I say between ourselves) than as a temporary expedient to quiet the minds of the Indians." He was not in the least concerned by the claims of the Shawnee in the Kentucky country but relied fully on the fact that the land had been ceded to the English by the Six Nations. He viewed with equanimity Dunmore's plan to offer protection to settlers below the Great Kanawha in spite of the express prohibition against such settlements. In 1773 he wrote to Crawford that he had heard that Dunmore would grant patents for lands situated south of the Ohio River and that, as it would be desirable to have the claims surveyed without delay, he had asked Thomas Bullitt, official surveyor for the colony of Virginia, to have ten thousand acres surveyed for him. He wanted these lands as near the Scioto as possible, "but for the sake of better lands, I would go quite down to the Falls [*at Louisville*], or even below; meaning thereby to get richer and wider bottoms, as it is my desire to have my lands run out upon the banks of the Ohio." Bullitt, probably under the influence of

[6] Butterfield, *Washington-Crawford Letters*, 25.

Richard Butler, was so considerate of the rights of the Shawnee to the Kentucky lands that he had promised not only to
make compensation for them, but also to preserve their hunting rights. As his attitude did not coincide with that of Dunmore he had been recalled by the governor in the fall of 1773.
Washington therefore requested Crawford, if he were going
down the Ohio in his own interests, to get Dunmore's permission to make the location.[7]

It was not, however, until the spring of 1774 that Washington's survey was finally made. It was made, together with
surveys for such other eminent Virginians as Patrick Henry,
Dr. Hugh Mercer, Colonel William Christian, Colonel William
Preston, and Dr. John Connolly, by the official surveying
party under John Floyd, which, in spite of the objections of
the Shawnee, had proceeded with its plans. The Shawnee had
given ample and emphatic warning that such trespasses would
mean war. "What we have seen," they told McKee, "as well
as the constant assembling of our Brethren with Red flags
[*surveyors*] convince us that war is still apparent in their
minds, otherwise such preparations wou'd be laid aside."
Floyd and his party, however, persevered and on April 26 were
on the Ohio at the mouth of the Little Guyandot. There the
members of one of his advance parties, which had been captured by the Shawnee and held for three days, reported that
the Indians had taken all their belongings and let them go
and had told them that George Croghan, the deputy superintendent of Indian affairs, had directed the Indians "to kill
all the Virginians they could find on the River & rob & whip
the Pennsylvanians." The more intrepid of the party nevertheless continued down the river, making surveys and locations as they went, while Captain William Russell of the
Fincastle County scouting forces waited breathlessly for news
of them. The captain wrote to his chief, Colonel Preston,
"May God of his Infinite Mercy Shield him, and Company,
from the present appending Danger." Russell engaged Daniel

[7] Butterfield, *Washington-Crawford Letters,* 3, 9, 30, 33.

Boone and Michael Stoner "to search the Country, as low as the falls" to warn these men of their danger, but the effort was unavailing. The expedition ended in July on the Kentucky River when Floyd and a few others, returning to the main party after an excursion, found that its members "had gone off in the greatest precipitation, leaving him only this notice, written on a tree, 'alarmed by finding some people killed, we are gone down.'" The Shawnee, after repeated, determined, but peaceful warnings, had at last struck in self-defense. Floyd, with the remnants of the expedition, abandoned further surveying and returned home overland.[8]

While Floyd's party had been assembling on the waters of the Ohio in April, another party, including the famous George Rogers Clark, was meeting at the mouth of the Little Kanawha. The object of this group was to descend the river in a body to make "a settlement in Kentucky." Between eighty and ninety had set out, when news was brought in that an advance group of their hunters had been fired on near the mouth of the Great Kanawha. Accepting this as a challenge instead of as a warning, the party immediately decided to conduct an expedition overland to surprise and destroy the Shawnee town called Horsehead Bottom near the mouth of the Scioto. They selected Captain Michael Cresap as leader of the enterprise.

Cresap was a trader and farmer of western Maryland who had failed in business and, in 1774, had removed to the Ohio Valley, where he hoped to secure a title to some lands and make a living for his family. Six or seven young men had accompanied him for the purpose of clearing the land and building houses. It was his plan, as soon as he and his hands had settled a plantation on the Ohio below Wheeling, to follow Clark to Kentucky. When approached by Clark and his party, who were determined to attack the Shawnee, he advised them to abandon the idea, warning them that although such an

---

[8] Thwaites and Kellogg, *Dunmore's War*, 7, 32, 50, 110, 114, 118, 121, 123, 125; *New York Colonial Documents*, 8:462; *American Archives*, fourth series, 1:707.

attempt in all probability would be successful, it would bring on a war for which they would be blamed, "and perhaps justly." They accepted his advice and returned to Wheeling "to hear what was going forward." "As it was early in the spring," if the Indians were for peace, they would still have ample time to return to Kentucky.[9]

The atmosphere at Wheeling in the spring of 1774 was war-like. This frontier town was at the junction of two routes of migration to the Ohio, the river route from Pittsburgh and the overland route from Cumberland and Redstone. It was filled with crowds of expectant emigrants, all touched with the Kentucky fever and anxious to be the first to find the best locations in the promised land. The situation at Pittsburgh was almost as belligerent. Feeling there was rendered more tense by the uncertainty as to which jurisdiction the settle-ment was subject, Pennsylvania or Virginia. Ever since 1772, when the British had abandoned the fort at this place, fron-tier anti-Indian sentiment had increased, and the settlement had become more and more the center of the disorderly ele-ments that congregate in frontier towns on the eve of anticipated excitements. It had long been expected that the Vandalia proprietors, a group of British and colonial land speculators who had petitioned the king for the formation of a new colony, would receive the benefits and ownership of these western lands with the establishment of their colony, an arrangement that would introduce the control necessary to restore order. In January, however, it had become apparent that colonial unrest was to cause the suspension of the activi-ties of the new colony. The moment was opportune for Vir-ginia to assert her jurisdiction. Crawford relayed to Washing-ton the information he had received from Williamsburg: "It is now without doubt that the new government is fallen through, and that Lord Dunmore is to take charge of so much of this quarter as falls out of Pennsylvania."[10] Dr. John Con-

[9] James, *Clark Papers, 1771-1781*, 5-7; Jacobs, *Michael Cresap*, 49.
[10] Butterfield, *Washington-Crawford Letters*, 40.

nolly at Pittsburgh was therefore commissioned by Dunmore a justice of the peace for the county of Augusta and given instructions for the establishment of the government. New militia officers were appointed, and under the energetic directions of Connolly, Pittsburgh assumed a martial air, while the Pennsylvania authorities, represented by Arthur St. Clair and supported by the fur traders, added interest to the situation by arresting Connolly and asserting Pennsylvania's rights. The Virginians in return were obliged to justify themselves by exaggerating the Indian danger.

When Clark and Cresap arrived at Wheeling they were informed by Connolly from Pittsburgh that a war with the Indians was feared and that they should await developments. The communication amounted to a request to hold their party in readiness to attack the Indians if help should be needed, and the frontiersmen at Wheeling needed little encouragement to comply. On about April 24 or 25, another letter arrived from Connolly, written on the twenty-first, more urgent in tone, which was seized upon by these Indian haters and interpreted as a declaration of war. The letter was addressed by Connolly to the inhabitants of Wheeling and, according to a contemporary report, asserted that he "had been informed, by good authority, that the *Shawanese* were ill disposed towards white men," and that he expected the people to be ready "to repel any insults that might be offered" by the Indians. The original of this message has not been preserved; the sources for the information it contained are vague; and there are no known accounts of Connolly's negotiations with the Indians that clarify the situation. It would seem, however, that Connolly had been in communication with the Shawnee, who, finding that his terms called for the unconditional occupation of Kentucky, in contrast with Bullitt's terms of the year before, indicated that they would oppose being deprived of their hunting rights. This understanding of the message was evidently in the minds of the members of Cresap's party at Wheeling, whose visions of Kentucky home-seeking ventures began to fade. Thus Clark says, "The reception of this letter was the epoch of open hostilities with the Indians. A new post was planted, a council was called and the letter read by Cresap. All the Indian traders being summoned on so important an occasion, action was had and war declared in the most solemn manner; and the same evening two scalps were brought into camp."[11]

On the night of the reading of Connolly's letter, news came in that a trader's party, including two Indians, one Delaware and one Shawnee, was descending the river. This party had been sent out by William Butler to take the place of one attacked and plundered by the Cherokee earlier in the month. The day following the receipt of this news, the party, according to one contemporary, was fired upon from the shore, and the two Indians were killed "by *Michael Cresap,* and a party he had with him; they also scalped the *Indians.*" McKee, at Pittsburgh, reported the story of "one Stephens" who was in the party. Stephens stated that on the way down the Ohio, near Wheeling Creek, he spied a canoe coming up the river. Suspecting it to be an Indian canoe, he made to the opposite side of the river to avoid it, but on approaching the shore he was fired on from the bank. The Shawnee Indian in his party fell at the first shot and the Delaware at the second. Stephens jumped into the river for safety, but he soon discovered that the occupants of the other canoe were white men and that one of them was Cresap. These men denied knowing anything about the party concealed near the bank, although from the circumstances Stephens was "well convinced that the above murder was done by some of said Cressop's associates." Stephens was taken into Cresap's canoe and observed the latter's threatening language to the effect that "he wou'd put every Indian he met with on the river, to death, and that if he cou'd raise men sufficient to cross the River, he wou'd attack a small village of Indians living on Yellow Creek."[12]

[11] James, *Clark Papers, 1771-1781,* 7; *American Archives,* fourth series, 1:468.
[12] *American Archives,* fourth series, 1:468; *New York Colonial Documents,* 8:463.

On the following day hostilities were renewed. Cresap learned that fourteen Shawnee Indians had stopped at his new plantation to ask for supplies, and he immediately set out in pursuit of them and soon overtook them. A skirmish took place near Grave Creek in which one Shawnee chief and one white man were killed and considerable plunder was taken from the canoes abandoned by the Indians. It seems probable that the Shawnee chiefs who were fired upon were those returning from the conference with McKee at Pittsburgh. After the attack they fled to the nearest Delaware towns, "greatly exasperated at this treatment, as they did not expect any such thing from the *English*."[13]

On the return of Cresap's party to Wheeling, "a resolution was adopted," according to Clark, "to march the next day and attack Logan's camp on the Ohio about thirty miles above us." "Logan's camp" was at the mouth of Yellow Creek, near what is now Steubenville, Ohio, and was inhabited by a group of Mingo Indians under the celebrated chief and orator, Logan. These Indians had committed even less offense than the Shawnee—they belonged to the Six Nations and made no claim to the lands south of the Ohio. Indeed, in 1765 they had insisted that the white trespassers on their lands in northwestern Virginia should be allowed to stay because the lands were about to be ceded by the Six Nations anyhow. The party set out accordingly, but it seems that a consciousness of the savagery and injustice of the act they were about to commit increased as they approached the town. They at last decided to abandon the expedition as "it was generally agreed that those Indians had no hostile intentions as they were hunting, and their party was composed of men, women and children with all their stuff with them. . . . In short, every person seemed to detest the resolution we had set out with."[14]

But the inhabitants of the Mingo town were not destined to escape violence from the whites. Across the Ohio, on the Vir-

[13] *New York Colonial Documents*, 8:463; *American Archives*, fourth series, 1:468.
[14] James, *Clark Papers, 1771-1781*, 7.

ginia side, was the farm of a white settler named Baker. For a long time amicable relations had been maintained between the two settlements, and the Indians often crossed the river to get liquor and other articles for their elders, and milk for their children. One of the latter was said to be the new-born son of the Pennsylvania trader, John Gibson, who afterwards became an officer in the Revolution and was later secretary and acting governor of Indiana Territory. The child's mother was Logan's sister. On the morning of May 3 a party of four Mingo, two men and two squaws, crossed the river to make a friendly visit to a group of whites assembled at Baker's. These Indians were aggrieved over an affair that had taken place the day before when some white men had crossed the river to examine land on the Indian side and, at night, on hearing the bell on one of their horses rattling violently, had surprised two Indians in the act of unspanceling the horse. Both Indians had been shot at and had fallen "as if dead." Just what happened when the four Mingo arrived at Baker's the day following is hard to tell. All chronicles agree that most of the Indians were made drunk and were unable to return the fire when they were attacked by the whites, and in several accounts reference is made to the fact that they were disarmed by being invited to partake in a contest of shooting at a mark. One chronicler states that the occasion for the first shot was the refusal of one drunken Indian to return a military coat belonging to one of the whites, in which he was swaggering around exclaiming, "I am white man." At any rate, all four of the Indians, men and women alike, were murdered. As the day passed, two more Indians crossed the river to see why the others did not return, and they, likewise, were killed. Disturbed by the shots and uneasy at the continued absence of their fellows, five more soon crossed and were met by a fire that killed two and wounded the other three. It was a bloody day at Baker's—eight or more unoffending Indians had been murdered, and one of them was Chief Logan's sister, Gibson's squaw and mother of the papoose supposed to be Gibson's son, who, strapped to his mother's back, escaped the bullet that laid her lifeless beneath him.[15]

The country was shocked and mortified by this atrocious act. Dunmore referred to it as "marked with an extraordinary degree of Cruelty and Inhumanity"; Thomas Jefferson characterized it as inhuman and indecent; and Clark said that the affair was even "more barbarous than related by Mr. Jefferson." Charles Lee denounced the war in general as "carried on by the governor of Virginia, at the instigation of two murderers on the frontier, and in spite of the declamations of the whole continent against the injustice of it. It was an impious, black piece of work."[16]

Shocking and unjustified as this act was admitted by all to be, no one dared to do anything in behalf of the outraged Mingo. Indian hatred was the spirit of the hour, and the whites must not be disunited even if mercy and justice must be sacrificed. Dunmore claimed that even if he could have had word of "this atrocious Action" immediately, "it would have been impossible for me to take any effectual Step, in the disposition which the People of the Back-Country were then, to bring these Offenders to Justice." Only the lone voice of Logan in behalf of his tribesmen was to be heard: "What did you kill my people on Yellow Creek for. The white People killed my kin at Coneestoga a great while ago, & I though[t nothing of that.] But you killed my kin again on Yellow Creek, and took m[y cousin prisoner] then I thought I must kill too."[17]

By the middle of May only the Mingo were at war. The Shawnee had had two of their tribe murdered and the Delawares one, but they were still for peace. It was not until peace overtures had been rejected by the whites and peace messengers insulted, that the former resorted to war, while no insults seemed sufficient to alienate the latter tribe. The massacre of

[15] Thwaites and Kellogg, *Dunmore's War*, 9-19.
[16] Thwaites and Kellogg, *Dunmore's War*, 378; Thomas Jefferson, *Writings*, 3:163 (edited by Paul L. Ford—New York, 1894); James, *Clark Papers, 1771-1781*, 8; *Lee Papers*, 1:149.
[17] Thwaites and Kellogg, *Dunmore's War*, 246, 378.

the Mingo tended, if anything, to bring the Shawnee and the whites closer together for the time being. There were among the Shawnee a few Pennsylvania traders, one of whom was Richard Butler. Upon hearing of the massacre of his people, Logan "raised a party to cut down the *Shawanese* Town traders at the *Canoe* Bottom, on *Hockhocking Creek,* where they were pressing their peltry." To protect the traders the Shawnee sent out five tribesmen to guide them in their return to the Shawnee towns from their camps on the Hockhocking. The Shawnee took the honorable attitude that the traders were in their care and that it was the Indians' duty to protect them. The Delawares informed McKee on June 1 at Pittsburgh that "the *Shawanese* had told the *Mingoes* that they had brought the traders amongst them, and were determined to protect them in their bosoms until they could return them safe home; and that if the *Mingoes* could not be satisfied without taking revenge upon the white people for the loss they had sustained, that they must look for it a greater distance than in their towns upon the people whom they had pledged their faith to preserve."[18]

When Butler and his fellows arrived in the Indian towns, Cornstalk, chief of the Shawnee nation, appointed a party in charge of his brother to conduct traders to Pittsburgh. With them he sent a warning letter to McKee stating that the late outrages "so close to each other, Aggravated our People very much; yet we all determined to be quiet till we knew what you meant ... The Traders that were amongst us were very much endangered by such doings ... we are convinced of their Innocence. We are Determined to protect them ... therefore we Request that you will present our good Intentions to the Governors of Virginia, and Pensylvania, and request that a stop may be put to such Doings for the Future.... I have with great Trouble and pains prevailed on the foolish People amongst us to sit still and do no harm till we see whether it

---

[18] *American Archives,* fourth series, 1:469; *Pennsylvania Archives,* first series, 4:481, 569.

is the intention of the white people in general to fall on us."[19]

Upon the arrival at Pittsburgh on June 16 of the traders and the Shawnee messengers, Butler waited upon Connolly and requested protection for the return journey of the Indians "that had so faithfully protected us." Connolly positively refused. A few days later Butler presented Connolly with Cornstalk's letter and again petitioned for protection to the messengers. Connolly again refused and "declared in a very ill-natured manner that he would not speak to them." He then actually sought to have them arrested and sent a party of forty militiamen to take them into custody. What would have happened if the attempt had not been frustrated can only be imagined. What actually did happen is told by Arthur St. Clair, justice of the county court of Westmoreland. When he heard of Connolly's intentions, St. Clair waited on him and demanded an explanation, and Connolly told him "that as the *Shawanese* had committed depredations on His Majesty's subjects, he had ordered out that party to make those prisoners who had escorted the traders." The traders were obliged to act at once to prevent an outbreak. As the militiamen surrounded the house of George Croghan, where the Indians were assembled, "Mr. *Butler,* and some other friends, conveyed the *Indians* and their presents over the river." Before spiriting the Shawnee away, the traders had raised money among themselves to reward the Indians for their fidelity, so that, according to Butler, they left "well satisfied" with their treatment. Connolly, however, sent two parties down the river in pursuit of them. The militiamen intercepted their game at Beaver Creek, where, after firing on the Indians and wounding one, they "ran off in the most dastardly manner." This encounter at Beaver Creek was the first revelation to this group of Shawnee of the perfidy of the whites, for they had been carefully guarded by Butler and the traders of Pittsburgh from knowing the spirit of hatred in which they were viewed by Connolly and his government. The episode was never forgotten by the

[19] *Pennsylvania Archives,* first series, 4:497.

Shawnee. St. Clair wrote of it, "What may be the consequence *God* knows."[20]

As soon as news was received by McKee of the series of outrages culminating in the Mingo massacre, he immediately called into council the Delawares and the Six Nations. The Delawares were entrusted to relay the negotiations to the Shawnee, to receive their answers, and to arrange for a conference between that tribe and the whites. At the first of the conferences on May 3, a speech of explanation and apology was made by McKee in which he assured the Indians that the government had not sanctioned the "breach of friendship" perpetrated and promised, on behalf of Virginia, that reparations would be made for this injustice. But McKee had no real authority to speak for Virginia. Connolly was her spokesman, and in his address, made on May 5, he assumed that the Kentucky country had been definitely bought from the Shawnee and that the legislature had the right to make rules and regulations for its settlement. Although he confirmed McKee's statement in regard to the innocence of the government in the affair, the only assurances he gave the Indians were that the legislature would direct the white men to be "kind and friendly towards you" and that it "will buy goods to clothe your people and children." The last pledge was probably interpreted by the Shawnee to mean that they were to be compensated for the Kentucky lands, but they placed no reliance on Connolly's promises on behalf of the legislature. "We look upon it all to be lies," they said, "and perhaps what you say may be lies also." They nevertheless promised not to take any notice of what the whites had done to them if the whites would reciprocate by not taking "any notice of what our young men may now be doing."[21]

The position in which the Shawnee Indians found themselves at this crucial moment in their history was a direct re-

[20] *Pennsylvania Archives,* first series, 4:570; *American Archives,* fourth series, 1:474, 483, 484.
[21] *American Archives,* fourth series, 1:476-480; *New York Colonial Documents,* 8:465.

sult of the British policy of divide and conquer and of the persistence of the Six Nations in their fidelity to the white man's cause. The isolation of the Shawnee from the other Indian nations, which signified the absence of the Delaware and Iroquois nations from the battlefields of 1774, was an important factor in the outcome of the struggle. It is of interest therefore to review briefly the means by which this policy was maintained and to note its effect on the nations concerned.

The Delaware Indians had been obliged, ever since their defeat in 1764, to submit to the domination of the Six Nations, and when war loomed between Virginia and the Shawnee they could not afford to risk their peaceful relations with their overlords by assisting the Shawnee cause. Moreover, their dealings with the whites had been on a more satisfactory basis than had those of the Shawnee. They, too, had suffered from the indiscriminate murders by the frontiersmen in the spring and summer of 1774, but they had been favored by greater efforts on the part of the whites to make reparations. It will be recalled that a Delaware had been killed by Cresap's men late in April. In June the Delaware chief, George White Eyes, who had been placed in charge of the messages sent by McKee to the Shawnee, returned to Pittsburgh to find that his house had been "broke open by the Virginians, & about £30 worth of his property taken." At about the same time, according to Lord Dunmore, a party of Delawares, who had come to Pittsburgh to trade, was fired upon, and two of them were killed. Steps had been taken immediately to discover the perpetrators of these murders, and at the same time an official letter of apology was sent to the Delaware nation.[22] It is apparent that such efforts were made, not primarily to bring the white murderers to justice, but to give the Delawares an ostensible reason to be friendly with the whites.

At the May conferences at Pittsburgh the meekness of this tribe was noticeable. "We cannot doubt of your uprightness

---

[22] *Pennsylvania Archives,* first series, 4:540; Thwaites and Kellogg, *Dunmore's War,* 381; *Pennsylvania Colonial Records,* 10:196-199.

towards us," they declared, "and that the mischief done to us, has been done contrary to your intent and desire . . . therefore it is incumbent upon us to aid you with our best assistance." When, late in the month, White Eyes returned from carrying the messages to the Shawnee and reported the equivocal attitude of that nation, the Six Nations peremptorily ordered all Delawares out of the Shawnee country. They stated that they were sorry that the Shawnee would not be reasonable "but since we think they will not, we must desire our brethren, the *Delawares,* to withdraw themselves from amongst them, that no evil may happen them by accident, which would give us great concern." To this command, White Eyes meekly acquiesced.[23]

The Delawares had thus, for their own preservation, cast their lot with the strongest party. They were, however, in mortal fear of the Shawnee, who looked upon them as traitors. In July, while Virginians were organizing to invade the Shawnee country, a threatening message was received by the Delawares to the effect that the Shawnee, after they had defeated the whites, "would then Blaze a Road . . . to New Comer's Town" to determine "whether the Peace was so strong Between the White[s] and the Delawares as the[y] Pretended." The whites could give them little assurance of protection, but during the ensuing struggle there were several individuals, mainly of the Pittsburgh trading interests, who seriously proposed rewarding the Delawares in a substantial way. One of them was Aeneas Mackay, who, on the basis of news and advice from Richard Butler, wrote to St. Clair in July, "It is absolutely necessary, that immediate application should be made to government in favour of the Delawares, that some steps may be taken to Reward the fidelity of that People, especially such of them as will undertake to Reconoture and Guard the frontiers of this Province, which they say they will do, from the hostile Designs of the Shawanese."[24]

[23] *American Archives,* fourth series, 1:477, 480.
[24] *Pennsylvania Archives,* first series, 4:552, 553, 556.

Such suggestions, however, were not received with much enthusiasm, because, if carried out, they would inaugurate a policy that would entail endless expense. As St. Clair wrote when he passed Mackay's letter on to Governor Penn, "The engaging the service of the Delawares to protect our Frontier would undoubtedly be good Policy, if it did not cost too dear. . . . but as they have offered, it should not be altogether overlooked; at the same time their Friendship should be secured on as easy terms as possible." One of the basic factors in this unwillingness to incur expense in behalf of the Indians was the ingrained feeling that if money was to be expended at all, it should be for the whites and not for the savage redskins, especially in times of war when it could find its way into the hands of hostile tribesmen. This attitude is illustrated by the effect on the commandant at Pittsburgh of the delivery of goods sent by traders to one of the Delaware towns; he was "enraged . . . to an exceeding degree, and he threatens 'the Persons who carried them shall be tried for their Lives on their Return.' " The rejection of all plans to give any real aid to the Delawares was made final by Governor Penn, who wrote to St. Clair in August, "You hint something in your last Letter about making Presents to the Indians, but, though such a Step at some future convenient Time might be very useful and proper, I am of Opinion it would be very unadvisable under the present Circumstances."[25]

It was not only in respect to holding the Delawares in check that the Six Nations rendered aid to the whites in the Shawnee disturbance; they were also instrumental in isolating the Shawnee from various other possible allies and in quieting the unrest of some of their own people. Their consistent support had been secured through the able and experienced management of Sir William Johnson and his son, Colonel Guy Johnson, who, after his father's death, succeeded him as superintendent of Indian affairs in the North. As soon as war became apparent, the former had assembled the Six Nations in

[25] *Pennsylvania Archives,* first series, 4:557; *Pennsylvania Colonial Records,* 10:203.

grand and solemn council at Onondaga, where they were convinced "that it was their duty and interest to calm their
people" and "to divert the attention of the other Tribes near
Ohio from the Shawanese." The first obstacle encountered by
the Six Nations in following this program was presented by
the Seneca, the most western tribe of the confederacy and also
the most wavering in its loyalty to the British, who were
loud in their protests against the deplorable trading conditions
and the insufferable arrogance of the frontiersmen. These conditions, they claimed, were the causes of the Shawnee revolt
and should be remedied before the Six Nations should be bur-
dened with the task of bringing about peace. To counteract
the effect of the outspoken talk of the Seneca, Sir William was
forced to resort to all the diplomacy of which he was capable.
His efforts were successful, though they cost him his life. He
succumbed, toward the close of the conference, to an illness
that had already confined him to his bed when the conference
had opened. The Six Nations, awed no doubt by the circumstances of the death of their lifelong friend at the crisis of his
career, agreed to send a party under the Seneca chief, Guyasuta, to bring the Shawnee to their senses.

When Guyasuta reached the Shawnee country early in
August, the tribe was already confronted with invasion from
Virginia. They entreated the Seneca chief to permit them as
a nation to attack their enemies; but Guyasuta and his party
were adamant and flatly refused to listen. They told the Shawnee that the matter would be submitted in the fall to a grand
council of all the northern nations, including the Seven Nations of Canada, at Onondaga, "where we shall determine
on measures to put a stop to these troubles." By the time the
council met in November the fate of the Shawnee had been
settled at the battle of Point Pleasant. The Shawnee proposals
for war were nevertheless discussed, and each nation arose
in turn and declared against them. The Shawnee were told,
"Quarrelsome people are dangerous, we advise you for your
good, for we pity you, and we know from our Superintendant,

that the King is inclined to desire you should be at peace."[26]

A similar fate met the Shawnee attempt to secure help from their other neighbors, the Lake Indians, and the tribes of the Miami and the Wabash. When Shawnee deputies sought to work on the Lake tribes—the Wyandot and the Ottawa— they were directed by Guyasuta and his Six Nations party to send a message to those tribes requesting them "to be quiet," and at the same time the Six Nations sent their own delegates to the Wabash tribes recommending them to remain at peace with the English. "From these circumstances," St. Clair wrote to the governor, "it is to be hoped the Fracas with the Shawanese will blow over without any very bad Consequences."[27]

Toward their own tribesmen on the Ohio, the Mingo, who had suffered heavily from white outrages, the Six Nations showed no more compassion than they had to the Shawnee. The Mingo were requested to abandon their homes and to return nearer to their own council fire. As few inducements seem to have been offered, these efforts were only moderately successful; Guyasuta reported on his return that he had been able to persuade only two families to come away. Later, however, Chief Brant of the Mohawk reported that others had deserted their homes in compliance with the command.[28]

What is to be said in extenuation of the policy of the Six Nations during this period? In the first place it seems probable that their opinion was influenced throughout by Sir William Johnson, in whom years of honorable dealing had taught them to place implicit confidence. Sir William had told them that the Shawnee were "a troublesome people, who have . . . at length excited the resentment of some Frontier Virginians, who struck them and fled, whilst without waiting for redress, they [the Shawnee] fell on the innocent Inhabitants . . . and now want you to countenance them in their Wickedness." It must also be remembered that the Six Nations believed the

[26] New York Colonial Documents, 8:474-484, 499, 527.
[27] Pennsylvania Archives, first series, 4:559.
[28] New York Colonial Documents, 8:480, 501, 519.

British when the latter assured them that the colonies would soon create a satisfactory Indian department. Finally, it should be noted that the confederacy stood firmly against any further provocation of the Shawnee and announced to the whites its firm determination that the Ohio River must be the ultimate and final bounds for the American people. The rapid overflow of the whites into the lands ceded at Fort Stanwix in 1768 was alarming even to the Six Nations, and as the Virginians prepared to punish the Shawnee, grave apprehension arose that the conquest of lands north of the Ohio might be the object. This apprehension was expressed in the November grand council by the Mohawk, Brant, who warned Johnson against undue encroachments on the part of Virginia. Johnson was alarmed and wrote to Dartmouth, "It has been the practice of some of the Colonies to acquire territory by conquest rather than purchase, and this renders every movement in that quarter suspected, and the Indians cant help believing, that it will be followed by other attempts on their Country or liberties." The Six Nations, although not willing to support the Shawnee in their quarrel over past grievances, were thus watchful that no further aggressions be made against them.[29]

In the spring of 1774 the Shawnee, cut off, as has been seen, from the support of other tribes, were marking time. The situation at the close of May was a precarious one. Peace was possible if Virginia made satisfactory reparations and if the Indians made no reprisals for the outrages committed. The relatives and friends of the murdered Shawnee, however, clamored for revenge. A council of the head men of the tribe was therefore called to meet at Wakatomica on the Muskingum, the village in which the murdered Shawnee had lived. At this council a small minority of the nation, consisting of the relatives of the dead men, desired immediate reprisals. The majority, trusting no doubt that the whites would not be angered at the just reprisals of a few Shawnee joined with

[29] *New York Colonial Documents*, 8:503, 516, 519, 521.

173

the belligerent Mingo, left the dissenters to seek their own vengeance. According to an unidentified contemporary, the Shawnee chiefs were "strong enough to prevail over their rash and foolish men who wanted to take revenge upon the white people for their loss, except two small parties, consisting of thirteen men altogether, who were friends to the *Indians* that suffered, and could not be restrained ... The above party have declared, as soon as they have taken revenge for their people, and returned, that they would then set down and listen to their Chiefs."[30]

With the memory of the fate of their deceased comrades urging them on, this mixed band of Mingo and Shawnee, under Chief Logan, set out silently and deliberately for the Ohio River, there to conduct a series of murderous raids on innocent and unsuspecting families. They avoided, however, any families known to reside in Pennsylvania, confining their attacks to the hated Virginians. By the middle of June thirteen lives had been taken in retaliation for the thirteen Mingo and Shawnee Indians who, according to the Indian count, had been similarly murdered by the whites. It was at last reported, on June 30, that "Logans party was returned, and had Thirteen Scalps and one prisoner: Logan says, he is now sattisfied for the loss of his Relations, and will sit Still untill he hears what the Long Knife ... will say."[31]

Logan did not have long to wait. The lives of innocent whites had been taken. According to Virginians and frontiersmen, ample cause had been given for war, and the Shawnee nation must be made to pay for the actions of thirteen of its members. Persons of thought and reflection, however, could not fail to see that the Shawnee nation, as a whole, was striving for peace. On June 10 McKee, at Pittsburgh, wrote, "To do the *Indians* justice, they have given great proofs of their pacific disposition, and have acted with more moderation than

---

[30] *Pennsylvania Archives,* first series, 4:499; *American Archives,* fourth series, 1:464.
[31] *Pennsylvania Archives,* first series, 4:533. The details of the massacres are in Thwaites and Kellogg, *Dunmore's War,* 36, and in *American Archives,* fourth series, 1:471.

those who ought to have been more rational." On June 21 the Delawares urged, "As things now seem to be easy, and all the Nations have now agreed to hold fast the Chain of Friendship and make their young men sit Quiet, we desire you to Consider of what you have to say when our Grand Children, the Shawanese, come to speak to you." The Moravian missionaries to the Delawares wrote that the Shawnee had accepted the proposals made to them, "so that we hope peace will be re-established"; and on June 30 the trader, John Montgomery, wrote to Governor Penn from Carlisle, "The Shawanees seem well Disposed and Inclineable for peace, and will Continue so, Unless provoked by the Virginians." Nevertheless, in spite of the obviously peaceful intentions of the Indians and their previous self-defensive plea, "We desire you likewise not to take any notice of what our young men may now be doing," the Mingo and Shawnee attacks were considered by the whites as having provided "good grounds to believe that hopes of a pacification can be no longer entertained," and on June 10 Dunmore ordered out the county militia of western Virginia with instructions to defend the Ohio River boundary by the erection of forts at strategic points on the river. The result was the collection of frontier militia at three points on the Ohio, that is, at Pittsburgh, Wheeling, and the mouth of the Kanawha, where forts were quickly constructed. These forts, if properly garrisoned and equipped with scouting parties, would block all attempts of the Indians to cross the Ohio River boundary and would thus maintain the basic contention of Virginian policy.[32]

The legislature of Virginia had failed to accept the governor's proposals to assume the financial obligations necessary for a move against the Shawnee, and it also refused to make any appropriations or to pass additional legislation to facilitate these defensive measures. Because of the expense involved in maintaining the new posts, the defensive aspect of the mili-

[32] *American Archives*, fourth series, 1:466; *Pennsylvania Archives*, first series, 4:496, 532, 533; *New York Colonial Documents*, 8:466; Thwaites and Kellogg, *Dunmore's War*, 33-35, 86.

tary preparations gradually gave way to plans for the invasion of the Indian country. A punitive expedition now and then would seem to be less costly and more likely to be approved by impecunious legislatures if the men who served thereon could be partially reimbursed by plunder from the Indian towns. Lord Dunmore stated that "the Expense of the Numerous scouting Parties in the Different Counties . . . Will soon exceed the Expences of an Expedition Against their Towns which will be more effectiaul," and in his letter calling for volunteers, Colonel William Preston explained that "the House of Burgesses will without all Doubt enable his Lordship to reward every Vollunteer in a handsome manner, over and above his Pay; as the plunder of the Count[r]y will be valluable, & it is said the Shawnese have a great Stock of Horses."[33]

Each of the commandants at the new outposts was therefore directed to adopt offensive tactics whenever possible. Dunmore sent word to Connolly at Pittsburgh on June 20, "I entirely approve . . . of marching into the *Shawanese* Towns, if you think you have a sufficient force," and to Colonel Andrew Lewis sent orders not to wait until the Indians attacked but "if you think you have forse enough . . . proceed derectly to their Towns & if possible destroy their Towns & Magazines and distress them in every other way that is possible." At Wheeling affairs moved quickly. By July 26 four hundred Virginia militiamen under Major Angus MacDonald had assembled and constructed a fort. The question of invading the Shawnee country was left to the men to decide, and, as an unidentified correspondent relates, "it was unanimously determined to cross the *Ohio,* and proceed to destroy the *Shawanese* Town called *Wagetomica*" on the Muskingum. By the middle of August the destructive work had been accomplished, and six Mingo towns had been laid waste in addition to this Shawnee village.[34]

At the Kanawha matters moved more slowly. Troops were

[33] Thwaites and Kellogg, *Dunmore's War,* 92, 98, 379.
[34] *American Archives,* fourth series, 1:473, 722; Thwaites and Kellogg, *Dunmore's War,* 86, 151-156.

assembled, however, with the intention of invading and laying waste the Shawnee country. But such a destructive invasion was not destined to take place, for the Shawnee were ready for the Virginian army when it reached its rendezvous at Point Pleasant. Assuming the offensive, the Indians crossed the Ohio on October 10 and attacked Lewis' camp on the Virginia side. The result of the battle of Point Pleasant is well known. The Indians were defeated although not so badly that they were unable to retreat in orderly fashion across the river. Seeing that it was hopeless to attempt to cope with the superior forces, the tribe sued for peace and accepted the terms offered by Lord Dunmore at Camp Charlotte, in Hocking County, Ohio, which involved complete surrender of all the points at issue. The basic articles in the peace settlement were the yielding by the Shawnee of their hunting rights in the Kentucky country and the promise of the whites to refrain from hunting north of the Ohio. Of equal importance to the Indians was the pledge of a definite settlement of trading conditions, which, however, was made dependent in its formation and operation on the discretion of the whites. "They Should promise to agree," the terms read, "to such regulations, for their trade with our People, as Should be hereafter dictated by the Kings Instructions." These provisions, together with a promise from the Indians to return all prisoners and stolen property, to refrain from molesting any boats on the Ohio, and to provide four hostages as a guarantee of good faith, constituted the conditions of peace.[35]

The humiliation of the Shawnee was complete. "We have made them sensible of their villainy and weakness," asserted Crawford. The war, claimed Dunmore, "has impressed an Idea of the power of the White People, upon the minds of the Indians, which they did not before entertain; and, there is reason to believe, it has extinguished the rancour so violently in our People against the Indians: and I think there is a greater

---

[35] Thwaites and Kellogg, *Dunmore's War*, 386; *American Archives*, fourth series, I:1014.

probability that these Scenes of distress will never be renewed, than ever was before."[36] Lord Dunmore was a poor observer and a false prophet. The American frontiersman never ceased to hold the Indian in contempt, and for over a century, scenes of distress never ceased to recur whenever Indians stood in the way of white men.

[36] Butterfield, *Washington-Crawford Letters*, 54; Thwaites and Kellogg, *Dunmore's War*, 386.

8

The Indians and
the Outbreak of Revolution
on the Frontier

THE AMERICAN REVOLUTION, coming close on the
heels of Dunmore's War, brought new and difficult problems
to the inhabitants of the upper Ohio Valley. A danger in every
American community in those anxious days of 1775 was that
of a Loyalist counter-revolt against the patriots, and in frontier communities the danger was doubly felt because of the
possibilities of alliance between the supporters of King George
and the redskins who ranged the neighboring forests. It was
to take the part of wisdom, then, for patriots to befriend the
Indians before their British rivals, with their long experience
and prestige among the tribesmen and their superior ability
to provide them with guns and ammunition, had made too
disastrous a use of their advantage.

Both the Six Nations and the Delawares were conscious of their past services to the British and of their right to a reward. In the early days of 1775 negotiations were going forward between the Delawares and the British that boded no good to the Revolutionists. Lord Dunmore gave assurances of reparations and protection to these Indians and promised them that he would interest himself in procuring a grant from the king for lands claimed by them. His agent, John Connolly, held a council of Delaware chiefs at Pittsburgh in June and reported that he had succeeded in winning them to the British cause. Connolly also organized a group of Loyalist sympathizers pledged to restore the king's power, if necessary supplies and men could be procured, and, after disbanding the garrison at Fort Pitt, or Fort Dunmore, as it was then called, he set out for Boston to solicit the assistance of General Gage. The plans formulated there for a conquest of the Ohio Valley by way of Detroit were thwarted by the American invasion of Canada. Connolly subsequently tried to reach Pittsburgh by ascending the Potomac and later, on November 19, 1775, was arrested near Hagerstown, Maryland. Letters were found on his person, one of which stated that he had "prepared the Ohio Indians to act in concert with me against his Majesty's enemies in that quarter."[1]

Confronted with these pretentious schemes, the Revolutionists obviously had to bestir themselves. The burden was assumed by Virginia. On June 24 the Virginia Revolutionary government appointed six commissioners to hold a council or treaty with the Ohio Indians and granted the commissioners permission to draw on the treasurer for two thousand pounds. The commissioners sent one of their members, James Wood, to call the tribes to Pittsburgh and to inform them of their peaceful intentions. The discoveries of Wood, on his tour of the Indian country, were significant. At Pittsburgh and in the Delaware and Mingo towns he found the seeds of hostility

[1] Thwaites and Kellogg, *Revolution on the Upper Ohio,* 35, 40, 73, 137, 140-142; *Pennsylvania Archives,* first series, 4:637; Siebert, *Tories of the Upper Ohio,* 2-4.

left in the minds of the Indians by the British; he discovered the attitude of the Wyandot to be most unfriendly; and in the Shawnee country he found that this tribe was in a state of distress over the encroachments of Virginians into its hunting grounds on the Kentucky River. At the close of his tour he informed the Virginia Provincial Convention that the "Indians are forming a General Confederacy against the Colony," and he advised two steps: the military occupation of Fort Pitt and the doubling of the appropriation for the treaty.[2]

So pressing was the need of immediate action to placate the Indians and foil the Loyalists that patriots could not wait for the Virginia convention to act. The members of the Revolutionary committee of safety of West Augusta, the Virginia district in which this part of western Pennsylvania was alleged to lie, consequently took up the negotiations with the Indians. After providing for the purchase of the necessary provisions out of their own pockets, they actually procured the aid of Connolly, whose influence with the red men was too important to be ignored, for the management of their conference with the Indians. The conference was held in July, and Wood reported that Connolly had "Conducted this Affair in the Most Open and Candid Manner."[3] It is probable that Connolly acquiesced in the proceedings because he felt that if the Indians assumed a warlike attitude, many frontier inhabitants who were of neutral or even of pro-Tory sentiment would of necessity be driven into the ranks of the Revolutionists. This conference was preliminary to the treaty of Pittsburgh held in September and October.

Fears of an alliance between the British and the Indians were widespread during the summer of 1775. Guy Johnson received orders from Dartmouth to take immediate steps to induce the Indians "to take up the hatchet" against the rebels. This was a direct authorization by the British government to the superintendent of Indian affairs to incite a Loyalist-In-

[2] Thwaites and Kellogg, *Revolution on the Upper Ohio*, 34-37.
[3] Thwaites and Kellogg, *Revolution on the Upper Ohio*, 38.

dian uprising. Dartmouth stated in justification that information had been received "of the Rebells having excited the Indians to take a part, and of their having actually engaged a body of them in arms to support their rebellion." Dartmouth referred to the facts that in March the Massachusetts Provincial Congress had accepted the offer of the Stockbridge Indians to serve as minutemen, and in May, Ethan Allen had invited the Indians to join in war against the king and had promised to provide the necessary knives and tomahawks. Dartmouth's order was a confirmation of the suspicions of Congress, voiced in July, that the British "will spare no pains to excite the several Nations of Indians to take up arms against these colonies." The American Indian commissioners were therefore instructed to seize any British agents found inciting the Indians against the colonies.[4]

Fortunately for the American cause in the upper Ohio Valley, other circumstances conspired to prevent the success of British efforts to get the Indians to join the Loyalists. The American invasion of Canada in 1775 blocked the St. Lawrence and depleted the stocks of Indian powder and other supplies at Niagara and Detroit. Although Guy Johnson sought to keep the Six Nations loyal to the king, he was forced by local patriot action to flee to Montreal. Before leaving, he assembled the Six Nations in council at Oswego, where they agreed to give assistance to British troops, but it is clear that the crisis was so sudden that he was unable to muster sufficient resources to insure their loyalty, and he succeeded in taking with him only a small portion of the New York Indians, most of whom were Mohawk. The rest of the Six Nations returned to their towns, then under American control, and told the American commissioners for the northern department at Albany on August 31 that Johnson had urged them to remain neutral. Another circumstance favorable to the patriots was their ability to establish actual military control of the upper

[4] *New York Colonial Documents,* 8:596; *American Archives,* fourth series, 1:1347, 1349; United States Continental Congress, *Journals . . . 1774-1789,* 2:174.

Ohio Valley, which was done by order of the Virginia Provincial Convention when Captain John Neville on September 11 occupied the old Fort Pitt with a body of Virginia militia.[5]

The Americans thus had control of the situation in the Ohio Valley in 1775, and it was therefore discreet, as well as safe, for them to treat the Loyalists as well as the Indians with some degree of indulgence. The American Indian agent, Richard Butler, not only permitted an invitation from the British to a council at Niagara early in 1776 to be communicated to the Seneca near Pittsburgh, but he even agreed that Guyasuta and his tribesmen should attend. Furthermore, the former British Indian agent at Pittsburgh, Alexander McKee, who was still loyal to the king, was placed on parole and permitted to represent the British among the Indians under certain restrictions. McKee's conduct in this arrangement was so honorable in Butler's eyes that the American agent spoke most highly of his British predecessor, commenting that "he has been much more quiet than some others that would fain be thought great friends now."[6]

The measures and arrangements of the patriot committees designed to placate the Indians and to prevent a Loyalist uprising culminated in the treaty of Pittsburgh of September and October, 1775. James Wood, the special agent sent west by the Virginia Provincial Convention, reported that the Indians expected a general council to be called at which the appropriate presents could be received; and the way had been paved for such a council by the preliminary treaty conference held by the West Augusta committee of safety in July. This committee subsequently sent a petition to Congress setting forth its fears of a rupture with the Indians unless a general council was held with them.[7]

The treaty of Pittsburgh that took place as a result of these reports, in the year of the battles of Lexington and Concord, was, like previous proceedings, conducted under the auspices

[5] *New York Colonial Documents,* 8:621, 630, 636, 658; Craig, *Pittsburgh,* 108.
[6] *American Archives,* fourth series, 5:815-817.
[7] United States Continental Congress, *Journals . . . 1774-1789,* 2:76.

of the West Augusta committee of safety and was therefore a Revolutionary affair. It was participated in by commissioners appointed by the rebellious colonies and by that Revolutionary body, the second Continental Congress. The commissioners for Virginia were Thomas Walker, Andrew Lewis, James Wood, John Walker, and Adam Stephen; for Congress, James Wilson and Lewis Morris. The Indian tribes represented were the Six Nations, the Delawares, and the Shawnee. The principal business was the settlement with the Shawnee of the outstanding issues of Dunmore's War, and the main accomplishment was the exclusion of the Shawnee from Kentucky and the establishment of the Ohio River boundary. The Indians were informed of the orders sent to the inhabitants in general and to the commanding officer of the fort at the Kanawha to prevent Indian trespasses south of the Ohio and white trespasses north of that river. At the same time a definite pledge was made by the whites that the Ohio River should be forever the boundary between them and the red men. This was the most important part of the proceedings to the Indians because they felt that it brought them security from future aggressions, and for that reason it won their promise of neutrality.[8]

In the generation of Indian conflict that followed, the Indians never ceased to remind the Americans of this solemn promise made by the latter to secure Indian neutrality. The boundary, agreed upon at the treaty of Fort Stanwix in 1768 and ratified by the Americans at the treaty of Pittsburgh in 1775, was to become the major bone of contention in Indian affairs and was not finally abandoned by all the tribesmen until the treaty of Greenville in 1795.

The Pittsburgh treaty council, however, accomplished more than the mere assurance of Indian neutrality. It was the occasion for the appearance, among the different tribes, of jealousies that, although they were not deliberately fomented

---

[8] Crumrine, *Washington County*, 187; Heckewelder, *Mission of the United Brethren*, part 3, p. 140. The proceedings of the treaty are printed in full in Thwaites and Kellogg, *Revolution on the Upper Ohio*, 70-125.

or encouraged by the Americans, did accrue to the benefit of the latter. The advantages of the phenomenon of "divide and conquer" thus first came to the attention of the Americans, who soon devised means of profiting thereby. In this connection two developments are to be noted—the bringing to bear of the influence of the Delawares and the Six Nations against the Shawnee and the alienation of the Delawares from the Six Nations. The Six Nations had never recognized the Shawnee claims south of the Ohio, so that the latter nation received no sympathy from the New York confederacy. Likewise, Chief White Eyes announced for the Delawares their acknowledgment of the rights of the white men and promised to uphold those rights. The subserviency of the Delawares to the Six Nations has been indicated elsewhere; with the rise of the new American power these Indians thought, as they had in the days of the French power in 1754, that the golden opportunity had come for deliverance from their ancient subjection. At the council, therefore, this tribe, with unwonted defiance, announced to the Six Nations, as well as to the whites, that it had received certain lands from the Wyandot nation lying between the Beaver and Cuyahoga rivers on the east and the Muskingum and Sundusky on the west. White Eyes gave voice to this defiance in no uncertain terms: "You say," he declared, "that you had conquered me [*the Delaware nation*] that you had cut off my legs—had put a petticoat on me, giving me a hoe and cornpounder in my hands, saying; 'now woman! your business henceforward shall be, to plant and hoe corn, and pound the same for bread, for us men and warriors!'—Look . . . at my legs! if, as you say, you had cut them off, they have grown again to their proper size!—the petticoat I have thrown away, and have put on my proper dress!—the corn hoe and pounder I have exchanged for these fire arms, and I declare that I am a man!" Then, with outstretched hand, he pointed beyond the Allegheny River, exclaiming, "And all the country on the other side of that river is *mine*." These claims were offensive to the Six Nations and thus could not be actively supported by the Americans for fear of offending these tribes, but no objection was advanced to them on the part of the whites. Indeed, the lack of concord among the Indians was no loss to the white man's cause, and the council closed in October with the Virginians distributing the goods and with all the Indians more or less reconciled to friendship for the American states.

At this first treaty or council of Pittsburgh the Americans gave the Indians of the upper Ohio Valley the presents and the assurance expected by the tribesmen, thus continuing British policy and ingratiating themselves with the Indians. But the facilities of the Americans for dealing with the Indians were not well organized, and the accomplishments at Pittsburgh could not therefore be viewed too optimistically. There was still danger, of which the Americans were only too conscious, that the tribes would join the British. The new Congress was weak and dependent upon the states and was therefore poorly equipped to combat effectively the century-old British Indian administration. The disastrous result of the American invasion of Canada early in 1776 made it doubtful whether or not Congress would be able to carry on at all. The retreat of the Americans at once reopened the St. Lawrence to British commerce; a steady channel for the supplying of goods to the British Indian agents was thus assured; and the tribes could rely upon more plentiful supplies at cheaper prices at Niagara and Detroit than at Pittsburgh. This superior ability of the British to provide the Indians with supplies continued throughout the war. It was an important factor in determining the attitude of the Indians of the Ohio Valley, and it reveals a great weakness in the American control of the Indians.

An example of the inability of Congress to deal satisfactorily with the Indians is found in the ineffective measures taken to promote contentment among the Delawares after the treaty of Pittsburgh. These Indians, under the leadership of their chief, White Eyes, made an appeal to Congress to assist them

in adopting an agricultural mode of life, but the only responses
of Congress were a promise in December to send them a minis-
ter and a schoolmaster to instruct them "in the principles of
religion, and other parts of useful knowledge," and a series of
resolutions passed on April 10, 1776, announcing that arrangements were being made to send to them "a sober man to instruct you in agriculture" and that the United States would
strive to put trade "on such a footing, as will secure the peace,
and promote the interest of all parties." Congress never could
and never did devise a plan for supplying the Indians satisfactorily—the program was left to be administered by the
Indian commissioners of the middle department and their
agent, George Morgan, who was appointed to succeed Butler.
Furthermore, when the Delawares sought from the Americans
a guarantee to the possession of the new lands received from
the Wyandot, Congress was forced to reply that as the Six
Nations claimed most of these lands, "we recommend it to you
to obtain their approbation of this grant to you from the
Wiandots in public council, and have it put on record."
Again, when a dispute arose over the ownership of Montour's
Island in the Ohio River, four miles below Pittsburgh, and was
referred by Richard Butler to Congress, that body did not
handle the matter to the satisfaction of the Delawares, who
were involved. John Montour was a half-breed Delaware who
had been granted a property right in this island by the Indians,
and when the island was surveyed by William Crawford for
certain other gentlemen, one of whom was Captain John
Neville, Virginia commandant at Fort Pitt, the Delawares
considered the action as a breach of the provisions of the
treaty of Fort Stanwix of 1768. Congress, however, merely resolved that the line settled on in the treaty of Fort Stanwix
"ought to be adhered to," but refused to acknowledge that the
attempted survey was unjustifiable.[9]

The Loyalist-Indian danger, which had been temporarily

[9] United States Continental Congress, *Journals . . . 1774-1789*, 2:433; 4:269, 270, 318; Savelle, *George Morgan*, 135; *American Archives*, fourth series, 5:817.

lulled by the invasion of Canada, had once more appeared and until the end of the war never ceased to be a factor. The Delawares were not the only Indians who required attention; when the Continental Indian commissioners arrived at Pittsburgh in the spring of 1776 to attempt to sustain Indian neutrality, they were so impressed with the difficulties of the situation and the weakness of the American position that all thought of civilizing the Delawares, or any other tribe, was set aside for the primary task of preserving the existence of the frontier itself. This feeling of pessimism experienced by the commissioners gradually deepened until it approached the proportions of panic. The Indian agent, George Morgan, upon his arrival at Pittsburgh that spring was so alarmed at the situation that he became convinced that the upper Ohio Valley was about to be invaded by the British and their Iroquois satellites then in council at Niagara, and that the designs of the enemy were against Pittsburgh. On May 16 he wrote in alarm to Lewis Morris, one of the commissioners, "This is a critical time, and unless the Commissioners can attend to their department, or I have full powers, you will hear of things going very wrong." Morgan was overwhelmed at the impoverished condition of the frontier, and he assumed that the British, aware of this condition, would immediately take advantage of it. His mistake was in failing to realize that the British had difficulties enough in attacking and defending more important positions in the East. Until this mistake was discovered, the American authorities in the West marshaled every resource for self-defense. Virginia militia were sent to garrison Fort Henry at Wheeling and Fort Randolph at the mouth of the Kanawha. Agents were sent by Morgan to Niagara and Detroit as well as among the Seneca, Delawares, and Shawnee. Morgan's request for more discretionary power was met in part by a series of resolutions by Congress throughout the year appropriating ten thousand dollars for another treaty at Pittsburgh; and in August Congress authorized the drawing of an order for fourteen hundred dollars for goods already purchased by Morgan for the treaty. In September the sum of four hundred dollars was advanced to Morgan, and the draft of over three thousand dollars by the commissioners at Pittsburgh was accepted; and in December over five thousand dollars more was advanced to the commissioners.[10]

Frontier fright, resulting from a consciousness of weakness, was undiminished by intelligence received from the Seneca and the Shawnee during the spring and summer of 1776 that they would remain neutral. The fact that the English were, for the time being, as much in need of peace on the frontier as were the Americans, had not yet been demonstrated. The commissioners at Pittsburgh admitted in their report to Congress on July 30, 1776, that they were pleased with the Indian assurances but that they were nevertheless disturbed by the fact that some of the Indians had joined the British forces "& we have reason to fear ... others amongst them may be induced [to] follow their example, the most ample promises are made to them [by] Colº Butler at Niagara, they purchase Goods & Merchandize [at the] English Garrisons at a price greatly inferior to those exacted of them by our Traders & of this we are but too sensible they complain loudly." The commissioners proposed that the local militia garrisoning the posts on the Ohio be supplemented by Continental troops at Congressional expense; at the same time they advised the purchasing of powder and other goods said to be at the posts on the Mississippi. "Presents," they said, "which bear no proportion to those received from our Enemies would rather disgust the Indians than conciliate their Esteem." A month later the commissioners repeated their suggestions for more troops and urged the construction by Congress of forts at Kittanning, Le Bœuf, and Presque Isle.[11]

The fears of the commissioners were fed by certain isolated attacks of irresponsible Indians. That these attacks were in

[10] *American Archives,* fourth series, 6:474; United States Continental Congress, *Journals . . . 1774-1789,* 4:329, 346; 5:595, 695, 739, 786; 6:998.
[11] Indian Commissioners to Congressional Committee on Indian Affairs, July 30, August 31, 1776, Morgan Letter Book, no. 2.

each case disavowed by the tribes to which these Indians belonged did not impress the commissioners. On July 30 they reported to Congress the murder by an unknown Indian of a white man named Crawford. "Much uneasiness," they said, "has been occasioned by this outrage, & frequent quarrels have arisen between our people & the Savages." During the same month Morgan had some difficulty in securing the release of two white prisoners from the Mingo on the Scioto, and a small war party of Cherokee and Shawnee, returning to the North after the severe defeat administered to the Cherokee by the Virginians at the battle of Long Island, killed two whites and captured the daughters of Colonel Callaway and Daniel Boone in Kentucky. Upon hearing of this, Captain Matthew Arbuckle, Virginian commandant at Fort Randolph, sent emissaries to the Shawnee town, who brought back the Shawnee chief with a report that the Kentuckians had recaptured the girls and had taken ample revenge by killing two Shawnee. He disavowed the act of his tribesmen and promised lasting peace. But Arbuckle put little faith in his words. "The peace with them," he said, "I Look upon it not to Be Lasting and am Ever on My Guard for fear of a Surprise, and the Trader's Gets Quantitys of Goods from the English at Detroit and has for Some time." At about the same time William Wilson, an agent of the commissioners, was in the Shawnee country when news was reported that whites had fired on a party of Shawnee and Cherokee. "I told the *Cornstalk*," Wilson wrote on September 26, "that I imagined the white people had sufficient reasons, or they would not have fired on them." But although Chief Cornstalk agreed with him, and it was apparent that the Shawnee nation desired to be peaceful, the haunting fear of attack from these Indians nevertheless persisted on the frontier, chiefly because it was known that the belligerent Cherokee had lately offered the tomahawk to the Shawnee.[12]

But it was the activities of the Mingo that caused the great-

[12] Indian Commissioners to Congressional Committee on Indian Affairs, July 30, August 2, 1776, Morgan Letter Book, no. 2; Thwaites and Kellogg, *Revolution on the Upper Ohio*, 186-189; *American Archives*, fifth series, 2:514.

est fear and panic. These Indians, it will be remembered, had become the sworn enemies of the Americans after the treatment they had received before and during Dunmore's War, and they felt themselves completely justified in wreaking vengeance on the hated whites. During the spring of 1776 their murderous raids became a source of horror to innocent frontier families. Their purpose was to drive from Kentucky the settlers who had been coming in since the close of Dunmore's War, and by October, 1776, they had caused the abandonment of all but three of the stations in Kentucky. In August of that year the Delawares brought in lurid and exaggerated reports of a party of Mingo who had just returned from Detroit, where "the commanding Officer there had deliver'd them the Tomahawk" and told them that if they met any Americans "they should strike their Tomahawks into their heads, cutt off some of the hair & bring it to him." The commanding officer was said to have "given each man the Bullets & half a pint of Powder." Such false reports were believed by the Americans, and from them sprang the famous stories of Governor Hamilton as the "hair buyer." The Mingo no doubt did receive supplies from Hamilton but simply as all other Indians received supplies for hunting purposes.[13]

By the end of the summer the feeling of panic received an added stimulus from the return of Matthew Elliott, who had been sent by the commissioners as special agent to the Shawnee and Delawares to invite them to the new treaty at Pittsburgh. Elliott was convinced that an Indian war was inevitable and that "if the Indians should come to the Treaty they will come in very large numbers & . . . they will come with an intention of destroying the Fort & Town." The Delawares and Shawnee had told him, moreover, that they had been summoned by the Wyandot to a council at Detroit, and this led him to believe the wild reports of the formation of a general confederacy among all the Indians. The fears of the commis-

[13] Thwaites and Kellogg, *Revolution on the Upper Ohio*, 205; Indian Commissioners to Congressional Committee on Indian Affairs, August 18, 1776, Morgan Letter Book, no. 2.

sioners were justified, and they reported to Congress in a letter dated August 31, "It is but too apparent to us that Lieutenant Governor Hamilton of Detroit has been straining every Nerve to excite the Indians to take up the Hatchet against the Americans." Circular letters were at once sent to all the county lieutenants on the frontier concerning the imminence of a general Indian attack, with the information that the Ottawa and Chippewa tribes were about to descend on Pittsburgh. "We do not however," they said, "give up all thoughts of a Treaty, but at the best we think it can only delay the blow." Letters imploring aid were hurriedly written to the governor of Virginia and to the convention of Pennsylvania, and dispatches were sent express to the committees of safety of the counties of Westmoreland, Bedford, and West Augusta and to the various county lieutenants with orders to have their militia in readiness and their guns and ammunition attended to. Arrangements were proposed to bring the panic-stricken Moravian Delawares into the settlements to safeguard them from the coming attack. Even the Delawares as a whole were reported on September 13 to be "ready enough to join the other Nations . . . & that they only waited until the other Tribes would begin the Attack."[14]

Suddenly the air cleared. Morgan and William Wilson, who had been sent by the commissioners in June to invite the Shawnee to the second treaty of Pittsburgh and who had been told that they must wait until the Shawnee had consulted the Wyandot, decided to risk the vengeance of the Mingo by undertaking a journey through Mingo territory to the Wyandot nation to ascertain the situation for themselves. The effect of the arrival of these men among this powerful nation indicates that this tribe was living in fear of a white attack at the very moment that the whites were panic-stricken in expectation of an attack from the Indians. "They said," Wilson wrote, "they

[14] Elliott to Indian Commissioners, August 31, 1776; Indian Commissioners to Congressional Committee on Indian Affairs, August 31, 1776; Indian Commissioners to Committee of Safety of Westmoreland County, September 1, 1776, Morgan Letter Book, no. 2. Duplicates of this letter were sent to the other counties.

had heard many bad reports . . . but my coming among them was a convincing proof that they were false." The trip thus dispelled from the Wyandot their fear of the Americans and made that tribe no longer an immediate menace to the frontier. It also had another effect that was favorable to the Americans: the Wyandot, before accepting the invitation to the treaty, insisted on conferring with Governor Hamilton and the rest of the tribes then assembling at Detroit. Wilson attended the conference, and his message was presented to the governor; and when Hamilton not only poured forth censure on Wilson, as was to be expected, but also publicly denounced his guide, the Delaware, George White Eyes, for his friendship with the Americans, all hope of reconciling the Delawares with England was destroyed for the time being. On the way back, White Eyes with mounting anger declared that "the Governour was a fool" and that if the Delawares "joined either side, it would be the *Buckskins* [*Americans*]." Other news from the Wyandot country helped to assuage the frontier panic. The Seneca chief, White Mingo, had returned from a mission to the Wyandot and reported to the commissioners that "about one half of the Indians are desirous of Peace, particularly the Wiandot Chiefs who are averse to War." The peace mission of the Seneca chief, who assumed the authority to speak for his fellow Iroquois, the Mingo, surprised the Wyandot and quieted their fears, since they had been led to believe that the Virginians were about to declare war on the Mingo. They were, however, afraid to come to the treaty council lest the whites punish them for not keeping their young warriors from joining the Mingo against the supposed Virginian attack.[15]

It should be emphasized that the British were not yet ready to encourage the Indians in general to attack the Americans, because the American blockade of the St. Lawrence still prevented the British from providing the necessary ammunition. Thus Hamilton reported to Dartmouth that he had told the

[15] Report of William Wilson, September 26, and of White Mingo, October 18, 1776, to Indian Commissioners, Morgan Letter Book, no. 2. Wilson's report is also in *American Archives,* fifth series, 2:514-518.

Indians assembled at Detroit "to content themselves, with watchfully observing the Enemy's motions," and that if they were attacked by the Virginians he would notify the whole confederacy, which could then unite its forces in defense. He added, however, that groups of Indians would probably persist in "falling on the scattered settlers on the Ohio . . . a deplorable sort of war, but which the arrogance, disloyalty, and imprudence of the Virginians has justly drawn down upon them." That he was actually dissuading the Indians from violence and deplored the attacks on Kentucky was, of course, not known to the American authorities. They had learned enough to abandon many of the preparations for a general Indian attack, and they were satisfied that the Delawares and the Shawnee would continue neutral "unless compell'd to a War by the more western Tribes." Although the Wyandot, Mingo, Chippewa, and Ottawa were "much more to be dreaded," and their true intentions could not yet be determined, the commissioners informed Colonel Aeneas Mackay that although a stockade at Kittanning was still desirable, "the taking Posts at Presque Isle & Lebouf must for the present be deferred."[16]

Although the second treaty of Pittsburgh was attended only by the Seneca, Delawares, and Shawnee, Morgan was justified in reporting to Congress on November 8, 1776, that the cloud that had threatened to break over the Ohio Valley "appears now to be nearly dispersed." The assembled tribes, he said, had resolved "to preserve inviolate the peace and neutrality they have engaged in with the United States." With the Mingo lay the cause of any remaining difficulty, and the Shawnee were enlisted in forewarning the Americans of their plans. Furthermore, the Seneca were engaged to deal finally with the Mingo; the Six Nations, Morgan stated, "have now deputed a principal chief and several warriors to go and remove the whole of them to the *Seneca* country; or at least to make

[16] "The Haldimand Papers," in *Michigan Pioneer and Historical Collections,* 10:268; Indian Commissioners to William Lochry, October 8, and to Aeneas Mackay, October 10, 1776, Morgan Letter Book, no. 2.

them sensible of their errors and engage them to desist." Thus the problem of the Mingo was in a fair way to be settled if the friendship between the United States and the Six Nations could be preserved, a requirement that was unfortunately not fulfilled. The crisis for the time being, however, was over. The frontiersmen, many of whom, as the result of the earlier reports, had fled in panic to safety in the East, were now encouraged by the friendly mood of the Indians. "God Grant," one of them prayed, "that temper may long Continue with them." The commissioners were satisfied and on October 8 declared that they would assuredly "be able at least to keep off a general Indian War with the Savages until the Spring, & we hope some Events will arise before that period which may convince the Indians that their true Interest will consist in an entire Neutrality."[17]

With the beginning of the campaign of 1777, however, the British, in view of the fact that the St. Lawrence had been opened, were at last prepared to make better use of their superior ability to supply the Indians. It was planned that upon the frontiers of New York, Pennsylvania, and Virginia, the tribesmen were to be induced to take up the hatchet, to harass the settlers, and to embarrass the general military plans of the colonies whenever possible. Instructions were sent to General St. Leger in New York and to Hamilton at Detroit to this effect. The orders of Hamilton, sent from London on March 26 to General Guy Carleton at Quebec and relayed to Hamilton, directed that the latter should assemble as many Indians as he could and, placing "proper persons" in command to "restrain them from committing violence on the well affected and inoffensive Inhabitants, employ them in making a Diversion and exciting an alarm upon the frontiers of Virginia and Pennsylvania."[18]

The intensity of the resulting Indian attacks on the Ameri-

---

[17] Morgan to President of Congress, November 8, 1776; Indian Commissioners to William Lochry, October 8, 1776, Morgan Letter Book, no. 2; Thwaites and Kellogg, *Revolution on the Upper Ohio*, 204.

[18] "The Haldimand Papers," in *Michigan Pioneer and Historical Collections*, 9:347.

can frontier varied. At no time, however, were they as severe as the Americans anticipated. The tribes of the upper lakes, including the Wyandot, assembled at Detroit in June, 1777, but no organized attack on the frontier resulted. Hamilton had urged the Indians to take up the hatchet and had used as arguments the encroachments of the Virginians on the Kentucky hunting grounds, the "grand operation" of Burgoyne, St. Leger, and Howe then going forward for the conquest of the colonies in New York, and the action of the Six Nations in actively supporting the British cause. But the Wyandot, after having tried unsuccessfully to persuade the Chippewa to take the responsibility for the decision, refused to accept the hatchet and war belt given them by Hamilton, on the grounds that the British should lead the way in fighting their own war, a proposal to which Hamilton was unable to agree because of a lack of sufficient troops and supplies. This decision did not, however, prevent independent parties of Wyandot from joining the Mingo in sporadic attacks upon the frontiers. At Niagara and Oswego in New York the Six Nations showed a more hostile disposition, because the British were actually engaged in a real offensive operation. By June, 1777, Guy Johnson was able to report that the Indians had "made several attacks along the back settlements from Fort Stanwix to the Ohio, with such success that the rebels have been obliged to detach General Hand with some troops to protect the frontiers and are in much consternation." Throughout the rest of the year the Six Nations, under the influence of the Mohawk chief, Brant, fought loyally for the British cause, confident that the colonists could not prevail against the power of the king's armies and that the ships of Indian goods safely in harbor at New York would bring them ample reward. Their hopes were dashed by the repulse of St. Leger at Oriskany, near Fort Stanwix, and by the defeat of Burgoyne at Saratoga in September, but their allegiance to the king remained.[19]

[19] Daniel Sullivan to Morgan, March 22, 1777, Morgan Letter Book, no. 1; Thwaites and Kellogg, *Frontier Defense*, 7-11; *Pennsylvania Archives*, first series, 5:446; *New York Colonial Documents*, 8:712.

The Indians and the Outbreak of Revolution

Nothing illustrates the weakness of the Americans in the face of the grave crises of 1777 so well as their complete inability to chastise the belligerent Mingo, who, released from the restraint placed on them by the Seneca, who had turned to the British, continued their raids throughout the year and gradually drew unto themselves adherents from other tribes. The main fruit of the second treaty of Pittsburgh in 1776 had been to assure the neutrality of all the tribes except the Mingo, and the Seneca chief, Guyasuta, had been sent to attempt to force these Indians to desist from their plundering and to return to the country of the Six Nations. But the Mingo were not to be silenced. They were a proud band, and they assumed, as Morgan wrote, "the air and authority of the Six Nations council."[20] These Indians desired, above all else, the expulsion of the whites from Kentucky. At the first treaty of Pittsburgh in 1775 they had refused to accept the terms offered them and from that day had resisted the settling of this new country from which the Shawnee had been expelled. By the spring of 1777 they had begun to gain more converts to their cause, largely because of the supplies available to all Indians from the British and because of the general expectation for the success of the plans of Burgoyne and his colleagues. The Six Nations of New York had also come out openly in support of the British cause and were urging the Mingo to do the same, and Morgan, at least, had doubts as to the sincerity of the Seneca in their former efforts to restrain that tribe. The nucleus of the Mingo Indians was a group that had separated from the main body of the Six Nations twenty or more years earlier; their fighting strength in 1777 amounted to about eighty men. During that spring, however, their power was greatly increased by the alliance with them of half the Shawnee nation, some Delawares, and a few scattered Wyandot.[21]

The Shawnee nation was split asunder on the issue of join-

[20] Morgan to Indian Agent of Northern Department, March 9, 1777, Morgan Letter Book, no. 1.
[21] Morgan to Indian Agent of Northern Department, March 9, 1777, Morgan Letter Book, no. 1; M. C. Darlington, *Fort Pitt*, 204.

ing the Mingo. There is no direct evidence to prove whether or not the disaffected group deliberately aspired at this time to reconquer the Kentucky hunting grounds, lost in Dunmore's War, or whether the British had as yet made them any promises in this connection. The peaceful and pro-American group was represented by the famous chief, Cornstalk. A schism also developed among the Delawares. Captain James O'Hara stated that the Munsee tribe, a division of the Delawares, "are much inclined to listen to the Mingoes," and the Delaware council reported to Morgan on February 26, "Some of our own foolish people who have been settled near the Mingo are corrupted by them." The Delawares likewise renewed their request for the construction of a garrisoned fort in their country and for a store of provisions and ammunition so that they might collect the friendly Indians together and thus render the outlying villages less likely to succumb to the blandishments of the Mingo. The Delaware defection was not so great as the Shawnee; on investigation, Morgan was informed by the Delawares that the Munsee intended to assemble at Shenango in what is now Mercer County "to be out of the way of bad people" and that they were "determined to be directed by the Delaware Council."[22]

Late in February, 1777, however, a mixed band of Mingo, Shawnee, Delawares, and Wyandot set out for Kentucky and opened a campaign of siege and terror. They besieged Wheeling, Boonesborough, and other stations, burned supplies, and carried off the horses, in order to prevent the raising of crops and to force the pioneers to abandon the country. Virginia was appealed to, and on March 12 the Executive Council resolved on a military expedition to destroy the Mingo towns. Accordingly Governor Patrick Henry sent orders to Colonel David Shepherd to march in command of three hundred men "with the utmost secrecy & expedition to punish the Indians of Pluggy's Town," one of the Mingo settlements. But the

[22] Shawnee Chiefs to Morgan, February 28, 1777; Delawares to Morgan, February 26, 1777; Morgan to Captain Pipe, April 7, 1777, Morgan Letter Book, no. 1; M. C. Darlington, *Fort Pitt*, 204.

Virginia expedition was not destined to take place; it was rendered too dangerous by the inability of the frontier troops to discriminate between the Mingo and the friendly tribes. "We could very easily chastise these People," Morgan wrote on March 9, "was it not for . . . our desire to avoid offending other Nations; for to distinguish between a Party of one & the other in case of meeting in the Woods would be impossible in many cases; and a single mistake might be fatal." To attack the Mingo, therefore, would be to plunge the frontiers into a general war in which all tribes would have to take sides. Governor Henry thought that the situation could be used to bring the Delawares and Shawnee into such a war on the side of the Americans and gave specific instructions for the protection of these Indians. "In one Word," said he, "support protect defend & cherish them in every Respect to the utmost." He also, however, instructed Shepherd to consult Morgan and John Neville, Virginia commandant at Fort Pitt, and if they discovered that the Shawnee and Delawares "will resent your March thro' their Country as an Injury, you are to lay aside the matter & not March."[23]

Morgan was aware that the American frontier was by no means prepared for such an expedition and that the difficulties in its way were insurmountable. He was certain that neither the Delawares nor the Shawnee would actively support the American cause so long as the British were able to supply the tribes more plentifully than the Americans and could foster the Indians' expectations for the success of a British invasion of the Hudson Valley. He therefore advised waiting until the outcome of affairs in the East should be favorable to the American cause. "Should it please God," he said, "to bless us with Victory to overcome our British Enemies on the Sea Coast, we shall have it in our power to take ample satisfaction of our Indian Enemy." Morgan also knew that the Indians

[23] Thwaites and Kellogg, *Frontier Defense,* 182, 244; United States Continental Congress, *Journals . . . 1774-1789,* 7:166; Henry to Shepherd, March 12, 1777; Morgan to Indian Agent of Northern Department, March 9, 1777, Morgan Letter Book, no. 1.

had not forgotten the years of contempt, trespasses, and assaults that had culminated in Dunmore's War. Nor had such trespasses ceased with the fine promises of the first treaty of Pittsburgh; "tomahawk claims" of speculators, some of whom were provided with Pennsylvania and Virginia land warrants, were common in the western country, and the practice of making them continued down into the year 1777. In March of that year Morgan wrote that care should be taken "to treat the different Nations in all respects with Justice, Humanity & Hospitality . . . for Parties have been hunting on their own Lands . . . These Steps if continued will deprive us of all our Indian Allies, and multiply our Enemies." He informed Congress that there was more to be gained by tact, forbearance, and calm investigation than by any expedition, and although he admitted that it was distressing to have to submit to the Mingo attacks, he declared that "it must be extremely injurious to the interest of the United States at this critical time, to involve ourselves into a general Indian War." He further recommended that Congress "appoint an Officer of Abilities to repair to this place to enquire into the true State of the Country & the real dispositions of the Indians . . . I believe it is more necessary to restrain our own people & promote good order among them than to think of awing the different Nations by expeditions." In April he reported that he had conferred with the friendly Shawnee and Delawares, who, he was convinced, "would wish our Success," but who deemed it unwise to attempt such offensive measures. Upon the receipt of these advices, Congress resolved that Virginia be requested to suspend the Mingo expedition and that a copy of Morgan's letter be sent to Governor Henry. The Virginia government in turn decided to abandon the expedition, and orders were sent to Shepherd, Neville, and Morgan to that effect. The Mingo thus escaped chastisement through the triumph of Morgan's policy of forbearance.[24]

Such a policy, however, was unnatural and could not pre-

[24] Morgan and Neville to Henry, April 1, 1777; Morgan to President of Congress,

The Indians and the Outbreak of Revolution

vail because the frontiersmen could not brook Indian attacks very long. A series of brutal assaults by whites upon innocent Indians in the latter half of 1777 put an end to all hopes of peace. The first of these was made in July on Indians who had arrived at Pittsburgh to attend a treaty; and by this action any gain the Americans may have made by the abandonment of the Mingo expedition was lost.

On June 18, 1777, Congress, upon the recommendation of Morgan, had ordered a third treaty to be held at Fort Pitt during the summer and had appropriated forty-two hundred dollars for the expenses thereof; at the same time the money that had already been authorized for co-operation with Virginia in the Mingo expedition was curtailed. Morgan had, indeed, already set the wheels in motion for this treaty. During March and April he had actually invited the Delawares, Shawnee, and Six Nations to assemble at Fort Pitt in July and had engaged the Delawares to summon the northern nations, including the Wyandot and Mingo. The Delawares declined to inform the Mingo, declaring it to be "useless to speak to them any more as they are determined not to listen to you or us," but they were successful in getting the Wyandot to promise to meet the Americans at the Delaware capital at Coshocton when they were summoned. The Pittsburgh treaty in July was, therefore, so far as the Wyandot were concerned, preliminary to the one to be held at Coshocton.[25]

It would have been too much, perhaps, to expect the Mingo to be present at the treaty, but Morgan counted strongly on the presence of their kinsmen, the Seneca. If the latter were placated, their influence in persuading the Mingo to be peaceful could be counted on. The Seneca, however, were part of the Six Nations' confederacy and, as has been noted, were fol-

March 15, 1777; Morgan to Shepherd, April 8, 1777, Morgan Letter Book, no. 1; Crumrine, *Washington County,* 187; United States Continental Congress, *Journals . . . 1774-1789,* 7:201; Thwaites and Kellogg, *Revolution on the Upper Ohio,* 247.
[25] United States Continental Congress, *Journals . . . 1774-1789,* 8:478, 493; Morgan to Delawares, March 6, 1777; Morgan to Robin, March 11, 1777; Delawares to Wyandot, March 26, 1777; Delawares to Morgan, March 29, 1777; David Zeisberger to Morgan, July 7, 1777, Morgan Letter Book, no. 1.

lowing their confederates in plans to co-operate with the British in the conquest of the Hudson Valley. As early as January 4, 1777, Morgan had reported to Congress a complaint from the Seneca "relative to our settling on their Lands." A month later a party of Seneca had set out from Niagara, at the instigation, no doubt, of the British, to warn off from Venango (now Franklin), at the forks of the Allegheny River and French Creek, certain frontiersmen who the Seneca alleged were trespassing on Indian lands. "The lands are ours," the message read, "and we insist on your quitting them immediately." According to Morgan, there had been no trespasses by the whites at Venango. Furthermore, the unpropitious manner in which the message had been delivered caused frontiersmen to experience genuine resentment. For the letter had been left, along with a war mallet and a tomahawk, on the dead body of Andrew Simpson on the road from Kittanning to Pittsburgh. At the same time Simpson's companion, Fergus Moorehead, was captured and turned over to the British. Moreover, in February a party of four Seneca had kidnapped Lieutenant Andrew McFarlane at his trading post near Kittanning and had taken him to the British at Niagara. These acts of apparently unprovoked hostility, coupled with the fact that General Washington had ordered Colonel Aeneas Mackay's western Pennsylvania regiment of seven companies, which was raised for service in the West, to join his army in the East, caused great uneasiness on the frontier. At the same time rumors were spreading that the Six Nations were preparing to attack Kittanning and overrun the frontier.[26]

Although Morgan co-operated in urging the retention of the troops ordered East and in the sending of reinforcements to Kittanning, he urged the same forbearance with the Six Nations that he was advocating with the Mingo. Thus he stated

[26] Morgan to President of Congress, January 4, February 14, March 2, March 24, 1777; Captain Samuel Moorehead to Morgan, March 21, 1777; David Sullivan to Morgan, March 22, 1777; Morgan to Westmoreland County Militia Officers, March 23, 1777, Morgan Letter Book, no. 1; Hildreth, *Pioneer History*, 116, 117; Thwaites and Kellogg, *Revolution on the Upper Ohio*, 245.

to Congress that the Six Nations were partially justified in their complaints of encroachments, which, he said, "we have undeniably made on their Lands, (tho' not at Venango)," and he advised that Pennsylvania be requested to remove the trespassers. Congress thereupon resolved that Pennsylvania should assure the Indians of satisfaction in the matter, but the resolution, which was sent to the Indian commissioners for the northern department, was, of course, a mere gesture. Morgan, at the same time, sent a message to the Seneca mildly rebuking them and promising them protection if they would come to the treaty at Pittsburgh. "It was certainly very foolish," he told them, "to deliver the Messages at Kittanning in the manner you did . . . You know I have never encroach'd on your Lands at Allegany & I have order'd the Settlers away from your Susquehanna Lands—I have no Settlement at Venango nor do I intend to settle there unless you force me to it." By this show of forbearance and frankness, Morgan succeeded in persuading the Seneca to be present at the treaty. But alas, the American cause would have fared better if the treaty had never been held. Frontier hatred at Pittsburgh, kindled by the murder of Simpson and the capture of McFarlane and Moorehead, could not contain itself in the very presence of the tribe that was held responsible, and the Seneca had scarcely arrived in Pittsburgh before they were fired upon by whites. Several Indians were killed. The Moravian chronicler, Loskiel, indicates the disastrous effect of this action on the Indians: "By this step," he says, "the savages were again enraged at the white people, considered them altogether as traitors, and vowed revenge." Governor John Page of Virginia immediately urged General Hand at Pittsburgh "to discover & bring to justice the perpetrators of the horrid murders committed on the Indians at their late Treaty at Fort Pitt . . . this affair . . . is a repetition of the same cruel & faithless behavior which the Cherokees experienced from us on a late similar occasion."[27]

[27] United States Continental Congress, *Journals* . . . *1774-1789*, 8:392; Loskiel,

The frontiersmen had, indeed, played straight into the hands of the British. In January, 1778, Morgan received a report from the Seneca country that the old chief, Guyasuta, had become one of the "warmest Enemies" of the Americans and that the Seneca were "determined to join the King of England's Troops" and "to exert themselves in committing Hostilities against the Frontier Inhabitants early in the Spring, with all their Abilities."[28] The third treaty of Pittsburgh was thus a failure. It not only alienated forever the Seneca tribe, but it also made impossible a meeting with the Wyandot, while the few meek Delawares who attended returned home conscious that they were incurring the contempt of the rest of the tribes.

The second injustice committed by the whites against the Indians was the murder of the Shawnee chief, Cornstalk, and his son, while they were held as hostages by the whites. It is of interest to review briefly the series of events that preceded this unwarranted action.

Plans for an invasion of the Indian country were revived as a result of the increased hostility of the Indians produced by the affair at the third treaty of Pittsburgh and by Governor Hamilton's continued activities among the tribes after the June council at Detroit. This hostility resolved itself into a series of attacks during July, 1777, one of which was that made on Fort Statler on Dunkard Creek, a branch of the Monongahela. It will be remembered that at the Detroit council, Hamilton had been unable to get the Wyandot to join the British in active warfare; nevertheless a band of these Indians now prepared to surprise the inhabitants of the upper Ohio Valley, and the Moravian missionary, David Zeisberger, reported that they had tried, unsuccessfully, to get converts from among the Delawares. Other acts of hostility, too nu-

Mission of the United Brethren, part 3, p. 122; Thwaites and Kellogg, *Frontier Defense,* 85; Morgan to President of Congress, March 24, April 1, 1777; Morgan to Captain Pipe, April 7, 1777, Morgan Letter Book, no. 1. The message to the Seneca was included in the letter to Captain Pipe.

[28] W. M. Darlington, *Gist's Journals,* 214-216.

merous to detail, were perpetrated at various places. The result was that Brigadier General Edward Hand, commander of the new Continental establishment created by resolution of Congress of June 3, determined to revive the expedition against the Mingo and sought to raise two thousand men from the frontiers of Pennsylvania. He was less impressed than Morgan by the possibility of drawing otherwise peaceful tribes into a general war, and he believed that the Indians could be forced to submission only by intimidation and a show of military power. The general opinion of him on the frontier is reflected in Loskiel's exaggerated report that after Hand's appointment to command, "a dreadful account was received, that an American general had arrived in Pittsburg, who denied quarter to any Indian, whether friend or foe, being resolved to destroy them all."[29]

Hand at first experienced a strange lack of support from the frontiersmen, some of whom protested that Pennsylvania did not have the constitutional power to order them to leave their homes unprotected. Fears for their own families and property were rekindled by the events of September, which included the destruction of the village of Wheeling, the siege of Fort Henry, the massacre of a foraging party from that fort under Captain William Foreman, and the abandonment of the garrison at Kittanning. They were further stirred by the recurring specter of a Loyalist-Indian uprising: in August a nest of Loyalists was surprised at and near Statler's Fort in Monongalia County, and messages were found at Kittanning offering two hundred acres of land to all who would join the British cause. George Morgan, in charge of the commissary department in the West, was under grave suspicion as a Tory during this period, and on September 1 Colonel James Perry refused to give a consignment of supplies for Fort Pitt into his hands because "the people in General are uneasy lest . . . it might fall into the hands of, or be destroyed by the Tories."

[29] Thwaites and Kellogg, *Frontier Defense,* 21-29, 36-43, 48-50; *Pennsylvania Archives,* first series, 5:443; Loskiel, *Mission of the United Brethren,* part 3, p. 127.

Morgan's arrest followed, but he was eventually acquitted. Hand received encouragement, however, from the raising of the sieges of Boonesborough and Fort Henry and from the news of Burgoyne's defeat on September 17, and in October he wrote to Colonel William Russell that he still hoped to drink his health "in pure element at Sandusky before Christmas." But his plans were doomed to failure by the impossibility of raising and provisioning a sufficient force, and late in October the orders for the expedition were countermanded.[30]

Although Hand's project was never carried out, it was the indirect cause of the unprovoked assault of the Virginia militia on the Shawnee chief, Cornstalk. When the Shawnee heard of Hand's projected invasion, Cornstalk and a companion went to Captain Matthew Arbuckle, commandant of Fort Randolph at the mouth of the Kanawha, "with strong protestations of friendship . . . to know the reason of it." Arbuckle learned from them that the peaceful Shawnee would probably be forced by the belligerent part of the nation and by British pressure to resist the Americans, and he therefore decided to detain the Indians as hostages to insure the good conduct of their tribe. Eight days later Cornstalk's son, Elinipsico, came to inquire why his father was detained, and he was also held as a hostage. Impartial witnesses agreed that such conduct was dishonorable. Captain John Stuart, who was present, says in his narrative that Cornstalk had made the visit as a friendly gesture "to communicate the temper and disposition of the Indians, and their design of taking part with the British," and another chronicler declares that Cornstalk was exerting all his influence "to prevent his brethren from again involving themselves, in a war with the whites." The poignantly tragic story is briefly concluded. On November 10 a party of militiamen crossed the Kanawha to hunt, and one of their number, a man named Gilmore, was ambushed and killed by

[30] Hand Correspondence, no. 14, 17, 20-22, 67, 68, 125, 141, 151, 152; Thwaites and Kellogg, *Frontier Defense*, 54-68, 82, 86-88, 106-112, 120, 134, 145-148; Withers, *Border Warfare*, 198-207, 219-228; Siebert, *Tories of the Upper Ohio*, 6; Savelle, *George Morgan*, 148-151.

The Indians and the Outbreak of Revolution

unknown Indians. Believing that the miscreants were Shawnee, probably those who had accompanied Cornstalk's son as far as the river bank the day before, the militia party rushed back to the fort to wreak vengeance on the hostages for the death of their comrade. As they approached the cabin in which the hostages were held, the interpreter's wife ran to the Indians to inform them that they were about to be killed. It is said that the young warrior, realizing his fate, "trembled exceedingly" and that Cornstalk "told him not to be afraid, for the great Spirit above had sent him there to be killed." With the death of these Indians the friendship of the Shawnee nation for the Americans perished forever. No one realized what had happened more completely than did General Hand. To the secretary of war he wrote, "From this event we have little reason to expect a reconciliation with the Shawanese . . . for if we had any friends among them, those unfortunate wretches were so."[31]

Shortly after this affair George Morgan revealed that the murder of Gilmore had been committed by Mingo and not by Shawnee, and this fact was admitted by Congress and by Colonels Fleming and Preston of Virginia in official apologies to the Shawnee nation. But the perpetrators of the murders went unpunished. General Hand was able to do nothing at the time in the way of bringing them to justice, and when the men accused were finally, through the insistence of Governor Henry, brought to trial in April, 1778, in the court of Rockbridge County, Virginia, they were acquitted because there were no witnesses against them.[32]

The general feeling of repugnance caused by these murders was due more to the fear of Shawnee retaliation than to sympathy for the "unfortunate wretches," and this fear promoted an intensified program of defense that gradually led to offen-

[31] Thwaites and Kellogg, *Frontier Defense,* 126, 149, 160, 188, 189; Withers, *Border Warfare,* 209.

[32] Thwaites and Kellogg, *Frontier Defense,* 176, 207, 234-237, 240, 259-261; "Early Days of Rockbridge County," in *Virginia Magazine of History and Biography,* 17:324 (1909).

sive measures. Colonel William Preston, convinced that the Shawnee would lose no time in making reprisals, petitioned the Council of Virginia for "some speedy measure for the Protection of the Frontier inhabitants," and on February 19 the Executive Council, with the approval of Governor Henry, gave directions for the necessary defense measures. Henry, at whose urgency the murderers of Cornstalk were brought to trial, deplored the necessity for this action and told Preston: "My Views go no further than defensive Operations. . . . offensive Measures set on foot against these Indians at this time after their late Treatment, would be too full of Injustice to escape general Execration." He likewise insisted upon a treaty with the Shawnee to be preceded by the mutual exchange of hostages. But to the frontier mind his attitude was one of mere sentimentality. Peace negotiations were futile. Preston and Fleming flatly informed him that the state should be prepared (as it obviously was not) to assume the financial burdens of such a treaty, if, indeed, it were not too late to bring one about, and, as Preston intimated, it was too late.[33]

Encouraged by Hamilton and by the former deputy of Sir William Johnson, Alexander McKee, who broke his parole and escaped from Pittsburgh in March, 1778, and made his way to the British at Detroit, the Shawnee sought revenge on the whites by a series of raids that continued with increasing intensity until the end of the Revolutionary War. On March 11 they accepted the war belt from Hamilton and on April 1 brought in their first prisoners. Four days later they brought in Boone and members of his party, whom they had captured at the Blue Licks in Kentucky while they were making salt, and Hamilton was greatly encouraged by Boone's account of the desperate condition of the people on the frontier. The focal point of Shawnee vengeance was, of course, Fort Randolph and the settlements on the Kanawha and its branch, the Greenbrier. On May 16 four hundred Shawnee appeared sud-

[33] David I. Bushnell, "The Virginia Frontier," in *Virginia Magazine of History and Biography*, 23:114, 118 (1915); Thwaites and Kellogg, *Frontier Defense*, 205-207, 223-225, 240.

denly before Fort Randolph and demanded its surrender and, upon the refusal of Captain William McKee, began a siege that lasted for a week. Finally, after destroying all the white men's cattle and horses, they abandoned the siege and began to ascend the Kanawha, with the intention of taking the upper stronghold by surprise. In the meantime they kept the communications between Fort Randolph and Fort Donnally on the Greenbrier closed. The frontiersmen held their breath in suspense. Preston wrote to Fleming on May 30, "I tremble for the fate of the Greenbrier people," and on June 2 he wrote, "I cannot express my Anxiety for the People in Greenbrier . . . Heaven Grant, that my apprehensions may be Groundless." But frontier ingenuity was equal to the occasion. In one of those thrilling episodes that enliven the pages of "border history," two scouts, John Pryor and Philip Hammond, made their way in disguise up the Kanawha through the Indian lines, and warned the defenders at Fort Donnally so that they were enabled to withstand the Shawnee attack until they were relieved by reinforcements under Samuel Lewis.[34]

The enthusiasm of the frontiersmen over the successful defense of Fort Donnally marked the transition from a state of fear of Shawnee vengeance to one of planning for the invasion of the Shawnee country. On June 14 Preston recommended for Governor Henry's approval, "a scheme that a number of young men have formed of embodying themselves into a Company or two and marching at their own Expence into the Indian Country & there annoy the Enemy." To this Henry, who, with reluctance, had begun to view offensive measures as necessary, replied, "I greatly approve the Spirit of the young men who are to go to the Enemys Country . . . It is bold of the men & commendable." On July 7 the Executive Council of Virginia abandoned its earlier policy of restraint and officially authorized General McIntosh at Fort Pitt to organize an expedition against the hostile Indians to "chastise them as they

---

[34] "The Haldimand Papers," in *Michigan Pioneer and Historical Collections*, 9:435; Kellogg, *Frontier Advance*, 62, 64, 66-73, 85, 98.

deserve." Thus did the murder of their kinsman, Cornstalk, and the frontier panic that it created, bring upon the luckless Shawnee the full military power of the frontiersmen.[35]

Up to this time, as has been pointed out earlier, Congressional policy had been weak, and Virginia had dominated events through her militia and her outposts on the Ohio at Fort Pitt, Fort Henry, and Fort Randolph. The determining factors in the invigoration of federal policy that was soon to take place, were, first, the desire of Virginia herself that Congress take over more control, and second, the complete failure of the old militia policy of defense, which was based on Lord Dunmore's contention that a line of forts along the Ohio garrisoned by militia would provide the necessary protection. With the spread of hostilities in 1777 and with the addition of the Shawnee to the hostile tribes in 1778, the inadequacy of this theory of defense became apparent, and in February, 1778, shortly before the Shawnee invasion of the Kanawha Valley, an event had occurred that demonstrated perfectly the need of a more effective policy.

While the Virginia militia officers were striving with the Shawnee on the Kanawha, General Hand was trying to maintain effective protection for the frontier at Pittsburgh. But the task was clearly hopeless because of the lack of an advanced federal fort to impress the Indians, and the inadequacy of the militia. Hand had to rely wholly on the militia forces, and his experience with them had been and continued to be humiliating. Refusals to obey orders, insistence on cheaper rates for provisions, short terms, furlough problems, and complaints as to salaries, were a few of his many difficulties. In fact the Congressional commissioners reported to Congress in 1778 that among the militia "a refactory and licentious Spirit is kept up, little compatible with the just Sense of military Subordination and Obedience." Hand was nevertheless obliged to continue to make the best of a bad situation.[36]

[35] Kellogg, *Frontier Advance*, 81, 90, 100, 104.
[36] Hand Correspondence, no. 54; Thwaites and Kellogg, *Frontier Defense*, 80; United States Continental Congress Papers, series 78, vol. 2, p. 437-444.

The Indians and the Outbreak of Revolution

In January, 1778, Hand learned that the British had deposited at the mouth of the Cuyahoga River a large amount of military stores, and, assuming that they were destined to be used by hostile Indians against the frontier, he determined on an expedition to destroy them. Within a month he was on his way with a force of five hundred, made up largely of Westmoreland militia. A thaw set in, however, and, after ascending the Beaver River as far as the Mahoning, the expedition was obliged to turn back. On their return trip they came upon an Indian camp about forty miles from the mouth of the Beaver where they found one Delaware with some women and children, and the militia, having been led by the scouts to expect a hostile group of warriors, impetuously killed the man and one of the women. The militiamen learned from the survivors that ten miles up the river some Munsee Indians were making salt. "I detachd a party," wrote Hand, "to Secure them, they turn'd out to be 4 Women & a Boy, of these one Woman only was Saved."[37] Among those who escaped death were relatives of the friendly Delaware chief, Captain Pipe. Thus ended the famous, or rather the infamous "squaw campaign," which was a final demonstration of the futility of relying upon the militia for frontier defense. It also helped to give rise to the idea that one or more strong forts stationed in the heart of the Indian country might, if properly garrisoned and supported by Congress, hold the Indians at bay much more effectively and economically than futile expeditions from the poorly equipped defense posts on the Ohio.

[37] Thwaites and Kellogg, *Frontier Defense,* 193, 215-220; Hand Correspondence, no. 98.

9

The Fort McIntosh-Fort Laurens
Indian Frontier
1778-1779

THE erection and attempted maintenance of the twin posts of Fort McIntosh and Fort Laurens during the years of 1778 and 1779 represents a distinct phase of American Indian policy. As has been pointed out, the need for a new policy developed from the fact, but recently realized, that the old measures neither provided an adequate system of defense nor made possible an effective means of offense. Ever since Dunmore's War, frontiersmen had faced the Indians behind a fringe of stations and forts placed, not in the Indian country, as Fort McIntosh and Fort Laurens were to be, but in the white man's country at the outer edge of settlement. Examples of these were Fort Wallace on the Conemaugh; Fort Hand, Fort Pitt, Fort Henry, and Fort Randolph, on the Ohio; and

Fort Donnally on the Greenbrier. Scouts from these posts were supposed to keep the country informed of the approach of the Indians. This meant that the frontiers would not know of an Indian invasion until the hostile army was at their very doors. Moreover, to make an efficient offensive stroke into the Indian country was almost impossible because the collection of a militia army large enough to accomplish a worthy objective would require resources in supplies and men that the frontier simply did not have. These points were clearly demonstrated by Hand's February expedition and by the Shawnee invasion of the Kanawha Valley in May.

A fundamental aspect of the Fort McIntosh-Fort Laurens movement was the assuming by the Continental government of the major share of the responsibility for protection against the Indians. The Continental Congress from 1775 to 1777 obviously had too much to do to add this western problem to its burdens. By the fall of 1777, however, the desolation caused by the belligerent Mingo, Seneca, and miscellaneous banditti had become so great, the clamors of the frontiersmen for protection so insistent, and the danger of Tory disaffection so real that on November 20, 1777, a special committee of Congress, to whom the flood of appeals from the frontier had been referred, reported that a dangerous spirit of hostility was in evidence on the Ohio frontier, caused by British machinations among the Indians. Resolutions were thereupon adopted by Congress appointing three commissioners to repair to Fort Pitt in order to investigate the causes of the trouble and to take measures to suppress them. They were also to cultivate the friendship of the Shawnee and Delaware Indians and to investigate the feasibility of assuming offensive military operations against the British and their Indian allies, with the conquest of Detroit as the ultimate objective.[1]

The commissioners arrived in Pittsburgh early in March, 1778, shortly after General Hand's return from the ignomini-

[1] *Pennsylvania Archives*, first series, 6:39, 68; 5:741; United States Continental Congress Papers, series 69, vol. 1, p. 439; United States Continental Congress, *Journals . . . 1774-1789*, 9:942-944.

ous squaw campaign. Although the Shawnee attack on Fort Donnally had not yet taken place, the commissioners saw at once the inadequacy of the militia system of defense. This system was too utterly extravagant, they reported, because to be effective it would require at least thirteen hundred militiamen on duty all the time. Militia troops were adapted only to "home Service, or short Excursions to the Indians Towns" and not to "a standing Defence of the Country, or for offensive Operations of any great Importance or Duration." In their two reports, made on March 31 and on April 27, they recommended to Congress several important changes in policy. One was the permanent stationing of two full regiments of Continental troops in the West, and another was the erection of a fort in the Indian country, preferably on the headwaters of the Scioto River.[2]

These recommendations were endorsed by Congress, and steps were soon under way to carry out the grand operations. Out of the proposal for the erection of a fort grew the conception of a conquest of Detroit under Continental auspices. Detroit was reported by the Congressional commissioners at Pittsburgh to be the source of all Indian attacks because it was at that point that the supplies for the tribesmen were received, stored, and eventually distributed to the Indians. If the expanded projects had been carried out, Fort McIntosh and Fort Laurens would have been but links in a great chain of forts immediately planned on by General Lachlan McIntosh, who was to be in charge of the expedition. As it turned out, however, the failure of the whole business made Fort Laurens the outermost post of the Continental advance. The reason for this failure was that the outburst of Indian war against eastern New York and the Pennsylvania frontiers, culminating in the Wyoming massacre of July 3, 1778, required the diversion of troops to the East and put a check on military plans in the West. Thus most of the troops destined

[2] United States Continental Congress Papers, series 78, vol. 2, p. 437-444; series 56, p. 93-95.

for the upper Ohio were sent up the Susquehanna, and the hopes of a panic-stricken western frontier, and of McIntosh himself, for a campaign against Detroit were disappointed.[3]

McIntosh, with his troops and supplies thus limited, was nevertheless determined to do something. If he could not get to Detroit he could at least occupy a post in the country of the friendly Delawares, and he clung to the hope that such a post would be but the beginning of a chain to Detroit, to which the remaining links would be added when Congress could provide the necessary assistance. In order to fulfill this plan he immediately set to work on the construction of a fort at the mouth of the Beaver River that could be used as a base for supplies for an advanced post to be erected sixty miles from it on the Tuscarawas River. He apparently did not doubt that he could protect this short communication from Fort McIntosh to Fort Laurens and thus adequately provide the garrison of the latter with supplies.[4]

Preparations were under way for this expedition throughout the spring and summer of 1778, and by early fall some of them were in a position to be carried out. These were the negotiations with the Delawares, to whom the commissioners, in compliance with the recommendations of Congress to cultivate the friendship of the Indians, had sent an invitation to attend a council at Pittsburgh. They had done this, of course, because it was necessary to have the assistance of at least one friendly tribe in the projected advance on Detroit. A crisis had been reached that year in the relations of the Americans with these Indians, whose solidarity had been shaken during the early part of 1778 by the conciliatory advances of the British, by the attack made on Captain Pipe's people during the squaw campaign, and finally by the reports of Alexander McKee and of his fellow-fugitives from Pittsburgh, Matthew Elliott and

---

[3] United States Continental Congress, *Journals . . . 1774-1789,* 11:587-591; 9:444; United States Continental Congress Papers, series 78, vol. 5, p. 155-157; vol. 20, part 1, p. 213-215; Kellogg, *Frontier Advance,* 15, 58, 61; *Pennsylvania Archives,* first series, 6:211, 495, 524, 528, 535, 556; Sipe, *Indian Wars,* 531-535.

[4] Kellogg, *Frontier Advance,* 294.

the Girtys, to the effect that the Americans were about to attack all Indian nations. This crisis had been averted, however, by the timely arrival of John Heckewelder, the missionary, at Coshocton in April, with messages of peace from Pittsburgh and denouncements of the stories of American intentions against the Indians; the Delawares, although they continued to be hard pressed by the British and the pro-British tribes, committed themselves once more to friendship with the Americans. The commissioners were thus able to proceed with their negotiations, with the result that on September 19 there had assembled at Pittsburgh the leading warriors of the Delaware nation to take part in the treaty to be known as the fourth treaty of Pittsburgh.[5]

Of this treaty George Morgan later said, "There never was a Conference with the Indians so improperly or villainously conducted." It provided for an offensive and defensive alliance between the United States and the Delawares and granted to American troops a free passage through the Delaware country in the proposed advance against Detroit. It also provided for the erection of a fort by the United States "for the better security of the old men, women, and children . . . whilst their warriors are engaged against the common enemy," and for further concessions to the Delawares. Morgan's characterization of the conference as a fraud was quite correct. The Indians had no understanding of the fact that the treaty was one of alliance and that the fort to be constructed was to protect their women and children while the warriors fought American battles. It is clear that, pro-Indian as some of the features of the treaty seemed to be, the articles were misrepresented to the tribesmen and that they did not know that in signing it they were "accepting the war belt," as they termed it. The work of the interpreters was quite deficient, if not de-

[5] United States Continental Congress Papers, series 56, p. 93-95; White Eyes and Killbuck to Morgan, March 14, April 6, 1778; Zeisberger to Morgan, April 6, 1778; White Eyes to Morgan, April 25, 1778; Proceedings of Council at Pittsburgh, April 26, 1778, Morgan Letter Book, no. 3; Heckewelder, *Mission of the United Brethren*, 170, 172, 180-182.

216

liberately deceptive. The Delaware, John Killbuck, expressed the Indian view of the affair in January, 1779: "I have now looked over the Articles of the Treaty again & find that they are wrote down false." McIntosh thus began his advance into the Indian country behind a false treaty and in doing so ran the risk of forcing one of the last friendly tribes into hostility against the United States. Had the Delawares known of the fate of their chief, White Eyes, who guided McIntosh and his army on this expedition, they would have deserted the Americans to the last man. It was given out that White Eyes had succumbed to small pox during the march, but actually, according to George Morgan, he was murdered by some of the militia, under circumstances that made it possible for him to be buried secretly. Thus was lost one of the most trusting Indian friends the American people ever had.[6]

The process of the American occupation of the Delaware country was an unexpected disillusionment to Indian preconceptions of the military power of the United States. The trouble was that McIntosh, instead of adopting the tactful manners of Morgan, assumed a bombastic air of superiority and marched into the Indian country as if he were Caesar occupying a conquered province. As a matter of fact, the army that the general took with him was so outrageously provisioned, and the horses were so weak from the lack of forage, which had been destroyed by the October frosts, that when he finally arrived at the site of Fort Laurens in November, he had become the object of Indian ridicule. McIntosh's successor, Brodhead, later denounced the movement heartily: "Gen'l. McIntosh," he wrote in April, 1779, "was more ambitious. He swore that nothing less than Detroit was his object, & he would have it in the winter season—in vain was the nakedness of the men—the scanty supplies worn out—Starved horses— leanness of the cattle and total want of forage—difficulty under such circumstances of supporting posts at so great a

[6] Kellogg, *Frontier Advance*, 203, 217; United States, *Indian Affairs, Laws and Treaties*, 2:1-3; Heckewelder, *Mission of the United Brethren*, 192, 193; Morgan to Congress, May 12, 1784, Morgan Letters, 1775-87 (Library of Congress).

distance in the enemies Country, and other Considerations urged."[7]

Brodhead was not exaggerating. The ridiculous nature of the American establishment of the Fort Pitt-Fort McIntosh-Fort Laurens chain in the Indian country is almost beyond belief. Fort McIntosh was erected at the mouth of the Beaver River in the early part of October, 1778, by Virginia militia, preparatory to the setting out of the larger expedition. It was erected, according to McIntosh, "for the Reception & Security of Prisoners & stores . . . with Barracks for a Regiment." At this post late in October arrived the twelve hundred men, mostly militia, who McIntosh fondly hoped would eventually be able to capture Detroit. Leaving 150 men there under the command of Colonel Richard Campbell, McIntosh proceeded up the Beaver and Mahoning rivers and late in November arrived at Coshocton, near which he built Fort Laurens. This fort was erected on the site of the present Bolivar, Ohio, on the Tuscarawas River. The army was but three days beyond Fort McIntosh when the horses became exhausted. The general complained, "They are tiring every day and Cannot Travel above four or five miles a day." The troops were depending on forage collected in western Pennsylvania and carried to them by pack horses and wagons. On November 14, after having traveled ten days from Fort McIntosh, the army had made only fifty miles. The general blamed "the scandelous Pack Horses that were imposed upon me" and wrote, "Above one half of them tires every day before we Travel two or three miles, and the woods is Strewed with those that have given out and dyed." Even at Fort McIntosh itself, forage conditions were deplorable. "My Waggon Horses," reported Campbell on November 10, "are droping down in the Geers for want of Forage." There was also a serious shortage of beef because of the lack of forage and of salt. John Irwin, deputy commissary general at Pittsburgh, reported on November 19 that "in a few Weeks more our Beeves in every Quarter will

[7] *Pennsylvania Archives*, first series, 12:110, 118, 146.

be wasted to mere Skeletons." As for provisions for the men, these very shortly began to give out, so that on November 18 Colonel Campbell reported that after making a survey of all the available supplies west of the mountains he had come to the conclusion that "there is not more than will Serve the army now under your Command Sixty Two Days."[8]

Thus it became apparent to McIntosh, after two weeks in the wilderness, that he must give up his dreams of the capture of Detroit and that he would not have time for more than the construction of Fort Laurens, after which he must disband his army and leave but a small garrison to protect the fort. He therefore on December 7 countermanded his orders to the Virginia counties of Washington, Montgomery, Botetourt, Greenbrier, and Rockbridge to supply two hundred militia each, to replace those whose terms would expire during the winter. Indeed he would not have been able to get the militia troops anyhow, because on November 20 Governor Henry of Virginia, at the order of the Executive Council of the state, had already countermanded McIntosh's orders. Colonel William Christian of Rockbridge County remarked, "It was well Gov[t] countermanded Macintoshs orders; because Men could not be got to go." Conditions are illustrated by the fact that after the completion of Fort Laurens in December the militia broke and rushed pellmell for home. Some accomplished the return trip in a day and a night; others returned more slowly under the greatest privations. While constructing the fort, the militia had been put on short rations for two weeks, and when they set out for home they had nothing to take with them. In fact, with sinister unanimity all the chronicles by participants in the expedition indicate that the returning militiamen were forced to subsist on the hides that had been left by the army on its way out. These they cut into strips and roasted. Others begged at farmhouses, or plundered the farm-

---

[8] Louis E. Graham, "Fort McIntosh," in *Western Pennsylvania Historical Magazine*, 15:93, 104 (1932); *Pennsylvania Archives*, first series, 7:132; Kellogg, *Frontier Advance*, 164-175.

ers' poultry without going through the formality of begging.[9]

Instead of covering himself with glory and reflecting honor on the United States for the Indians to behold and respect, McIntosh accomplished quite the opposite. To the redskins the spectacle of this bedraggled army, subsisting on short rations and appealing to them for provisions instead of bringing the long-expected Indian supplies, was most disillusioning. It was consequently the height of folly for McIntosh to assume the attitude of a *conquistador* and to deliver bombastic and threatening speeches to the Indians. On the twenty-second of November, the day after the army's arrival at the site of Fort Laurens, he called the near-by Delawares together and informed them that he was on his way to Detroit. "I have ordered," he regally declared, "Great Guns, Waggons, Horses, Cattle and flour enough to be got ready to take that place and am determined never to leave this Country untill that is done." He then gave the rest of the Delaware nation, the Shawnee, the Wyandot, the Chippewa, and the Ottawa the impossibly short time of fourteen days to come to Fort Laurens to make their peace, and solemnly warned them that "if any nations or Tribes refuses this offer now, I will never make it again nor rest or leave this Country, but pursue them While any of them remain upon the face of the earth for I can fill the woods with men as the Trees, or as the Stones are on the Ground." Then, after revealing his weakness by asking the Indians for supplies and promising to pay for them, he again denounced all enemy Indians, stating "that any nation or people who would not afterwards Join us heartily by taking up the Hatchet with us, and Striking, such refractory People Should be looked upon as Enemys to the United States of America." Upon this declaration, the Indians are said to have "Set up a General Laugh."[10]

Thus did McIntosh succeed in undoing all that had been accomplished by Morgan's years of painstaking efforts to

[9] Kellogg, *Frontier Advance*, 157-163, 182-185.
[10] Kellogg, *Frontier Advance*, 178-180.

cultivate the friendship of the Delawares. When Morgan, disgusted with the policy of attempting to build forts in the Indian country and to induce the Indians to take up arms in support of the United States without the necessary means of establishing an adequate trading system, finally resigned his post as Indian agent in May, 1779, he took the opportunity openly to denounce McIntosh to Congress, although McIntosh had retired two months before. At that time Morgan stated that an agent was unnecessary at Pittsburgh "further than to act under the sole direction of the Officer commanding in the Department—which from the conduct of General McIntosh . . . Colᵒ Morgan begs leave to decline."[11]

The subsequent history of Fort McIntosh and Fort Laurens was what the strange nature of their erection might lead one to expect. The communications between the two posts were so precarious that the garrison at Fort Laurens was dependent in large part upon the game and wild fowl brought in by the Delaware Indians. Few military enterprises in history ever reached such dismal depths as that from which Colonel John Gibson, commandant at Fort Laurens, and his little garrison were eventually rescued by fortuitous circumstances. Less than a month after McIntosh had left Gibson in charge, there was not enough clothing to keep the soldiers warm. On January 1, 1779, Gibson wrote to McIntosh at Pittsburgh, "Unless a Supply of Cloathing soon Arrives, I shall not have fifty men fit for duty in a short time." Three weeks later he wrote, "We have not a single nail to make a Sentry Box or a door for the Stores." The Delawares soon began to be insolent as the Americans went about begging for supplies. On January 23 certain Delawares at the Indian village of Goshgoshunk (Coshocton), shot and killed John Nash, one of the soldiers in a detachment sent by Gibson to buy corn and skins from the Indians. On the next day Indians shot three horses belonging to the Americans and carried off several saddles, blankets, and other articles. On the twenty-seventh two more American

[11] Kellogg, *Frontier Advance*, 277, 345.

soldiers were fired on and severely wounded. Chief Killbuck was profuse in his apologies, but the fact that Delawares were killing American soldiers and stealing American property in the central town of the Delaware nation is indicative that there was a serious defection within the tribe.[12]

The privations of the Fort Laurens garrison were soon intensified by siege. Late in January Gibson was informed by David Zeisberger that a band of belligerent Indians, led by Simon Girty, was about to attack the fort. These Indians were mostly Mingo and Wyandot; the Delawares were not yet willing to go so far as to take part in a concerted action against the Americans. Gibson at once dispatched Captain John Clark and fifteen men to Fort McIntosh for help. When four miles out, Clark was attacked by Girty's Indians, who killed two men, wounded four, made one a prisoner, and carried off all the letters entrusted to Clark by Gibson. The party thereupon beat a hasty retreat to Fort Laurens. Hearing of the siege and of the repulse of Captain Clark, McIntosh at Pittsburgh sent Major Richard Taylor with a guard of one hundred men to carry supplies by boat to Fort Laurens by the roundabout way of the Ohio and Muskingum rivers. The land route was too precarious. After getting twenty miles up the Muskingum, Taylor gave up and returned to Pittsburgh with all the supplies. He had lost two of his men in attacks by the Indians.

In the meantime conditions at Fort Laurens continued to be deplorable. On February 23 a detachment of nineteen men from the beleaguered post stole out to haul in wood. The party was ambushed; seventeen of its members were killed, and the other two were captured. Conditions inside the fort had become so bad, according to one report, that the soldiers, after being forced to live on one half a biscuit a day, were compelled finally to wash their moccasins and broil them for food. Because of these conditions McIntosh was obliged to march

---

[12] The account of conditions at Fort Laurens, January-March, 1779, in this and the two following paragraphs is based on letters in Kellogg, *Frontier Advance*, 190, 210, 212, 221, 224, 240-242, 256-258, and on "Letters from the Canadian Archives," in *Illinois Historical Collections*, 1:381-386.

to the relief of the fort with two hundred militia, three hundred Continentals, and the much-needed supplies. Upon his arrival at Fort Laurens late in March, 1779, the Indians dispersed, and the starving soldiers were so rejoiced that they fired off guns with such effect that the incoming pack horses stampeded and destroyed over half the flour. The soldiers so glutted themselves on the provisions that a general sickness followed, in which three men died.

After the withdrawal of McIntosh's relieving expedition, it was seen that conditions at Fort Laurens had not substantially improved. In fact this expedition did not even accomplish one of its most elemental purposes, that is, the escorting of adequate provisions for the garrison. Not only was a large part of the flour destroyed by the stampede of the pack horses, but also a great portion of the rest of the supplies was unfit for use. On April 29 Major Frederick Vernon, who had taken over the command of the fort, reported, "The greatest part of the pork is not fit for consumption, but necessity obliges us to eat it. Should you not send us provisions in a very short time, necessity will oblige us to begin on some cowhides which the Indians left, which will keep us gnawing two or three days . . . There is not one pair of shoes in the garrison fit to wear." Even the danger of siege was not permanently dispelled by the relieving expedition. When the Indians dispersed late in March, they repaired at once to the temporary British post on the Sandusky and petitioned the British commandant, Captain Henry Bird, for more help to pursue their activities against Fort Laurens. Reluctantly did Captain Richard B. Lernoult, who lacked sufficient troops even for his own immediate purposes at Detroit, give his consent to Bird for a renewal of the siege of Fort Laurens. The plan was to co-operate with Alexander McKee so as to join the Shawnee to the Wyandot and Mingo, and, when McIntosh's force had withdrawn, to attempt to put an end to the feeble garrison.[13]

[13] Kellogg, *Frontier Advance,* 269, 298; "The Haldimand Papers," in *Michigan Pioneer and Historical Collections,* 10:310.

The factors that saved Fort Laurens from a second siege in 1779 were the effect on the Wyandot and the Mingo of George Rogers Clark's victories on the Wabash, and the new danger to the Indian country from Kentucky. On February 25, Clark had consummated his amazing occupation of Vincennes, entailing the capture of the entire British garrison. The effect on the Indians was electrifying. From many sources arose British laments. Captain Lernoult at Detroit declared "This most unlucky shake . . . has greatly damped the spirit of the Indians"; Alexander McKee later reported, "This unlucky event has not only discouraged many tribes well disposed, but inclined others who were wavering to stand neuter"; and General Frederick Haldimand in September informed the British Cabinet, "It is much to be apprehended that our Indian allies have it in contemplation to desert us."[14]

Bird, with the help of McKee, managed to collect about two hundred Indians, mostly Shawnee, but the Wyandot and Mingo, influenced by the effect of Clark's victories on the Indians to the south and west, were noticeably absent. Indeed on April 1 there had appeared at Fort McIntosh the Wyandot chief Half-King, who announced through an interpreter, "My Father the English that sets here with me is not good for he wants to work my ruin . . . he is good for nothing & I will not listen any more to his speeches." He offered free passage through the Wyandot country for the American army on its way to Detroit. Thus when Bird tried to recruit the Wyandot for the second siege of Fort Laurens he found them unresponsive. Bird lamented, "Orontoni and his Brother [*Wyandot leaders*] are either Rascals or Cowards they tell me their heads are down. You may depend on it . . . Dugantait [*Half King*] has made Peace on a Belt with the Rebels . . . He is gone to Detroit to persuade all he can to follow his example. . . . The Half King & his People who sit still positively by his orders, are absolutely undeserving your attention—Our Enemies will

[14] "The Haldimand Papers," in *Michigan Pioneer and Historical Collections*, 10:328, 341, 359.

meet with little or no opposition in their progress to Detroit." And when Bird sought to influence the Mingo, he found that Half-King was also opposing him there. It was reported at Fort Pitt in June by Delaware emissaries that "when Captn Bird had come to the Mingoe Towns, to gather men to go with him to Fort Lawrence . . . the Half King went there, made a speech & turned back again; after which they, the Mingoes, told Captn Bird that he would be obliged to go alone to that place, they having no inclination to go with him."[15]

At the last minute an unforeseen event dispersed beyond hope of recall the two hundred Shawnee collected by Bird. This was the sudden expedition of Colonel John Bowman of Kentucky against the Shawnee towns in May, 1779, in which much damage was done. The first news of Bowman's approach sent the Shawnee rushing to the defense of their homes. "News flew," reported Bird, "that all the Towns were to be attack'd & our little body separated in an Instant past reassembling."[16]

It might be thought that Clark's victories and the appearance of a determination on his part to add Detroit to his "conquests" would result in a co-operation movement from Kentucky and western Pennsylvania against that post, in which the Fort McIntosh-Fort Laurens spur would play a most important part. But this was not to be. A new commandant came to Fort Pitt with new ideas, and Fort McIntosh and Fort Laurens were cast into the discard. General McIntosh, disgusted with his failures, retired in March and gave way to his chief critic, Colonel Daniel Brodhead, who scornfully referred to Fort McIntosh as the "Hobby Horse" at Beaver Creek and who believed that Niagara and not Detroit was the more sensible objective for American frontier armies. This belief, to whatever degree it was held by Brodhead and the

[15] "The Haldimand Papers," in *Michigan Pioneer and Historical Collections*, 10:328, 336; 19:413; Kellogg, *Frontier Advance*, 266, 363.

[16] "The Haldimand Papers," in *Michigan Pioneer and Historical Collections*, 10:336; 19:413; Kellogg, *Frontier Advance*, 33, 365; "Letters from the Canadian Archives," in *Illinois Historical Collections*, 1:343, 357; *The Remembrancer; or, Impartial Repository of Public Events . . . 1778-1779*, 7:340 (London, 1779); Withers, *Border Warfare*, 271.

commander-in-chief, General Washington, was dictated by considerations of expediency as well as of military principle. It was clear that the resources of the East would, by the application of this theory, be made more readily available for use, since the British and Indian headquarters at Niagara were nearer the eastern centers of population. Furthermore, Clark's victories relieved the situation in the latter quarter and made possible the evacuation of Fort Laurens without loss of prestige. It was thought also that the capture of Niagara would, by stopping the British supplies to the western nations, bring the Indians quickly to terms. Hence the year 1779 witnessed John Sullivan's grand Susquehanna campaign against the Six Nations and Brodhead's supporting expedition up the Allegheny.

Thus the ground was prepared for administering the last rites to the outpost that was Fort Laurens. Although relieved from siege by the exploits of McIntosh, Clark, and Bowman, the fort was still, less than two months after McIntosh had brought in his supplies, in such a deplorable condition that Major Vernon had to send most of his garrison back to Fort McIntosh. The reason for most of the difficulty was that the people of western Pennsylvania simply would not provide the Continental commissaries with supplies. On May 6 Brodhead wrote to Washington from Fort Pitt, "How to support it [*Fort Laurens*] I know not. I can take no Salt Provisions from here without robbing the artificers & the few Troops on the Frontier of eleven Barrels of Pork just now arrived . . . nor have I a single pound of fresh meat to issue to them." Two weeks later Brodhead wrote Washington again: "I should not have had it in my power to have sent the smallest supplies of salt provisions had I not by the most unweried exertions collected about three thousand weight of Bacon & pork and robbed Fort McIntosh of some stinking Beef." But the increasing friendliness of the Indians came to Brodhead's rescue and enabled him to evacuate the fort with good grace and at the same time to augment his forces for the Allegheny campaign that he was preparing. On June 5 he informed Washington, "As to the holding or evacuating Fort Laurens, I shall be the better able to determine after some conversation with the Chiefs of the Wyandotts." Shortly after this he received enough assurances from the Wyandot to take positive action. Hence on July 16 the last of the troops from Fort Laurens were ordered into Fort McIntosh. As for the latter post, it was not to be an integral part of western Indian administration again until after the close of the Revolutionary War.[17]

The abandonment of the Fort McIntosh-Fort Laurens line in July, 1779, represents the abandonment by the Continental government of the policy of placing stations in the Indian country when it had not sufficient resources to sustain them. From this time until the end of the Revolution, the United States had to let the northwestern frontier take care of itself and was able to lend it only a modicum of support. There was more than enough trouble on the war frontiers of the East to absorb the military resources of the American people. Thus the years from 1779 to 1782 represent a new and bloody phase of American Indian relations.

[17] *Pennsylvania Archives,* first series, 7:516, 569; 12:114, 128, 141; Kellogg, *Frontier Advance,* 293, 310, 324, 346, 389.

10
George Rogers Clark

WHILE McINTOSH was attempting to further American prestige in the Ohio Valley during 1778, developments were taking place to the west that enlarged the sphere of the contest with the Indians by bringing into its vortex the tribes on the Wabash and Maumee rivers and on Lake Michigan. Problems of Indian administration were thus complicated for the officials of the middle department, whose headquarters were at Fort Pitt and Fort McIntosh in western Pennsylvania. This enlargement, although operating throughout 1778 and 1779 to the benefit of the Americans under the immediate influence of George Rogers Clark's victories, was destined in 1780 to reveal that it had only served to increase the number of tribes that American Indian policy had offended and alienated. Clark's victories were brilliant but not of lasting effect. For the moment he deceived the Indians into a friendly attitude by his daring bluff, his good fortune, and the ease with which he was able to augment his funds from outside sources. He was able therefore temporarily to win the friendship of the tribes in the Northwest, and, as it has been seen, his successes were also instrumental in influencing the Indians to refrain from lending their support to the British in the Ohio Valley for a second siege of Fort Laurens. But his exploits did not bring to the tribesmen those fundamental necessities for Indian tranquillity: the forbearance of the frontiersmen and a settled and efficient trading system. Consequently the British, whose policy was based on a recognition of these necessities, were gradually able to neutralize the effects of Clark's "conquest" of the Northwest. The artificial nature of American influence in the upper Ohio Valley provides the background for the theme of the present chapter.

It is misleading to say that Clark "conquered" the Old Northwest, or that he "captured" Kaskaskia, Cahokia, and Vincennes. It would be more accurate to say that he assisted the French and Indian inhabitants of that region to remove themselves from the very shadowy political rule of the British. Few conquerors have been able to count on the general assistance of the inhabitants of the towns they were capturing in driving out the alien military rulers, to profit by the almost universal mutiny of the very troops they were attacking, or to finance their campaigns with other than their own or their country's resources. All these things Clark was able to do. It should also be stated, however, that few "conquests" have been followed by such a sudden and complete disappearance of the power of the "conquerors" and of any respect for them among the "conquered."

Clark's campaign arose out of Kentucky's determination to be rid of the Indian attacks with which it had been plagued ever since the first settlements in 1775 and which had made the year 1777 one of horror in western annals. It will be re-

membered that 1777 was the first year in which the British
governor at Detroit had had liberty to put British control of
the St. Lawrence into effective use in supplying the Indians.
The attacks of the bands of Mingo, Shawnee, Wyandot, Chippewa, and other Indians had reduced Kentucky to a population of one hundred fighting men huddled in the three fortified
stations of Boonesborough, Harrodsburg, and St. Asaphs. The
defeat of Burgoyne at Saratoga at the climax of this year of
bloodshed gave Clark his opportunity. On December 10, 1777,
"Burgoynes army having been Captured and things seeming
to wear a pleasing aspect," Clark outlined his plans for a
campaign to Governor Henry.[1]

These plans were based on the sound contention that the
removal of British influence from the Illinois and the Wabash
country would stop once and for all the Indian attacks on
Kentucky. They were based also on the belief that the white
inhabitants of the Old Northwest, who were mostly French
and who had brought the Indians of that region under their
influence by their trading system, could be won to the American cause. The publication in May, 1778, of the Franco-
American treaty of alliance greatly encouraged Clark in this
belief. Before he had received authorization and aid for his
excursion from the government of Virginia, he had sent spies
to Kaskaskia, who reported on their return that, notwithstanding the efforts of the British to inflame the minds of the
French against the Americans, there were "traces of affection
in some of the Inhabitants." Clark wrote in his memoir that
before setting out for Kaskaskia he had learned "that the
French Inhabitants in those Western settlements had great
Influance among the Indeans in Genl and [were] more beloved by them (the Ind^s) than any other Europeans. that
their Commertial Intercours was universal throughout the
West and N Western Cuntrey and the governing Interest on
the Lakes was mostly in the Hands of the English not much
beloved by them." He added, "Fort[u]nately I had Just Re-

[1] James, *Clark Papers, 1771-1781*, 218.

ceived a Let^r from Col^l Campbell Dated Pittsburgh informing
me of the contents of the Treaty between france and America."
Clark was not, however, laboring under any delusions. He
knew that the French did not have a very high opinion of the
aggressive American frontiersman. He therefore planned with
Machiavellian tact to use this situation to his own advantage
by displaying the traits, unusual on the frontier, of leniency
and graciousness. Referring to the spies he had sent out, he
wrote, "No part of their information pleased me more than
that of the Inhabitants Viewing of us as more savage than
their Neighbours the Indians, I was determined to improve
upon this . . . as I conceived the greator the Shock I could
give them at first the more sensibly would they feel my lenity
and become more valuable friends."[2]

The ensuing events proved that Clark had not planned un-
wisely. Selecting Kaskaskia as his first objective because it
did not, like Vincennes, have a garrison, he approached it in
July, 1778, with a force of 175 volunteers and with the hope
that if he were successful, he would have paved "our way to
the possession [of] St. Vincent [*Vincennes*]." Preserving the
utmost secrecy at it approached, the little army suddenly descended upon the town, frightened all the inhabitants into
their houses, cut off all escape, captured the British commandant, the Chevalier Philippe de Rastel de Rocheblave,
and took control of the goods of the leading merchant, Gabriel
Cerré. According to his plan, Clark gave the panic-stricken
French time to nurse their fears of the complete dispersion of
their community and the plundering of their property, and
then confounded them by informing them of his intentions
toward them. "I asked them," he wrote in his narrative,
"whether or not they thought they were speaking to savages
. . . did they suppose that we ment to strip the women and
children or take the Bread out of ther mouths or that we would

[2] The account of the campaign in this and the two following paragraphs is based on
Clark's "Memoir, 1773-1779," and other papers, in James, *Clark Papers, 1771-1781*,
31, 50-53, 120, 122, 218, 224-239. The letter from Campbell is printed in Thwaites
and Kellogg, *Frontier Defense*, 298.

condesend to make war on the women and Children or the Church that it was to prevent the effution of Innocent blood by the Indians through the Instigation of their Com^{dts} and Enemies that caused us to visit them, and not the prospect of Plunder . . . that as the King of France had Joined the Americans their was a probability of their shortly being and [*sic*] end to the War (this information very apparently effected them)." He thereupon ostentatiously granted them freedom to move about at will and to practice their own religion. He gave them a pledge of security to their persons and property and released the imprisoned French militia. Clark's own soldiers were under the strictest discipline not to molest the inhabitants. Great was the rejoicing of the French at Kaskaskia, and in order to prove their gratitude, they offered to embody their own militia and bring about the conversion of the near-by villages of Prairie du Rocher, St. Phillippe, and Cahokia, a project that was carried out with characteristic Gallic spirit. All the inhabitants of these towns took the oath of allegiance to the United States, and the "conquest" of the Illinois country was thus completed.

Clark then turned his attention to the Wabash country. He sought information from Father Pierre Gibault (whose jurisdiction included the parish of Vincennes), to whom Clark had shown the greatest respect, and who had in turn shown himself to be a strong American sympathizer. What must have been Clark's surprise when Father Pierre informed him that "he did not think it was worth . . . while to cause any Military preparation to be made at the Falls [*of the Ohio*] for the attack of St Vincenes." Clark was told that Edward Abbott, the British governor of Vincennes, had just left there for Detroit and that "when the Inhabitants was fully acquainted with what had past at the Illinois and the present happiness of their Friends and made fully acquainted with the nature of the war . . . their Sentiments would greatly change." Father Pierre finally proposed to relieve Clark of all responsibility in the matter and declared that he had no doubt that he could bring Vincennes "over to the American Interest" without military assistance. In July, 1778, the priest set out upon his mission to convert the people to the American cause. He was accompanied by a lay adviser, Dr. Jean Baptiste Laffont, and was armed with letters from Clark denouncing Hamilton and the British government for setting the Indians against innocent inhabitants of the frontier. Gibault and Laffont were able to accomplish their task at Vincennes, and all the people accepted their proposals "except a few Europanes . . . that amediately left the Cuntrey." The oath of allegiance was administered to them in the church, and after an officer had been elected, the fort was taken possession of "and the American Flag displayed to the astonishment of the Indians and every thing setled far beyond our most sanguine hopes." Having accomplished their purpose, Father Pierre and his party were back in Kaskaskia by August 1. Thus, without even the use of an American army, was the Wabash country "conquered."

Clark then turned to the Indian problem. He was apparently convinced that Cerré, the trader, had placed his St. Louis and New Orleans trading facilities at the disposal of the British and was thus in part responsible for the British success in winning over the Indians. This was the reason for Clark's sequestration of the stores belonging to Cerré, who happened to have been in St. Louis at the time of Clark's entry into Kaskaskia. Clark, however, had no evidence against Cerré except a letter from Governor Hamilton to Rocheblave in which the merchant was "alluded to with much affection," and the veiled insinuations of the inhabitants of Kaskaskia, most of whom were in debt to Cerré. The trader, therefore, had relatively little difficulty in proving his innocence. With much pride and some warmth, according to Clark, "he defied any man to prove that he ever Incouraged an Ind^n to war . . . that their was a number in Town that was much in Debt to him perhaps the object of some of them to get clear of it by Ruin-[in]g of him." He was then confronted with his accusers, who with much embarrassment withdrew their accusations.

Clark therefore restored his liberty and property, where-upon the trader took the oath of allegiance to the United States and was subsequently, according to Clark, "of Infinite service to us."[3]

But it took more than Cerré to back Clark's operations with sufficient goods and credit. The goods required to placate the Indians and to supply the troops would soon exhaust local stores and must, moreover, be paid for. The answer to the problem was Oliver Pollock, American merchant at New Orleans, whose supplies and credit were placed at Clark's disposal. In 1785 Clark, in paying tribute to Pollock, acknowledged that his own success in the West was largely due to the financial help of this New Orleans trader. "The invoice Mr. Pollock rendered upon all occasions in paying those bills," Clark stated, "I considered at the Time and now to be one of the happy circumstances that enabled me to keep Possession of that Country." In the hurry of his preparations at Williamsburg for his western venture, he had given little thought to finances, and he was told that Pollock would take care of them. Having captured Kaskaskia, Clark, taking advantage of his sudden prestige, paid his bills by drawing on the credit of the state of Virginia, assuring those from whom he purchased that Pollock would accept the drafts on the state for more goods at New Orleans. Thus he wrote to Pollock on July 18, 1778, "I have succeeded agreeable to my wishes. & am Necessi[t]ated to draw Bills on the State and have reason to believe they will be accepted by you." Later, when Pollock began to complain that his own creditors would not accept these drafts on Virginia and that no efforts were made on the part of Virginia to honor them, Clark was concerned and protested that it was only the absolute necessity of distributing goods among the Indians and of thus neutralizing the effect of the British trade that had driven him to make use of Pollock's credit. By February 5, 1779, Clark had drawn on Pollock to the amount of forty-eight thousand dollars. But for the

[3] James, *Clark Papers, 1771-1781*, 235-237.

time being, his bluff worked, and traders accepted his notes and made deliveries of goods.[4]

Having thus brought the traders to his side, as well as the Church and the populace in general, Clark had little difficulty in handling the Indians. The suddenness of his arrival had created great consternation among the tribes, and Clark claimed, without any strong regard for accuracy, that this was because the Indians "were generally at War against us" and the "French and Spainyards appearing so fond of us confused them." They therefore, he said, "counciled with the French Traders to know what was best to be done, and of course . . . [were] advised to come and selicit for peace, and did not doubt but we might be good Friends." The first in the procession of Indian tribes that began to come in to Cahokia and make their peace with Clark late in August, 1778, were the more docile tribal remnants of the Kaskaskia, Peoria, and Michigamea. Following them came bands of Chippewa, Ottawa, Potawatomi, Missisuaga, Winnebago, Sauk, Foxes, Osage, Iowa, and Miami. With each of these tribes solemn ceremonies were held in which the tribesmen expressed their repentance, threw down the English war hatchet, and pledged peace and friendship with the Big Knife, their new American protectors. The Americans, in turn, rebuked the Indians for favoring the British, told these credulous natives of the forest a garbled version of the origin of the Revolution designed to show the Indians the tyranny that would fall on them if the British conquered the Americans, forgave them, and distributed presents in such a way as to show American generosity. As a consequence of these negotiations, together with those at Vincennes, "a boundary seemed to be now fixed betwen the British Emisaries and our own at the heads of the Waters of the Lakes and those of the mississippi."[5]

---

[4] James, *Clark Papers, 1771-1781*, lxvi, lxvii, 55, 330. Pollock's connection with the American cause is described at length in James A. James, "Oliver Pollock, Financier of the Revolution in the West," in *Mississippi Valley Historical Review*, 16:67-80 (1929).

[5] James, *Clark Papers, 1771-1781*, 123-129, 239-258.

At Vincennes the Indian problem was more difficult because the tribes on the Wabash, unlike those on the Illinois, were numerous and vigorous. On the lower Wabash near Vincennes were the Piankashaw, whose chief, Tobacco's Son, was known among the tribes as "the Grand Door to the Waubash" and whose position corresponded with that formerly held by Pontiac in the North. According to Clark, "Nothing of Importance was [to] be undertaken by the League on the Waubash" without the consent of this chief. This meant that the Ouiatenon Indians—better known as the Wea—who inhabited the upper Wabash, would be governed by the decision of the Piankashaw. Clark had therefore focused his attention on this chief and directed Father Pierre to show him much deference, and after the return of the priest with the news of the acceptance by the Wabash people of the American cause, Clark sent Captain Leonard Helm to Vincennes as "Agent for Indian affar[s] in the Department of the waubash." Helm was instructed to touch Tobacco's Son "on the same spring" as Father Pierre had done. As a result of Helm's diplomacy, Tobacco's Son was converted and announced that "his Ideas was quite changed and that he [would] tell all the Red people on the waubash to blody the Land no more for the English." "In a short time," according to Clark, "almost the whole of the Various Tribes of the different Nations on the waubash . . . Came to St Vincenes and followed the example of their grand chief . . . the British Interes Dayly lost ground in this Quarter and in a short time our Influance Reach[ed] the Indians [as far] as the River St Joseph and the Border of Lake Michigan." When Governor Hamilton at Detroit sought to prepare the way for a reconquest of the country by sending Pierre Joseph Céloron with supplies to the Wea towns in August, 1778, Captain Helm immediately sent a detachment up the Wabash with such effect that Céloron fled back to Detroit, much to Hamilton's disgust.[6]

---

[6] James, *Clark Papers, 1771-1781,* 124, 130, 176-179, 241, 259; "The Haldimand Papers," in *Michigan Pioneer and Historical Collections,* 9:486, 493, 495.

A temporary British restoration soon set in, however, under the forward pushes inaugurated in the fall of 1778 by Governor Hamilton. This movement by Hamilton was a premature one, because he was unsupported by sufficient British troops and supplies to warrant retaining control of such an exposed position as Vincennes, and he was afterwards severely rebuked by his superiors for his rashness. He set out from Detroit, however, in September, 1778, with a force of about one hundred whites and sixty Indians, and goods to be used in enlisting Indians on the way. When he reached Vincennes on December 17, he had a combined force of five hundred. There Captain Helm was forced to surrender with his small force of thirty-five men, while the French and the Indians meekly acquiesced in the reversion to British rule and took oaths of allegiance to the king. Hamilton thereupon began to erect a strong fortification and sent emissaries to Henry Stuart, British southern Indian superintendent, to make plans for a co-operation with the southern tribes in the spring in order "to concert a general invasion of the frontier."[7]

The situation was critical for Clark, who, at Kaskaskia, was greatly alarmed because he foresaw the reconquest of Kentucky by the combined forces of the northern and southern Indians. "We now Viewed ourselves," he wrote, "in a very critical Situation in a manner cut off from any Intercourse betwen us and the continent   that G Hamilton in the Spring by a Junction of his Northward and Southern Indians which he had prepaird for would be at the Head of such force that nothing in this Quarter could withstand his arms." Knowing that he could not raise troops from Kentucky in time to recapture Vincennes and hearing that Hamilton's forces had been temporarily divided and reduced, he decided to resort to a strategem and cross the "drowned lands" between Kaskaskia and the Wabash in the late winter and to count on the loyalty of the French to aid him in surprising Hamilton and

[7] James, *Clark Papers, 1771-1781*, 176-184; "The Haldimand Papers," in *Michigan Pioneer and Historical Collections,* 9:490-497.

his forces. "I knew," he said, "that a number of the Inhabitants wished us well . . . and also learned that the Grand Chief the Tobacos Son had . . . openly declared in Counsell with the British that he was Brother and Friend to the big knife." He was able to augment his troops, which had dwindled to about one hundred men, with French volunteers, by skillfully playing off the zeal of the loyal people of Cahokia against the inhabitants of Kaskaskia, who had failed to rush to arms at the time of a reported attack by an overwhelming British force.[8]

Then followed that historic winter march of Clark and his band of 270 French and Americans from Kaskaskia to the very gates of Vincennes. They arrived on February 23, 1779, and not the slightest leak of information forewarned the unsuspecting Hamilton. Clark distributed his troops on the hills overlooking the town in such a way as to make them appear an army of a thousand. As it happened, the British did not see them and were not warned of their presence by the French, who were notified just before the attack. Consequently when Clark and his men suddenly appeared in the streets of Vincennes, the British were taken completely by surprise. Lieutenant Colonel J. M. P. Le Gras and Captain François Bosseron of the Vincennes militia at once turned over to Clark the powder and shot that they had concealed from the British, and Tobacco's Son appeared and offered the assistance of his Piankashaw warriors in the siege of the British fort. Clark accepted the former, as his own shot and powder had been destroyed in the march, but he ostentatiously declined the latter in order to show the Indians that he did not need their help. On the morning of February 25, after a two days' siege, Hamilton was forced to surrender. It developed after this capitulation that a strong factor in bringing it about had been the treachery, as Hamilton called it, of the besieged militia from Detroit, half of whom were French and who had informed Hamilton that "it was very hard to be obliged to fight against

[8] The account of Clark's occupation of Vincennes contained in this and the two following paragraphs is based on James, *Clark Papers, 1771-1781,* 97-100, 138-151, 170, 185-193, 267-297, 345.

their countrymen and relations [*of Vincennes*], who they now perceived had joind the Americans."

Exhilarated by his success, Clark prepared for the conquest of Detroit and sent to Kentucky for supplies. He distributed the British spoils at Vincennes among the soldiers so as to keep them from clamoring openly for more worlds to conquer, and, in order to keep his plans secret, he circulated the information that he was not going to Detroit. The Detroit militia were given their liberty, and they returned to their homes where they "made great havack to the British interest" and secretly prepared the people for the American conquest. To make the victory seem even more overwhelming, Clark dispatched Captain Helm and the Vincennes militia officers, Le Gras and Bosseron, up the Wabash to intercept ten British boats laden with goods and provisions, whose French guardians greeted the officers with shouts of "Vive le Congress." Clark then clinched his victory by renewing the treaties with the Indians of the Wabash and stationed Captain James Shelby in the Wea towns with a small garrison.

Clark's "conquests" provided an unparalleled opportunity for the Americans to promote their cause among the Indians and to put an end to British influence in the West. That they were unable to profit by their advantages is ample testimony to the inadequacy of their policy and to the artificiality of the position of supremacy in which Clark's victories placed them. The augmentation of Indian regard was an important result of the victories, but the Americans proved themselves unable to make it a permanent one.

This regard manifested itself, on the part of the Wyandot and other northern tribes, in a willingness to befriend their one-time enemies, and the way was paved for a reconciliation with them by the sending of messages inviting them to a council to be held at Pittsburgh. These messages were delivered by the Delaware half-breed, John Montour, who had deserted the Delaware nation to join the British as a result of the murder of his fellow tribesmen during Hand's "squaw campaign." His services were enlisted at the suggestion of George Morgan, who had shown his understanding of the reason for Montour's delinquency and had therefore retained his respect. On January 4, 1779, the American fur trader to the Wyandot, John Dodge, wrote to Montour, "You may depend on it that you will be treated by the Americans as a friend now. It is therefore the desire of Colonel George Morgan and also of your friend John Dodge that you might come as soon as possible to this place, where you . . . will be treated well and receive an immediate employ." Dodge asked Montour to sound out the Ottawa, Potawatomi, and Chippewa. Captain John Killbuck, head chief of the Delaware nation, also urged Montour to come over to the United States and to bring the Wyandot with him. "You shall be treated very kindly," he wrote. "As you know and understand matters better than others you will endeavour to explain to the Wyandots and other nations what a strong chain of friendship we have made with the United States, and encourage them to take hold of it likewise."[9]

Montour was persuaded to deliver the messages, and, in view of Clark's occupation of Vincennes, the Wyandot, after some deliberation among the various branches of the tribe, made their decision in favor of the Americans. At the end of May, therefore, Montour was able to report that the Wyandot had agreed to come to the treaty at Pittsburgh. With them they sought to bring the Ottawa, Chippewa, Potawatomi, and other western tribes, and although these tribes did not agree to take part in the treaty, they did agree to drop the British war hatchet and befriend the Americans. The decision of the Ottawa tribe was made known to the British directly by these Indians themselves. "We now tell you," they said, "that we are going to our brothers the Virginians, with whom we will make peace & receive that which is good." Lernoult, the British commandant, was, of course, angry, and he replied emphati-

[9] Morgan to John Jay, May 28, 1779, Morgan Letter Book, no. 3; "Letters from the Canadian Archives," in *Illinois Historical Collections,* 1:379, 380; Kellogg, *Frontier Advance,* 193.

cally, "Children! You are welcome to do so, you know that I am not afraid of you, I have before now fought with you & have conquered, & am able to fight you again, and even both you and the Americans together." The Wyandot peace messages were delivered to Brodhead by the Delaware, Big Cat, in June, 1779, but there was some delay in the preparations for the meeting at Pittsburgh, and when it did finally take place in the middle of September, events were to transpire that proved that British influence was not dead among the Wyandot and might easily revive.[10]

The Delaware nation was also temporarily affected by the rising tide of American success. After the retirement of McIntosh, who, according to Brodhead, was "almost universally Hated by every man in this Department both Civil & Military" and, according to John Dodge, "got the Ill Will of all his Officers, the Militia in protickaler," George Morgan lent his efforts during the two months before his own resignation toward checking the discontent among the Delawares fostered by McIntosh's deception at the fourth treaty of Pittsburgh. He informed Brodhead, McIntosh's successor, that he had invited the Delaware nation to send chiefs to Philadelphia as the only method of restoring its confidence in the United States. Brodhead was inclined to view the Indian problem from Morgan's point of view, and he adopted a friendly attitude toward the Delawares and insisted that the emissaries to Philadelphia be received with great cordiality. So impressed were the Delawares at Pittsburgh with Brodhead's sincerity that they conferred upon him the name of one of the four great kings of their nation, that of Machingwe Keesuch, the Great Moon. This was a title of honor second only to that of Taimenend ("the affable one"), which they had conferred on Morgan.[11]

[10] "The Haldimand Papers," in *Michigan Pioneer and Historical Collections*, 10:328; 19:423; Kellogg, *Frontier Advance*, 266, 309, 324, 346, 363, 380; "Letters from the Canadian Archives," in *Illinois Historical Collections*, 1:435; *Pennsylvania Archives*, first series, 7:516; Kellogg, *Frontier Retreat*, 67, 70.

[11] Kellogg, *Frontier Advance*, 200, 209, 216, 230, 238, 260, 261, 282; Brodhead to

Council Fires on the Upper Ohio

On their pilgrimage to the East, the trusty Delawares were beset on every side by threats against their lives. Brodhead reported that several groups of frontiersmen had "assembled to murder the Delaware chiefs now on their way to Philadelphia: Should they effect their malicious purpose, there will be an end to negotiation, and a general war with the Savages will be the inevitable consequence of their barbarity." Before they reached Philadelphia the Delawares were conducted, at Morgan's request, to his home at Princeton, New Jersey, where a petition to Congress in behalf of these Indians was drawn up. The petition struck directly at the heart of their greatest grievance, the failure of the United States to fulfill its promises to make permanent trade arrangements, and also voiced an insistence that Congress and General Washington "give such orders as will prevent any further Infringment of the Friendship & Alliance subsisting between the Delaware Nation and the United States." The Delawares declared a willingness to adopt the white man's way of life, if the white man would undertake to teach the Indians, and they sent the son and the half-brother of John Killbuck and the son of George White Eyes to Princeton to begin the process. In view of the fact that they would no longer need so much land, they also promised to cede a large part of their territory to the United States. But the United States could answer the appeals of the Delawares with nothing but excuses and promises of trade when the British were defeated. The reply of Congress was designed to convince the Indians that England was responsible for the shortage of goods and that more goods could be expected now that France was the ally of the United States. Promises were made to educate the three Indian boys at Princeton, and "when the Country Shall be restored to quiet to encourage & promote your Civilization by inducing Ministers Schoolmasters, Tradesmen & Husbandmen to reside among you."[12]

Delawares, April 2, 1779, Morgan Letter Book, no. 3.
[12] Kellogg, *Frontier Advance*, 296-298, 301, 307, 313, 317-321, 323, 340-342; Morgan to John Jay, May 16, 1779, Morgan Letter Book, no. 3.

This reply was, of course, a blow to the Delawares. "We are very sorry," they said, "you have it not in your Power to supply our Wants . . . We are in great distress for Cloathing in particular and for Powder and Lead . . . true we need not be at a loss if we go to Detroit . . . But we submit, and hope it will not be long before you get rid of all your Enemies, and that you will soon be able to s[u]pply our Wants." The future was not bright for the Delaware nation. The disappointed Indian delegates returned to their homes and were forced to resort to strategy on the way to avoid attacks on their lives by hostile frontiersmen. President Joseph Reed informed Colonel Brodhead in July, 1779, that it was with great difficulty that the Indians got back as "there were several Parties made up to destroy them on their Return, which were disappointed by the Indians taking an unexpected & circuitous Route."[13]

The American hold upon the Indians of the Northwest was greatly weakened by the inability of American Indian policy to produce payment for past Indian supplies, to say nothing of providing for future ones. The loss of control was most marked in the Illinois country and on the Wabash, where Clark's financial credit was about to collapse and where the disillusioned French of Vincennes, Kaskaskia, and Cahokia clamored in vain for payment of the debts that they had so willingly incurred to make Clark's success possible. As early as April 29, 1779, Clark reported that traders demanded prices five hundred per cent higher when goods were to be paid for in his paper money. He wrote that "people conceived it to be of no value, and both French and Spaniards refused to take a farthing of it." Provisions had tripled in price in the last two months and were "to be got by no other means than my own bonds, goods, or force." Merchants who were still loyal to Clark came to the rescue, but their loans were not sufficient to bolster American credit. By November 15, 1779, the dollar at Kaskaskia had depreciated to more than fifteen to one. The

[13] Kellogg, *Frontier Advance,* 344, 351-353; *Pennsylvania Archives,* first series, 7:569.

only resource was an appeal to the loyalty of the French and the holding out of the hope that the end of the war would bring the much desired gold and silver. John Todd, civil commandant at Kaskaskia, addressed the people at his post, "The only method America has to support the present just War is by her Credit.... There is no friend to American Independence who has any Judgment but soon expects to see it equal to Gold & Silver."[14]

Oliver Pollock at New Orleans continued to hold the bag, waiting for real value to fly in. While he paid his boatmen and traders "silver dollars for Paper Currency Dollar for Dollar," Clark's notes were not accepted by anyone at New Orleans. Pollock therefore accumulated great quantities of American currency, which formed the basis for his later contest with Congress. His labors for the United States as well as his plight are described in simple and direct terms in his letter to Governor Henry of July 17, 1779. "Being already drained of every shilling I could raise for the use of your's and the rest of the United States," he said, "I went first to the Governor of this place, and then to every merchant in it, but could not prevail upon any of them to supply said goods." He was therefore forced to mortgage his own private assets in order to meet his obligations and to cover personally such notes on Virginia and Congress as were protested by New Orleans merchants.

The situation was aggravated by the passage of a law by Virginia requiring all currency bearing dates of April 20, 1777, and April 11, 1778, to be paid into the Continental loan offices by June 1, 1779, after which date they would be worthless. Although John Todd, the lieutenant of Virginia's Illinois County, did his best to gain an extension of time, his efforts were fruitless. The French at Kaskaskia refused to trade except for cash. The only resort of the Americans was impressment, accompanied by offers to pay with the hated paper

[14] The account of the recession of American influence in the Northwest contained in the remainder of this chapter is based on the introduction and on letters and papers in James, *Clark Papers, 1771-1781,* xcvii, xcviii, cv, 114-154, 169-174, 300, 308, 324-326, 331, 344-346, 356, 379, 386-391, 430-450, 460.

money—methods that were anything but agreeable to the populace. Richard McCarty, a merchant of Kaskaskia, vehemently denounced his countrymen: "We are become the Hated Beasts of a whole people by pressing horses, Boats, &c, &c, &c, Killing Cattle, &c, &c, &c, for which no valuable Consideration is given; even many not a Certificate; which is hear looked on as next to nothing."

At Vincennes the situation was remarkably similar. There, as at Kaskaskia, the leading citizens, Lieutenant Colonel Le Gras and Captain Bosseron, lent their credit to the United States. But when the Americans resorted to the more forceful methods of impressment and the political dictation of the value of the paper currency, the inhabitants petitioned the governor of Virginia on their own behalf, saying, "As soon as we had furnished provisions and goods for this money, the Virginians appeared to think they could take by force our property, our supplies, and even the little we had reserved to keep ourselves alive. . . . after these first injuries, they have perpetrated others of a more serious character, by killing our cattle in the fields, and our hogs in our yards, taking our flour from the mills, and the corn in our granaries, with arms in their hands threatening all who should resist them and the destruction of the fort we built at our own expense."

Thus disappeared the allegiance of the French, who had once welcomed Clark to their towns with open arms, and with it went that of the Indians; for the French, having no goods, were no longer able to trade. In no case is the blighting effect of American frontier impecuniosity on the Indian civilization more directly and clearly revealed. The French at Vincennes complained in August, 1780, that the Americans had carried off with them all the available ammunition, so that the Wabash Indians were obliged to resort to the bow and arrow. Of these Indians the French said, "They abandon the cultivation of their fields to us, and on our side we wish to help them in their need by our works, our industry, and our commerce with them." This consideration of the Indians is in striking contrast with the arrogance of the Americans.

The state of Virginia could do little to improve the situation. The war in the East absorbed all its energies so that the authorities could supply the West with neither troops nor money. In spite of this condition, Colonel Le Gras of Vincennes loyally continued to put his financial resources behind the American cause. On August 1, 1780, he informed Clark that the governor and Council of Virginia had refused to pay him; that he had "nevertheless furnished this very day one hundred weight of flour to discharged soldiers going to the Falls of Oyo not knowing who shall pay for it . . . having advanced all my fortune to the State I will be obliged to go again to Virginia, if not paid, or go and hide myself in Some remoted part of the world, not being able to pay my debts."

The recession of American influence in the Northwest is also illustrated by the failure of Clark to complete his plans against Detroit. After his capture of Vincennes, everything had indicated the success of those plans, and Clark had figured that three hundred men would be sufficient for his purpose. As has been seen, he had released the Detroit militia captured at Vincennes, on the ground that his "good treatment of the Volunteers Inhabitants of Detroit would Promote my Interest there." Upon their being discharged, according to Clark, "they went off huzzaing for the Congress and declared though they could not fight against the Americans they would for them." Captain Helm at Vincennes reported to Clark on May 31, 1779, that at Detroit sedition and defiance of the British by the French were rampant. The British flag was insulted, and even small children went through the streets with cups of water, drinking to the health of the Americans and babbling, "Success to Clack Success to Clack." Captain Carney, Helm's informant, who had been sent to Detroit as a spy, reported, "Its not safe for a person to spake dispicably of the Americans . . . there is a Room for you and an other for me in every principle Gentlemans house in the Village furnished with Bowls and Glasses and Called Col⁰ Clarks & Capᵗ Helms

Rooms." Nor were these reports the results of wishful thinking on the part of the Americans; for Captain Lernoult, the commandant at Detroit, informed Lieutenant Colonel Bolton on March 26, "The Canadians [*French*], exceedingly assuming on our bad success and weakness, not one of them will lend a hand."

Clark, however, was unable to raise a sufficient force for the accomplishment of the task. On July 1, with a small party of horsemen, he arrived at Vincennes, which he had designated as a place of rendezvous for the troops. There he awaited the arrival of Colonel John Bowman and Colonel John Montgomery, from whom he expected to receive enough men to make up an adequate army. Bowman, who had raised 296 men for an expedition against the Shawnee, did not receive Clark's instructions in time and proceeded on his original expedition, much to Clark's chagrin. Only 30 men from Kentucky joined Clark at Vincennes, and these, with the 150 men that Montgomery brought from Kaskaskia, were not enough. The expedition was therefore abandoned. "Never," Clark lamented, "was a Person more mortified than I was at this time to see so fair an oppertunity to push a Victory; Detroit lost for want of a few Men."

The hollowness of Clark's conquest was thus fully demonstrated by the temporary nature of its effect on the Indians and by its failure to give a sufficient impetus for the success of a final venture against British strongholds. It fell short of the latter accomplishment by a narrow margin, however, and the immediate influence on the Indians of Clark's victories, though not to be a lasting one, did provide an opportunity for the carrying out of an expedition directed toward Niagara that was to prove a temporary setback to British influence in the East.

11
Indian War,
1779-1782

THE expedition of Colonel Daniel Brodhead against the Seneca Indians, a tribe of the Six Nations, in August, 1779, was the one outstanding accomplishment of the Americans made possible by Clark's victories in the Northwest and by the subsequent friendliness of the northern Indian tribes. The trend of events was to prove, however, that even this spurt was of little lasting benefit to the United States, and it was followed by a general chaos on the frontiers that lasted until the year 1782.

Brodhead, in command of the western department, with headquarters at Pittsburgh, was highly encouraged by the favorable turn of events following Clark's victories, by which peaceful relations with the Indians to the west of Pittsburgh seemed to be assured. He therefore turned his attention to northwestern Pennsylvania and sought to co-operate with General John Sullivan in destroying the most powerful tribes in the North, the Six Nations, and in thus completing the general conversion of the Indian tribes of North America to the American interests.

As late as March 21, 1779, Brodhead had favored a campaign against the Wyandot and had at that time expressed his fears that the frontiers of the upper Ohio would once again be forced to experience a season of attacks from the Detroit Indians. But with the final conversion of the Wyandot to the American cause toward the end of May, he felt justified in changing his mind and his plans. On June 5 he informed Washington, "It would give me great pleasure to make one grand push against the Mingos [*Iroquois*] . . . who will not and ought not to be treated with but at the point of the Bayonet." As the Ottawa, Chippewa, and Potawatomi joined the Wyandot in their new friendship, Brodhead became even more optimistic and envisioned leading a grand Indian army against the Six Nations. By the middle of July he had convinced Washington, who until that time had favored an expedition against Detroit, that a campaign against the Mingo by way of the Allegheny would be a more effective move. Washington, in fact, viewed the scheme with some enthusiasm and pointed out that it "would operate as an useful diversion in favour of the expedition under General Sullivan." Brodhead thereupon set about with great eagerness to put his plans into effect.[1]

The difficulties encountered in attempting to fulfill the few requirements for the success of the Allegheny expedition are an indication of the inefficiency of American Indian policy. One of these requirements was the active co-operation of the Delawares and the Wyandot. On April 15 Brodhead had written to President Reed of Pennsylvania, "I am persuaded the

[1] Kellogg, *Frontier Advance*, 262, 371, 388; *Pennsylvania Archives*, first series, 12:108, 127.

Delawares may be engaged to fight against the Six Nations though more numerous than themselves, provided they are well supplied and we have the means, that is Indian goods, Trinkets and black Wampum to pay them for their services." On June 25 he wrote Washington that he hoped to have enough such supplies for the Indians, but added that he was not then "in possession of a single article to pay them." Washington was not very encouraging on this score, and President Reed was emphatic in his refusal to lend assistance. His reasons were that supplies were impossible to secure and that "the People in the Back Counties" could not be expected to furnish any aid, "so violent are the Prejudices against the Indians." This aversion of frontiersmen to furnishing supplies to the Indians was elemental and was a barrier to amicable Indian relations throughout the history of the frontier.[2]

A second requirement for the success of the expedition was the full co-operation of the frontier in providing men for the expedition. This assistance was rendered necessary by the inability of Congress and the states to furnish enough men from the East. On April 17 Brodhead had only 722 regular troops distributed at the posts of Fort Laurens, Fort Randolph, Fort McIntosh, Fort Hand, and Fort Pitt, and at Wheeling and Hollidays Cove (opposite what is now Steubenville, Ohio). Before setting out on his expedition he evacuated Fort Randolph, Fort Laurens, and Fort Hand and erected Fort Armstrong and Fort Crawford on the Allegheny. He also reduced the garrison at Fort McIntosh to forty men. He took 605 troops with him, and the indications are that the militia were extremely backward in turning out. On May 31 he informed Colonel Lochry of Westmoreland, "Your inhabitants are regardless of everything but their own convenience and security, but they may yet learn the fruits of such dirty policy and inattention to the general good of their Country."[3]

[2] *Pennsylvania Archives,* first series, 7:466, 569; 12:107, 132; Kellogg, *Frontier Advance,* 305, 388.

[3] Kellogg, *Frontier Advance,* 411; *Pennsylvania Archives,* first series, 7:664; 12:123, 145, 151.

This inattention was universal among the frontier people and continued throughout the preparations for the campaign.

One of the reasons for the attitude of the frontiersmen was the fact that western Pennsylvania was subject to such severe Indian attacks during that season that most of the inhabitants did not dare leave their farms to join the army. Many others were fleeing to the East. Early in the spring a band of Seneca had killed or carried off eighteen persons at Turtle Creek, twenty miles east of Pittsburgh, and during April attacks were made as far south and east as the Cheat River and the Great Glades of the Youghiogheny River in Garrett County, Maryland. Sewickley, Hannastown, and Ligonier were likewise the scenes of hostilities that spring, and the inhabitants of Bedford County, who had long considered themselves protected from Indian attacks, were no longer immune. According to Lochry, the frontiers had "stood as long as they can," and the inhabitants "are now removing & evacuating the country." The climax of these attacks was the siege of Fort Hand on the Conemaugh on April 26 and 27 by a band of over one hundred Indians. The siege was raised, however, by the heroic measures of Lochry, who brought to the rescue a large body of county militia. The Indians nevertheless succeeded in destroying a surprising number of cattle and hogs. Thus Brodhead's army of six hundred men that set out up the Allegheny on August 11, 1779, had few supplies with which to enlist the active support of the Indians and had practically no militia, unless the two companies of rangers raised by Lochry at the time of the siege of Fort Hand, which were paid by Congress, be counted.[4]

Before setting out, Brodhead sent scouts ahead to carry letters announcing his approach to Sullivan on the Susquehanna. He had but a month's provisions for the accomplishment of his purpose, which was to prevent future hostilities on the part of the Seneca and to "revenge the past, to carry

[4] "The Haldimand Papers," in *Michigan Pioneer and Historical Collections,* 19:374, 384; Kellogg, *Frontier Advance,* 35, 241, 284, 292, 295, 299-301; *Pennsylvania Archives,* first series, 7:445.

the war into their own country, and strike a decisive blow at their towns." At the mouth of French Creek, on the site of the present city of Franklin, the little army surprised a hunting party of Seneca, and a hot skirmish took place in which several Indians, but no white men, were killed. Brodhead proceeded up the Allegheny but met with no opposition, as most of the warriors were away fighting against Sullivan, and the rest were warned of Brodhead's approach. On reaching the deserted upper Seneca towns he destroyed eight of them. At the town farthest north, Yoroonwago, just below the New York line, he destroyed one hundred and thirty houses and five hundred acres of growing corn and took plunder, including furs, to the amount of thirty thousand dollars. On his return, the towns of Connewango (on the site of Warren), Buckaloon, and Mahusquechikoken (twenty miles above Franklin) were put to the torch. Although his lack of resources prevented him from effecting the hoped-for junction with Sullivan, Brodhead was convinced that he had prevented a general descent of the Six Nations on the upper Ohio by way of the Allegheny. "From the great quantity of Corn in new Ground," he wrote, "& the number of new houses Built & Building it appears that the whole Seneca & Muncy nations intended to collect to this settlement which extends about eight Miles on the Allegheny River . . . I have a happy presage that the counties of Westmoreland, Bedford & Northumberland, if not the whole western Frontiers will experience the good effect of it [*the expedition*]." How much truth there was in this claim is uncertain, but it is probable, in view of the rising tide of British military success in the East and the great numbers of reinforcements and new supplies of Indian goods arriving in Canada, that the Seneca had planned to expand the domain of their old hunting grounds.[5]

The effect of Brodhead's coup, though temporary, was widespread. It has been said of his campaign that "dread of

[5] *Pennsylvania Archives,* first series, 12:119, 155-158; Kellogg, *Frontier Retreat.* 55-66.

American prowess was enhanced, and the baleful influence of the Five Nations upon the western tribesmen was severed." Confronted with starvation by the destruction of their corn by Brodhead and Sullivan, great numbers of Iroquois flocked to Niagara seeking food from the English, and General Haldimand actually became apprehensive for the safety of Niagara. Thus in the summer of 1779 the Indian situation seemed to be anything but discouraging to the United States: the Wyandot had abandoned their alliance with the British; the Shawnee had been beaten in May by Colonel John Bowman's expedition; and to the northeast of Pittsburgh the Six Nations had been severely drubbed by the Sullivan-Brodhead expeditions. But the tide was about to turn. None of these victories was as real as it seemed. Sullivan had not captured Niagara, and the British still enjoyed the uninterrupted passage of the St. Lawrence-Great Lakes route and were thus able to do what the Americans could not do for the Indians of the Northwest, that is, to deliver them supplies. As for the Shawnee, Bowman's punishing of them was merely a temporary inconvenience and only served to increase their hatred of the Americans. Nor, as the sequel will show, were the Six Nations entirely eliminated as factors in the Revolutionary War. Brodhead's achievement, according to one historian, "marks the high tide of success upon the Fort Pitt frontier; thereafter, the fortunes of the American cause in that region began to ebb."[6]

Before he set out up the Allegheny, Brodhead had planned to pay his respects to Detroit. He had made arrangements to meet the Wyandot in September, 1779, at what was to be the fifth treaty of Pittsburgh. Like McIntosh the year before at the fourth treaty of Pittsburgh, Brodhead hoped to enlist the active support of the Indians in the advance to Detroit. Unlike McIntosh, he did not deceive himself and the Indians by forcing an agreement that provided the basis for a futile

[6] Kellogg, *Frontier Retreat*, 16, 78; "The Haldimand Papers," in *Michigan Pioneer and Historical Collections*, 19:478.

and disastrous advance into the Indian country. The Wyandot were not even willing, as the Delawares had been, to let the American army pass through their country, but told them to go to Detroit by way of Lake Erie. Thus when Brodhead told the Wyandot, "You ought to assist your Brothers of the United States to destroy them [*the British*]," he got a direct refusal. "Be cautious," replied the Wyandot, Half King, "not to go the nighest way to where he [*the British*] is, lest you frighten the owners of the lands who are living through the country between this and that place [*Detroit*] . . . go by water, as it will be the easiest and best way." This opposition clearly made the expedition impossible as the United States was no more capable of conquering Detroit by way of Lake Erie in 1779 than it was to be in 1812. Thus at the fifth treaty of Pittsburgh little more was accomplished than the formal exchange of pledges of mutual friendship and of condolences for past tragedies.[7]

In this situation Brodhead vainly appealed to eastern sources for aid. He knew that the chief reason for the unwillingness of the Indians to fight for the United States was that they were not getting any supplies. They could hardly be expected to fight American battles without the necessary guns, ammunition, and provisions. As he informed George Morgan, "I conceive it to be next to an impossibility to carry on a secret expedition against that place [*Detroit*], whilst the English have goods to engage the Indians in their interest, and we have nothing but words." As before, Brodhead appealed to President Reed of Pennsylvania: "The Delawares, Wyandots, & Maquichees tribes of the Shawnese Nation," he wrote, on September 23, "seem disposed for peace . . . And if I was possest of a few Goods & some trinkets, I should doubtless engage them to go against the Enemy. Indeed, the Delawares seem ready to follow me wherever I go." At the same

[7] Kellogg, *Frontier Retreat*, 67, 70. The material from here to the end of this chapter has appeared in but slightly different form in Randolph C. Downes, "Indian War on the Upper Ohio, 1779-1782," in *Western Pennsylvania Historical Magazine*, 17:93-115 (1934).

time he appealed to the Continental authorities by writing to Timothy Pickering, secretary to the board of war, asking him "if possible [to] enable me to engage one nation of Indians to wage war against the other."[8]

Brodhead was, of course, asking too much. In spite of the peacemaking of the fifth treaty of Pittsburgh, disconcerting evidence was beginning to come in that the Wyandot were resuming hostilities because they found no supplies coming from the Americans and because George Rogers Clark had failed in his plans to extend his conquests to Detroit. In the East, British armies were overrunning South Carolina, so that on October 18, 1779, General Washington advised Brodhead to moderate his plans. "It is not in my power," wrote Washington, "circumstanced as things are at this critical moment to say how far it may be practicable to afford sufficient aid from hence." Brodhead was, therefore, instructed to occupy himself with collecting information about routes and about the status of the defenses at Detroit so that when the advance on Detroit eventually did take place, he would be ready. To this he replied with characteristic zeal that he would "endeavour to have everything in perfect readiness" for the advance.[9]

Another unfortunate incident occurred in this month of October, 1779, which illustrates how isolated the upper Ohio really was. This was the destruction by the Indians of a five-boat convoy of provisions and supplies ascending the Ohio River at a point opposite what is now Cincinnati. This convoy was bound for Pittsburgh and contained a large amount of supplies for military uses. They had been bought by the government of Virginia at New Orleans and entrusted to the protection of Colonel David Rogers and a detachment of sixty men. Rogers made the supreme mistake of landing his boats at the Ohio River crossing at the mouth of the Licking River after having sighted an Indian band that he judged to be smaller than his. He ran into a well-planned ambush of over

---

[8] *Pennsylvania Archives,* first series, 7:710; 12:159, 160.

[9] *Pennsylvania Archives,* first series, 12:164, 184; Kellogg, *Frontier Retreat,* 101.

130 Indians led by Simon Girty. Girty's band descended upon Rogers' party with fury and succeeded in killing about forty men, including Rogers himself, and in carrying off several as prisoners. Only one boat escaped into midstream; the rest were plundered and sunk. The disaster was of great significance not only in depriving the militia of western Pennsylvania and Virginia of supplies, but in counteracting in some degree the effect of Clark's victories earlier in the year.[10]

During the winter of 1779-80 developments took place that showed plainly the impotence of the United States on the northwestern Indian frontier and that forecast the failures of the years that followed. These developments demonstrated how impossible it was to make the frontiersmen assume more than what they judged to be their share of the responsibilities in the capture of Detroit. The frontier required a Continental army from the East and, lacking one, refused to expose itself to Indian attacks by permitting its fighting men to be appointed to remote forts on the Allegheny far removed from the homes and firesides of its families. The zealous Brodhead did not thoroughly understand the situation and proceeded on the assumption that the local militia would do just as he directed, even when he sought to make them do what they thought Congress should do.

A part of Brodhead's plan for the campaign of 1780 was to concentrate the Continental troops at Fort Pitt. In doing this he felt it necessary to call in the Continentals at the Allegheny River posts of Fort Armstrong and Fort Crawford and to substitute militia troops or rangers, as they were called, from Westmoreland County. He therefore issued orders to Captains Joseph Irwin and Thomas Campbell, over the head of militia Colonel Archibald Lochry, to station small detachments of rangers at these two posts. The Allegheny River was part of the northern boundary of Westmoreland in that day, and, if militia were placed at these remote posts, protection

---

[10] Kellogg, *Frontier Retreat*, 79-94, 104, 123; "The Haldimand Papers," in *Michigan Pioneer and Historical Collections,* 19:497.

would be drawn away from the centers of settlement, which would then be exposed to the murderous attentions of stray bands of Indians. Captain Irwin, supported by his son-in-law, Colonel Lochry, refused to obey Brodhead and kept the rangers in posts nearer home, that is, Hannastown and Fort Wallace on the Conemaugh. On appeal to President Reed of Pennsylvania, Irwin and Lochry were sustained.[11]

Brodhead retaliated with the only weapons at his disposal. If the militia officers were to do without Continental orders, they could also do without Continental supplies. To be sure, it was by resolution of Congress that the rangers were to be provided from Continental stores. But supplies were scarce, and Brodhead, of course, felt that the Continental troops should have first chance at what there were. Hence, when, on December 13, 1779, Lochry requested Brodhead "to Give Orders for their [*the militia*] Being Regularly Supplyed in Provitions," the latter had a ready answer. "As to the Provisions," he said, "I do not know where they are to be supplied; and, as you seem to be vested with authority to station the Troops, you will, doubtless, be able to get them supplied, by directing your orders to the proper Commissaries." The result was that the Westmoreland rangers had to be quartered on the people of the county.[12]

This was not Brodhead's only weapon. Having failed to get the rangers stationed on the Allegheny, he sought to have them dismissed from militia service so that they might be reenlisted as Continental troops. He therefore wrote to Lochry on December 29, 1779, "I think it adviseable to discharge the Ranging Companies so soon as they are mustered and paid ... I wish you to impress on the minds of the officers of these Companies that they cannot now more essentially serve their Country than by encouraging their men to enlist during the war." Brodhead's officers thereupon went out and succeeded in enlisting a few of the rangers. Such cavalier actions

[11] Kellogg, *Frontier Retreat*, 79, 98; *Pennsylvania Archives*, first series, 7:770, 771; 12:163, 169, 170.
[12] *Pennsylvania Archives*, first series, 8:42, 50, 78.

enraged Lochry. The implication behind Brodhead's conduct was that the frontiersmen were obstructing the efficient administration of Indian affairs. Lochry informed Brodhead that he would resist any attempt to take militiamen away from his service. He wrote to President Reed asking for orders to re-enlist the rangers for another year. When Captain Campbell and Captain Irwin were arrested by Brodhead's order for not permitting the departure of the rangers who had enlisted as Continentals, Lochry refused to permit his captains to be taken to Pittsburgh. The incident was finally closed when President Reed, on February 14, 1780, came to the assistance of Lochry and forbade the taking of troops from ranging service before their terms expired. Brodhead had failed completely to compel the frontiersmen to sustain an aggressive Indian policy that Congress would not support. During the entire winter of 1779-80 he was obliged to leave Forts Armstrong and Crawford ungarrisoned.[13]

The year 1780 brought additional humiliations to Brodhead. It began with roseate expectations on the part of the colonel that Detroit would be in his hands before the end of the year. On April 4 he wrote to George Rogers Clark, "I think it is probable that before next Winter I shall have the pleasure of taking you by the hand somewhere upon the waters of lake Erie."[14] It ended with the utter failure of any expedition of any kind even to get started. The basic reason for this failure was the adverse fortunes of American armies in the East. On March 14 Washington advised Brodhead to drop all ideas of an advance on Detroit and to confine himself to short excursions against hostile tribes. In June the situation in the East was so bad that disastrous orders were issued to all Continental commissioners in the West to cease to draw on Congressional funds. Nor could the commonwealth of Pennsylvania do any better. On April 29 President Reed informed Brodhead that the legislature had voted four companies for the frontiers

---

[13] *Pennsylvania Archives,* first series, 8:65, 66, 68, 78, 109; 12:186, 202.
[14] *Pennsylvania Archives,* first series, 12:216.

but that they could not possibly be sent because the eastern armies were using all the supplies. The predicament of the eastern government was well described by Reed's letter of April 8 to the Reverend Joseph Montgomery of Sunbury. "The Frontiers," he wrote, "exclaim with Anguish, & we are now reduced to the painful Necessity of listening to Distress we cannot relieve & Claims we cannot satisfy—the poor People like the Waggoner in the Fable, must put their own Shoulders to the Wheel as well as call on Hercules—On these Occasions our Aid is so distant that I do not recollect any Instance when it has proved effectual."[15]

According to Washington's order of March 14, the program for the year 1780 was modified to the conducting of whatever short excursions against hostile tribes Brodhead judged necessary. The three groups of Indians that occupied Brodhead's attention this year were the Six Nations, the Shawnee, and the Wyandot. As for the Six Nations, the fact that they caused Brodhead concern is in itself testimony that the Susquehanna-Allegheny expeditions of 1779 had not completely accomplished their purpose of permanently silencing these Indians. Less than six months after his return from the destruction of the Seneca towns, Brodhead advised President Reed by letter of February 11, 1780, "I sincerely wish to see a reinforcement from the main Army, for I am really apprehensive of a visit from Niagara." Early in May the visit came, when warriors of the Six Nations appeared among the settlements on Brush Creek, a branch of the Monongahela east of Pittsburgh, and spread destruction. From then until the burning of Hannastown by Guyasuta in 1782, the western Pennsylvania frontier was never without the menace of the depredations of these warriors, who were supposed to have been silenced in 1779. Throughout all these years this menace had the effect of permanently preventing the men of Westmoreland County from joining any of Brodhead's expeditions that would take them

---

[15] Kellogg, *Frontier Retreat*, 147; *Pennsylvania Archives,* first series, 8:170, 217, 218; 12:234.

far from home. Brodhead's comment of May 13, 1780, to Washington on the Brush Creek attack was equally true of the seasons that followed. He wrote that it "will probably prevent my receiving any aid from the militia of that County." It is clear that the Six Nations needed another lesson from the Americans, but Congress would not help Brodhead give it.[16]

Something, however, had to be done. This was clear from the effects of the murderous attacks of the Indians, whose early spring "visits" spread terror throughout the upper Ohio Valley. A meeting of county militia officers was arranged "to establish either some general defensive plan, or to consult & fix upon some well calculated offensive operations against one or more of the hostile Tribes." Just what decision was reached is not certain, but Brodhead, who was present, felt warranted in making preparations for a short expedition against the Shawnee and in setting May 22 as the date, and Wheeling as the place, for the rendezvousing of 825 militia. It was hoped that the expedition would be at an end in time for the militia to return to harvest their crops and that it would be a "home stroke" from which "a lasting tranquility will ensue to the inhabitants of this Frontier."[17]

But the effort failed. Its success would have required the arrival of the artillery and supplies promised by the Continental authorities. The clothing situation was so bad that, at the request of his officers, Brodhead, on April 27, sent a special party to Philadelphia to get the clothing long overdue from headquarters. He postponed the expedition till June 4, pending their return. As for the artillery and other military stores, Brodhead, after sending a pressing call, was obliged to do without them because he could not get them transported over the mountains from Carlisle. Another element necessary to the success of this expedition was the presence of four regiments from the eastern Pennsylvania militia that had been promised. But at the last moment the crisis in the East pre-

[16] *Pennsylvania Archives,* first series, 8:106; 12:205, 233; M. C. Darlington, *Fort Pitt,* 235.
[17] Kellogg, *Frontier Retreat,* 154; *Pennsylvania Archives,* first series, 12:219, 223.

vented the sending of these troops. And finally the attack of the Six Nations made it impossible for Westmoreland to contribute any militia to the venture. Brodhead therefore countermanded his orders to the militia, adding the significant remark: "In the meantime I shall endeavor to give every possible protection to the Settlements and amuse the Indians by speeches." Accordingly he sent Major Geoffrey Linctot among the tribes with speeches "threatning them with the force of France, Spain & America, if they did not immediately desist from further hostilities."[18]

A second time in this year of stalemate did Brodhead attempt the impossible. In the middle of July, 1780, he called for a rendezvous of the militia at Fort McIntosh on August 10 to attack the Wyandot at the same time that George Rogers Clark was to attack the Shawnee. In order to tempt the frontiersmen to part with the supplies necessary for the expedition, he devised an ingenious paper-money scheme. The Continental purchasing agents were to pay for the supplies with certificates that were either to be redeemed in gold after three months or to draw interest in paper at five per cent. But the frontiersmen were not to be deceived. On July 31 Brodhead, in announcing the postponement of the Fort McIntosh rendezvous, wrote to the militia officers, "I have the mortification to assure you that the public Magazines are quite empty & that I cannot yet see a prospect of obtaining a sufficient supply for the sustenance of the Troops."[19]

In making his third and last attempt that year, Brodhead was obliged to resort to the most desperate of all expedients for the collection of supplies, that of impressment. He was reluctant to use this weapon and did so only after receiving express authority from President Reed and from the Continental board of war. On September 23 Brodhead wrote to Richard Peters of the board of war, "This Day the last meat

[18] *Pennsylvania Archives,* first series, 8:217, 300; 12:226, 231, 233, 237, 238; Kellogg, *Frontier Retreat,* 178-180.
[19] *Pennsylvania Archives,* first series, 12:243, 244, 246-254; M. C. Darlington, *Fort Pitt,* 236; Sparks, *Correspondence of the American Revolution,* 3:32-34.

that could be obtained by purchase is issued to the Troops, and to-morrow a party will march out with a Commissary to purchase or take—I think it must be by force—some Cattle &c." The experiences of these impressment parties, one under Captain Uriah Springer, one under Captain Samuel Brady, and one under Major William Taylor, were most illuminating. In the middle of October, Springer stated that the people above Redstone actually intended to rise up in arms against him. Others upon the approach of the troops drove their cattle into the mountains. It was useless. By November 3 Brodhead had to yield to the people. "It is clear to every body," he wrote to Ephraim Blaine of Cumberland County, "that a supply of meat cannot be had even for ready money equal to half the present consumption, to say nothing of what quantity ought to be laid in to enable me to act vigorously the ensuing campaign." The impressment parties could not even get enough food for themselves. Disgusted with this turn of affairs, Brodhead called in the parties and decided that the only way to provision Fort Pitt was to send men out to hunt for game and wild fowl.[20]

To this miserable depth had affairs sunk in Pittsburgh in the closing years of the Revolution. By December, 1780, the American force at Fort Pitt was almost as pitifully impotent as that at Fort Laurens had been two years before. Parties were sent to range the hunting grounds as far down the Ohio as the Little Kanawha in search of game for the garrison. North of the Ohio the aid of the Moravian Indians was sought. But even these efforts proved futile, and only four hundred pounds of wild meat were delivered to Fort Pitt by December 16. "This being a subversion of my intentions," Brodhead wrote to Captain Samuel Brady on December 16, "has determined me to recall both the officers and soldiers." Obviously the third rendezvous named by Brodhead in August had long since been given up.[21]

[20] *Pennsylvania Archives,* first series, 8:408, 536; 12:260, 262-264, 266, 274-278; Kellogg, *Frontier Retreat,* 270, 278, 281, 284, 291, 293-295, 300, 301, 306, 309.
[21] Kellogg, *Frontier Retreat,* 308-311.

The more closely the situation at Pittsburgh in the fall of
1780 is analyzed, the more convincing is the conclusion that
the frontier might have gone over to the British if the latter
had been successful in the East. The American garrison at Fort
Pitt was reduced to the most humiliating privations and weakness and would have been an easy prey to a popular uprising
in behalf of the triumphant British. Brodhead reported to
Washington on September 14, "The whole Garrison, with
Serjeants to lead them, came to my quarters a few days ago
to represent that they had not rec'd any bread for five days
together." Disaffection among the inhabitants was widespread. On September 23 Brodhead reported certain of his
officers as saying, "Should the Enemy approach this frontier
& offer protection, half the Inhabitants would join them," and
a few weeks later he was even more convinced that the people
only awaited an opportunity to declare for the British cause.
He informed Peters on December 7, "I learn more and more
of the disaffection of many the inhabitants on this side the
mountain. The King of Britain's health is often drunk in companies; & I believe those wish to see the Regular Troops removed from this department, & a favorable opportunity to
submit to British Government." Desertions were frequent and
it was utterly impossible to find new recruits for the declining
garrison.[22]

In the early months of 1781 the Americans were confronted
with a new misfortune which had been brewing for some time.
This was the loss of the friendship of the Delaware Indians,
the last tribe on which the United States could really count.
Gradually the effect of Clark's activities was wearing off, and
the respect of the Delawares for the United States was not increased by Brodhead's failure to make good an agreement he
had made with them in the summer of 1779 to re-establish Fort
Laurens. The Delawares were disappointed, and the episode
constituted the first in a chain of events that led directly to

[22] *Pennsylvania Archives*, first series, 12:265, 274; Kellogg, *Frontier Retreat*, 286,
302.

their abandonment of the Americans. The next episode was the invasion in 1779 of the Delaware hunting grounds west of the Ohio by squatters. Brodhead could meet the situation only by making extravagant promises that would pacify the Indians for the time being. Thus in telling them of his measures to expel the squatters he said, "You may depend I will punish them so severely that they will never venture to behave so again." When in the fall of 1779 the Delaware nation, confronted with a winter of starvation and exposure, made representations at Pittsburgh and asked to be allowed to go again to Philadelphia to represent their situation more directly, Brodhead dissuaded them by the statement that he would soon "strike the Warpost."[23]

This was a dangerous promise and Brodhead knew it. He did not fail to inform the board of war that, unless something was done for the Delawares, "they will be compelled to submit to such terms as our enemies may impose on them." In the spring of 1780 he blandly assured the Delawares that the time had almost come for him to strike. "I am only waiting," he told them, "to receive a letter from our great Warrior, but I am weary of sitting here & am now standing with my Tomhawk in my hand." Each time during 1780 that Brodhead planned the advance, as already narrated, the Delawares were informed, and each time they were disappointed. And with each disappointment the British pressure increased. On April 23, 1780, the Delawares wrote, "I am so much mocked at by the Enemy Ind[s] for speaking so long to them for You. Now they laugh at me, and ask me where that great Army of my Brothers, that was to come out against them so long ago, and so often, stays so long. . . . They further desire me to tell You now to make haste and come soon, the sooner, and the greater Your Number the better." In June the Delawares spoke thus to the free-lance colonel, Augustin Mottin de la Balme, "If our father [*the French*] is allied to the Americans, why do

[23] *Pennsylvania Archives*, first series, 12:158, 167, 174, 176, 182, 183, 188-190; Kellogg, *Frontier Retreat*, 96, 97.

264

these allow us to be in want of everything ... our urgent needs will finally force us to lend an attentive ear to their [*the British*] proposition ... Last year they [*the Americans*] made us a thousand promises at Philadelphia, now these are not even thought of." With the failure of Brodhead's third attempt to advance, in the fall of 1780, the Indians finally saw that the United States was powerless to act offensively, and Brodhead gave up all hope of retaining their friendship. He wrote to Washington on September 16, "As no supply of Goods has yet been sent for the Delaware Indians ... I conceive they will be compelled to make terms with the British or perish." When Congress in March, 1781, finally refused to re-establish Fort Laurens, Brodhead informed the president of Congress, "We may now expect a general Indian war." His expectation was justified; for he had already been informed by the Moravian, John Heckewelder, that the Delaware council had made the fatal decision and that parties were being organized to attack the American frontier.[24]

Brodhead decided to strike first. With a band of 150 Continentals and about the same number of militia he set out from Pittsburgh on April 7, 1781, for Coshocton, the central town of the Delawares, located on the Tuscarawas River in what is now Ohio. Although the inhabitants were not surprised, the town itself was destroyed, as was the neighboring village of Lichtenau, and fifteen warriors were killed after they had been captured. Twenty other prisoners were captured, and plunder in the form of peltry and livestock that sold at Wheeling for eighty thousand pounds was taken. Brodhead wished to make a more complete job of it and proposed the destruction of more Delaware towns and warriors, but his troops, feeling that they had accomplished enough, were unwilling to accompany him. They therefore returned to Pittsburgh. The expedition was characterized by excessive cruelty in the killing of captured Indians and in the infamous murder by Martin Wetzel

[24] *Pennsylvania Archives*, first series, 8:708; 12:190, 269; Kellogg, *Frontier Retreat*, 166, 172, 337-340, 345; Alvord, *Kaskaskia Records*, 164.

of a Delaware peace emissary. It was claimed that these cruelties were justified as retaliation for previous killings by the Delawares of innocent whites.[25] In a narrow sense the expedition was probably successful. It caused the Indians more direct loss than that suffered by the whites. But it did nothing to lessen the danger from the new Delaware enemies; it only increased their rage and their determination to make reprisals.

There is another factor to be considered in determining the net utility of Brodhead's Coshocton campaign. This was its effect upon the second attempt of George Rogers Clark to get the upper Ohio frontier to co-operate with him in a campaign against Detroit. This endeavor was a complete failure and was accompanied by that humiliating disaster known as Lochry's defeat. One of the factors that made the attempt a failure was, of course, the unwillingness of practically all the men of western Pennsylvania and northwestern Virginia to leave their homes exposed to the menace of the Six Nations and the now belligerent Delawares, and another factor was Brodhead's insistence on his Coshocton venture, which, instead of being a help to Clark, robbed him of three hundred men and of supplies that he greatly needed.

A more fundamental reason than either of these for Clark's failure to make a successful drive against Detroit was the ever present inability to get help from the East. The initiative for the projected expedition was taken by the government of Virginia with the acquiescence of Congress. It was Governor Thomas Jefferson's plan that the entire two thousand men who were to constitute Clark's force were to be recruited from the frontier country. But the plans, which were first publicly broached in December, 1780, were scarcely two months old when the negative action of the four Virginia counties of Greenbrier, Frederick, Berkeley, and Hampshire, which were to furnish over nine hundred men, put a decided damper on Clark's hopes. The protests of these counties against contributing to Clark's army were based on the fear caused by the

[25] Kellogg, *Frontier Retreat*, 376-380, 382; *Pennsylvania Archives*, first series, 9:161.

invasion that was already taking place in eastern Virginia and on the dread of the Tories nearer home and of the Indians to the northwest. Jefferson, anxious "to prevent anything like commotion or opposition to Government," quietly acceded and was able to make arrangements with Congress by which Clark was to get the assistance of two hundred regulars at Pittsburgh. This nullified some of Clark's losses but still left him to recruit six or seven hundred men from some other source. He complained bitterly, but derived comfort from the expectation of finding the extra men in the Pittsburgh area.

But success was not to be. The arrangements to give Clark two hundred Continental troops did not fit with Brodhead's plans against the Delawares. Brodhead therefore declined to permit these troops to join Clark and was later entirely supported by Washington. Clark then turned to the inhabitants of the upper Ohio in an effort to raise five hundred men. Here he was again destined to be disappointed. As in other regions and in other years, the people of the frontier were disinclined to bear what they thought was more than their just burden.[26]

Clark's efforts to raise men were completely wrecked in a sea of factionalism. A controversy was raging in southwestern Pennsylvania that had its roots in the boundary dispute between Virginia and Pennsylvania. The boundary line had been settled in 1779 by agreement between the two commonwealths, but in 1781 it had not yet been run. The Virginia faction, led by Colonel Dorsey Pentecost, was organized under the old county of Yohogania. The Pennsylvania faction was led by James Marshel, lieutenant of militia of the newly created county of Washington. When Clark appeared on the lower Monongahela, the two factions at once took sides, Pentecost and the Virginia group supporting Clark, Marshel and his Pennsylvanians opposing him. Marshel took the position that had been taken by the opponents of Brodhead. "There is a greater necessity," he said, "for the service of the Militia of

[26] James, *Clark Papers, 1771-1781,* 485, 490, 501-503, 507, 510, 517, 560; Kellogg, *Frontier Retreat,* 331, 340, 342, 344, 372; Daniel Brodhead, "Correspondence," in *Olden Time,* 2:389 (1847); *Pennsylvania Archives,* first series, 9:51, 52, 57, 79, 161.

this frontier County against the Immediate Enemies of the Country, and it would have a greater tendency to promote our own safety, than their best services with General Clark at Kaintucky possibly Could do."[27]

Pentecost, however, proceeded to recruit the militia of Yohogania County. Meetings of "the Principal People" were held, and these resulted in the decision to aid Clark by drafting one-fifth of the men of the county for the expedition. By July 27 these men, the number of whom is not recorded, were assembled and ready to accompany Clark. Marshel, relying upon his Pennsylvania commission, branded their movement as seditious. He sought to break the Yohogania militia movement by proceeding to organize the militia of Washington County for home defense. He divided the county into battalion districts and ordered elections of officers in each. By August he was able to report that he hoped "Shortly to have the Militia in full form" and that Clark's expedition "is on the Eve of falling totally through, and I am to bear the blame." The fact that President Reed later rebuked him for his action made little difference; he had succeeded in keeping most of the militia for "home defense."

A similar contest took place in Westmoreland County, although the affair was not complicated by the boundary dispute. Here, Colonel Archibald Lochry, the commander of the militia, took the side of Clark and, supported by President Reed, proceeded to do his best to find recruits. He told Clark on May 11, 1781, "Nothing Could Give Me Greater Pleashure than assisting you in the Intended Expadition—Contious there is no other way of retaliating On the savages But By Entring their Cuntery." Lochry, however, was also opposed by a "home defense" faction, led by Christopher Hays, who claimed that Lochry's endeavors were "Contrary to the will and Pleasure of the Major Part of the Inhabitance" and that

[27] The controversies over the raising of militia described in this and the three following paragraphs are based on letters in: *Pennsylvania Archives,* first series, 9:52, 193, 233, 247, 307, 315-317, 333, 343, 368, 369, 371, 404, 445; James, *Clark Papers, 1771-1781,* 549, 566, 569, 570, 580.

they were "to the Great Disadvantage of the Distressed Frontiers." This group, according to Lochry, was responsible, by its
insinuations, for the fact that he was able to enlist fewer than
one hundred men to take part in Clark's expedition.

Filled with anger and at the head of but four hundred
troops, Clark set out down the Ohio early in August, 1781. He
could only heap coals of wrath upon the people of western
Pennsylvania, whom he deemed responsible for his failure to
raise enough troops. "The anxiety I have," he wrote to Governor Jefferson on August 4, "and the probabillity of loosing
the fair prospect I had of puting an End to the Indian war
Occasion me to View such Charracters in a most Dispickable
light and to make this Representation. I do not suppose I shall
have anything more to do with them, but should it be the
case and had [I] power [I] should take the necessary steps
to teach them their duties before I went any farther."

Students of the life of George Rogers Clark have never
sufficiently emphasized how close he and his expedition came
to utter destruction as they descended the Ohio River in 1781.
Almost as soon as he left Wheeling his force began to be depleted by desertion. He was, therefore, obliged to hasten his
descent to get the men so far from home that they could not
desert. In the meantime the British and Indians were gather-
ing to destroy his force. Indian scouts were watching his every
move. At the mouth of the Great Miami, the half-breed
Mohawk chief, Joseph Brant, with a band of about thirty
warriors, was waiting, but his force was not strong enough to
attempt to stop Clark. Brant had expected a large band of
Shawnee and Wyandot led by Alexander McKee and Captain
Isidore Chene, and a few British rangers under Captain Andrew Thompson. Mismanagement and bad weather delayed
these reinforcements, and they joined Brant at the Great
Miami a few days too late. The British-Indian force was
probably a little smaller than Clark's but was unencumbered
with boats and supplies. What might have taken place if the
British and Indians had been a few days earlier can only be

imagined. William Croghan at Pittsburgh wrote shortly after Clark had left that place: "From Every Account we have the Indians Are preparing to receive him And if they should attack him in his present Situation, either by land or Water, I dread the Consequences."[28]

Lochry, however, was not so lucky as Clark. The latter had set out from Wheeling only one day ahead of Lochry, who was descending the river from Pittsburgh. It was but common sense that with so much danger the two forces should combine. Arrangements were made for their union, but so great was Clark's haste that Lochry could never catch up. Obstructed by sand bars and by the lack of skilled pilots, harassed by the shortage of horse-feed and of ammunition for the hunt, Lochry hastened from one rendezvous to another only to find, pinned to a tree, a note from Clark telling of the necessity of his departure and assigning a new time and place for their junction. Frantically Lochry sent messengers express to Clark begging him to wait. One of these messengers was captured by the ever watchful Brant. Using him as a decoy, Brant on August 24 lured Lochry's men to land in an ambush near the Great Miami. Every soldier in Lochry's band of almost one hundred either was captured or died a wretched death at the hands of Brant and his ninety warriors, and Lochry himself was killed. The rest of the story of the final failure of Clark in this grand campaign of 1781 is a part of Kentucky history.[29]

In the meantime, back at Pittsburgh, Brodhead was making another of his futile efforts to accomplish something against the Indians. This time it was the Wyandot who were to be punished, in an excursion against the Sandusky to be led by Colonel John Gibson. Everything was in readiness for the advance early in September, 1781, when an event occurred that showed the people that Brodhead's Coshocton expedition for the destruction of the Delaware towns earlier in the year had

[28] James, *Clark Papers, 1771-1781,* 583, 588; "The Haldimand Papers," in *Michigan Pioneer and Historical Collections,* 10:547; 19:617, 647, 658.
[29] "The Haldimand Papers," in *Michigan Pioneer and Historical Collections,* 19:655; Draper MSS, 6NN164-170.

not silenced that nation sufficiently. This event was the attack of a small army of Indians led by the Delaware, Buckonga-helas, and the Wyandot, Half-King, against Wheeling. Only the alertness of the missionary, David Zeisberger, in warning Brodhead of the impending attack saved the upper Ohio from a more sanguinary visit. So great was the shock to the frontier that once again Brodhead found himself unable to get the militiamen to leave their homes for a remote objective.[30]

Instead the frontiersmen turned their wrath upon the Delawares, whom they held responsible for the Wheeling scare. Thus Colonel David Williamson of Washington County organized a military expedition to accomplish the object that Brodhead was supposed to have accomplished in his Coshocton expedition of the spring of 1781. When Williamson arrived at the Delaware towns in October, he found them completely and seemingly permanently deserted. The Delaware nation in the course of the year 1781 had migrated to the Sandusky River and, in September, as a punishment to Zeisberger for his duplicity in giving warning of the attack on Wheeling, had forcibly compelled the Moravian Delawares to accompany them. Thus did the Delaware Indians do voluntarily what the Americans had attempted to force them to do. That their retreat to the Sandusky was to make them no less a menace to the American frontiers was left to the events of the year 1782 to demonstrate.[31]

There was no truce in the Northwest following the surrender of the British at Yorktown in October, 1781. Encouraged by Clark's and Brodhead's failures and by their own successes, the Indians continued to ravage the frontier, and, under British leadership, they set about to organize the greatest force ever assembled in the Northwest up to that time. The Ameri-

---

[30] Kellogg, *Frontier Retreat,* 557, 573; Butterfield, *Washington-Irvine Correspondence,* 74; Draper MSS, 14S116-120.

[31] Butterfield, *Expedition against Sandusky,* 33; Draper MSS 31J56-58; "The Haldimand Papers," in *Michigan Pioneer and Historical Collections,* 10:518. A good summary of the events of 1782 is in Milo M. Quaife, "The Ohio Campaigns of 1782," in *Mississippi Valley Historical Review,* 17:515-529 (1931).

cans, still unsupported from the East, frantically sought to anticipate the Indians by striking first. They did, and in Crawford's defeat and torture suffered the worst blow of the Revolutionary War in the Northwest.

Frenzy is the word that best defines the state of mind on the upper Ohio and that characterizes American actions in 1782. The Moravian massacre that preceded Crawford's defeat is ample testimony to the fact. This example of valor was the frontier reaction to the unexpectedly early appearance of Indian hostility in February, 1782, when the chastened Delawares sought revenge for the years of American duplicity. Their attacks included such well-known episodes of border warfare as the murder of John Fink on February 8 and the capture two days later, on Raccoon Creek, of Mrs. Robert Wallace and her three children, who were afterwards killed when the whites pursued their captors. Frontiersmen were convinced that Indians were using the Christian Delaware towns on the Tuscarawas in their operations against western Pennsylvania and Virginia. Consequently Colonel David Williamson again organized his Washington County militia and repeated his foray of the preceding fall. This time he found at the town of Gnadenhutten, near Coshocton, ninety unfortunate Moravian Delawares who, to avoid starvation in their camps on the Sandusky, had returned for some of the stores abandoned in their sudden migration the year before. Williamson also found four hostile Indians with the Moravians and unmistakable evidence that belligerents who had committed some of the recent outrages had been at Gnadenhutten. These discoveries apparently produced a surge of frenzied wrath in the frontiersmen, and on the morning of March 8, 1782, the ninety Indians were slaughtered.[32]

It is obvious that such futile strokes had a wrong objective. The Delawares no longer lived on the Tuscarawas but had removed to the Sandusky, from where, with the neighboring

[32] Butterfield, *Expedition against Sandusky,* 33-36; Butterfield, *Washington-Irvine Correspondence,* 99; Draper MSS, 3E61.

Wyandot, they continued to raid the western Pennsylvania frontier. Clearly it was time for an expedition to attain an objective not yet reached during the Revolution, if a stop was to be put to Indian hostilities.

Hence it fell to Brodhead's successor, General William Irvine, to encourage an effort against the Delaware and Wyandot Indians on the Sandusky. It would be a mistake to say that Irvine undertook the expedition on his own initiative. Washington could spare no troops or supplies from the East, and Irvine was under express orders not to attempt any offensive operations "except upon a small scale." Crawford's Sandusky expedition was thus entirely a militia affair. As preparations got under way in the spring of 1782, Irvine was only the nominal director of arrangements; the militia officers of Westmoreland and Washington counties made the real decisions. The expedition was neither recruited, commanded, supplied, nor in any way paid for, by Congress. The militia, who were all mounted, were to be volunteers who "would equip themselves and victual at their own expense." Their "pay" as soldiers was to be in the form of exemption from two months' militia duty. They chose their own commanding officer, Colonel William Crawford, and made Williamson second in command. As Irvine said, "Nor are we in such a situation that I could take a single continental soldier along." Compensation for losses was to come from plunder.[33]

Thus an untrained band of militia, numbering about four hundred and inspired by revenge for the continuing Indian attacks and by fear of more to come, rendezvoused on May 21 at Mingo Bottom on the Ohio near Steubenville. Setting out on May 25, the mounted army proceeded rapidly westward in the hope of completely surprising the Sandusky Indians. All precautions for secrecy were rendered ludicrous because the Indians had no trouble in reconnoitering Crawford's

[33] The account of Crawford's expedition in this and the two following paragraphs is based on Butterfield, *Washington-Irvine Correspondence*, 94, 113-118; Brackenridge, *Indian Atrocities*, 10, 18-25; Butterfield, *Expedition against Sandusky*, 55, 61-77, 139, 153, 159, 202-217, 311-317, 379-392.

movements from the very day he left Mingo Bottom. Consequently on June 4 Crawford was confronted on the upper Sandusky by an Indian force more numerous than his own, with British reinforcements rapidly approaching from Detroit. On that day the Americans in pitched battle held their own. But on the next day the arrival of the British reinforcements and of Shawnee warriors from the south made it necessary for Crawford to order a retreat.

The retreat was a rout. In confusion the army broke into fleeing parties. Harassed by the Indians as far as the Olentangy, a branch of the Scioto, the Americans suffered repeated losses. The main party, led by Williamson, arrived back at Mingo Bottom late in June. In the meantime a small party under Crawford lost its way on the upper Sandusky and fell into the hands of Delaware Indians. The ensuing torture of Crawford was the supreme act of contempt for the American cause shown by the Indians during the war. It was considered by the Delawares as just retribution for the recent murder of their kinsmen at Gnadenhutten.

To this depth had the power of American arms on the frontier sunk in 1782. The frontier was wide open. Irvine at Pittsburgh could do nothing. Hence on July 13, 1782, there appeared before Hannastown, county seat of Westmoreland, Guyasuta and his band of Seneca. The town was burned to the ground, and much of the surrounding country was devastated. Relatively few whites were killed. Wheeling was then attacked but without the success experienced at Hannastown. The greatest British-Indian army raised in the course of the Revolution in the Northwest turned aside from its objective, the destruction of Wheeling, and centered its attentions on Kentucky. The bloody defeat of the Americans at the Blue Licks in August was the result of this effort.[34]

From July until mid-October, 1782, the upper Ohio frontier went through another series of abortive attempts to produce

[34] Butterfield, *Expedition against Sandusky,* 268; Butterfield, *Washington-Irvine Correspondence,* 176, 250, 381, 394; Hassler, *Old Westmoreland,* 176-181.

an expedition. Crawford's disaster was so humiliating that
something had to be done. Congress finally agreed to produce
soldiers and supplies, and Irvine went through the motions of
organizing for another assault upon the Sandusky. But
August 1, the first date of rendezvous, came and went, and the
eastern troops had not come. On August 25 Irvine wrote to
his wife, "There has been a great talk of the militia going on
another expedition but it will all end in talk. They will not
accomplish it. They are now afraid to go without regular
troops." On September 10 he confided, "There never was so
much talk of one [*an expedition*] as at this moment, and I am
sure it will end like the rest—all talk . . . I will not go into the
Indian country without a sufficiency of regular troops which I
really have not got. But I must talk of it, prepare for it, etc.,
etc., or it would not do here." With the commanding officer
writing this way, it could hardly be expected that an efficient
expedition would take place. Indeed, when troops from the
East were at last on the way, Irvine actually hoped that they
would not arrive; and he informed the secretary of war on
September 12 that things were so quiet and the season for
expeditions so far advanced that "I now almost wish they
may not come." September 15, another day of rendezvous,
went by, and still the help from the East had not arrived. A
resurgence of Indian attacks came in the latter part of the
month, and Irvine began to feel an interest in a campaign. He
named October 20 as the next day for a rendezvous. But on
October 19 the news of the preliminary peace treaty with
England arrived. At once the feeling of panic disappeared. As
Irvine reported to George Rogers Clark on November 7, "This
news gained universal belief with the country and I fear would
have mutilated my plan [even] if the report had proved
premature." A rush of squatters to the north of the Ohio had
begun before the news was a week old. There was nothing to
fear from Indians unsupported by the British, and the Americans, though beaten, could now breathe easily.[35]

[35] Draper MSS, 2AA70, 74; Butterfield, *Washington-Irvine Correspondence*, 134,

The long, sordid contest was at an end. Almost at the lowest tide of effectiveness of its Indian policy, the United States was presented with victory in the shape of new boundaries that included the very lands that the Indians had just successfully defended. The vanquished had become the victors. Perplexed, the Indians turned to the British for an explanation; the tribesmen had no intention of giving up their hunting grounds. A new phase of the struggle between the red men and the white in the Old Northwest had opened.

182, 184, 185, 255, 256, 259, 316, 317, 319, 335-339, 392, 396, 398, 400; James, *Clark Papers, 1771-1781*, 221.

12

The Revival
of American Aggression,
1782-1789

PEACE returned to America in 1782, but a strange peace it was for the Indians. The conflict between the British and the Americans in the battlefields of the East was at an end, but the peace that came to the frontiers of the West was an anomalous one indeed. For reasons of political expediency in Europe, England had yielded up the American Northwest, leaving the Indians to come to whatever terms they could with the United States over the disposition of the lands involved. The Indians were thus confronted with the astounding facts that the Americans had conquered the British and now owned the unconquered Indian hunting grounds north of the Ohio, and that Kentucky was lost to the red men forever. It was inconceivable to the tribesmen that the Americans could be called victors in the very year of their most humiliating defeats. The Indians, wrote Haldimand on October 23, 1782, "are Thunder Struck at the appearance of an accommodation So far short of their Expectation from the Language that has been held out to them, & Dread the Idea of being forsaken by us, & becoming a Sacrifice to a Vengeance which has already in many Instances been raked upon them."[1]

In order fully to understand this abnormal situation, the fundamental basis of the relationship between the British and the Indians must be kept in mind. From the days of 1777, when the British had pledged the Six Nations their territorial integrity, to the days of 1782, tribe after tribe had cast its lot with the British, and until the very moment of the announcement of peace, the British had stood loyally by the Indians. Although British support had never been up to Indian expectations and although in 1781 and 1782 there had been a noticeable decline in British attentions, there had never been the slightest indication to the tribesmen that their allies would desert them. They therefore continued to expect British support in the defense of their claims in the Northwest.

By the treaty of peace the Americans were relieved of a tremendous restraint. Racial hatred on the frontier, fed by the memory of the bloodshed of years of war, could now find a freer vent; vengeance could be taken; and reparations could be demanded in the form of cessions of land. It is true that the semblance of peace came to the frontiers of the upper Ohio. But it was a peace brought on by circumstances and not by the wishes of the frontiersmen themselves. It was a peace that came amidst preparations for war. It was a peace with the English, but not a peace with the Indians. Thus in the very months in which the treaty was being negotiated, Clark and his Kentuckians were going ahead with their preparations for an expedition against the Shawnee towns in retaliation for the massacre of the Blue Licks.

Clark's second expedition against the Shawnee actually

[1] "The Haldimand Papers," in *Michigan Pioneer and Historical Collections*, 10:663.

took place, therefore, after peace had been decided upon with England. On November 1, 1782, he crossed the Ohio with one thousand volunteers and in ten days reached Chillicothe, the central town of the Shawnee, at what is now Piqua, Ohio. Although the Indians, who had been warned of his approach, escaped with but a small loss, the town and five other villages were put to the torch, and ten thousand bushels of corn and quantities of provisions were destroyed. A detachment under Colonel Benjamin Logan then destroyed the store of British supplies at the portage at the head of the Great Miami, and although Clark failed to entice the Indians into a general engagement, their spirits, according to a somewhat exaggerated statement of Daniel Boone, were "damped, their connexions dissolved, their armies scattered & a future invasion [was] entirely out of their power."[2]

Confronted by this menace from the American frontier, the Indians naturally turned to their British allies for protection. Their desires were threefold. In the first place, they needed a continuation and improvement of trade. In the second place, because of the activities of the Kentuckians against the Shawnee and Miami, the Indians wanted the pledge of British troops in case of further invasion. Finally, they wanted the English to use their influence to promote a confederacy of all the tribes in order to increase the effectiveness of resistance to the Americans. Thus in April, 1783, the Wyandot appealed to Arent De Peyster, commandant at Detroit, "We don't know how to act 'till we hear from you, and as we have gone on hand in hand together, we hope to continue so, and that you'll not allow your poor children to be crushed under the weight of their enemies, but we expect you will be so good as to call the rest of your children about you, letting them know how its like to be with us, and that we want their assistance as soon as possible. We are likewise in hopes to see you here on this ground with as many of your own People as can be spared . . . for Fath[e]r depend upon it we have great reason to expect

[2] James, *Clark Papers, 1781-1784,* lvi, lvii, 140, 152, 157.

them [*the Americans*] shortly—Father! Should a Treaty of Peace be going on we hope your children will be remembered in the Treaty."[3]

The British had no intention of deserting the Indians, for to do so would be to see them destroyed, and their destruction would mean the loss of the fur trade and an added impetus to the westward rush of the American pioneer, with the inevitable restriction of the possibilities of expansion of British influence and empire. The British knew that the Indian nations were as determined as even the proudest white nations could be to protect their hunting grounds from invasion. They knew that a contest for Indian rights would be far bloodier than the Revolutionary one because the Indians would be unrestrained by the British. Haldimand wrote to Lord North on October 19, 1783, "In case things are carried to extremities, the Indians seem determined to defend themselves and to make the Americans feel the difference of a war carried on in their own manner from the late one, which was subject to the restraints imposed upon it by His Majesty's officers."[4]

Thus a new note appeared in British Indian policy with the coming of peace. Having failed in suppressing the rebellion and in reconquering the West, having been forced by diplomacy to preserve peace with the Americans and to be generous to them, the British now sought to curb Indian aggressiveness in order to protect the Indians themselves and to preserve the fur trade. In so doing they were to meet two of the Indians' three requirements—a continuation of supplies by means of the fur trade, and the encouragement of an Indian confederacy to resist American encroachments. Although the Indians long believed the contrary, the British had no intention of providing troops, because to do so would have meant a continuance in times of peace of a war-time alliance. It must be emphasized that the great consideration of the British was not a humani-

[3] "The Haldimand Papers," in *Michigan Pioneer and Historical Collections*, 11:355.
[4] Burt, "Western Posts," in Canadian Historical Association, *Report of the Annual Meeting*, 1931, p. 67.

tarian interest in the Indians, but the preservation of the fur trade. The loss of Indian friendship would be the loss of perhaps the most important reason for the retention of Canada.

The British therefore met the first requirement of the Indians by a continuance, without interruption, of the old-time trading system. It was only gradually, however, that they undertook to fulfill the second requirement, that of encouraging the confederacy. At first they attempted to convince the Indians of the need of moderation in resisting the Americans and of the feasibility of a defensive policy only. De Peyster in December, 1782, had relayed a message from Haldimand to the Indians: "Children! I have another Message from the Commander in Chief to you which is that you will not push the War into the Enemies Country but defend your own, in which he is ready to give you every assistance in his power." The advisability of adherence to such defensive tactics was, of course, increased by the assurance of lasting peace early in 1783. When the Shawnee, smarting under Clark's destructive blow, appealed to the British for aid in retaliating, Haldimand instructed De Peyster, "Nothing can be more natural than this desire Yet under the express orders I have received . . . it is impossible I can comply with their Request."[5]

The Indians were restless and, in spite of British warnings, made certain moves toward retribution. Alexander McKee therefore went among the tribes in the early part of 1783 to attempt to bring them to their senses, and he achieved some success. Of all the tribes, the Miami were the most insistent upon retaliation, and De Peyster was obliged to lavish more goods on them to keep them from going against Kentucky. "In general," he reported to Haldimand on May 3, 1783, "the Indians are well disposed . . . I doubt not however, that I shall find some difficulty to restrain the Wabash Indians, but nothing shall be neglected that may in any wise contribute to bring it about." The Indians, in fact, were still possessed by

[5] "The Haldimand Papers," in *Michigan Pioneer and Historical Collections,* 10:660; 11:328, 342.

the great fear that peace might mean the loss of their lands through American aggression. Speaking in the spring of 1783 of the Indian attitude toward the treaty of peace, De Peyster wrote, "They seemed satisfied with it, & I really believe will conform to it, provided the Enemy let them alone which it is past a doubt they will not." General Allan MacLean, at Niagara, reported in May, "They [*the Iroquois*] are pleased with the Peace, but they seem to be very anxious & uneasy, they have heard of certain pretended Boundaries, to which they never can agree if true, but they do not believe it."[6]

The anxiety of the Indians could not be removed by exhortations of restraint, nor could restraint be imposed by mere words pledging the Indians a vague support from the British in the matter of the retention of their hunting grounds. They were uneasy in the face of declining British support and of rising American aggressiveness. A movement of self-defense therefore began that was to characterize the contest in the Northwest until 1795, a movement of confederation by which the Indians sought to present a united front to the oncoming Americans, to alienate no lands but by the common consent of all nations, and, if need be, to unite their warriors on a common battlefield in defense of a common cause.

The Indian confederation originated under the joint auspices of the British Indian superintendent, Sir John Johnson, and his wards, the Six Nations. The Indian leader was Captain Joseph Brant, or Thayendanegea, the brilliant chieftain of the Mohawk nation. By the end of July the Six Nations had made plans for a grand council of thirty-five nations to be held on the Sandusky River in the Wyandot country early in the fall, for the purpose of forming a general confederacy. Thus originated the first of a long series of councils in the Northwest that were to culminate in the Indian War of 1790-94. It must be noted that this movement for Indian confederation took place during that interlude of uncertainty

[6] "The Haldimand Papers," in *Michigan Pioneer and Historical Collections,* 11:359, 362, 367; 20:110, 117, 122.

when the Indians feared for the status of their lands because they had heard vaguely that the treaty of peace forfeited these lands entirely to the Americans and because they feared lest the English might desert them in their hour of need. As Haldimand stated, the object of the Indian confederacy was "to defend their country against all invaders." On the one hand they were to "keep a watchful eye over the conduct of the Americans settled on the frontiers of this country"; and on the other they were to seek, by means of Brant's maneuvering, to obtain from the English an effective guarantee of the Ohio River boundary. The Indians were not destined to obtain this guarantee, and the British were eventually to let the tribesmen fight the matter out alone at the battle of Fallen Timbers in 1794. For the time being, however, the British lent their support, though cautiously, to the confederation movement.[7]

At the council of Sandusky in September, 1783, the confederacy was definitely informed by the British that the Ohio River was their boundary. The British assumed, since no cessions had been made by the Indians since the treaty of Fort Stanwix of 1768, when the Ohio River had been designated as the boundary between the whites and the Indians, that the Americans would not push their claims further without direct negotiations with the Indians. At the council the Indians were also told by Sir John Johnson that although they must cease their warfare, they must be ready at any time to resume the battle at the moment that their lands were invaded by the Americans. The superintendent adroitly omitted to mention whether or not the British would support the Indians in such an encounter and created enough of an impression of British sincerity to induce the Indians to give up any insistence upon further armed support. Thus Sir John assured the confederacy that he would "take the Tomahawk out of their hand; though he would not remove it out of sight or far from

[7] Manley, *Treaty of Fort Stanwix*, 18; Burt, "Western Posts," in Canadian Historical Association, *Report of the Annual Meeting*, 1931, p. 67.

them, but lay it down carefully by their side, that they might have it convenient to use in defence of their rights and property if they were invaded or molested by the Americans."[8]

The downfall of the Indians after the first grand council at Sandusky in 1783 was but a matter of time. The English had managed to inform the tribes of the terms of the treaty of peace without incurring their ill will. The Indians were deceived into thinking that, although their lands belonged to the Americans, the British would help the Indians keep the latter from taking possession, and they had also been led to believe that the boundary of the Ohio River would be kept inviolate. The tribesmen furthermore felt reassured by the fact that the war ax had not been taken from them. "Though at present unemployed," said John Dease, Johnson's relative and subordinate, in 1784, "they often Look Wishfully at it [*the ax*] & keep it Close to their Sides." But while the British congratulated themselves on the success of their diplomatic measures with the Indians and while the Indians permitted themselves to be lulled into a feeling of false security, American policy overcame its pitiable weakness and began to take on the form of renewed aggressiveness reminiscent of the days of General McIntosh. This new form was embodied in the Ordinance of October 15, 1783, by which Congress for the first time made known the American interpretation of the new Indian boundary in a declaration that wrested from the Indians all lands between the Ohio River and Lake Erie east of the Great Miami and Maumee rivers.[9]

For imperial aggressiveness and outright effrontery this document takes a front rank in the annals of American expansion. To the Indians it could mean nothing less than an open declaration of war. In section three of the ordinance, Congress announced that the Indians, by breaking their

[8] *Pennsylvania Archives*, first series, 10:554. The proceedings of the council are printed in full in "The Haldimand Papers," in *Michigan Pioneer and Historical Collections*, 20:174-183.

[9] Manley, *Treaty of Fort Stanwix*, 19. The Ordinance of 1783 is in United States Continental Congress, *Journals . . . 1774-1789*, 25:681-693.

pledges of neutrality given in 1776, and by supporting the British cause, had forfeited all rights to their lands. It was further asserted, however, that the United States was willing to be generous and would insist on the cession of only part of these lands. "As the Indians," the ordinance read, "notwithstanding a solemn treaty of neutrality with Congress at the commencement of the war . . . could not be restrained from acts of hostility and wanton devastation . . . so consequently with a less generous people than Americans, they might be compelled to retire beyond the lakes, but as we prefer clemency to rigor . . . & as we are disposed to be kind to them, to supply their wants and partake of their trade, we from these considerations and from motives of compassion draw a veil over what is passed, and will establish a boundary line between them and us, beyond which we will restrain our citizens from hunting and settling." Congress could not afford to be too aggressive. Although the annexation might be allowed to be offensive to the Indians, it should not be so grasping as to bring the forest natives in united and confederated force upon the frontiers in a general Indian war. The lands of the Northwest must therefore be occupied by degrees.

This policy of carefulness originated as the result of the attempt in 1783 of the state of New York to expel the Iroquois and of the scare caused by the unexpected resistance of the Indians and their British friends. The reception given by the Indians to the instructions concerning their expulsion was so hostile that General Philip Schuyler in a letter to Congress on July 29 had immediately advised a retraction to avoid an Indian war, and his advice was given more weight by the strong endorsement of General Washington. The commander-in-chief had become firmly convinced that the United States could accomplish a more effective destruction of Indian civilization by a modified advance than by a complete occupation of all the Indian lands, which could only be accomplished through the suppression of a general Indian uprising.[10]

[10] Manley, *Treaty of Fort Stanwix*, 28-32; Washington, *Writings*, 8:479-484 (Sparks edition).

The policy of Congress towards the Indians was further moderated as the result of General von Steuben's visit to General Haldimand and by the missions of John Joseph Bull, Ebenezer Allen, and Ephraim Douglass to the various Indian tribes. Steuben had been sent by Washington in July with instructions to devise with Haldimand measures for receiving possession immediately or "at an early day" of all British military posts in the territory ceded to the United States. These were the posts of Michilimackinac, Detroit, Niagara, and Oswego. Washington was anxious that the American forces should take possession the moment the British withdrew, so that there would be no danger of the posts being seized by the Indians for use against the Americans. Haldimand, however, politely declined to make arrangements and protested that no instructions on the matter had as yet been received from the king. No communications were permitted with the Indians, and Steuben was not allowed to go to Detroit. It was thus apparent to Congress that the British intended to retain a strong influence among the tribes and that if an Indian war were to be avoided, it would be prudent to let discretion temper American aggressiveness.[11]

A similar lesson was drawn from the visits to the tribes of the Congressional agents, Bull, Allen, and Douglass. During the spring of 1783 there had occurred a series of ferocious Indian attacks that took a toll of over forty lives on the frontiers of western Pennsylvania and Virginia. That the Indians felt justified in these attacks is borne out by the fact that when they had ceased fighting at the suggestion of the British the year before, white settlers had at once swarmed into their territory in increasing numbers. These attacks, however justified they may have been, aroused the wrath of the frontier, and at the request of President John Dickinson of Pennsylvania, Congress sent Douglass to the Northwest and Bull and Allen to New York to announce the declaration of peace

[11] Washington, *Writings*, 8:461-464 (Sparks edition); Sparks, *Correspondence of the American Revolution*, 4:39-43; Burt, "Western Posts," in Canadian Historical Association, *Report of the Annual Meeting*, 1931, p. 66, 67.

and to summon the Indians to treaties for the cession of lands. The Indians were to be reminded that "the U. S. are a compassionate and merciful people—that they are disposed to pity the I[ndians] and to forgive their past folly, on condition that they immediately desist from further hostility, and hereafter conduct themselves as a people disposed to Enjoy the blessings of Peace."[12]

But the Congressional bark was stronger than its bite, and the results of these journeys only proved further that the Indians must still be handled with discretion. It was found that the Iroquois "are well disposed for peace, but are ready for War, and will desolate the Frontiers of Pennsylvania if the United States resolve to conquer their lands"; and Douglass was informed by the Delawares that the preliminary articles of peace had "never been communicated to them by authority," and that "the accidental information they had occasionally received had been in some respects contradicted by the Officers of the Crown; particularly that part which related to the evacuation of the posts on the Lakes." De Peyster, at Detroit, told Douglass that he would not allow him to inform the Indians of the American plans, "especially as he had uniformly declared to them, that he did not know these Posts were to be evacuated by the English." Douglass thereupon proceeded to Niagara and sought with even less success to get General Allan MacLean to permit him to address the Indians. MacLean emphatically reminded Douglass that the state of New York was attempting to effect the removal of the Indians by violence and that the Indian resistance to this attempt was ample evidence that Douglass' message to the tribesmen could not be permitted. He assured Douglass that the Indians had been informed that they could no longer count on British help in war and that if the tribesmen persisted, "the British Troops would join the Americans to punish

[12] Butterfield, *Washington-Irvine Correspondence*, 109, 185, 193, 196, 231, 261, 320; *Pennsylvania Archives*, first series, 10:45, 168; Clarence M. Burton, "Ephraim Douglass and His Times," in *Magazine of History with Notes and Queries*, extra numbers, vol. 3, no. 10, p. 33 (1910).

them." The British thus prevented the carrying to the Indians of the peremptory warnings of Congress.[13]

These were, then, the circumstances that produced the Ordinance of October 15, 1783, and that determined the new American policy of modified aggression into the Indian lands of the upper Ohio, New York, and Pennsylvania. Under instructions of Congress, following up the ordinance, five commissioners, Arthur Lee, Richard Butler, George Rogers Clark, Oliver Wolcott, and Benjamin Lincoln, were chosen to go to the various tribes to impose upon them the new cessions of land. At the same time that arrangements were being made for these commissioners to treat with the Indians, state commissioners in the various states involved were also attempting to negotiate with the tribes. But the Indians were determined to treat with the United States as a whole, and, further, to get the United States to treat with the confederacy rather than with separate tribes. They were encouraged in this determination by the failure of New York to accomplish its original intention of expelling from the state four of the Six Nations.

In October, 1783, the Mohawk chief, Brant, informed General Schuyler, who was acting as intermediary between the Indians, New York, and Congress, that the Indians were disposed to treat with the representatives of Congress. New York, however, persisted in making arrangements for its own treaty, and Brant finally acquiesced in meeting the state commissioners, although he made it plain that no matters of importance could be discussed. Congress even warned the Oneida and Tuscarora that the New York treaty had not been "authorised by Congress." When, early in September, the meeting with the New York commissioners actually took place at Fort Stanwix, Brant told them that "it was the Voice of our Chiefs and their Confederates that We should first meet Commissioners of the whole thirteen States and after that if any Matters should remain between Us and any particular State,

[13] United States Continental Congress Papers, series 78, vol. 1, p. 433-435; *Pennsylvania Archives*, first series, 10:83-90.

288

that we should then attend to them." Remonstrances from the
New Yorkers were to no avail, and the conference broke up
pending the Congressional treaty, which was to be held at the
same place.[14]

Throughout the negotiations leading up to the Congressional treaty at Fort Stanwix, Brant proceeded on the fundamental assumption that the treaty was to be with the whole
confederacy. Congress had originally shown a desire to frus-
trate this movement towards Indian confederation by encouraging separate treaties but had been obliged to abandon
the attempt because such negotiations would take too much
time and money. The Ordinance of 1783 had therefore provided for a single treaty, probably in the interests of economy and
time. Further acquaintance with the tribal divisions of the
Indians, however, brought the United States to a different
attitude, and on March 19, 1784, Congress reversed its action
and directed the commissioners "to treat with the several nations at different times and places." But a month later Congress was again obliged to suspend these instructions because
it was anxious to get matters settled with "utmost dispatch."[15]

Circumstances, however, made it possible for the commissioners to attempt to break the confederacy. Brant had, with
great difficulty, brought about the assembling of delegates of
the western nations at Niagara early in September, 1784; the
commissioners, ignoring Brant, had sent their own messenger,
James Deane, to summon the western nations to meet at Fort
Stanwix on September 27. Deane committed the tactical error
of not summoning them through the medium of the Iroquois,
and the effect of his instructions was further weakened by the
fact that they were not committed to writing—the British had
informed the Indians that General Washington had advised
General MacLean "that no attention might be paid to any
verbal message as every transaction that related to public

[14] *Pennsylvania Archives*, first series, 10:88; Manley, *Treaty of Fort Stanwix*,
34-56, 59, 61, 70-72.
[15] *Pennsylvania Archives*, first series, 10:122; United States Continental Congress,
Journals . . . 1774-1789, 26:153, 238.

business with the Indians should be sent in writing." As a result the western delegates arrived at Niagara in response to Brant's invitation long before the Congressional commissioners were ready for them and were left on the hands of the British, who could hardly be expected to support Indians for an American treaty. The tribesmen were forced to wait while Brant went through the process of putting off the New Yorkers at Fort Stanwix; the result was that by the time the Continental commissioners were ready for the Indians, most of the western tribesmen had gone home. Consequently when the nations assembled early in October to meet the United States commissioners, the only western Indians present except the Iroquois were a few Shawnee. Thus from the Indian point of view, since the whole confederacy was not represented, there could be no valid treaty.[16]

The American commissioners nevertheless persisted in forcing a treaty on the Iroquois. In so doing they assumed a domineering tone, and, by taking advantage of the Indians' weakness, exacted a cession of land from the Iroquois that the confederacy never recognized as just or valid. With telling effect the treaty of 1783 between the United States and Great Britain was read to the warriors assembled at the treaty ground on October 11, so that, in the words of the Americans, "the Indian nations will perceive that the King of Great Britain renounces, and yields to the United States all pretensions, and claims, whatsoever, of all the country South, and West of the Great Northern Rivers, and Lakes, as far as the Mississippi." As a gesture of generosity, the commissioners thereupon invited the Indians to propose such a boundary line "as will be just for you to offer, and honorable for the United States to agree to."[17]

[16] Manley, *Treaty of Fort Stanwix*, 69, 72-74; "Treaty of Fort Stanwix in 1784," in *Olden Time*, 2:416 (1847).

[17] The proceedings of the Congressional treaty discussed in this and the three following paragraphs are in Manley, *Treaty of Fort Stanwix;* "Treaty of Fort Stanwix in 1784," in *Olden Time*, 2:404-432 (1847). See also United States, *Indian Affairs, Laws and Treaties*, 2:3, 4; *American State Papers, Indian Affairs*, 1:10.

The Revival of American Aggression

Justice, to the Iroquois, was the retention of the old boundary of the first treaty of Fort Stanwix in 1768, and this was what the British had encouraged them to insist upon. With what trepidation was their reply to the Americans made! Completely lacking in the arts of diplomacy, they confessed that they had been deserted by Great Britain. They announced that their only reliance was the Great Spirit. "Certainly the Great King did not look up to that Great Spirit," said the Mohawk, Aaron Hill, head of the Iroquois delegation, "otherwise common justice would not have suffered him to be so inattentive, as to neglect those who had been so just, and faithful to him." But Justice was hiding her eyes to what went into the scales at this treaty of Fort Stanwix. "We Indians love our lands," announced the Seneca chief, Cornplanter, "we warriors must have a large country to range in, as indeed our subsistence must depend on our having much hunting ground." In their weakness the unfortunate tribesmen could only plead. Cornplanter concluded by proposing a boundary line not much different from the 1768 line, to "continue forever, as the sun which rolls over from day to day."

This was too much for the Americans. In their reply the Iroquois were told in plain words that they would be forced to submit—that they had been utterly perfidious in supporting the British in the Revolution and in thereby breaking their neutrality pledges of 1775 and 1776. "You are mistaken," said the commissioners, "in supposing that . . . you are become a free and independent nation, and may make what terms you please. . . . You are a subdued people. . . . When we offer you peace on moderate terms, we do it in magnanimity and mercy. If you do not accept it now, you are not to expect a repetition of such offers. . . . We shall now, therefore declare to you the condition, on which alone you can be received into the peace and protection of the United States." The terms were thereupon dictated, and there was nothing for the Iroquois to do but to surrender. There was no reply to the open and avowed argument of force. Cornplanter thereupon arose and said,

"You have this day declared your minds to us fully, and without disguise. We thank you for it; this is acting like men, for thus men speak."

In this way did the once imperial Iroquois confederacy resign from the hegemony of Indian politics in the North. The treaty included a definite and final relinquishment by the Iroquois of their historic claims to lands west of the states of New York and Pennsylvania. The compensation consisted of a vague promise that the United States "will order goods to be delivered to the Six Nations for their use and comfort." Finally, Aaron Hill and five others were held as hostages until "all the prisoners . . . taken . . . in the late war from amongst the citizens of the United States shall be delivered up." So dishonorable did Brant consider this action that he immediately suspended all the preparations he had been making to visit England and bent every effort to return the so-called prisoners, many of whom preferred the Indian life, in order to effect the release of the hostages.

The Iroquois were thus left to deal alone with New York and Pennsylvania, with whose Indian lands Congress, of course, had no right to interfere. These states were quick to appropriate most of the Iroquois land. Pennsylvania accomplished the cession of every square inch of Indian hunting ground within the boundaries of the commonwealth in her own treaty of Fort Stanwix, held at the close of the Continental treaty.[18] New York was less hasty but hardly less drastic and kept as close to the heels of the retreating Indians as could be done without raising the danger of goading them into confederated war.

The treaties at Fort McIntosh were in effect repetitions of those at Fort Stanwix. The Continental commissioners, intent upon breaking the Indian confederacy, dealt merely with the Wyandot and Delawares and a few wandering Ottawa and Chippewa, all of whom were bound by the agreement at Sandusky in 1783 not to cede any lands except with the consent

[18] *Pennsylvania Archives*, first series, 11:508.

of all. The Wyandot and Delawares were officially represented because the land in question belonged to the Delawares through a grant from the Wyandot, the original owners or claimants. It was force alone that exacted from these tribes a cession that was never recognized as valid by the rest of the confederates, and it was apparent to all who understood Indian affairs that the treaty could not be binding. Alexander McKee, at Detroit, wrote Sir John Johnson on April 24, 1785, "It is indeed evident that the transactions at those two Meetings can not be permanent, as it will be found that refractory tribes will never tamely submit to be deprived of A Country on which they think their existence depends."[19]

By December 30, Arthur Lee, Richard Butler, and George Rogers Clark had assembled the Indians at Fort McIntosh at the mouth of the Beaver River. The commissioners lost no time in showing the Indians what they could expect. The opening speech, made on January 8, 1785, was, in effect, an impressive and overwhelming announcement that the Indians had no friends. The American treaty of alliance with France was read, and the Indians were informed that the king of France had "renounced forever" any claim to lands in the United States. The treaty of peace of 1783 with Great Britain was also read, and the Indians were solemnly informed: "The King of Great Britain in his treaty with the U. States, has not stipulated any thing in favour of you & of the other Indian Nations who joined him in the war against us. You are therefore left to obtain peace from the U. States, & to be received under their government and protection, upon such conditions as seem proper to Congress, the Great Council of the U. States." It was then impressed on these western tribes that the Six Nations had surrendered at the treaty of Fort Stanwix and that therefore the confederacy was broken.[20]

[19] Draper MSS, 23U24, 125.

[20] Draper MSS, 1W26, 27. The proceedings of the treaty of Fort McIntosh described in this and the two following paragraphs are in "Memorandum of the Proceedings at Treaty of Fort McIntosh," Pickering Papers. See also United States, *Indian Affairs, Laws and Treaties*, 2:4, 5; *American State Papers, Indian Affairs*, 1:11.

There was nothing left for the Indians to do but to throw themselves on the mercies of the commissioners and plead for their lands. Their only arguments were their own needs, the fact that they actually resided on these lands, and the traditions handed down from their fathers. As the Delaware spokesman quaintly put it, "I think as the old men in former times did. They were old, I am young: nevertheless, I think that the grant was good, and that the country is mine. And as our children grow up, we tell them that the country is ours." To these statements the Wyandot gave their strong endorsement: "Attend to what my nephew (the Delaware) has said to you. Believe him; for he has spoke the truth . . . I set him down in *this land. The rest belongs to the Wyandots.*"

To these pleas the American commissioners turned deaf ears and in no uncertain terms informed the Indians that the red men had no rights. "You have been particular," they said, "in describing to us the claim and title of each particular tribe . . . The detail of these claims and title may appear to be of consequence among yourselves. But to us & to the business of the Council Fire to which we have called you, they have no relation; *because* we claim the country by conquest; and are to give not to receive. It is of this that it behooves you to have a clear and distinct comprehension." The terms of the treaty, dated January 21, 1785, were then dictated to the tribesmen, and they could do nothing but accept. The treaty was falsely declared to be "between the commissioners plenipotentiary of the United States of America, of the one part, and the sachems and warriors of the Wyandot, Delaware, Chippewa and Ottawa nations, of the other." By it, these four nations were made to acknowledge that, outside of the reservation bounded by the Cuyahoga, the Maumee, and Lake Erie, and on the south by the line drawn through the central part of what is now the state of Ohio, all the lands of the Northwest belonged to the United States. The thing that came nearest to compensation was the distribution of goods after the signing of the treaty "in pursuance of the humane and liberal views of Congress." Although not stated in the treaty, the promise was made to the Indians by the commissioners that they might continue to hunt in the ceded lands while the game was plentiful and until the whites had settled there.

The effect of the treaty of Fort McIntosh, like that of the treaty of Fort Stanwix, was to increase the discontent among the Indians. At first they were disposed to quarrel among themselves and to blame the warriors who had attended the treaties for their submission and for opening the country to American surveyors and settlers. But anger quickly gave way to a desire to renew the confederacy and to preserve a united front in defense of the Ohio River boundary. McKee informed Johnson on May 29, 1785, "The impolicy of exacting or enforcing such terms upon the Indians was visible by the disgust shown upon this occasion by all Nations."[21]

The Pennsylvania commissioners, following along in the wake of the Congressional agents, repeated the process they had gone through at Fort Stanwix of negotiating with the Indians present after the latter had dealt with the national commissioners. On January 25 the Delaware and Wyandot chiefs formally deeded to the commonwealth of Pennsylvania "all that part of the said Commonwealth not yet purchased of the Indians." The wording saved the Pennsylvania commissioners from offending the Iroquois, and the fact that in the negotiations they recognized the Delaware and Wyandot claims pleased the latter tribes. There was apparently no friction. The action of the Iroquois in ceding the same lands was, however, cited, and the Indians were given presents in payment for their claims.[22]

Having dealt with the Iroquois, Delaware, Wyandot, Chippewa, and Ottawa tribes, the American commissioners turned their attentions to the more western tribes, that is, the Shawnee, Miami, Wea, Piankashaw, Potawatomi, Kickapoo, and others. This final treaty was to be held at Vincennes, on the

[21] Draper MSS 23U17, 22, 23.
[22] The proceedings of the Pennsylvania treaty of Fort McIntosh are in Bausman, *Beaver County*, 2:1203-1210.

Wabash, a place central to the tribes concerned. It was to arrange a ratification of the Fort McIntosh cession and, in accordance with the doctrine that the United States owned the lands, to allot hunting grounds to each tribe. It was not destined, however, to be successful in its object, because the commissioners found that the hostility of the tribes in the Wabash country made it inexpedient to transport their goods and themselves to Vincennes. The treaty was therefore held at the mouth of the Great Miami at the hastily constructed Fort Finney, and with but one tribe, the Shawnee, present.

During the preparation for the treaty, the suspicion and hostility of the western Indians threatened to make the negotiations a complete failure. The hopes of all the interested tribes that the United States would conduct a general treaty with the confederacy had been raised to a high pitch immediately upon the close of the war, but when the treaties of Fort Stanwix and Fort McIntosh were negotiated with separate tribes with the deliberate purpose of breaking the Indian confederacy, the western nations assumed a suspicious and unfriendly attitude, and in conseqeunce, all tribes but the Shawnee failed to appear at Fort Finney. The Americans were made aware of this attitude by plain-spoken replies to their invitations to the treaty. A general Indian council was actually in session at Detroit to discuss the Fort Stanwix and Fort McIntosh treaties when the American commissioners' invitation was received, and in a united reply the Indians rebuked the United States for dealing with separate tribes at the previous treaties and stated that those treaties had not yet been considered and approved by the confederacy. They then declared that when the council had finished its business in its own time, it would be ready to treat, and expressed the hope that the next spring would be soon enough. Briefly, the result of the Detroit council of 1785 was a repudiation by the western Indians of all partial treaties in general and of the treaties of Fort Stanwix and Fort McIntosh in particular.[23]

[23] Draper MSS, 23U28, 30.

When the Shawnee finally assembled at Fort Finney on January 28, 1786, the terms proposed to them were: the retention of hostages until the return of all prisoners; the acknowledgment by the Shawnee that the United States was sovereign over all lands ceded by Great Britain; the recognition of the United States as protectors; the consent that all crimes, even those committed on whites by Shawnee in the Shawnee country, were to be punished by American law; and the grant to the United States of all Shawnee claims east of the Great Miami.[24]

Stung by what seemed to them the monstrosity of these terms, the long suffering Shawnee balked, and the chief, Kekewepellethe, answered in heroic terms, saying that it was "not the custom of the Shawnese to give hostages . . . and as to the lands, God gave us this country, we do not understand measuring out the lands, it is all ours. You say you have goods for our women and children; you may keep your goods, and give them to the other nations, we will have none of them." This was strong language for Indians to use to Americans and as usual it gained the tribesmen nothing but threats of force. Richard Butler immediately replied with much heat, repeating his charges of Shawnee perfidy and declaring that the Indians would either have to submit or expect to be destroyed. "The destruction of your women and children," said he, "or their future happiness, depends on your present choice. Peace or war is in your power; make your choice like men, and judge for yourselves." There was, of course, no choice. Kekewepellethe found it necessary to apologize for his action and agreed to furnish hostages. "Brethren," he said in closing, "you have every thing in your power—you are great, and we see you own all the country; we therefore hope, as you have everything in your power, that you will take pity on our women and children. . . . and we agree to all you have proposed, and hope, in future, we shall both enjoy peace, and be secure."

---

[24] The proceedings at the treaty of Fort Finney described in this and the following paragraph are in Butler, "Journal," in *Olden Time*, 2:433-464, 481-532 (1847). See

The Shawnee returned home, but the methods of intimidation used to force them to accept the terms of the treaty were viewed by them as justification for subsequently repudiating their agreement. They thereupon adopted that attitude of proud belligerency that had long since been forced upon them. In the meanwhile Indian depredations into Kentucky had continued, and although these were carried on by Mingo and Cherokee, the Shawnee were blamed by the frontiersmen for tolerating the hostile attacks. Resentment flared high, and the attitude taken by the Shawnee after the treaty of Fort Finney gave the Kentuckians an excuse to strike at that tribe. During the summer of 1786, therefore, determined plans were made for expeditions against the Shawnee, and by fall the Kentucky militia was ready to strike. On September 14 General George Rogers Clark, having assembled officers and troops at Clarksville, across the Ohio from Louisville, issued orders to Colonel Benjamin Logan to proceed against the Shawnee for having broken the treaty of Fort Finney. Logan suddenly descended upon the Shawnee towns on the Great Miami early in October, burned seven of them, killed ten chiefs, and did much damage to the crops and cattle. And as if this unjust attack were not enough, the Shawnee were made victims of a disgraceful incident that took place on the expedition—the murder of Melanthy, friendly Shawnee chieftain, under a flag of truce. "Melanthy," Colonel Harmar wrote on November 15, 1786, "would not fly, but displayed the thirteen stripes, and held out the articles of the Miami treaty, but all in vain; he was shot down by one of the party, although he was their prisoner."[25] From that time until the battle of Tippecanoe the Shawnee were determined to deliver their people from such insults, and the Indian confederacy had no more loyal supporters than the Shawnee nation—the people of Tecumseh and his brother, the Prophet.

also United States, *Indian Affairs, Laws and Treaties*, 2:12; *American State Papers, Indian Affairs*, 1:11.

[25] Virginia, *Calendar of Virginia State Papers*, 4:204, 205; W. H. Smith, *St. Clair Papers*, 2:19.

The Revival of American Aggression

The Indians in general, discontented with the entire trend of events since the signing of the peace between England and the United States, believed that a new deal was now in order, and the confederacy decided to reject the false treaties of 1784, 1785, and 1786 and to request a reopening of the whole issue before a grand treaty council between the United States and the united Indian confederates. A preliminary Indian council had been held by the Iroquois at the British Fort Schlosser on the Niagara peninsula in March, 1786, at which that tribe had determined to send a message to the United States renouncing the treaty of Fort Stanwix and asking for a new treaty council in order to make a more just settlement in regard to the New York lands. This message bespoke the spirit of what was to come in the grand council.[26]

The Indians attempted to assemble for their grand treaty at the Shawnee town of Wakatomica but were frustrated by the invasion of Benjamin Logan and his Kentuckians. They managed to meet, however, in satisfactory numbers at Detroit in December, 1786, and at this historic council the Indian union of 1783 was solemnly renewed. The lead in the proceedings was taken by the Six Nations, and the Mohawk, Brant, was one of the chief figures and spokesmen. Brant, in an attempt to gain British endorsement of the entire Indian program from the very source of British policy, had gone to England late in 1785 and, on January 4, 1786, had presented his message to Lord Sidney, colonial secretary. He had pleaded for a more generous treatment from the British than had yet been evidenced and had asked for assurances of the continuation of their alliance. The answer was noncommittal, but Brant was encouraged by the British protestations of friendship and had returned to America determined to push his advantage to the utmost.[27]

The keynote speech at the Detroit council of 1786, probably made by Brant, is one of the strongest and most eloquent ever made in defense of Indian union. The speaker called before the

[26] Draper MSS, 23U32.　　　　[27] Stone, *Life of Joseph Brant*, 2:248, 253.

view of the assembled tribes the history of the Indian race in America since the coming of the white man and made it plain to them that the continued retreat of the Indians was due to their fatal inability to co-operate with each other against a common enemy. "It is certain," he said, "that before Christian Nations Visited this Continent we were the Sole Lords of the Soil! . . . the Great Spirit placed us there! and what is the reason why we are not Still in possession of our forefathers birth Rights? You may Safely Say because they wanted that Unanimity which we now So Strongly and Repeatedly recommend to you. . . . Therefore let us . . . be unanimous, let us have a Just sense of our own Value and if after that the Great Spirit wills that other Colours Should Subdue us, let it be so, we then Cannot reproach our Selves for Misconduct . . . The Interests of Any One Nation Should be the Interests of us all, the Welfare of the one Should be the Welfare of all the others."[28]

As the result of these eloquent exhortations, an address asking for a new council was drawn up for submission to Congress. The address was signed by ten tribes constituting all the nations of the upper Ohio and Great Lakes country. These were the Iroquois, Wyandot, Delaware, Shawnee, Ottawa, Chippewa, Potawatomi, Miami, and Cherokee tribes and the Wabash confederates (Wea and Piankashaw). It was an important address as it was the first official information to the United States from the confederacy that the Indians desired a reconsideration of the treaties of Fort Stanwix, Fort McIntosh, and Fort Finney. Besides giving voice to the displeasure of the Indians at not being included in the treaty of peace with Great Britain and at the unwillingness of the United States to deal with the confederacy, the message asked that until a new treaty council could be held, Congress withdraw the surveyors who were engaged in laying off into the well-known "Seven Ranges" part of the lands allegedly ceded at the treaty of Fort McIntosh. These proposals they believed were reason-

[28] Draper MSS, 23U45.

able; if they were rejected by the United States, the tribesmen, they stated, would have no alternative but to fight.[29]

It took this document a surprisingly long time to reach Congress. And it took Congress more time to act upon it. The result was that the movement for the new council was not really under way until 1788 and did not reach fruition until the treaty of Fort Harmar in January, 1789. In the meantime the settling of the Indian lands north of the Ohio had proceeded so rapidly that a reconsideration of terms was rendered futile. By the time of the Fort Harmar treaty, actual settlements at Marietta and Cincinnati had taken place.

At the same time the American policy of divide and conquer had slowly but surely made its progress, so that when the tribes finally met the United States for a reconsideration of the treaties of settlement, various schisms among them had destroyed their united front. The first rift occurred when the Wyandot and Delawares found themselves unable to put the confederacy's insistence on the Ohio River boundary into effect because they had been forced to agree to the cession of lands north of the Ohio at the treaty of Fort McIntosh. If they had actually attempted to stop the surveying and settling of the ceded lands they would have precipitated a war in which their people, who were closest to the Americans, would be the first to be struck and possibly destroyed. These helpless tribes were thus exposed to the opprobrium of their colleagues, who blamed them for the breakdown of union. In a feeble effort to keep the peace, however, the Wyandot and Delawares warned the United States not to proceed too swiftly with the surveying of the western lands: "What you said about dividing the land," they told one of Butler's messengers in the fall of 1786, "we will always stand to it. But its best not to let it be divided yet.... If we were to force this work of the land now, it might do mischief; its best to let the land alone till every thing is right."[30]

Thus the confederate Indian council at Detroit in Decem-

---

[29] *American State Papers, Indian Affairs*, 1:8.   [30] Draper MSS, 1W246, 247.

ber, 1786, developed into a quarrel between the Wyandot and the Delawares on the one side, and the rest of the tribes on the other, and this discord brought about a fatal mistake by the confederacy: in its message to Congress there is a strange omission of any specific boundary line. Thus the Americans could now conduct a new treaty with all the tribes without conceding in any way the Ohio River claim and could accuse the Indians of deception in not stating officially their fundamental object. The United States, therefore, proceeded to follow up the surveying of the lands with actual settlement.

The second rift that appeared among the Indians was one that developed in the Iroquois nation between the Mohawk leader, Brant, who was the prime mover in the confederacy, and the Seneca under Chief Cornplanter. The Seneca, who, like the Wyandot and the Delawares, would be in a precarious position in the case of war with the United States, had been inclined from the first to abide by the decision of the treaty of Fort McIntosh in regard to their lands. Furthermore, Cornplanter made numerous attempts during the years 1786 and 1787 to get Congress to guarantee trade and protection for his people and did in fact succeed in getting that body to make a statement to the effect that the Seneca hunting grounds would remain inviolate: "The United States will take care," the statement said, "that none of their Citizens shall intrude upon the Indians within the bounds which in the late treaties were allotted for them to hunt and live upon." In gratitude Cornplanter returned to the West and attempted, much to Brant's distress, to win over the western nations, and Chief Guyasuta undertook an unsuccessful mission to attempt to enlist the Shawnee and Mingo. Congress, pursuing its policy of soothing the Seneca, instructed General Harmar to construct a new post, to be known as Fort Franklin, at the junction of French Creek and the Allegheny, and when this was accomplished in April, 1787, the reconciliation between the United States and the Seneca nation was complete. At the council at Canadasaga, near Geneva, New York, early in 1788, Brant was therefore utterly unsuccessful in getting any support for the confederacy from the Seneca. Captain Jonathan Heart, who had erected Fort Franklin, wrote to Harmar in the spring of 1788 that "the conduct of the Senecas along the Allegheny bears the strongest marks of friendship," and that these Indians, at least, could be prevented from joining with Brant.[31]

Another rift in Indian unity during the years immediately preceding the treaty of Fort Harmar occurred when the tribes of the Wabash and Maumee valleys resented an attempt made by Brant in 1788 to avoid a war by pledging the confederacy to a slight compromise on the Ohio River boundary. These tribes, the Shawnee, Miami, and Kickapoo, represented the extreme left wing of the confederacy, which refused to make any concessions regarding the boundary. When Brant, therefore, attempted to come to terms with the Seneca, Delaware, and Wyandot Indians, who represented the right wing in favor of conciliation with the United States, by ceding the land bounded by Pennsylvania, the Ohio, the Muskingum, and a line from the headwaters of the Cuyahoga to the mouth of French Creek, the Wabash-Maumee nations were angered. These tribes had pledged firm allegiance to the old boundary at the time of the original formation of the confederacy at the Sandusky council in 1783, and they had refused attendance at the treaty of Fort Finney in accordance with this allegiance. Their adherence to it had been stiffened by a filibustering expedition of George Rogers Clark against Vincennes in 1786 for the purpose of putting an end to Indian raids in Kentucky, and Harmar had not dared to disturb their already ruffled feelings by mentioning boundary matters when he extended the authority of Congress to Vincennes in 1787. The Miami were not even present at Harmar's Vincennes council of September 5, 1787, which was attended by the Piankashaw and the Wea.

A meeting of the confederacy had been called for October,

[31] United States Continental Congress Papers, series 56, p. 371, 395-397, 407-410; *Pittsburgh Gazette*, August 12, 1786; Draper MSS, 1W216, 307-309, 379, 380.

1788, in the Miami country to prepare for the treaty of Fort Harmar, but it was a failure, as Brant had anticipated: "The Hurons [*Wyandot*], Chippewas, Ottawas, Pottawattamies, and Delawares," he wrote, "will join with us in trying lenient steps, and having a boundary line fixed; and, rather than enter headlong into a destructive war will give up a small part of their country. On the other hand, the Shawanese, Miamis, and Kickapoos, who are now so much addicted to horse-stealing that it will be a difficult task to break them of it, as that kind of business is their best harvest, will of course declare for war, and not giving up any of their country, which, I am afraid, will be the means of our separating. They are, I believe, determined not to attend the treaty with the Americans." This statement was a prophecy. What happened was told to General Arthur St. Clair, governor of the Northwest Territory and new administrator of Indian affairs, by a trader named Wilson, who received the information from a Delaware. St. Clair, in relaying the information to the secretary of war, Henry Knox, wrote, "I can not learn any thing of consequence ... further than that there had been little unanimity amongst them; that the Kickapoos and Piquas (a tribe of the Twightwees [*Miami*]) particularly would agree to nothing that was proposed, and would propose nothing themselves; that the Wyandots presented them with a large string of wampum, taking hold of one end of it and desiring them to hold fast by the other, which they refused to do; that they [*the Wyandot*] then laid it on the shoulder of their [*the Miami*] principal chief, recommending to them to be at peace with the Americans, and to do as the Six Nations and the others did, but, without making any answer, he turned himself on one side and let it fall to the ground; that they, the Wyandots, got up and told them they had been a long time there talking to them and advising them for their good, they would now leave them to talk by themselves, and immediately left the council-house."[32]

[32] Stone, *Life of Joseph Brant*, 2:278; W. H. Smith, *St. Clair Papers*, 2:102.

The Revival of American Aggression

The treaty of Fort Harmar was thus conceived and prepared for in circumstances of the most unfortunate misunderstanding between the contending powers. The object of the Indians was union and the Ohio River boundary. The object of the United States was Indian disunion and the Fort McIntosh boundary. The Indians, victims of the policy of divide and conquer, were hopelessly disunited, while the Americans on the other hand were able to deliberate in full strength and with one voice. Those Indians who straggled into Fort Harmar were mainly of the Seneca, Wyandot, and Delaware tribes and were mere remnants of these. According to Timothy Pickering in 1792, Heckewelder could not find among the signers of the treaty "the name of even one Great Chief"; only the most inconsiderable tribe of the Delawares was present; and only one of the principal Ottawa chiefs, one of the two principal chiefs of the Potawatomi, and one of the three Shawnee chiefs, attended.[33]

The Indians, almost, it seems, without encouragement from Governor Arthur St. Clair, the American dictator of terms, began to apologize for their delay and backwardness, to denounce Brant, and to quarrel among themselves. The Wyandot blamed Brant for keeping the western nations from being present and actually accused him of organizing these tribes to attack the Americans at Pittsburgh and at Fort Harmar. St. Clair then asked the Wyandot what they would do if Brant did strike. The Wyandot turned upon the Iroquois who were present and demanded that, since all the trouble was caused by their brethren, they give the answer. This demand greatly irritated Cornplanter and his Seneca, and on December 19 he replied to the Wyandot, accusing them and Brant for the failure of the great confederacy to meet the Americans at Fort Stanwix in 1784. Cornplanter, by thus denouncing the oppo-

[33] "Miscellaneous Memorandum," Pickering Papers. The account of the treaty of Fort Harmar in this and the following paragraphs is, unless otherwise stated, based on material in Draper MSS, 23U79, 91-97, 104-107, 115-126, 138-142. The text of the treaty is also in United States, *Indian Affairs, Laws and Treaties*, 2:13-18, and in *American State Papers, Indian Affairs*, 1:5-7.

nents of the Fort Stanwix treaty, played straight into the hands of the Americans. "I now tell you," he announced, "that I take Brant & set him down in his chair at home and he shall not Stir out of his house but will keep him there fast, he shall no more run About amongst the Nations disturbing them and causing trouble."

Cornplanter then appealed to the Americans' sense of fair play, and seldom has an Indian made an appeal with greater eloquence: "Father, you told me that all this land is yours I hope you will take pity on the Native inhabitants of this Country, as they took pity on you when you first arrived at this Island . . . I hope you will satisfy the Minds of all that are uneasy, let them know the Boundary line of your land and they will soon acquaint all the Nations with it, in order that they may be Satisfied."

St. Clair thereupon dictated the terms of two treaties, one with the Iroquois and one with the rest of the tribes. The same boundaries and the same reservations of posts in the lands set aside for the Indians were named as in the treaties of Fort Stanwix and of Fort McIntosh. Additional terms, however, made concessions. The Indians would be permitted to hunt within the ceded territory if they would "demean themselves peaceably" and molest no Americans. Strict punishment was declared necessary for all horse thieves, both Indian and white. All traders in the Indian country were obliged to get official licenses from the governor of the Northwest Territory. The United States pledged itself to warn the Indians of any hostile movements against them, and the Indians gave a reciprocal pledge and likewise acknowledged that their remaining lands should be ceded to no other nation than the United States. Finally, in addition to the goods distributed at the treaty, the Six Nations were compensated to the amount of three thousand dollars.

Money compensation, however, meant practically nothing to the Indians, and the other concessions were mostly of the paper variety. Recognizing defeat, the Indians turned to their only real friend, the Great Spirit. After the terms had been read, Shendeta, the Wyandot chief, arose and said, "We cannot Say any thing farther to day, it is to be hoped the Great Spirit above will teach us the way how to speak and to declare our sentiments to you to-morrow." On December 29, Shendeta sought to describe to the whites the Indian view of the occupation of the land by the white man.

Shendeta said that he had dreamed of the past and that in this dream he saw "that the Wyandot nation Was the first man that the Great Spirit Placed upon this Ground." The Delaware nation was the second. The Wyandot sent the Delawares to the seashore to look out and see when great beasts should come into the country out of the water, and the first beasts they saw were the French. Then they espied others, the British, who asked to "remain only one night on shore," and when the Delawares applied to the Wyandot, permission was given. Thus the British begged for a little ground large enough to make a fire on, that is, "as much as one Cow hide could cover." This was granted, and when it was done, the British gave the Delawares some liquor, which made them "a little Giddy & foolish, and in the mean time you cut this cow hide into a String that covered a Considerable Quantity of Ground, and that is the way you first took me in for a piece of land in this Country." When the Delawares came to their senses they saw what had happened and said, "You have Cheated me for once, is this the way you are going to treat me always while you remain in this Country?" The British denied this but soon proposed to buy another strip, as much as a man could walk in a day, and hired their swiftest runners to deceive the Indians again. Since then the British, and after them the Americans, had continued to take land; but the Indians could not explain the reason. "How you advanced so far this way I cannot tell, as I have not dreamt of it." "This," he concluded, "is the finishing of the Dream. I am but a foolish man that you see here Standing." This talk was the preface to Shendeta's subsequent plea for a reconsideration of the terms. As with

Cornplanter, his main weapon was merely a plea for justice. Presenting the wampum belts representing former treaties and the establishment of the Ohio River boundary, Shendeta said, "Let the Ohio be the Boundary line as it was concluded upon before, We are poor helpless people."

From the day of this plea until January 4, 1789, there were no sessions, and no records were kept of proceedings. There was plenty of time for the emotional effect of Shendeta's appeal to wear off. Some events transpired that made the Indians decide to offer again the land north of the Ohio and east of the Muskingum, instead of insisting upon the Ohio River boundary. Thus on January 4 they returned to the council with the compromise but with stronger language to denounce the previous treaties with the Americans. "We don't understand," they said, "how you came to get this land from our Father [*the British*], as none of us Know any thing about it. ... when the Great Spirit made the land it was for the Indians and not for the white people. We are very sorry that you did not make enquiry amongst us Indians before You entered into that business to Know whether we had given the right of the land to our Father, as you very well Know that this Country did belong to us Indians." They thereupon made the offer of the Muskingum boundary.

But all this oratory had no effect on St. Clair. In his reply on January 6 he flatly rejected the proposals. "Truly," he said, "if this is what we have been waiting for, our time has been spent to very little purpose." As for the complaint that the Indians had been cheated by the British, that was not the fault of the Americans, whom, St. Clair said, the British would not allow to take part in Indian affairs. There could be no argument; the Indians must forfeit their lands because they had fought for the British and lost. That was final.

There was nothing for the Indians to do but to accept the fact. They asked the Americans not to occupy the land right up to the boundary, and since they were going to have to come under American influence, they asked also for the establishment of a trading system, including regulation of prices, licensing of traders, and provisions for smiths to repair their guns. Cornplanter was eager to adopt the agricultural economy of the whites: "We Shall want our hoes & other Articles mended," he said, "& for that purpose we would wish to have a Blacksmith Settled amongst us."

Thus the treaty closed in humiliating defeat for the Indians and in triumphant success for the Americans. St. Clair sent the redskins back to the forests with these words, "I fervently pray to the Great God that he will be pleased to bless the Good Works we have been about and to extend to your Nations the Glorious light of the Gospel of peace & the Blessings of Civilization." How strangely these words compare with those in which St. Clair on May 2, 1789, reported the proceedings to George Washington, the new president of the United States. "The reason," he said, "why the treaties were made separately with the Six Nations and the Wyandots, and more westerly tribes, was a jealousy that subsisted between them, which I was not willing to lessen by appearing to consider them as one people . . . I am persuaded their general confederacy is entirely broken: indeed, it would not be very difficult, if circumstances required it, to set them at deadly variance."[34]

---

[34] W. H. Smith, *St. Clair Papers,* 2:113. Following the federal treaty there was also drawn up at Fort Harmar a treaty between Pennsylvania and the Indians, by which the Seneca ceded the title of the Erie Triangle to the commonwealth. See *Pennsylvania Archives,* first series, 11:529-533; 12:100-102.

13
The War
for the Ohio River Boundary,
1789-1795

THE UNITED STATES would have begun war against the tribes on the Wabash and the Maumee in 1789 directly after the treaty of Fort Harmar, if it had been able. By that treaty the United States had isolated those tribes and had fulfilled Secretary of War Knox's hope, expressed in December, 1788, that St. Clair would be successful in making peace with some of the tribes so that "it would be more easy to punish the Wabash and more westerly Indians, if they should persist in their predatory incursions and murders." And individuals of these tribes had resumed their attacks with the coming of the spring of 1789 to such an extent that Major John F. Hamtramck, commandant of the federal Fort Knox at Vincennes, reported on April 11 to General Josiah Harmar,

The War for the Ohio River Boundary

"Every thing draws a picture of hostility in this quarter." Four days later Major John P. Wyllys, commandant of the federal Fort Steuben at the Falls of the Ohio (near Louisville), declared that Indian attacks into Kentucky from "that nest of villainy the Miami Village" were so frequent that communications with Fort Knox could not be maintained without fifty or sixty troops accompanying all convoys.[1]

The reason for the hostility of the members of these tribes is not hard to discover. As they were served by British traders, they devoted themselves whole-heartedly to the ideal of the Indian confederation and to the preservation of the Ohio River boundary. The fact that the United States had repudiated that boundary at the treaty of Fort Harmar meant nothing to them because that treaty was negotiated with only a fragment of the confederacy, and they themselves had not been present. The actual attacks on Kentuckians and on river immigrants to Kentucky dated from 1786 when the Indians had been alarmed by the advent of squatters in Vincennes and by George Rogers Clark's subsequent unsuccessful and repudiated filibustering expedition in support of the squatters. The benevolent purpose of the establishment in 1787 of federal forts at Vincennes and at the Falls of the Ohio (Fort Knox and Fort Steuben) had been misinterpreted by these bands of Indians, and between May and September of 1788 four federal detachments passing between those posts had been attacked. This had led Kentuckians to a resumption of the filibustering method, and in August, 1788, Patrick Brown at the head of a band of sixty frontiersmen appeared at Vincennes, defied Hamtramck's orders to desist, and attacked some friendly Piankashaw. If Brown had attacked Wea or Miami Indians he would have had more justification, but his choice of a friendly tribe only increased the number of enemies of the white race.[2]

The result was that the year 1789 saw many more Kentucky

[1] Draper MSS, 1W482, 486; 2W25, 34, 78.

[2] Draper MSS, 1W418-423, 442, 445-455, 462; W. H. Smith, *St. Clair Papers*, 2:89.

freebooting expeditions, as well as the beginning of the conversion of the federal government to the endorsement of such
tactics. Kentuckians had expected much from the adoption
of the new United States Constitution, and one of their number, Colonel George Clendenen, had predicted in December,
1788, that "the next year will put an end to Indian Hostilities,
as the General Government will take the business up, and the
settlements west of the Ohio will be greatly strengthened."
But the disillusionment that came with the Indian attacks
in the spring of 1789 precipitated action on the part of the
Kentuckians. On August 2 there set out from Clarksville on
the Ohio, opposite Louisville, Major John Hardin and about
two or three hundred Kentuckians. They were bound for
that "nest of infamy," the Wea towns. Their visit was not
altogether satisfactory, as they killed only twelve Indians and
destroyed no villages, but their conduct was so mortifying to
Hamtramck that the latter's report, together with a report to
the effect that three more filibustering expeditions were in
preparation, produced a strange reaction from Harmar. He
actually suggested that there might have been a secret federal
endorsement of the Kentucky filibuster policy. "Will you be
pleased," he wrote to Knox on October 19, 1789, "to give me
particular and especial directions how to act with the inhabitants of Kentucky? Perhaps they may be secretly authorized
to form these expeditions." Harmar was most anxious to receive authorization from the government to proceed against
the Indians. On November 9 he wrote to Captain Joseph
Asheton at Fort Steuben, "If the word *March!* is given by the
proper authority, a speedy movement shall be made against
the savages."[3]

The question of war in the Wea and Miami country awaited
the decision of President George Washington, who considered
the Kentuckians partly to blame for the Indian attacks. Pressure, however, was gradually exerted on him, and he was also

[3] Virginia, *Calendar of Virginia State Papers*, 4:533, 542; Draper MSS, 2W89,
93-95, 114, 116, 120.

not unaware that Mississippi River politics and diplomacy in 1789 and 1790 required a friendly Kentucky. The first pressure made itself felt late in 1789 when Virginia and Kentucky leaders asked him to assume the burden of sustaining the frontier scouts formerly supported by Virginia. Early in the spring of 1790 Washington acquiesced on this point, but he nevertheless insisted upon a safeguard against the abuse of federal aid, in the form of close federal supervision of troops. From this concession it was but a few steps to a general endorsement of Kentucky's filibustering methods. The next step was taken on April 13, when Knox issued an order to Harmar declaring that the continuation of Indian attacks authorized investing the federal district judge of Kentucky, Harry Innes, with the power of calling out scouts. In April Harmar consented to and co-operated in a filibustering excursion led by General Charles Scott against a nest of Indian banditti stationed at the mouth of the Scioto, who had been raiding emigrant and supply boats on the Ohio River. The expedition was a failure and was followed on May 12 by an Indian attack on a federal convoy of six boats under Ensign Asa Hartshorne. In this encounter five white men were killed and eight were made prisoners. This event so exasperated Knox that on June 7 he authorized Harmar to confer with Arthur St. Clair, governor of the Northwest Territory, on the advisability of extirpating "utterly, if possible," these banditti with the use of one hundred federal troops and three hundred Kentucky militia. By the time Harmar and St. Clair met, however, the latter had found cause to engage the federal and Kentucky troops against more Indians than the mere banditti who were interfering with Ohio River transportation.[4]

President Washington had instructed St. Clair on October

[4] Draper MSS, 2W148-150, 187-190, 200, 268-273; Richardson, *Messages and Papers of the Presidents*, 1:65; *American State Papers, Indian Affairs*, 1:85, 91, 92, 97, 107, 108; W. H. Smith, *St. Clair Papers*, 2:146. The adverse effect of the Indian attacks upon the trading activities of Colonel John May in the summer of 1789 is described in his "Journal," in *Pennsylvania Magazine of History and Biography*, 45:119 (1921).

6, 1789, to discover "whether the Wabash and Illinois Indians are most inclined for war or peace." "A war with the Wabash Indians," he wrote, "ought to be avoided by all means consistently with the security of the frontier inhabitants, the security of the troops, and the national dignity. . . . If, however . . . they should continue their hostilities . . . you are hereby authorized and empowered, in my name, to call on the lieutenants of the nearest counties of Virginia and Pennsylvania, for such detachments of militia as you may judge proper." The fact that Washington thus referred the question of war to St. Clair was unfortunate because St. Clair did not really expect peace with the Miami tribe. On January 26, 1790, he wrote to Knox, "The Miamis, and the renegade Shawanese, Delawares, and Cherokees . . . I fear are irreclaimable by gentle means. The experiment, however, is worth the making; and, at any rate, I do not think we are yet prepared to chastise them." He took the view that any Indians under the British influence would be hostile. Thus, with his mind half made up, he authorized Hamtramck at Vincennes to send an emissary to the tribes in question. The emissary, Captain Pierre Gamelin, took St. Clair's message to the Wea, who referred him to the Miami, who, in turn, referred him to the confederacy and to the British. The Wabash-Maumee Indians denied the validity of the treaty of Fort Harmar and made it clear that they would deal with the Americans only through the confederacy and with assurances of trade equivalent to that with the English and a guarantee against future incursions by Kentuckians on their hunting grounds north of the Ohio.[5]

St. Clair was in Kaskaskia when he heard of the results of Gamelin's mission. He at once decided for war, because, as he told Knox, "there was not the smallest probability of an accommodation with the Indians." He had no idea of taking up the negotiations himself, but left Kaskaskia on June 11 and traveled by way of Kentucky to Fort Washington (Cincin-

[5] *American State Papers, Indian Affairs,* 1:93, 94, 97; W. H. Smith, *St. Clair Papers,* 2:132, 155-160; Draper MSS, 2W182, 192.

nati), where he spread the news of his decision for war and received the enthusiastic endorsement of all Kentuckians. He reached Fort Washington on July 13, and he and Harmar spent the next two months there organizing an expedition. On September 26 everything was in readiness, and Harmar at the head of 1,133 militia and 320 regulars started up the Great Miami. The ascent was slow, and by the time the troops had reached the Maumee country on October 18, all the Indians had fled. Five Miami towns near what is now Fort Wayne, Indiana, were destroyed. Two skirmishes with Indians took place, one on the eighteenth and one on the nineteenth, but both were failures. The first failed because Harmar's troops were unable to discover the whereabouts of the Indian army, and the second failed for the opposite reason: the troops found the Indians, who ambushed them and drove the terror-stricken militia back to the main camp. In this engagement forty militiamen and twenty regulars were killed. On October 21 the army started for home.[6]

Even without these unfortunate skirmishes the expedition would have been worthless, for the burning of towns meant little to the Indians. But the events of October 22, the day after the commencement of the return, made the expedition really a failure. Early in the morning of that day, Harmar, thirsty for vindication, sent a detachment of regulars and militia under Major John P. Wyllys back to the Miami villages. This detachment took the Indians by surprise, but the foolhardy militia chased the fleeing Indians so far that other Indians, observing what was happening, closed in on the outnumbered regulars, and a great slaughter ensued, in which 183 men, including Wyllys, were killed, and 31 were wounded. In the meantime Hamtramck was supposed to lead a detachment up the Wabash from Fort Knox to join with the conquering Harmar. But it was not Harmar's fault that the junction did not take place. Hamtramck got his 330 men a few

[6] W. H. Smith, *St. Clair Papers,* 2:159; *American State Papers, Indian Affairs,* 1:94, 102; Draper MSS, 2W285; Denny, "Military Journal," in Historical Society of Pennsylvania, *Memoirs,* 7:345-350.

days on the way when he discovered that he was not going to be supported with enough rations. The men refused to go on half rations, and the whole force returned to Fort Knox without having seen an Indian.[7]

Thus did the much touted Kentucky and Pennsylvania frontiersmen acquit themselves on the field of battle. The fault lay not merely in the lack of training and discipline of the militia but also in the lack of equipment. There was as yet no highly elaborate federal commissary department as was to be provided in later expeditions. According to Harmar's aide, Ebenezer Denny, the federal authorities expected that the Kentuckians and Pennsylvanians who had been loud in clamoring for a war would furnish "active riflemen, such as is supposed to inhabit the frontiers." The frontiersmen, on the other hand, thought that the federal government would assume the burden of the defense of the West. "Their whole object," said Denny, "seemed to be nothing more than to see the country, without rendering any service whatever." They took neither camp kettles nor axes. When they were asked why they brought useless firearms with them, they said that "they were told in Kentucky that all repairs would be made at Fort Washington."[8]

The Indian problem was now further from an amicable settlement than it was before Harmar set out. As in the days following Braddock's defeat, the Indians were convinced that they were a match for their white opponents. They "were much elated with there [*sic*] success," said Rufus Putnam of Marietta, "& threatened there should not remain a Smoak on the ohio by the time the Leaves put out." The United States Congress, on the other hand, stimulated by the massacre of thirteen inhabitants of the "Big Bottom" on the Muskingum by Wyandot and Chippewa banditti on January 2, 1791, appropriated three hundred thousand dollars for a new cam-

[7] *American State Papers, Indian Affairs*, 1:106; *American State Papers, Military Affairs*, 1:26, 28; Denny, "Military Journal," in Historical Society of Pennsylvania, *Memoirs*, 7:351, 352; Draper MSS, 2W246, 361-369.
[8] *American State Papers, Military Affairs*, 1:20, 24.

paign. Governor St. Clair was to lead the expedition from Fort Washington and was enabled to call three thousand men to the field. Precautions, however, were taken to assure a larger nucleus of regulars than had been available in Harmar's campaign and to place less reliance on the militia.[9]

Before calling out troops, St. Clair was to await the outcome of the mission of peace emissaries who were to be sent to the Wabash tribes and to the Iroquois. The former tribes were to be invited again to accept the Ohio River boundary; the latter, to take up arms against the western tribes if peace overtures failed. The peace plans were ill conceived and poorly executed and served to alienate Indian good will instead of fostering it. Thomas Proctor, the agent chosen to visit the Wabash Indians, sought to get some Iroquois to accompany him to those tribes in order to help him convince them of his sincerity. While the Iroquois were preparing to accede to his request, a message came from St. Clair urging the Iroquois to take up the hatchet against the Wabash tribes. This action completely discredited Proctor, for although the Iroquois were not disposed to go to the aid of the Wabash Indians, they had nothing but contempt for those who sought to set them against members of their own race. They therefore refused to have anything more to do with the peace plans. In May, 1791, Proctor, unable to accomplish his mission, retired from the Iroquois country in confusion.[10]

The road was now clear for the militarists. It had been planned that if St. Clair was not ready to advance in May, Kentucky mounted militia under Brigadier General Charles Scott were to attack the Wea so as to prevent incursions on the frontiers from that source. Accordingly, late in May, Scott, at the head of seven hundred Kentuckians, visited the upper Wabash, destroyed four or five Wea towns, killed thirty-

[9] Buell, *Memoirs of Rufus Putnam*, 113; United States, *Statutes at Large*, 1:222-224; *American State Papers, Indian Affairs*, 1:121.

[10] *American State Papers, Indian Affairs*, 1:129, 139, 146, 147, 164, 171-174, 197; W. H. Smith, *St. Clair Papers*, 2:181, 192; "Colonial Office Records," in *Michigan Pioneer and Historical Collections*, 24:192, 235, 236.

two warriors, and brought back fifty-eight prisoners. As St. Clair was still unready early in August, Lieutenant Colonel James Wilkinson of Kentucky led five hundred militia to the same region, but lost himself and his troops in the bogs and morasses of the upper Wabash country. He returned without having damaged anything but his own self-esteem.[11]

St. Clair and his army finally got under way on October 4. Exactly one month later he succumbed to an ambush executed at sunrise by the confederated Indian army led by the Miami chief, Little Turtle. In this action 630 Americans were killed and only 150 Indians. The American dead included thirty-seven officers, one of whom was Major General Richard Butler, second in command to St. Clair. The wounded brought the casualty list to 913, nearly half the army. When it is considered that all the supplies, including the artillery, were lost, it is fair to say that St. Clair's defeat was the worst defeat ever suffered by the American army in proportion to the numbers engaged. It is significant to note that whereas the advance from Fort Hamilton, the second post on the march, to the scene of action, took a month, the same distance was covered in only two days by most of the fleeing survivors.

What were the causes of this disaster? St. Clair considered himself under unalterable orders to erect a chain of military forts from Fort Washington, near the mouth of the Miami, to the rapids of the Maumee where the British had a fort called Fort Miamis. He was originally directed to set out from Fort Washington in July, but delays in getting supplies prevented him from leaving that post until September and from leaving Fort Hamilton until the fourth of October. The result was that the frosts destroyed the grass, which was the

[11] The material on St. Clair's expedition and the events leading up to it in this and the three following paragraphs is based on *American State Papers, Indian Affairs,* 1:131-133, 137, 138, 186, 187; Denny, "Military Journal," in Historical Society of Pennsylvania, *Memoirs,* 7:362-375; Winthrop Sargent, "Diary while with General Arthur St. Clair's Expedition against the Indians," in *Ohio Archaeological and Historical Publications,* 33:253, 256-269 (1924); St. Clair, *A Narrative of the . . . Campaign, passim;* Benjamin Van Cleve, "Memoranda," in *American Pioneer,* 2:150-153 (1843); W. H. Smith, *St. Clair Papers,* 2:262-267.

only source of food for the horses and cattle. Blundering in the quartermaster's department resulted in the failure to provide adequate supplies and arms. The morale of the army, two-thirds of which was made up of militiamen and from which many had deserted, was undermined mainly by the fact that during their six months' service the troops received their monthly pay of three dollars but once, and also by the fact that the army was on short rations and subject to rigorous and non-military services made necessary by mismanagement. St. Clair himself was not as experienced in frontier and Indian warfare as was General Butler, though he was probably a more able commander. He declined to accept Butler's opinions and advice on certain technical matters, and the resulting estrangement continued throughout the campaign. Butler declined to divulge to St. Clair information that came to him concerning the concentration of the Indians around the camp during the night that preceded the attack. At no time during the expedition did St. Clair have sufficient knowledge of the numbers and location of the Indians opposing him.

An incident took place a few days before the action that was an important factor in bringing about the defeat and that was traceable to the general lowering of the morale caused by mismanagement. On October 31 one hundred Kentucky militia refused to march any farther. Declaring that they would plunder the first military convoy of provisions that they met in order to be able to reach Kentucky in safety, they started back toward the Ohio. St. Clair, concerned for the safety of his supplies and afraid that more of his army would proceed to desert, decided to deal with the defection with an iron hand. He ordered Major Hamtramck and the first regiment of regulars, the best regiment in the American army, to march twenty miles south, or until they overtook the deserters and met the convoy. The wording of St. Clair's orders was faulty. He meant to say that if the provisions and deserters were not reached before Hamtramck had gone twenty miles, the latter was to turn back. The result was that on the fourth of November the army lacked its most effective regiment. Little Turtle and his army had struck a tremendous blow for Indian unity. The Indians' hopes of successfully preserving their civilization were revived to the highest point, much as they had been in the days immediately following Braddock's defeat in 1755. As Rufus Putnam said, "The Indians began to believe them Selves invinsible, and they truly had great cause of triumph."[12] As in 1755, the frontiers receded. The settlers abandoned their farms on the Allegheny, the Muskingum, and the Great Miami and found shelter south and east of the Ohio at such places as Pittsburgh, Wheeling, and Louisville, or they collected at the posts in the Indian country at and near Marietta and Cincinnati. Considering the work involved and the money spent, the American occupation of the upper Ohio had made remarkably little progress since the "conquest" and annexation of that country from England.

As in the days following Braddock's defeat, success went to the Indians' heads. The Americans could now be made to compromise and to cede back to the tribes some of the lands allegedly given up by the Indians at Fort Harmar. But the Indians had no use for peaceful measures. "After two successful general engagements," wrote the British agent, Alexander McKee, "in which a great deal of blood has been spilt, the Indians will not quietly give up by negotiation what they have been contending for with their lives since the commencement of these troubles."[13] The defeat of St. Clair was a complete justification to the Indian mind of the insistence by the confederacy on the Ohio River boundary. This confederacy, which had threatened to disappear in the years immediately following the treaty of Fort Harmar, found new life as those tribes, such as the Delawares and the Wyandot, who had been willing to give up the Ohio River boundary, now joined the ranks of their more hostile brethren.

The formal resuscitation of the confederacy took place at a

[12] Buell, *Memoirs of Rufus Putnam,* 116.
[13] Stone, *Life of Joseph Brant,* 2:333.

grand Indian council held in August and September, 1792. The council was the first formal assembling of the tribes since 1788 and was called for the purpose of making a united response to American overtures for peace. These overtures were brought by Captain Hendrick Aupaumut, an Indian from the reservation at Stockbridge, Massachusetts, who had been working to assemble the northwestern Indians all summer. But in spite of anything Captain Hendrick could do or say, the confederacy insisted upon complete expulsion of the Americans from north of the Ohio. In justifying themselves they called up to memory all the deceit and cruelty and land robbery they had suffered from the Americans. They told of the Moravian massacre of 1782, the murder of the Shawnee chief, Melanthy, in 1786, and the faithless way in which the Americans had rewarded the Delawares for their services in the Revolutionary War. "And since that," they added, "every time the Big knifes get ready to come against us, they would send [a] message to us for peace.—Then they come to fight us."[14]

The confederacy was not going to be duped again. Captain Hendrick might be sincere, but the Indians were taking no chances. They entrusted their reply to Iroquois messengers, who carried it to the American agent to the Iroquois, General Israel Chapin. It was delivered in a council at Buffalo Creek on November 16, 1792. The Iroquois told Chapin that the lands north of the Ohio must be given up by the United States.

[14] The complete report of Captain Hendrick's work is in United States Continental Congress Papers, series 167, p. 283-348. See also Hendrick to Timothy Pickering, December 11, 1792, Pickering Papers. Captain Hendrick was the fifth American agent sent to the Indians in 1792. The others were Captain Peter Pond, William Steedman, Captain Alexander Trueman, Colonel John Hardin, and Brigadier General Rufus Putnam. None of them accomplished anything substantial. Pond and Steedman were stopped by the British; Trueman and Hardin were killed; and Putnam met a few Indians at Vincennes and drew up a treaty that was recognized by neither the United States nor the Indian confederacy. See *American State Papers, Indian Affairs,* I:227, 229-236, 238, 243, 283-295, 321-324, 338; Mann Butler, *A History of the Commonwealth of Kentucky,* 220 (Louisville, 1834); Buell, *Memoirs of Rufus Putnam,* 268, 270-279, 293, 296-307, 320, 327, 335-368, 370, 376.

"We do not want compensation," they said, "we want restitution of our Country which they hold under false pretences." They even insisted that the Shawnee be compensated for the Kentucky lands of which they had been deprived in Dunmore's War. If the United States cared to consider these terms it must send its agents to the Sandusky rapids in the spring, there to make a lasting peace. And it must send "men of honesty not proud land jobbers." For the moment the Indians, confident of British backing, felt themselves masters of the situation.[15]

Galling as this Indian arrogance was to American militarists, the counsels of the peacemakers and the advocates of economy prevailed. Early in 1793 three commissioners, Timothy Pickering, Beverly Randolph, and Benjamin Lincoln, were instructed to do what American Indian commissioners had never done before—penetrate far into the Indian side of the frontier to offer to make a formal treaty of peace with the red men. American abasement went even further. According to Knox's instructions of April 26, 1793, the commissioners were authorized to make real concessions to the Indians. In the first place they were to give back to the Indians, if the Indians should require such a restitution, most of the lands ceded at Fort Harmar, that is, all but the lands that had been granted to the two private companies that had been organized to settle the Northwest Territory—the Ohio Company and the Symmes Associates. Minor concessions included a federal guarantee of the Indians' possession of their country, the evacuation of Fort Harmar and Fort Washington, and the outright gift of fifty thousand dollars down and an annuity of ten thousand dollars in case the Indians were willing to let the treaty of Fort Harmar stand.[16]

Late in July, 1793, the American commissioners arrived at

[15] *American State Papers, Indian Affairs*, 1:324, 337; Cruikshank, *Correspondence of . . . Simcoe*, 1:227.
[16] The negotiations between the United States and the Indians described in this and the three following paragraphs are in *American State Papers, Indian Affairs*, 1:340-342, 352-357.

322

Detroit. On the thirtieth, delegates from the confederacy, which was keeping headquarters at the Maumee Rapids, appeared before the commissioners and asked point-blank whether or not the United States was prepared to accept the Ohio River boundary. "If you seriously design to make a firm and lasting peace," the Indians added, "you will immediately remove all your people from our side of that river." This was the ultimatum that Knox said would justify the announcement of the utmost concessions the United States would make. The commissioners therefore announced their willingness to give up all the lands ceded at Fort Harmar save that sold to the Ohio Company and the Symmes Associates. They declared also that they were prepared to abandon the doctrine, held by the United States since the treaty with England in 1783, that the king of England had by that document ceded the Indian title to lands within certain boundaries to the United States. The commissioners openly said that their predecessors at Fort Stanwix, Fort McIntosh, and Fort Harmar had "put an erroneous construction on that part of our treaty with the King." They said, "As he [*the king*] had not purchased the country of you, of course he could not give it away; he only relinquished to the United States his claim to it."

The reply of the Indians was received by the Americans on August 16. The red men rejected all compromise and insisted on the complete evacuation of all lands north of the Ohio. The Indian mind could not understand how the United States could recognize the justice of the Indian claims and at the same time expect the Indians to give up some of their lands. They said: "You ... [have] agreed to do us justice, after having long, and injuriously, withheld it—we mean in the acknowledgment you have now made, that the King of England never did, nor ever had a right to give you our country, by the treaty of peace. And you want to make this act of common justice a great part of your concessions: and seem to expect that, because you have at last acknowledged our independence, we should, for such a favor, surrender to you our country." As for accepting compensation for the lands of the Ohio Company and the Symmes Associates, the Indians told the United States to keep the money and give it to the land companies and those who were settling on the land. "Money, to us," they said, "is of no value, and to most of us unknown: and as no consideration whatever can induce us to sell the lands on which we get sustenance for our women and children, we hope we may be allowed to point out a mode by which your settlers may be easily removed, and peace thereby obtained. . . . We know that these settlers are poor, or they would never have ventured to live in a country which has been in continued trouble ever since they crossed the Ohio. Divide, therefore, this large sum of money, which you have offered to us, among these people: give to each, also, a proportion of what you say you would give to us, annually, over and above this very large sum of money: and, we are persuaded, they would most readily accept of it, in lieu of the lands you sold them. If you add, also, the great sums you must expend in raising and paying armies, with a view to force us to yield you our country, you will certainly have more than sufficient for the purposes of re-paying these settlers for all their labor and their improvements."

This was the end of negotiation. The Americans could now say that they had offered to be reasonable and that the Indians had chosen not to be. The commissioners began their long journey back across Lake Erie. In a parting message to the confederacy they said, "The negotiation is . . . at an end. We sincerely regret, that peace is not the result; but, knowing the upright and liberal views of the United States, which, as far as you gave us an opportunity, we have explained to you, we trust that impartial judges will not attribute the continuance of the war to them."

As soon as news was received of the outcome of the peace negotiations, General Anthony Wayne, the new commander of the American army, was authorized to renew hostilities against the Indians. By the time the commissioners made their report, however, it was too late in the year to administer an effective stroke. During the spring and summer, Wayne had marched his army from his headquarters at Legionville to Fort Washington, and he got the signal to advance early in September, 1793. But he did not make the mistake St. Clair had made of trying to conduct a fall campaign on frosted forage. He marched the army from near Fort Washington to a position six miles north of Fort Jefferson, where he built Fort Greenville and settled down for the winter.[17]

The contrast with St. Clair's campaign is apparent. An improvement in the quartermaster's service was to be expected after the result of the mismanagement in the previous disaster. Moreover, Wayne had more money to draw on. Although he had not quite twice as many troops at his disposal as St. Clair, he had over three times as large an appropriation from Congress. The officers of Wayne's army were paid from ten to thirty per cent more than those of St. Clair's, and the privates were paid a higher bounty for enlisting, although their monthly pay, in spite of the serious effort of the House of Representatives in 1794 to raise it from three to four dollars, was the same. The troops moved more slowly, and the actual invasion of the Indian country was carried out in the summer season when there were available an abundance of vegetables for the men and ample forage for the horses. Above all, the army was well disciplined, adequate in numbers and morale, and admirably provided with scouts. It is perhaps fair to say that in this last provision is to be found the greatest single factor accounting for Wayne's success. Wayne knew the numbers of the Indians opposing him, and he was informed of their whereabouts. St. Clair thought that the only way to learn the plans of the Indians was to send an emissary to associate with them and pick up information. This, of course, was impossible, as Wayne knew. As a matter of fact, the approved frontier method was to stalk individual Indians, to capture

[17] Stillé, *Anthony Wayne*, 326-328; *American State Papers, Indian Affairs*, 1:359.

them, and to bring them into camp, there to extract the desired information. By the skillful use of this device, Wayne was able to advance, flanked, as it were, by Kentucky scouts. He was thus at no time in danger of being ambushed.[18]

Meanwhile in western Pennsylvania every effort was being made to keep the Iroquois neutral. The Mohawk, Brant, was enlisted for the furthering of this purpose. Brant had returned from the Detroit conferences still convinced that peace could be maintained, and through his efforts another conference with the Iroquois was scheduled to take place at Fort Franklin at Venango on May 15, 1794. By that date, however, the British had convinced Brant that the confederacy would be supported by English troops in resisting Wayne. Hence the meeting never took place, and Brant went off to join the confederates.[19] A matter that arose in the spring of 1794 and that all but provoked the Iroquois to take up arms was the attempted occupation of Presque Isle by the state of Pennsylvania. The federal rights to the Erie Triangle, which included Presque Isle, were acquired by Pennsylvania as the result of a resolution of Congress of September 4, 1788. The Indian rights were allegedly acquired by Pennsylvania at Fort Harmar in 1789. In 1792 the exchange of deed and payment with the United States was completed, and on April 18, 1793, the Pennsylvania legislature directed Governor Thomas Mifflin to lay out and survey a town at Presque Isle. Nothing further was done in 1793, but on February 28, 1794, the legislature authorized Mifflin to call out militia to protect the surveyors from possible Indian attacks. Captain Ebenezer Denny was appointed to head the militia, and by the middle of May, Cussewago (Meadville) and Le Bœuf (Waterford) were under military control. Secretary Knox, greatly alarmed at the possibility of an Indian war in New York and Pennsyl-

[18] *Annals of Congress*, 3 Congress, 1 session, 4:112, 272; "Daily Journal of Wayne's Campaign," in *American Pioneer*, 1:315-322, 351-357 (1842); 2:290-292 (1843); James McBride, *Pioneer Biography: Sketches of the Lives of Some of the Early Settlers of Butler County, Ohio*, 1:87 (Cincinnati, 1869).

[19] *American State Papers, Indian Affairs*, 1:478-481.

vania, corresponded at great length with Governor Mifflin.
The Iroquois, supported by the British, claimed the Fort
Harmar cessions to be a fraud, and at Buffalo Creek on June
18, 1794, called upon both British and American agents to accompany an Indian delegation to Presque Isle and Le Bœuf
to request the whites to withdraw from all lands north of Fort
Franklin. Reluctantly the American agent to the Iroquois,
General Israel Chapin, accompanied the Indians and the British to Le Bœuf, where on June 26 Denny and Andrew Ellicott,
official Pennsylvania surveyor, were ordered by the Indians to
withdraw. Ellicott, although he insisted on the validity of the
Fort Harmar document, consented to advance no farther and
promised to refer the whole matter to the president of the
United States.[20]

These developments engrossed the Indians for the time
being and thus kept Wayne from being embarrassed by
complications on the western Pennsylvania frontier. By the
end of July, 1794, he was joined by a body of a thousand
mounted Kentucky volunteers under General Charles Scott
and was ready to advance from Fort Greenville. He proceeded
directly to the Indian villages on the Maumee River at the
mouth of the Au Glaize River, the center of the Indian confederacy, which he occupied on August 8. He was unopposed in
this occupation and apparently approached the settlement
so rapidly that the inhabitants did not have time to destroy
their corn and other abundant supplies of fresh vegetables.
He at once began the construction of Fort Defiance at this
point, which, with Fort Adams, twenty-four miles in advance
of Fort Recovery, which was constructed on the extreme
upper waters of the Wabash in Ohio, made a total of eight
federal posts in the chain from Fort Washington. At the Au
Glaize, Wayne's army turned sharply to the right and descended the Maumee to the Rapids, or Roche de Bout, as the

[20] *Pennsylvania Archives,* second series, 6:630-650, 658, 663, 668, 669, 673, 678, 680, 683, 690, 691, 692, 700, 701-705, 716-721, 794-798; Denny, "Military Journal," in Historical Society of Pennsylvania, *Memoirs,* 7:382-384; *American State Papers, Indian Affairs,* 1:503-506.

French called it, where the Indians had congregated near the fortified post maintained there by the British. After four years of effort, an American army had at last on August 18, 1794, arrived at its objective, which was to penetrate the very heart of the Indian country. The nineteenth was occupied in building a temporary post, Camp Deposit, and in reconnoitering the position of the Indian enemy. On the next day, the twentieth, the army, three thousand strong, advanced against the Indians at Fallen Timbers.[21]

What had the Indians been doing in the meantime? It is important, in considering their uncompromising attitude, to emphasize the effect on them of British encouragement since 1783. It is true that Alexander McKee, British Indian agent at Detroit, had entreated the Indians to accept the compromise offered by the Americans in the Detroit conferences in 1793. But it was the same McKee to whom the Delaware, Buckongahelas, pointed, on August 9, 1793, in the presence of the confederacy at the Maumee Rapids, when he said, "That is the Person who advises us to insist on the Ohio River for the line." What Buckongahelas meant was that the British had, ever since the treaty of Fort Stanwix of 1768, told the Indians that the Ohio should be the permanent line between the white race and the red. He meant that the English had pledged the red men that line during the Revolution. He meant that that line had been the basis for the formation of the Indian confederacy under the auspices of Sir John Johnson at the Sandusky in 1783. He meant that the English had constantly encouraged the Indians to deny the validity of the treaties of Fort Stanwix of 1784, of Fort McIntosh, and of Fort Harmar. He meant that in July, 1791, McKee had urged the Indians to ask for a neutral Indian barrier state bounded by the Ohio River, so that the English might use this neutral territory for purposes of bargain in the diplomatic maneuvering then going on between England and the United States. He meant also that at the council at the Au Glaize in September,

[21] *American State Papers, Indian Affairs,* 1:490-492.

1792, after the Americans had rejected the barrier state, the British had endeavored to persuade the confederacy to get the United States to ask England to intervene in the red men's behalf in defense of the latter's territorial rights. Finally, he meant that it was now the turn of the British to aid the Indians in taking for themselves a step that was only slightly more drastic than the measures formerly urged on them by the British.[22]

And in the preparation for the war that must inevitably follow the collapse of the negotiations at Detroit, the British gave the Indians every reason to expect the king's help in the moment of conflict. The British agents in Canada committed the fundamental error of leading the Indians actually to expect war between the United States and England as the outcome of the negotiations being carried on in England by the American commissioner, John Jay. Canadian officials felt that war between England and America would be the natural result of the complications growing out of the war declared in 1793 between England and revolutionary France, because the United States was bound in alliance to France by the treaty of 1778.

The men responsible for spreading this belief among the Indians were the two governors of Canada, Lord Dorchester (Guy Carleton), governor of Quebec, and John Graves Simcoe, governor of Upper Canada. The most outspoken utterance in regard to the probability of war was a speech made by Lord Dorchester at Quebec on February 10, 1794, on the occasion of the formal presentation to him by the Indians of the lower St. Lawrence Valley of the proceedings of the confederacy that had culminated in the breakdown of negotiations with the United States commissioners at Detroit in August, 1793. The speech seems to have been the result of its author's sincere belief that the movements of Wayne's army, certain hostile appearances on the Lake Champlain frontier, the vociferously

[22] Cruikshank, *Correspondence of . . . Simcoe,* 2:16, 34; 1:177, 188, 190, 201, 207; Bemis, *Jay's Treaty,* 117-119.

pro-French feeling in the United States, and American resentment at British interference with commerce on the high seas, would produce an Anglo-American war. Dorchester told the Indians: "From the manner in which the People of the States push on, and act, and talk on this side and from what I learn of their conduct towards the Sea, I shall not be surprised if we are at war with them in the course of the present year ... There is no Line between them and us. I shall acknowledge no Lands to be theirs which have been encroached on by them since the year 1783; they then broke the Peace, and as they kept it not on their part; it doth not bind on ours ... we have acted in the most peaceable manner, and borne the Language and Conduct of the People of the United States with Patience; but I believe our Patience is almost exhausted."[23]

Dorchester's actions immediately following this speech inspired the Indians with the utmost confidence of a successful resistance to Wayne. On February 17, 1794, exactly one week after the Quebec speech, Dorchester ordered Simcoe to reestablish the old English Fort Miamis at the Maumee Rapids as a challenge to the erection by Wayne of Forts Greenville and Recovery in the fall of 1793. Simcoe was delighted and, armed with Dorchester's speech, he went at once to Detroit to supervise directly the building of the fort. On his way he interviewed Brant at the latter's home on Grand River near Niagara. What happened may be judged from Brant's letter to Joseph Chew of March 25: "His Excellency Governor Simcoe," wrote Brant, "has just now left my House on His Way to Detroit with Lord Dorchester's Speech to the Seven Nations, and have Every reason to believe when it is delivered that Matters will take an immediate Change to the Westward as it will undoubtedly give those Nations high spirits, and Enable them by a Perfect Union to Check General Wayne if he advances any further, which appears to me will be the case as affairs now stand." On April 14, 1794, Simcoe met the delegates of the Miami, Shawnee, Delaware, Mingo, and

[23] Cruikshank, *Correspondence of ... Simcoe,* 2:149.

Wabash tribes at the Au Glaize and read Lord Dorchester's speech to them. To the unfortunate Indians this rash act of Governor Simcoe was the formal pledge of support, and the establishment of Fort Miamis showed that the English were putting their pledge into actual operation. It was all they needed, and they immediately prepared to set forth to battle. "We salute you," they replied to Simcoe, "& thank you for your speech you have sent us, which was delivered by our Father at Quebec to the Seven Nations . . . You have set our hearts right, and we are now happy to see you standing on your feet in our Country."[24]

The actions of the British led by Dorchester and Simcoe had an electrifying effect. Brant, whose loyalty to the confederacy had been lagging ever since the failure of peace in August, 1793, revived his enthusiasm and called upon all the tribes to rush to the support of the tribes on the Maumee. He construed the erection of Fort Miamis to mean "a certainty of Great Britain being engaged in Hostilities with the United States." He was prevented, however, from joining the confederates in arms by the fear of exposing the Iroquois country in New York and Pennsylvania to American attack. From the shores of Lake Erie came the Wyandot and Ottawa, from Lake Huron came the Chippewa, and from Lake Michigan came the Potawatomi. By the middle of June one of the largest Indian armies ever assembled had gathered at the rendezvous at Fallen Timbers, near Fort Miamis. All accounts agree that the number of warriors was almost two thousand. The Indians expected to smash Wayne's army much as they had that of St. Clair over two and a half years before. If properly directed they might have done so. They fully expected not only proper direction but also military support from the British, whose agents worked indefatigably during the spring months of 1794 to assemble and provision the tribes.[25]

[24] Cruikshank, *Correspondence of . . . Simcoe*, 2:2, 39, 68, 79-83, 104, 105, 122, 154, 194; "Colonial Office Records," in *Michigan Pioneer and Historical Collections*, 24:656.

[25] The material on the preparations for the Indian campaign in this and the two

Guided by McKee, the Indians at the Au Glaize sent out, on May 7, a call to the Lake Indians that the time to assemble was at hand. On May 24 they likewise called upon the English to fulfill at once Lord Dorchester's and Simcoe's promises. "When you filled the Pipe of the three Nations [*Miami, Delawares, and Shawnee*]," they said, "you told them you would rise & go along with us; make haste then & get up & bring your children along with you, as we expect they [*the Americans*] are all now collected at Greenville." In response to these urgings, the British commandant at Detroit, Colonel Richard G. England, issued orders that every means should be used to send all available Indians to the Au Glaize. In the meantime Fort Miamis was garrisoned, and a blockhouse and storehouse were built on Turtle Island at the mouth of the Maumee.

The tragedy and the irony of the situation become more apparent when the reader observes that at the very moment when the Indians were being pushed headlong into war by Dorchester, Simcoe, and McKee, the British Cabinet was ordering these same officials to pursue a contrary procedure. On July 10, 1794, Simcoe wrote to McKee that Jay's treaty would be fruitless and that war was inevitable. On July 4 Lord Dundas, British secretary of war, wrote to Simcoe that Jay's treaty would probably be successful, and that peace was all but assured. He stated that, although Simcoe might continue with the occupation of Fort Miamis, he must be prepared to abandon it soon, along with Detroit.

Oblivious to the doom that was awaiting them, the Indians prepared for Wayne. Having attained their maximum force by the middle of June, and knowing that such numbers could not stay long in the field, they prepared for immediate action. At the moment of advance, lacking white leadership in the form of British troops, they drafted all white traders among them, and with this motley array of leaders, the Indians, two thousand strong, advanced in two divisions against the Ameri-

following paragraphs is based on Cruikshank, *Correspondence of . . . Simcoe*, 2:232, 247, 250-253, 259, 262, 265, 278, 285, 294, 300; 5:86, 92, 95.

cans. Unkind, indeed, was the fate that decreed that the destiny of the Indians should be entrusted to such a force. The Indians had a different task before them in 1794 than they had had in 1790 and 1791 against Harmar and St. Clair. The main part of Wayne's army was safe in the protection of Fort Greenville. Until the beginning of a forward movement (which did not take place until late in July), no encounter such as those that took place on the previous occasions was possible. The most effective thing to do, granting that the Indians could not conduct a siege because of the lack of provisions, was to capture sufficient American provisions en route and to deliver such a paralyzing stroke or series of strokes to the supplies that Wayne could not support his large army and would be forced to retire. According to McKee, the Indians had actually planned to do this. But their impetuosity and their need for action quickly frustrated an effective coup. They blasted every hope of success by throwing themselves into a futile frontal attack on Fort Recovery on June 30 and July 1, with the sole effect of capturing or killing about three hundred horses and some cattle. Colonel England, who was stationed at Detroit and who watched the progress of the army, prophesied the outcome correctly on the night of June 28 when the Indians abandoned their Fabian tactics and decided to attack the fort. "Cutting off the Communication between the Forts and the Ohio," he wrote, "is the only object by which we could promise success but as the Northern Indians take the lead we are forced to comply to change our Course tomorrow for Fort Recovery where nothing effectual can be done but on the contrary the means perhaps of discovering our Force and put the enemy on their guard." This is precisely what happened. Colonel England reported, "It has all the ill consequences of a defeat, without materially weakening the Americans." "I must observe with grief," lamented an unknown officer, "that the Indians had never it in their power to do more—and have done so little."[26]

[26] The material on the Indian campaign and on Wayne's attack in this and the

The attack on Fort Recovery was the beginning of the end. If it was a victory at all, it was a Pyrrhic one. Wayne was at once on his guard, and there was no chance for a surprise. Above all, the Indians, having captured no supplies, had no means of subsistence. The Indian army at once broke up, never again to assemble in such force. The confederacy had failed. The issue of Fallen Timbers and the treaty of Greenville had been decided.

As the Indian army disintegrated, the impotence of the English became at once apparent. They could not supply the Indians, to say nothing of reinforcing them with an army of their own. McKee could do absolutely nothing to keep the Chippewa, Wyandot, and Potawatomi warriors from going home. Moreover, the Indians were annoyed with England for not taking part in the actual fighting. "I conceive," stated McKee to the colonel, "there would have been little difficulty in stopping all the Indians here, Provided I had been authorized for that purpose, but we must in that case have taken an active share in the contest and become at least auxiliaries in the War." Nevertheless, McKee struggled valiantly to hold the Indians together on the Maumee and reported to Simcoe on July 26 that the dispersion was checked. To do this he was compelled to be far more lavish in supplying food than ever before. But the Fort Recovery campaign had made the Indians apprehensive about the possibility of British military aid. As Wayne advanced, the tribes made insistent demands and, as usual, got vague promises that they interpreted as pledges. Thus in the latter part of July the Miami chief, Little Turtle, visited Colonel England to discover, according to the colonel's report, "what assistance he and the other Indians were to expect from us." The Wyandot were even more peremptory. On August 5 a delegation led by Chief Crane presented their demands. "They were very peremptory and pointed," said England, "in their demands for

following paragraphs is, unless otherwise stated, based on Cruikshank, *Correspondence of . . . Simcoe*, 2:306, 314, 315, 330, 334, 344, 353, 357-362, 368, 374, 382, 395; 3:7-11, 21, 75, 99, 180; 5:90, 93, 94.

assistance in the Field from their Fathers and seemed discontented at its being so long delayed."

Through McKee's efforts the English were able to keep thirteen hundred warriors assembled at Fallen Timbers to wait for Wayne. But fate decreed that even that number was not available for action when Wayne finally attacked on August 20. The Indians had been waiting for the American army for three days without food. An American had been captured on August 17, who said that Wayne would attack the next day. The Indians, fasting, as was their custom before battle, waited for him throughout the days of August 18 and 19. The twentieth was stormy, and the Indians, unable to resist longer the pangs of hunger, went off in large parties to get food at Fort Miamis, four miles down the river. In their absence, Wayne attacked, and in the two-hour battle that ensued, the tribesmen, only eight hundred in number, were crushed by superior strength before the warriors below could come to their help. Wayne knew that the Indians were at Fallen Timbers, and it is probable that he deliberately delayed his attack so as to create the situation that actually occurred. Colonel England was disgusted with the Indians and stated that they did not offer the Americans adequate resistance. "The Indians," he wrote to Simcoe, "on this occasion have forfeited every pretension to a Warlike or Gallant Character."

The battle of Fallen Timbers, considered by itself, was not an overwhelming or crushing defeat for the Indians. Not more than fifty of them seem to have been killed. According to McKee, the Indians, on the afternoon of August 20, after the battle, "were still in spirits and determined to give them [*the Americans*] another brush." But the defeat assumed more the aspect of finality when it became apparent that the British guns at Fort Miamis were to be silent and that war was not to take place between the United States and England. On August 21 and 22 Wayne laid waste all crops and property for several miles down the river. He even approached within pistol shot of the British fort. But although he and the British commandant, Major William Campbell, exchanged insults on paper and demanded surrender of each other, not a shot was fired. It was then that the spirits of the Indians began to fall, and from then on their disillusionment was rapid. On October 10, 1794, at the Wyandot village of Brownstown near Detroit, in the presence of the remnants of the confederacy, Brant, according to Lieutenant William Wayne, a British officer who was present, "demanded that assistance which had this later spring been promised them by Lord Dorchester from their allies, the British." There was much point in this demand because the Americans could still have been thoroughly whipped. The chain of American forts extending rather precariously through the wilderness from Fort Washington on the Ohio to Fort Wayne on the Maumee was not strong enough to withstand the attacks of the confederated Indians, who, with proper support, could have destroyed every bit of the provisions sent out. But Simcoe had no answer for Brant. The Indians dispersed for the winter, and in the spring the answer came in the form of Jay's treaty: peace between the United States and England and the final surrender of the British posts to the Americans. As Brant told Chew on January 19, 1796, "This is the second time the poor Indians have been left in the lurch."[27]

The second time indeed—but was it to be the last? The Indians had confided in the French and then in the English— not because they chose to, but through the force of circumstance. They must now place their trust in the Americans. How long would it be before this third trustee would leave them in the lurch? The answer was temporarily withheld.

For the moment the tribesmen went "sneaking off" to the American camp at Greenville where Anthony Wayne and his aides cultivated Indian resentment against the British by ascribing all the red men's ills to their trust in the king. As for the confederacy, it was in ruins. "I have," boasted Wayne

[27] Cruikshank, *Correspondence of . . . Simcoe,* 2:396; 3:78, 96, 98, 124, 131, 140, 151; Bemis, *Jay's Treaty,* 180; "Indian Affairs," in *Michigan Pioneer and Historical Collections,* 20:434 (Lansing, 1892).

in his report to Knox on December 23, 1794, "succeeded in dividing and distracting the counsels of the hostile Indians, and hope, through that means, eventually to bring about a general peace." At the treaty council, held at Greenville in July and August, 1795, Little Turtle spoke for the confederacy that was then but a memory. "I expected," said the great Miami chief, "in this council that our minds would have been made up, and that we should speak with one voice." At another time he said, "This is a business of the greatest consequence to us all: it is an affair to which no *one* among us can give an answer. Therefore, I hope we will take time to consider the subject, that we will unite in opinion, and express it unanimously."[28]

But this hope was a forlorn one. By the treaty document, dated August 3, 1795, and signed by Little Turtle and most of the rest of the leaders of the confederacy that a year ago had had high hopes of Indian destiny, the Ohio River boundary was given up forever. Money was paid, and annuities were promised, to each tribe. Trade was opened, and an effective system of trade control was pledged. The offer was made to civilize the Indians according to the white man's ways.[29]

The treaty of Greenville marked the end of the contest for the control of the upper Ohio. Never again were the Indians to menace the white man's supremacy in that region. Never again was the cry of "Indian!" to spread terror and panic among the frontier inhabitants. The land that the Indians had vainly fought to retain became the basis for a new civilization. Forests, fields, and streams were no longer homes for abundant game but instead sustained farms, villages, and towns. The vestiges of the little towns and villages of Indian huts and wigwams were soon lost as the recurring seasons alternately brought forth and shed their verdure. The bustling activity of the white men's towns replaced the Indian settlements. Whereas once the appearance of Indians in the streets caused

[28] *American State Papers, Indian Affairs,* 1:548, 571, 574.
[29] United States, *Indian Affairs, Laws and Treaties,* 2:30-34; *American State Papers, Indian Affairs,* 1:562, 563.

sensations of distrust and apprehension among the white people, there was now only a feeling of curiosity and amusement as some forlorn representative of the race straggled into town. Indian affairs in western Pennsylvania were no longer a problem.

To the west, on and near the western shores of Lake Erie and on the waters of the Wabash and the Maumee, the shattered tribes reassembled in an effort to preserve their civilization and to live in peace with the Americans. Some Indians found their way to Canada, and others trekked beyond the Mississippi. But most of them remained on the eastern frontier and hoped against hope that the white men had made their last advance. Wayne had promised them satisfactory trading conditions in the form of the new factory system, which had already been inaugurated among the southern Indians in 1795. Never before had the British or the American governments undertaken to exercise a complete monopoly of trade. The Indians thought that now, perhaps, the end of conflict had come.

Of course, the end had not come. With the floodgates open, emigrants poured into the upper Ohio Valley. Ohio became a state. Soon the irresistible advance of population approached the waters of the Wabash, where now lived the Shawnee with their new leaders, Tecumseh and his brother, the Prophet. While there still lived those who could remember the beginning of the struggle west of the mountains, these two great Indian leaders began their attempt to restore the ancient confederacy and to prepare it for its last great test—that of November 7, 1811, at the battle of Tippecanoe.

Bibliography

Bibliography

Printed works that were used only once or twice, and then incidentally, are not included in the following bibliography. Bibliographical data for such works appear in the footnotes.

SOURCE MATERIAL

MANUSCRIPTS

Bouquet, Henry. Papers. British Museum, Additional Manuscripts, 21631-21659. The Library of Congress has photostatic reproductions of virtually all the documents bearing upon Pennsylvania.

Draper Manuscripts. State Historical Society of Wisconsin. Madison.

Hand, Edward. Correspondence and Papers. Four folio volumes. Library of Congress.

Morgan, George. Letter Books, 1769-79, numbered 1, 2, and 3. Carnegie Library of Pittsburgh.

Morgan, George. Letters. Library of Congress.

Pickering, Timothy. Papers. Massachusetts Historical Society. Boston.

United States. Continental Congress. Papers. Library of Congress.

PRINTED SOURCES

Alvord, Clarence W., *Kaskaskia Records, 1778-1790*. Springfield, 1909. 1, 681 p. (*Illinois Historical Collections*, vol. 5).

Alvord, Clarence W., and Clarence E. Carter. *Trade and Politics, 1767-1769*. Springfield, 1916. xviii, 760 p. (*Illinois Historical Collections*, vol. 11).

American Archives. Edited by Peter Force. Fourth series, Washington, 1837-46. 6 vols. Fifth series, Washington, 1848-51. 2 vols.

Bibliography

American State Papers. Documents, Legislative and Executive, of the Congress of the United States. Washington, 1832-61. 38 vols. *Indian Affairs,* vol. 1; *Military Affairs,* vol. 1.

Bouquet Collection, Calendar, in Canadian Archives, *Report,* 1889. Ottawa, 1890.

Brackenridge, Hugh H., ed. *Indian Atrocities.* Cincinnati, 1867. 72 p.

Buell, Rowena, ed. *The Memoirs of Rufus Putnam and Certain Official Papers and Correspondence.* Boston and New York, 1903. xxxvi, 460 p.

Butler, Richard. "Journal of General Butler," in *The Olden Time,* 2:433-464, 481-531 (1847). Reprint, Cincinnati, 1876.

Butterfield, Consul W., ed. *The Washington-Crawford Letters,* 1767-81. Cincinnati, 1877. xi, 107 p.

Butterfield, Consul W., ed. *Washington-Irvine Correspondence.* Madison, 1882. vi, 430 p.

Canadian Archives. "Letters from the Canadian Archives," in *Illinois Historical Collections,* 1:290-457. Springfield, 1903.

Carter, Clarence E., ed. *Correspondence of General Thomas Gage with the Secretaries of State,* 1763-75. New Haven, 1931. 2 vols.

"Colonial Office Records." *See* Great Britain. Public Record Office.

Cruikshank, Ernest A., ed. *The Correspondence of Lieutenant Governor John Graves Simcoe.* Toronto, 1931. 5 vols.

"Daily Journal of Wayne's Campaign, from July 28th to November 2d, 1794, Including an Account of the Memorable Battle of 20th August," in *The American Pioneer,* 1:315-357 (1842).

Darlington, Mary C., comp. *Fort Pitt and Letters from the Frontier.* Pittsburgh, 1892. 312 p.

Darlington, Mary C., ed. *History of Colonel Henry Bouquet and the Western Frontiers of Pennsylvania, 1747-1764.* n.p. ᶜ1920. 224 p.

Darlington, William M., ed. *Christopher Gist's Journals, with Historical, Geographical and Ethnological Notes.* Pittsburgh, 1893. 296 p.

Denny, Ebenezer. "Military Journal of Major Ebenezer Denny," in Historical Society of Pennsylvania, *Memoirs,* 7:205-409. Philadelphia, 1860.

Dinwiddie, Robert. *The Official Records of Robert Dinwiddie,*

Bibliography

1751-58. Richmond, 1883-84. 2 vols. (Virginia Historical Society, *Collections,* vols. 3, 4).

Forbes, John. *Letters of General John Forbes Relating to the Expedition against Fort Duquesne in 1758.* Compiled by Irene Stewart. Pittsburgh, 1927. 88 p.

Galbreath, Charles B., ed. *Expedition of Celoron to the Ohio Country in 1749.* Columbus, Ohio, 1921. 140 p.

Goodman, Albert T., ed. *Journal of Captain William Trent.* Cincinnati, 1871, 117 p.

Great Britain. Public Record Office. "Colonial Office Records," in *Michigan Pioneer and Historical Collections,* 23:603-680; 24:1-699; 25:1-698. Lansing, 1895, 1896.

"The Haldimand Papers," in *Michigan Pioneer and Historical Collections,* 9:343-658; 10:210-672; 11:319-656; 19:296-675; 20:1-673. Lansing, 1886, 1888, 1888, 1892, 1892. Additional sections of "The Haldimand Papers," not used in this work, appear in other volumes of the *Collections.*

James, James A., ed. *George Rogers Clark Papers, 1771-1781.* Springfield, 1912. clxvii, 715 p. (*Illinois Historical Collections,* vol. 8).

James, James A., ed. *George Rogers Clark Papers, 1781-1784.* Springfield, c1926. lxv, 572 p. (*Illinois Historical Collections,* vol. 9).

Johnson, William. *The Papers of Sir William Johnson.* Prepared for publication by the Division of Archives and History, New York. Albany, 1921-33. 8 vols.

Kellogg, Louise P., ed. *Frontier Advance on the Upper Ohio, 1778-1779.* Madison, 1916. 509 p. (*Wisconsin Historical Collections,* vol. 22).

Kellogg, Louise P., ed. *Frontier Retreat on the Upper Ohio, 1779-1781.* Madison, 1917. 549 p. (*Wisconsin Historical Collections,* vol. 24).

Kenny, James. "Journal to Ye Westward," 1758-59, in *The Pennsylvania Magazine of History and Biography,* 37:395-449 (1913).

Kenny, James. "Journal of James Kenny, 1761-1763," in *The Pennsylvania Magazine of History and Biography,* 37:1-47, 152-201 (1913).

Bibliography

The Lee Papers, 1754-1811. New York, 1872-75. 4 vols. (New York Historical Society, *Collections*, publication fund series, vols. 4-7).

Le Roy, Marie, and Barbara Leininger. "Narrative," in *Pennsylvania Archives*, second series, 7:401-412.

"Letters from the Canadian Archives." *See* Canadian Archives.

Massachusetts Historical Collections. Fourth series, vols. 9, 10. Boston, 1871. These volumes comprise a collection of letters relating to the French and Indian wars, which are called the Aspinwall Papers, from their collector, Thomas Aspinwall.

[*New York Colonial Documents*]. *Documents Relative to the Colonial History of the State of New York*. Albany, 1853-87. 15 vols.

Pennsylvania Archives. First series, Philadelphia, 1852-56. 12 vols. Second series, first edition, Harrisburg, 1874-93. 19 vols.

[*Pennsylvania Colonial Records*]. Harrisburg, 1851-53. 16 vols. The *Minutes of the Provincial Council* constitute the first ten volumes of this set.

Post, Christian F. "Journal of Christian Frederick Post, from Philadelphia to the Ohio," 1758-59, in Reuben G. Thwaites, ed., *Early Western Travels*, 1:175-291. Cleveland, 1904.

Pouchot, M. *Memoir upon the Late War in North America, between the French and English, 1755-60*. Translated and edited by Franklin B. Hough. Roxbury, Mass., 1886. 2 vols.

Pritts, Joseph, ed. *Incidents of Border Life*. Lancaster, Pa., 1841. 511 p.

Richardson, James D., comp. *A Compilation of the Messages and Papers of the Presidents*, 1789-1897. Washington, 1898. 10 vols.

Rogers, Robert. *A Concise Account of North America*. London, 1765. vii, 264 p.

Rogers, Robert. *Journals of Major Robert Rogers*. Edited by Franklin B. Hough. Albany, 1883. 297 p.

St. Clair, Arthur. *A Narrative of the Manner in which the Campaign against the Indians, in the Year One Thousand Seven Hundred and Ninety-one, Was Conducted*. Philadelphia, 1812. 273 p.

Smith, James. *An Account of the Remarkable Occurrences in the Life and Travels of Col. James Smith*. With notes by William M.

Bibliography

Darlington. Cincinnati, 1870. xii, 190 p. (*Ohio Valley Historical Series,* no. 5).

Smith, William H., ed. *The St. Clair Papers.* Cincinnati, 1882. 2 vols.

Sparks, Jared, ed. *Correspondence of the American Revolution; Being Letters of Eminent Men to George Washington.* Boston, 1853. 4 vols.

Stuart, Charles. "The Captivity of Charles Stuart." Edited by Beverly W. Bond, Jr., in *The Mississippi Valley Historical Review,* 13:58-81 (1926).

Thwaites, Reuben G., and Louise P. Kellogg, eds. *Documentary History of Dunmore's War, 1774.* Madison, 1905. xxviii, 472 p.

Thwaites, Reuben G., and Louise P. Kellogg, eds. *Frontier Defense on the Upper Ohio, 1777-1778.* Madison, 1912. xvii, 329 p.

Thwaites, Reuben G., and Louise P. Kellogg, eds. *The Revolution on the Upper Ohio, 1775-1777.* Madison, 1908. xix, 275 p.

"Treaty of Fort Stanwix in 1784," in *The Olden Time,* 2:404-432 (1847). Reprint, Cincinnati, 1876.

"The Treaty of Logg's Town, 1752," in *The Virginia Magazine of History and Biography,* 13:143-174 (1905-6).

United States. Continental Congress. *Journals of the Continental Congress, 1774-1789.* Washington, 1904—To be complete in 34 vols.

United States. *Indian Affairs, Laws and Treaties.* Compiled and edited by Charles J. Kappler. Washington, 1903-29. 4 vols.

Virginia. *Calendar of Virginia State Papers and Other Manuscripts.* Richmond, 1875-93. 11 vols.

Washington, George. *The Diaries of George Washington, 1748-1799.* Edited by John C. Fitzpatrick. Boston and New York, 1925. 4 vols.

Washington, George. *The Writings of George Washington.* Edited by Jared Sparks. New York, 1847. 12 vols.

SECONDARY MATERIAL

Alvord, Clarence W. *The Illinois Country, 1673-1818.* Springfield, 1920. 524 p.

Alvord, Clarence W. *The Mississippi Valley in British Politics.* Cleveland, 1917. 2 vols.

Bibliography

Bausman, Joseph H. *History of Beaver County, Pennsylvania.* New York, 1904. 2 vols.

Bemis, Samuel F. *Jay's Treaty: A Study in Commerce and Diplomacy.* New York, 1923. xvi, 388 p.

Burt, A. L. "A New Approach to the Problem of the Western Posts," in the Canadian Historical Association, *Report of the Annual Meeting,* 1931, p. 61-75. Ottawa, 1931.

Butterfield, Consul W. *An Historical Account of the Expedition against Sandusky under Col. William Crawford in 1782.* Cincinnati, 1873. x, 403 p.

Carter, Clarence E. *Great Britain and the Illinois Country, 1763-1774.* Washington, 1910. ix, 223 p.

Craig, Neville B. *The History of Pittsburgh.* New edition, annotated by George T. Fleming. Pittsburgh, 1917. xxiv, 310 p.

Crumrine, Boyd, ed. *History of Washington County, Pennsylvania.* Philadelphia, 1882. 1002 p.

Donehoo, George P., ed. *Pennsylvania: A History.* New York and Chicago, 1926. 7 vols.

Fernow, Berthold. *The Ohio Valley in Colonial Days.* Albany, 1890. 299 p.

Hanna, Charles A. *The Wilderness Trail.* New York and London, 1911. 2 vols.

Hassler, Edgar W. *Old Westmoreland: A History of Western Pennsylvania during the Revolution.* Pittsburgh, 1900. vi, 200 p.

Heckewelder, John G. *History, Manners, and Customs of the Indian Nations Who Once Inhabited Pennsylvania and the Neighbouring States.* Revised edition, Philadelphia, 1876. 465 p. (Historical Society of Pennsylvania, *Memoirs,* vol. 12).

Heckewelder, John G. *A Narrative of the Mission of the United Brethren among the Delaware and Mohegan Indians.* Philadelphia, 1820. 429 p.

Hildreth, Samuel P. *Pioneer History: Being an Account of the First Examinations of the Ohio Valley.* Cincinnati, 1848. xiii, 525 p.

Hodge, Frederick W., ed. *Handbook of American Indians.* Washington, 1912. 2 vols. (Bureau of American Ethnology, *Bulletins,* no. 30).

Bibliography

Jacobs, John J. *A Biographical Sketch of the Late Captain Michael Cresap*. Cincinnati, 1866. 158 p.

James, Alfred P. "The First English-speaking Trans-Appalachian Frontier," in *The Mississippi Valley Historical Review*, 17:55-71 (1930).

Kellogg, Louise P. *The French Régime in Wisconsin and the Northwest*. Madison, 1925. xv, 474 p.

Loskiel, George H. *History of the Mission of the United Brethren among the Indians in North America*. London, 1794. 3 parts in 1 vol.

Manley, Henry S. *The Treaty of Fort Stanwix, 1784*. Rome, N. Y., 1932. 126 p.

Parkman, Francis. *The Conspiracy of Pontiac*. Boston, 1917. 2 vols.

Savelle, Max. *George Morgan, Colony Builder*. New York, 1932. xiv, 266 p.

Siebert, Wilbur H. *The Tories of the Upper Ohio*. Charleston, W. Va., 1914. 13 p. (Reprint from the biennial report, 1913-14, of the Department of Archives and History of the state of West Virginia).

Sipe, C. Hale. *The Indian Wars of Pennsylvania*. Second edition, Harrisburg, 1931. 908 p.

Stillé, Charles J. *Major-General Anthony Wayne and the Pennsylvania Line in the Continental Army*. Philadelphia, 1893.

Stone, William L. *Life of Joseph Brant*. Albany, N. Y., 1864. 2 vols.

Volwiler, Albert T. *George Croghan and the Westward Movement, 1741-1782*. Cleveland, 1926. 370 p.

Withers, Alexander S. *Chronicles of Border Warfare, or a History of the Settlement by the Whites, of North-western Virginia*. Edited by Reuben G. Thwaites. Cincinnati, 1895. xx, 447 p.

Index

Index

Index

306; desire to deal with Congress, 288-289; disagrees with Senecas, 302-303; fears failure of Confederacy, 304; goes to England, 299; leader of Indian Confederation, 282-283, 299-300; meets New Yorkers, 288-290; plans to attack Clark's expedition, 269; pro-British, 196, 326, 330-331; quoted, 172; returns captives, 292; warns Virginia, 173

British, condemned by Indians, 307-308; defeat French at Great Meadows, 69; Delawares appeal for aid in Ohio Valley, 83-85; economy toward Indians, 106-122; failure of Loyalist-Indian uprising, 182-183; fear desertion by Indians, 224; fear of Franco-Shawnee alliance, 25-28, 38-39; improvement in Indian relations, 45-48, 53; Indian relations after Revolution, 280-284, 286-287, 291, 299, 322, 326-336; Indians incited against Colonists, 180-182, 193-197, 204-205, 208-209, 213, 223; Indians request help in war against French, 49-51; lose control of Wabash and Illinois country, 231-236, 238-239; muddling in Indian affairs, 123-151; neglect of Indians, 58-59, 66-67, 78; plan of reconciling Indians, 97-105; plan to conquer Ohio Valley, 180; refuse appeal of Shawnee, 33-34, 57-58; refuse to surrender forts to Americans, 286-290; removal of troops from Fort Pitt demanded by Indians, 94-95; support needed by Cherokee and Iroquois, 146; surrender to French at Great Meadows, 70; withdraw from frontier posts, 132. *See also* Indian land, Indian trade

Brodhead, Colonel (later General) Daniel, denounced McIntosh, 217-218; 225; disagreeableness of, 256-258; discouraged by Washington, 255, 258-259; expedition up the Allegheny, 226, 248-253, 259; fears Indian attack, 259; honored by Indians, 241; lack of understanding of, 256; laments lack of supplies, 226, 254-255; leads an attack on Delawares, 265-266; organizes impressment parties, 261-262; plans for campaign of *1780*, 256-257; promises Delawares protection, 264-265; quoted, 241-242, 260, 263; refused help by Wyandot, 254; to attack Shawnee, 260; to attack Wyandot, 261

Brown, Patrick, attacks Piankashaw, 311

Brush Creek, attack on, 259-260

Buckongahelas (Delaware) leads attack on Wheeling, 271; quoted, 328

Bull, John Joseph, visits Indian tribes in New York, 286-287

Bullitt, Colonel Thomas, 156-157, 160

Burgoyne, General John, 196-197, 206, 230

Butler, Colonel John, 189

Butler, General Richard, approves British council at Niagara, 183; deals with Indians as American commissioner, 288-297; death of, 318; influence of, 156-157, 169; protected by Shawnee, 165-166; quoted, 152-153; relationship with St. Clair, 319; succeeded by Morgan, 187

Butler, William, 161

Callaway, Colonel, 190

Camp Deposit, erection of, 328

Campbell, Captain Donald, 108, 110

Campbell, John, agent of Baynton and Wharton, 129

Campbell, Richard, at Fort McIntosh, 218; reports lack of supplies, 218-219

Campbell, Thomas, 256, 258

Campbell, Major William, 336

Canadasaga, council at, 302-303

Captain Pipe, 211, 215

Captives, 190; from Wea towns, 318; murder of Delawares, 265-266; taken by Delawares, 272; taken by Girty's band, 256; taken by Seneca, 251; taken by Shawnee, 208. Return of, 119; a cause of Pontiac's War, 98; demanded by Americans, 292, 297; de-

Index

manded by British, 100-101, 105, 121-122; heartbreaks caused by, 107; presents in exchange for, 115-117, 127

Carleton, Guy, 195; prophecy of Anglo-American war, 329-332

Carlisle, Indian council at, 66-67

Carlyle, Major John, 64

Carney, Captain, informer, 246-247

Cartlidge, Edmund, complains of rum trade, 21-22; envoy to Shawnee, 30-31; trades in Ohio Valley, 20, 32

Cavilier, 25-26

Céloron de Blainville, Pierre Joseph, 45, 53-54, 236

Cerré, Gabriel, 231, 233-234

Chapin, Israel, 321, 327

Chartier, Peter, Chartier's Town named for, 19; leads Indians, 31, 33, 40-41, 43; reports on Indian conditions, 37; trades in Ohio Valley, 20, 32, 35

Chartier's Town, 19, 40; council at, 34

Cheat River, squatters at, 138

Chene, Captain Isidore, 269

Cherokee Indians, battle of Long Island, 190; propose to unite with Iroquois in war, 146-147

Chippewa. *See* Lake Indians

Christian, Colonel William, 157; quoted, 219

Cincinnati, settlements at, 301

Clark, George Rogers, 228-247; at Wheeling, 160; attack on Shawnee, 278-279, 298; attack on Vincennes, *1786*, 303; deals with Indians as American commissioner, 288-297; goes to Kentucky, 153, 158; quoted, 161-162, 164; results of victories, 224-226, 248, 263; to attack Shawnee, 261; unsuccessful plan for conquest of Detroit, 239, 246-247, 255, 266-270

Clark, John, 222

Clendenen, Colonel George, quoted, 312

Cleveland, Benjamin, 13

Clinton, Governor De Witt, 59

Colonies, prepare defense program, 207-208, 210; refuse to control Indian trade, 131; relationship with Indians,

179-338; weakness of, in Indian affairs, 186-187, 197, 207, 211. *See also* Congress, names of colonies

Confederacies, Indian, Iroquois, 8-9; Ohio Indians and tribes on Miami and Wabash, 145, 147; Shawnee and Seneca, 148-149

Indian Confederation, appeal to Congress, 300-302; attempt at restoration of, 338; attempts to break up, 289, 292-293, 296, 306, 309; encouraged by British, 280-281, 326; dissent in, 301-306, 309; failure of, 334, 336-337; formation of, 282-283; Indians desire for Americans to deal with, 288, 290, 296; new life of, 320-321; rejects treaties, 299-300; renewal of, 299-300; rumors of formation of, 151, 181, 191

Conferences. *See* name of place

Congress, Continental, abandons policy of building stations in Indian country, 227; action concerning land encroachment, 203; apology to Shawnee, 207; appropriates funds for attack on Indians, 275; appropriates fund for Indian gifts, 188-189, 201, 243; approves military plan of commissioners, 214; assumes responsibility of protection against Indians, 213; attempts to warn Indians against aggression, 286-287; failure in Indian affairs, 186-187, 210, 239; participation in treaty of Pittsburgh, 184; petition to, in behalf of Delawares, 242-243; recommends cultivation of Indian friendship, 215; sends commissioners to investigate Indian affairs, 213-214

Connolly, Dr. John, 157; commanded to march against Shawnee, 176; cruel treatment of Shawnee, 166; justice of peace, 159-160; part in American Revolution, 180-181; promises peace to Indians, 167; warns Wheeling, 160-161

Continental Army, 256-257, 267

Index

Index

Index

Frontier, alarms on, 195, 202, 237; chaos on, 248, 259-276; impoverishment of, 188, 208, 259; success on, 252-253

Frontiersmen, aversion to furnishing supplies for Indians, 250; failure as soldiers, 316; lack of co-operation for expeditions, 250-251, 256, 266-267, 271; Hand asks aid of, 205-206; need of, for war, 160, 250, 266; organize against Shawnee, 209-210; supported by government in land occupation, 155-156. *See also* Settlers

Fur trade, decrease in, 132. *See also* Indian trade

Gage, General Thomas, aid of, enlisted, 180; embarrassed by Croghan, 129; guarantees safety of Indian goods, 127; offers to evict squatters, 137; prevents traders from going to Indian country, 128; proposal of trade control by colonies, 131; recognizes Shawnee discontent, 144-145; realizes failure of British trade plan, 130; sees futility of eviction of squatters, 138; warned of Indian trouble, 136, 145

Galasko, 75

Galissonière, Marquis de la, 53

Gamelin, Captain Pierre, 314

Gaustarax, 144, 148-149

German Flats, congress of, 133; results of, 146-148

Gibault, Father Pierre, aids Clark in capture of Vincennes, 232-233, 236

Gibson, Colonel John, 130; commandant at Fort Laurens, 221-222; death of squaw, 163-164; to lead expedition against the Sandusky, 270

Gifts, Congress appropriates fund for, 188-189, 201; from colonists, 186; from Pennsylvania, 136, 140-141; seven thousand pounds a year from British, 126; to Delawares, 169-170. *See also* Indian trade

Gilmore, ——, murder of, 206-207

Girty, Simon, leads attack against Fort

Laurens, 222; leads attack on supply boats, 255-256; warns Indians, 216

Gist, Christopher, 56, 59, 63-64

Gladwin, Henry, 120

Gordon, Patrick, attempts to control Indian trade, 21-25, 28, 30-31, 35

Great Meadows, 69

Guyasuta, burns Hannastown, 259, 274; emissary to Mingo, 172, 197, 302; enemy of Americans, 204; instigates revolt against British, 108; rebukes Shawnee, 142; speaks for Iroquois, 141; to attend Niagara council, 183; visits Shawnee, 171, 302

Haldimand, General Frederick, fears for safety of Niagara, 253; quoted, 224, 278, 280-281; refusal to give British forts to Americans, 286

Half-King (Iroquois). *See* Tanacharison

Half-King (Wyandot). *See* Dunquat

Hamilton, Governor James, 59, 191; conquers Vincennes, 237; denounced by Clark, 233; dissuades Indians from attacking, 193-194; failure to help Indians in war, 57-58; lack of understanding in Indian affairs, 55-56; prepares for reconquest of Illinois country, 236; reprimands Delaware, 193; starts Indian uprisings, 192, 195-196, 204, 208; surrender at Vincennes, 238; urges Pennsylvania help in Indian affairs, 66-67; urges return of captives, 116

Hammond, Philip, saves Fort Donnally, 209

Hamtramck, John Francis, leads unsuccessful detachment, 315-316; mortification of, 312; ordered to capture deserters, 319-320; ordered to send emissary, 314; quoted, 310-311

Hand, General Edward, desire to revive Mingo expedition, 205-206; difficulties with militia, 210-211; encouraged, 206; realizes sad state of Indian affairs, 207; "squaw campaign," 211,

Index

213-215, 239-240; to protect frontiers, 196; urged to punish murderers, 203

Hannastown, destruction of, 259, 274

Hardin, John, attacks Indians, 312

Harmar, Colonel, consents to filibustering expedition, 313; constructs Fort Franklin, 302; defeat of, 14; leader of expedition to Maumee country, 315; quoted, 298; seeks government permission to march against Indians, 312

Harrisburg, 50, 73

Hartshorne, Ensign Asa, 313

Hays, Christopher, 268

Hays, Lieut. William, 90

Heart, Captain Jonathan, 303

Heckewelder, Rev. John, brings message of peace to Delawares, 216; warns frontier of Delawares, 265

Helm, Captain Leonard, agent of Indian affairs at Vincennes, 236; quoted, 246; sent up the Wabash, 239; surrenders to British, 237

Hendricks, James, 36

Henry, Patrick, 157, 200, 230; approves offensive war, 209; countermands McIntosh's order, 219; insists on punishment of Cornstalk's murderers, 207-208; orders expedition against the Mingo, 198-199

Hillsborough, Earl of, approves Johnson's plan, 146, 148

Holderness, Earl of, 63

Horse stealing, 107-108, 304, 306

Horsehead Bottom, 158

Hostages. See Captives, return of

Hostilities. See names of tribes; Uprisings; Wars

Howe, Lord, 196

Hudson Valley, British invasion in, 199-202

Hunters, destruction of, 11-14

Hunting grounds, Croghan's plan for, 124-125; encroachments on 11-14, 114-115, 137. See also Indian lands; names of tribes

Hutchins, Thomas, 112

Illinois Country, conquest of, by Clark, 229-232

Illinois Indians, French influence on, 150; incensed, 145; refuse to come to Onondaga, 149; reprimanded, 147; trade with, 127-129, 131, 142

Impressments, 261-262

Indian attacks. See names of tribes; Uprisings

Indian councils. See name of place

Indian lands, American gains from Revolution, 277, 284-286, 288; cession at treaty of Fort Stanwix, 124, 141-145; cessions demanded by treaty of Fort Harmar, 306, 308; encroachments on, 113-114, 134-135, 196; government supports occupation by frontiersmen on, 155-156; Indian fear of losing, 77-80, 87-89, 103, 282-284; Indian view of land occupation by whites, 307-308; new cessions ordered by Congress, 288-297; Northwest to be occupied by degrees, 285-286, 288, 295; payment for, 138-141; rapid settlement of, 301-302. See also Hunting grounds; names of tribes; Settlers; War for the Ohio River boundary

Indian policy, American aggression in, 284-309; British policy after Revolution, 280-284; inefficiency of American, 186-187, 210, 239, 249-250
1720-1745, 17-41
1745-1754, 42-74
1755-1758, 75-92
1758-1765, 93-122
1765-1774, 123-151
1778-1779, 212-227

Indian trade, Americans lack of supplies for, 243, 250, 254-255; Americans promise improvements in, 337-338; bad for British, 65; bad for French, 53-54; British desire for continuance of, after war, 280-281; British government abandons control of, 131-132; British promise for improvement in, 98-100, 103, 105; British supremacy over colonies in, 186, 189, 195, 199,

358

Index

253-254; Croghan's plan for, 125-126; embargo, 110-112; failure of Pennsylvania government to control, 20-23, 39-40, 52, 124; failure of policy of few trading posts, 128-130; improvement in, for British, 42-43, 47, 127-128; Iroquois control of, 21, 23, 28; lamentable state of, 129-133; need for more trade by Indians, 108-109, 129-130, 142, 279, 309; opened on the Wabash, 128; price control urged, 24; traders prohibited from Indian country, 107-108. *See also* Gifts; names of Indian tribes; Ohio Company; Rum traffic

Indians, appeal to British, 279-280, 299; arrogance of Americans toward, 245-246; chosen people, 4-5; civilization of, 1-15, 117-119; colonists fear Indian alliance with British, 179-181, 186, 191-192, 201-202, 205; condition of, at outbreak of Revolution, 179-211; cruelty of, 80-81; discontented in relation with Americans, 288-336; effect of George Rogers Clark's victories on, 224; effect of McIntosh on, 220; effect of their own success, 320-322; failure to understand outcome of Revolution, 277-282, 299, 308; jealousies among tribes, 185-186; make peace with Clark, 235; military control of Indian affairs, 132; mistreatment of, 200; promise of neutrality of, 184, 194-195, 197; pride offended, 115-117; reaction to British victory over French, 119-120; reason for defeat of, 15; recession of American influence on, 243, 246-247; refusal of peace overtures, 321-324; result of lack of neutrality of, 285, 291; revolt against British economy, 110-122; starvation among, 253; tribes represented at treaties of Pittsburgh, 184, 194. *See also* Confederacies; names of tribes

Innes, Harry, 313

Intermarriage, 84, 107, 117

Iroquois Indians, appeal for aid against

French, 62; appeal for aid against western nations, 146; as traders, 21-23; disappearance of supremacy of, in Ohio Valley, 72-74; expedition against, 249; fight for British, 196-197; influence on western Indians severed, 253; land cessions, 173, 290-292; murder of, 139; neutrality of, 38, 71, 73-74, 78, 124, 134, 326; order Delawares from Shawnee country, 169; overlords, 19-20, 27, 44, 134-135, 141-145, 148, 170-172; payment for land of, 140-141, 145, 148, 306; promise to send Shawnee from Ohio Valley, 28; rebuked by Johnson, 149; refusal to aid in conference with Wabash Indians, 317; sponsors of Indian confederation, 282, 299; supremacy of, in Ohio Valley, *1745-1754*, 42-72, 94; war on frontier, 259-276; warn French, 63. *See also* Indians

Irvine, General William, helpless in frontier warfare, 274-275; organizes expedition against Delawares, 273, 275

Irwin, John, reports lack of supplies, 218-219

Irwin, Joseph, 256-258

Jay, John, 329

Jay's treaty, 332, 336

Jefferson, Thomas, plan for Clark's attack, 266-267; quoted, 164

Johnson, Guy, ordered to incite Loyalist-Indian uprising, 181-182; quoted, 196; succeeds father, 170

Johnson, Sir John, at Sandusky, *1783*, 328; British Indian superintendent, 282; urges hostilities against Americans, 283-284

Johnson, Sir William, 79, 84, 109-111, 121, 130; advice sought by Gage, 129; arranges land settlement, 134-135, 148; capture of Niagara, 97; death of, 171; demands honesty in dealing with Indians, 173; fears war, 139, 145, 150; influence on Indians, 47, 96, 127; mas-

Index

ter at treaty of Fort Stanwix, 142-143; opens trading posts, 128; ordered to evict squatters, 137, 154; pacifies Iroquois and Cherokee, 147; plans to demand return of captives, 98; plans uprising of Indians against each other, 145-146, 148; present at Indian council at Detroit, 108; quoted, 14, 133, 153; rebukes Iroquois, 149; receives money for Indians, 140; secures Iroquois support, 170-172; warned against bribery, 106; works for neutrality, 124

Joncaire, Chabert de, 27, 108

Joncaire, Philippe Thomas de, 58

Jumonville, Ensign Coulon de, 69

Kaskaskia, Clark at, 237-238; Clark's campaign against, 229-232

Kekewepellethe (Shawnee) submits to Americans, 297

Kenny, James, 97, 114-116

Kentucky, attempts to end raids in, 303; filibustering policy of, 312-313; promised land, 159; surveying in, 156-158; uprisings in, 198-199, 229-230, 237, 274, 298, 311-312. See also Boone, Daniel; Indian lands; Shawnee Indians

Kickenapaulin, 90

Killbuck (Delaware) quoted, 217, urges Wyandot-American friendship, 240

King, Thomas (Iroquois) 78, 117

Kissinaugtha (Shawnee) 142

Kittanning, 43-44, 135; abandoned, 205; attack feared on, 202; need for American fort at, 189, 194, 202

Kittiuskund, 84, 94

Knox, Henry, 310, 313, alarmed over possible war, 326-327, peace moves of, 322-323, quoted, 304

Kuskuski, 96, capital of Iroquois, 43; English seizure of, 92; transfer to Delawares, 94

La Demoiselle (Indian) 46

Laffont, Dr. Jean Baptiste, 233

Lake Indians, called to fight, 332; cession of lands of, 292-294; colonists fear of, 192, 194; confer at Fort Pitt, 102-103; friendly to Americans, 240, 249; gather for attack, 96; influenced by British, 105; refuse help for Shawnee, 172; to attack Pittsburgh, 192

Langlade, Charles, 57

Lawoughgua, 122

Lawrence, Thomas, 49

Lee, Arthur, deals with Indians, 288-297

Lee, Charles, quoted, 164

Leininger, Barbara, 75-76

Lenape. See Delaware Indians

Lenni-Lenape. See Delaware Indians

Le Gras, Colonel J.M.P., 238-239, 245-246

Lernoult, Captain Richard B., 223-224; warns Ottawa, 240-241

Le Roy, Marie, 75-76

Le Tort, James, 20-21, 32

Lewis, Major Andrew, attacked by Shawnee, 177; ordered to march against Shawnee, 176

Lewis, Samuel, saves Fort Donnally, 209

Lincoln, Benjamin, Indian commissioner, 288-297; peace commissioner, 322-325

Linctot, Geoffrey, warns Indians, 261

Little Turtle (Indian) demands British aid, 334; quoted, 337; victory of, 320

Livingstone, James, 114

Lochry, Captain Archibald, 250, 256-258; aids Clark in raising militia, 268-269; defeat of, 266, 270; saves Fort Hand, 251

Logan, Benjamin, attacks British supplies, 279; attacks Shawnee, 298-299

Logan, James, 35; opinion on Indian conditions, 24-27, 34

Logan (Mingo Chief) camp, 162; desire to attack traders, 165; leads party to avenge murders, 174; rebukes white men, 164

Index

Logstown, 56, 66; burning of, 70; gifts delivered at, 51, 58; importance of, 43-44

Loskiel, Bishop, quoted, 203, 205

Louisburg, 50, 88

Lowrey, Lazarus, 32, 65

Loyalist-Indian alliance, 179-211

Loyparcowah, 35

McCarty, Captain Richard, 245

McCullough, John, 118

McDonald, Angus, attempts to expel settlers, 113-114; commander at Wheeling, 176

McFarlane, Andrew, 202-203

McIntosh, General Lachlan, 228; aids Fort Laurens, 222-223; character of, 217-218, 220, 241; deceived Indians, 217; denounced, 221; deplores lack of supplies, 218; gives up idea of the capture of Detroit, 219; plans for forts, 214-217; quoted, 218; threatens Indians, 220; organizes expedition against Shawnee, 209-210

Mackay, Aeneas, 194; army ordered east, 202; quoted, 169

McKee, Captain Alexander, 127; allowed to represent British among Indians, 183; arranges conference, 167; commissary for Fort Pitt, 128; guides Indians into war, 332, 335; incites Shawnee uprising, 208; insists on Ohio River boundary for Indians, 328; quiets Indians, 281; quoted, 161, 174-175, 224, 293, 295, 320, 334-335; Shawnee appeal to, 154, 165-166; warned by Shawnee, 157; warns Indians, 215-216; warns of impending war, 139; works against colonists, 213, 269

McKee, Thomas, 116

McKee, William, 209

Mackey, Alexander, 136

MacLean, General Allen, quoted, 282; refusal to allow Douglass to address Indians, 287

Maddox, John, 22, 24

Mansker, Casper, 13

Marietta, settlements at, 301

Marshel, James, 267-268

Massachusetts, accepts offer of Indian help, 182

Maumee Indians. See Wabash Indians

Melanthy (Shawnee) murder of, 298, 321

Mercer, Hugh, 95, 97-100, 157

Miami Indians, desire for retaliation, 281; pro-French, 45, 57, 61-62, 65; refuse to help Shawnee, 172; trading conditions of, 46, 55-56

Mifflin, Thomas, 326-327

Militia, bad spirit of, 210-211; erect Fort McIntosh, 218; gain right of passage through Delaware country, 216; inadequate in frontier wars, 211, 213-214; lack of supplies for, 218-222; need for, on frontier, 189, 198, 202, 205-206, 213, 250, 256, 260; refuse to go to frontier, 219; sent east, 202, 214-215. See also Virginia

Mingo Indians, 9; expedition against, 198-201, 205, 249; lands taken, 114; massacre of, 162-165; migration to Ohio Valley, 18-20; murderous raids of, 190-191, 196-198, 206-207; ordered away from Ohio, 172, 194-195; plea for settlers, 140; refuse to aid British, 224-225; six towns destroyed, 176; strengthened by alliance with Shawnee and Delawares, 197-198; support French, 45, 74; unfriendly to colonists, 201. See also Delaware Indians; Shawnee Indians

Miranda, George, 35

Monckton, General Robert, 102, 105-107, 113

Money, American, spurned by Indians, 324; weakness of, 243-245

Monongahela Valley. See Redstone; Settlers

Montcalm, 81

Montgomery, John, joins Clark at Vincennes, 247; quoted, 175

361

Index

Montour, Andrew, 53, 59, 63, 67, 95, 97, 101

Montour, John, property rights of, 187; urged to join colonists, 239-240

Montour's Island, 187

Moorehead, Fergus, 202-203

Moravian Delawares, massacre of, 272, 321; migration to Sandusky, 271

Moravian missionaries, 175

Morgan, Colonel George, 198, 204-205, 207, 240; arrest of, 205-206; demands third treaty at Pittsburgh, 201; denounces McIntosh, 221; fears Loyalist-Indian danger, 187-189; friendship for Delawares, 220-221; honored by Indians, 241; houses Delawares, 242; quoted, 197, 199, 202, 216-217; satisfaction with second treaty of Pittsburgh, 194-195; secures release of prisoners, 190; succeeds Butler, 187; travels to Wyandot country, 192-193; urges retention of troops on frontier, 202; urges Seneca to come to Fort Pitt, 203; warns against expedition to the Mingo, 199-200

Morris, Lewis, 184, 188

Mound Builders, 16

Munsee Indians (Delawares) alliance with the Mingo, 198; attack on, 211

Murder, convictions for, 138; of Indians, 139, 161-162, 168, 190, 201, 203, 298; of settlers, 206-207, 221; scalping, 161; "squaw campaign," 211. See also Captives; names of tribes

Murray, Captain William, 129; consoles Indians, 137; Fort Pitt commandant, 128; orders squatters to leave, 136-138

Nash, John, 221

Netawatees. See New Comer

Neutrality. See Indians; names of tribes

Neville, Captain John, 187, 200; occupies Fort Pitt, 183

New Castle, 43

Newcheconer (Shawnee) 35

New Comer, effect of Anglo-French peace on, 119-120; pleas for trade, 129-130

New York, fails to enact treaty with the Indians, 288-289; fails to expel four tribes of the Iroquois, 288; seizes Iroquois land, 292

Niagara, councils at, 183, 188, 289-290; hostility of Indians at, 196

Norris, Isaac, 66

O'Hara, General James, quoted, 198

Ohio Company, 59-61, 63-64, 322-324

Ohio Valley, American influence in, 229-247; British and colonists vie for control of, 179-183; departure of Shawnee from, 41-43; English flag raised in, 93; ignored by Shawnee, 17-18; Indian war in, 259-276; migration to, by Shawnee, 18-41; slowness of American occupation in upper part of, 320; supremacy of Iroquois in, 42-74

Onas. See Penn, William

Onondaga, councils at, 149, 171

Opakeita, 30

Opakethwa, 30

Opessah, 18

Ordinance of October 15, 1783, circumstances producing, 286-288; provisions of, 284-285, 289

Orontony (Wyandot) 46, 224

Oswego, council at, 182; hostility of Indians at, 196

Ottawa, friendship with Americans, 240-241. See also Lake Indians; Pontiac

Page, Governor John, resents murder of Indians, 203

Patten, John, 67

Patterson, James, 32

Paxinoso, 76-77

Penn, Governor John, against Indian gifts, 170; co-operation sought in Indian trade, 127, 131; orders squatters

Index

to evacuate Monongahela Valley, 137-138

Penn, William, 18, 35, 76

Penn's Creek Massacre, 75-76

Pennsylvania, expedition from, 205-206; gifts for Indians, 49, 136, 140; negligence in Indian affairs, 58-59, 66-67; seizes Delaware and Wyandot lands, 295; seizes Iroquois land, 292; should remove squatters, 203. *See also* British; Fort Presque Isle; Rum traffic

Pentecost, Dorsey, 267-268

Perry, Colonel James, 205

Peter, Captain (Indian) 92

Peters, Richard, 37, 48, 66

Philadelphia, council at, 241-242

Philadelphia conference of *1747,* 55

Pickering, Colonel Timothy, 255; peace commissioner, 322-325; quoted, 305

Picoté, Marie François, Sieur de Bellestre, failure of attack of, 56-57; surrenders Detroit, 103-104

Pisquetomen, 84-85, 89-90

Pitt, William, 89

Pittsburgh. *See* Fort Duquesne, Fort Pitt; Treaties

Point Pleasant, battle of, 171, 177

Pollock, Oliver, financial aid of, 234-235, 244

Pontiac, 104, 118, 120, 144; influence of, 108

Pontiac's War, 99, 124, causes of, 98, 106, 114, 119-120, 125; end of, 123; nonparticipants in, 134

Population, increase in Indian, 45

Post, Christian Frederick, 116; ordered out of Indian country, 94-95; sent to the Ohio to prevent Indian hostilities, 90-92; visits Delawares, 84-89

Potawatomi. *See* Lake Indians

Pouchot, M.——, 81

Preston, Colonel William, 153, 157; apology to Shawnee, 207; fear of Shawnee attack, 208; quoted, 176, 209

Princeton, council at, 242

Prisoners. *See* Captives

Proctor, Thomas, 317

Prophet (Shawnee) 298, 338

Pryor, John, saves Fort Donnally, 209

Putnam, Rufus, quoted, 320

Queen Allaquippa. *See* Allaquippa

Raids. *See* names of tribes; Uprisings

Randolph, Beverly, peace commissioner, 322-325

Redstone, squatters at, 136-138, 141; trading post at, 129

Reed, Joseph, 257-259, 268; Brodhead's appeal to, 249-250, 254; quoted, 243; sanctions impressment, 261; upholds Lochry, 258

Religion, Indian, 117-118

Rocheblave, Philippe de Rastel, 231

Rogers, David, 255-256

Rogers, Major Robert, 103-104

Rum traffic, importation prohibited in western Pennsylvania, 34-35; Indians and traders agreement on, 32; negligence in curbing, 21-23, 30-31, 39, 105, 133; rum as reward for captives, 102; trade to be purged of, 66

Russell, William, 157

St. Clair (Delaware) 304

St. Clair, Arthur, 160; decision to war on Indians, 313-315; defeat of, 14, 318-320; dictator at treaty of Fort Harmar, 305-306; expedition contrasted to Wayne's, 325; leads expedition, 317-318; new administrator of Indian affairs, 304; quoted, 166-167, 170, 172, 309; rejects Indian proposals, 308

St. Lawrence, blockade of, 193; used to supply Indians, 195, 230, 253

St. Leger, Major Barry, 195-196

St. Pierre, Legardeur J. de, 64

Sandusky, council at, 283-284, 292, 303; Delawares migration to, 271

Scarouady, asks suppression of rum

363

Index

trade, 52; joins Washington, 69-71; presided over Shawnee, 44; repudiated by Iroquois, 71, 73; warns British to improve trade, 51

Schuyler, General Philip, 285, 288

Scott, Charles, joins Wayne, 327; leads expedition, 313, 317-318

Seneca Indians, ally of British, 197, 201-202, 204; attack Americans, 202, 204, 251; attacked at Fort Pitt, 203; attacked by Brodhead, 251-252, 259; deplore trading conditions, 171; friendly to Americans, 302-303; neutrality of, 189; resent land encroachments, 202-203. *See also* Guyasuta; Iroquois

Settlers, Indians proposal for removal of, 324; north of Ohio, 275; ordered off Seneca lands, 203; settle on Indian lands, 301-302; Virginians, 153-154. Monongahela Valley, 113-114, 135-138; denounced by Croghan, 139; to abandon settlements, 139-140; to remain, 141

Sharpe, Governor Horatio, 89

Shawnee Indians, 9; appeal to British, 33-34, 57, 154; appeal to Iroquois, 144; attack settlers, 208-209; chiefs of, attacked, 162, 173-174; defeated by Bowman, 253; departure from Ohio Valley, 41-43; enemies of Americans, 206-208; failure to select Ohio Valley, 17-18; French alliance, 25-27, 36-40; frightened by Clark, 279; frontiersmen attack on, 190, 209-210, 225; isolation of, 167-168, 170-173; loss of hunting grounds of, 10-12, 134-135, 141-145, 153-154, 156-157, 160, 167, 177, 181, 184, 198, 297, 322; migration to Ohio Valley, 18-41; Mingo alliance, 197-198; neutrality of, 71, 73, 189, 194; protect traders, 165-166; reconciled with English, 46; Shawnee war (Dunmore's War) 152-178; strike at whites, 157-158; submit to British, 122, 177; threaten Delawares, 169; warned by Johnson, 143. *See also* Indians

Shelburne, Lord, authorizes purchase of land, 141-142; demands that squatters be evicted, 137

Shelby, Captain James, 239

Shendeta (Wyandot) plea for lands, 307-308

Shepherd, Colonel David, expedition against the Mingo, 198-200

Shikellamy, 29

Shingas, 86, 88, 95; reasons for siding with French, 77-78; request for British teachers, 83-84

Sidney, Lord, 299

Simcoe, John Graves, prophesy of Anglo-American war, 329, 332; reads Dorchester's speech to Seven Nations, 330-331; to reconstruct Fort Miami, 330

Simpson, Andrew, 202-203

Six Nations. *See* Iroquois

Skaggs, Henry, 13

Smith, James, 80-81, 88

Springer, Uriah, 262

"Squaw campaign." *See* Hand, General

Stanwix, General John, attends conference, 100-101; replaced at Fort Pitt, 102

Steuben, Friedrich Wilhelm, Baron von, emissary to British, 286

Stevens, Francis, 32

Stirling, Sir Thomas, impending occupation of Fort de Chartres, 128, 142

Stockbridge Indians, aid Massachusetts, 182

Stoner, Michael, 158

Stuart, Charles, 77, 83, 88

Stuart, Henry, 237

Stuart, John, quoted, 206

Studebaker, Elizabeth, 121

Stump, Frederick, murders ten Iroquois, 139-140

Sullivan, Major General John, campaign against Six Nations, 226, 249, 251-253

Supplies, military, Brodhead's lack of, 250-251, 254, 257, 260-262; destruction of, by Indians, 255-256; lack of,

Index

for Fort Laurens, 221-223, 226; lack of, for militia, 218-220; St. Clair's lack of, 319

Susquehanna Valley, Delawares in, 35-36; Delaware migration from, 41; Shawnee liking for, 17, 18; Shawnee refusal to return to, 30, 33; settlers ordered off Seneca lands, 203

Symmes Associates, 322-324

Tanacharison, 44, 61, 72; advises Ward, 64-65; assists British, 68-70; complains against Washington, 70-71; death of, 73; repudiated by Iroquois, 71; warns French, 63

Tarentum, 19

Taxation, colonies adverse to, 131

Taylor, Major Richard, 222

Taylor, Major William, 262

Teaffe, Michael, 65

Tecumseh (Shawnee) 298, 338

Teedyuscung, 84, 86

Thomas, Governor George, concern over Indian affairs, 36-39, 41

Thompson, Captain Andrew, 269

Thonissahgarawa (Iroquois) 142

Ticonderoga, 88, 97

Tippecanoe, battle of, 298, 338

Tobacco's Son, friendship for Americans, 238; influence of, 236

Todd, John, 244

"Tomahawk claims," 200

Tostee, Peter, 40

Traders, worthy of licenses, 32. See also names of individuals

Treaties, denounced by Indians, 299, 308; unsuccessful attempts at peace treaties, 321-324; urged with Shawnee, 208; with Wabash, 239

    Albany, treaty of 1754, cause for Indian revolt, 77; repudiated, 89, 100, 113

    Coshocton, treaty of, 201

    Easton, treaty of 1757, 84, 86, 89, 91

    Fort Finney, treaty of, 296-298, 303

    Fort Harmer, treaty of, British agitation against, 327-328; conception of and preparation for, 301, 303-305; Indian participants in, 305; lands ceded by treaty to be restored, 322-323; results of, 309-311; terms of, 306, 307, 326

    Fort McIntosh, treaty of, 292-295; British agitation against, 328; effect of, 295-296, 300-302

    Fort Stanwix, treaty of 1768, boundary agreement of, ratified by Americans, 184; breach of, 187; results of, 10, 124, 141-145, 148, 173, 283, 291

    Fort Stanwix, treaty of 1784, 289-293; British agitation against, 328; opponents of, denounced by Cornplanter, 305-306; renounced by Indians, 296, 299-300

    Fort Stanwix, Pennsylvania treaty of, 292, 295

    Franco-American, 230-231

    Greenville, treaty of, 184, 334, 337

    Iroquois. See Treaties, Fort Stanwix, treaty of 1784; Treaties, Pennsylvania-Iroquois

    Lancaster, treaty of, 38, 40, 55, 60, 99

    Logstown, treaty of 1748, 51-52

    Logstown, treaty of 1752, 59, 61

    Pennsylvania-Iroquois, 28-29

    Pittsburgh, first treaty of, 183-186, 200; preliminary to, 181; refusal of the Mingo to comply to, 197; representatives at, 184

    Pittsburgh, second treaty of, funds appropriated for, 188-189; Indians invited to, 191-193; results of, 194-195, 197; uselessness of, 191-192

    Pittsburgh, third treaty of, failure of, 203-204; Indians invited to, 201, 203

    Pittsburgh, fourth treaty of, Delawares at, 215-216; injustices of, 216-217, 241, 253-254

    Pittsburgh, fifth treaty of, plans for,

Index

239-241, 253; results of, 254-255
Treaty of August 1, *1739*, 36
Treaty of *1765*, 121-122
Winchester, treaty of, 63, 66
Trent, Captain William, 101; ambassador to the Indians, 61-63; sent to forks of the Ohio, 64-65
Turtle Island, blockhouse at, 332

Uprisings, Indian, 36-37, 145-146, 189-190, 251-276, 286; against Fort Laurens, 221-223; incited by British, 195-196, 204-205. *See also* Kentucky; names of tribes

Vaudreuil, Marquis de, 26, 81
Venango, trespassers on Seneca land at, 202-203
Vernon, Major Frederick, 223, 226
Vincennes, Clark's reconquest of, 237-238, 246, 303; Clark's victory at, 224, 229, 231-233; council at, *1787*, 303; plans for treaty at, 295-296; rendezvous for attack on Detroit, 247; spoils of, distributed, 239; taken by British, 237
Virginia, approves defense measure, 208; authorizes offensive war, 209-210; legislature refuses financial aid for war against Shawnee, 175; military expedition against the Mingo curtailed, 198-201; retains militia for home defense, 268; seeks to woo Indians to side of colonists, 180-181; weakens American credit, 244-246. *See also* British; Settlers
Virginians, Indians dislike for, 174

Wabash country, conquest of, 232-233, 236; hostility of tribes in, 296
Wabash Indians, deny validity of treaty of Fort Harmar, 314; fear of trouble with, 281; peace overtures toward, 317; refuse to help Shawnee, 172; re-

sort to bow and arrow, 245. *See also* Illinois Indians
Wagetomica, destruction of, 176
Wallace, Mrs. Robert, capture of, 272
Wampum, 8
Ward, Ensign Edward, prevents Indian disillusionment, 64-65, 67-68
Warriors, census of, 44
Wars, against eastern New York and Pennsylvania frontier, 214-215; averted, 140-141, 192-195; Croghan warns British against, 136; fears of, 138-140, 145, 191-192, 202; inevitable, 151; Iroquois desire for, 146-147; prophecy of Anglo-American, 329-330 American Revolution, frontier help refused by East because of, 258-260, 266, 272-273; Indian conditions at outbreak of, 179-211
Dunmore's War, 11, 152-178, 198, 200; causes of, 124; settlement of, 184, 322; war declared, 161
Indian War, *1779-1782*, 248-276
Indian War, *1790-1794*, 282
King George's War, 47
King William's War, 18
War for the Ohio River boundary, *1789-1795*, 310-338
Washington, George, advises Brodhead to moderate plans, 255, 258; approves gradual occupation of Indian lands, 285; approves sustainment of frontier scouts, 312-313; battle at Great Meadows, 68-70; desires land in Kentucky, 156-157; favors conquering Fort Niagara, 226; inexperience of, 70-71; orders frontier army east, 202; quoted, 314; upholds Brodhead, 248, 267
Wauntaupenny (Indian) 84
Wayne, General Anthony, campaign of, 15, 324-325, 327-328, 334-336; Indians resistance to, 330-333; influence on Indians, 336-338
Wayne, William, quoted, 336
Wea Indians, expedition against, 317-318

366

Index

Weiser, Conrad, appointment as Pennsylvania Indian interpreter, 29; deplores British-Indian relations, 52; explains Shawnee discontent, 40; influence of, 46-47; urges giving of presents to Indians, 49-51

West Augusta committee of safety, conducts treaty of Pittsburgh, 183-184; urges general Indian council, 183; warned of approaching attack, 192

Westmoreland County, attempt to raise men for Clark in, 268-269; fails to aid Brodhead, 261

Wetzel, Martin, murders Delaware, 265-266

Wheeling, attacked, 271, 274; besieged, 198; destruction of, 205; inhabitants warned, 160; raiding party from, 176, 260; warlike atmosphere of, 159

White Eyes (Delaware) 168-169; appeals to Congress, 186-187; denounced by Hamilton, 193; murder of, 217; speaks for Delawares, 185

White Mingo (Seneca) 193

Whites, injustice of, reviewed by Indians, 321. See also Captives; Murder

Wilkinson, James, 318

Will, Captain (Shawnee) 11

Williamson, Colonel David, organizes attack on Delawares, 271-272; second in command in Delaware attack, 273-274

Wilson, William, in Shawnee country, 190; in Wyandot country, 192-193

Wolcott, Oliver, deals with Indians, 288-297

Wood, James, representative at treaty of Pittsburgh, 184; sent to Indian country by Virginia, 180-181, 183

Wraxall, Peter, 79

Wyandot (Indians) cession of lands, 292-295; fear to attend treaty of Pittsburgh, 193; friendship with colonists, 239-241, 249, 253; invited to Pittsburgh council, 239-240; no longer menace to frontier, 192-193, 227; offer Americans free passage through country, 224; plan attack in Ohio Valley, 204; refuse army passage through land, 254; refuse to aid British, 196, 204, 224; settlement on Shenango, 43; summon Shawnee and Delawares to Detroit, 191; to meet Americans at Coshocton, 201, 204; trade with British, 45-48; unfriendly to colonists, 181, 255. See also Lake Indians

Wyllys, Major John P., detachment slaughtered, 315; quoted, 311

Wyoming Massacre, 214

Yorktown, surrender at, effect of, in Northwest, 271-272

Zeisberger, David, informer, 204, 222, 271

OHIO INDIAN COUNTRY

The Upper Ohio Valley in the 18th Century Showing
Important Purchases from the Indians

Purchase Lines ————————
Modern State Lines ————————

0   25   50   75   100
SCALE OF MILES

MICHIGAN

Detroit

LAKE ERIE

Fallen Timbers • Ft. Miami
Ft. Defiance
Sandusky
River
1795
Maumee
Ft. Wayne
Cuyahoga River

• Crawford's Defeat

Ft. Recovery
(St. Clair's Defeat)
GREENVILLE TREATY LINE
Ft. McInto

INDIANA

Ft. Laurens
Schoenbrunn
Wakatomica
• Pluggy's Town
Coshocton • Gnadenhutten
Pickawillani
Chillicothe, or
Ft. Piqua
Greenville •
Ft. Jefferson
Lichtenau
Wakatomica
Ft. Henry
(Wheeling)

OHIO

Ft. St. Clair
1795
1795
Scioto River
Muskingum River
Camp Charlotte
Marietta
Ft. Harmar
Miami
Ft. Hamilton
1768
Ft. Finney
Ft. Washington
(Cincinnati)
Ohio River
SURRENDERED IN 1768
Pt. Pleasant
(Ft. Randolph)

GREENVILLE TREATY LINE

BOUNDARY OF INDIAN LAND CLAIM
Ft. Steuben
Ohio River
Licking River
Maysville
Kanawha River

WEST VIRGI

Louisville
Blue Licks •

KENTUCKY
• Lexington
• Boonesboro
1768
Kentucky River
Big Sandy River
1768
River
APPROXIMATE LINE
Greenbria
Harrodsburg •
• Danville

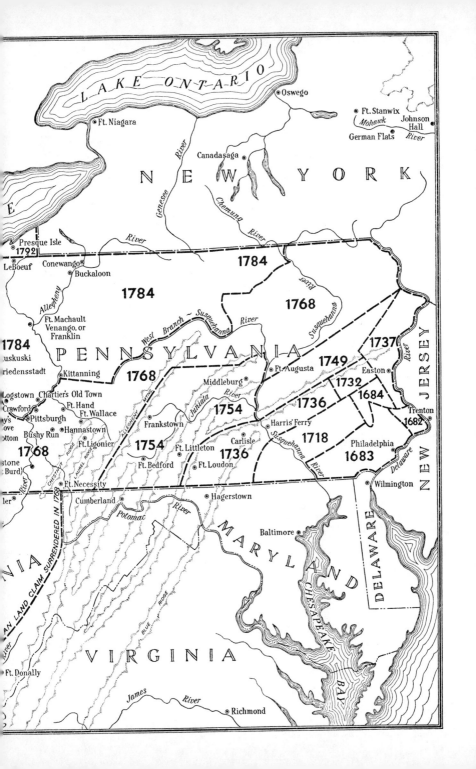